REMARKABLE TRIALS

OF ALL COUNTRIES:

PARTICULARLY OF THE

UNITED STATES, GREAT BRITAIN, IRELAND
AND FRANCE:

WITH NOTES AND SPEECHES OF COUNSEL.

CONTAINING

THRILLING NARRATIVES OF FACT FROM THE COURT ROOM,

ALSO

HISTORICAL REMINISCENCES OF WONDERFUL EVENTS.

COMPILED BY
THOMAS DUNPHY,
OF THE NEW YORK BAR,
AND
THOMAS J. CUMMINS
OF THE NEW YORK PRESS.

NEW YORK:
DIOSSY & COMPANY,
LAW BOOK PUBLISHERS.
1870.

CONTENTS

PREFACE.

The present work is intended to supply a deficiency which has long been felt in American literature. A collection of celebrated trials, published at such a price that they can be reached by all, must prove invaluable not only to the legal profession, but to the public generally. We have seen with what genuine interest the advent of a well-written romance is received among us, but in this volume we have compiled and culled out, not fictitious gems to please the fancy, but stern realities taken from the court-room—histories of crime and its deplorable results. Each trial is a work of wonderful interest in itself. Added to most of them are the speeches of counsel, eloquent, learned, and famous. In the trial of Francois Benjamin Courvoisier for the murder of Lord William Russell in London, we give the speech of Mr. Charles Phillips, who defended the prisoner for his life. This speech created at the time a vast amount of speculation and criticism throughout Great Britain, in consequence of the knowledge which Mr. Phillips possessed of his client's guilt when delivering his masterly effort.

The Helen Jewett and Colt cases are remembered by many of the old citizens of New York. Their barbarity, and the extraordinary circumstances which surrounded them, caused the greatest excitement in the public mind at that period.

The other cases in this volume will be found equally interesting, and it is not necessary to here allude to them at any length. If errors occur, the public must look back for redress to the chroniclers of the periods in which those trials took place.

THOMAS DUNPHY.
THOMAS J. CUMMINS.

REMARKABLE TRIALS.

CHARLOTTE MARIANE D'ARMANS CORDAY.

THE ASSASSINATION OF MARAT (LEADING SPIRIT OF THE FRENCH REVOLUTIONARY PARTY OF 1793,) BY CHARLOTTE CORDAY.

LAMARTINE'S HISTORY OF THE LIFE, TRIAL AND EXECUTION OF THE FRENCH HEROINE.

THE history, trial, and execution of Charlotte Corday is known almost to every reader; her early secluded life; her devotion to liberty; her determination to strike at what she believed to be the cause of the sufferings of France—the carrying out of her project unaided, unassisted by a single human being—the courage and determination exhibited in stabbing Marat—her arrest—her trial—her remarkable beauty, and lofty bearing on her way to the guillotine—her execution—group together a character the most remarkable and prominent which figured in that small party,who,"cast by Providence into the very centre of the greatest drama of modern times, comprised in themselves the ideas, the passions, the faults, the virtues of their epoch; and whose life and political acts formed, as we may say, the nucleus of the French Revolution, and who perished by the same blood which crushed the destinies of their country."

This young French heroine was born at St. Saturnin des Lignarets, in the department of Orne, July 28, 1768; guillotined at Paris, July 17, 1793. Her bearing on the scaffold sent a thrill even through the hearts of her executioners. A young German enthusiast, Adam Lux, a deputy from the city of Mentz, on witnessing the execution, conceived a romantic passion for her, and when her head fell, he cried, with a voice hoarse with emotion, "She is greater than

Brutus." He wrote a pamphlet, suggesting that a statue with such an inscription should be erected to her memory. He was arrested and guillotined. André Chénier, who had paid a glowing poetical homage to her heroism, shared the same fate before a year had elapsed. When Vergniaud was informed of Charlotte's death, he exclaimed, "She has killed us, but she teaches us how to die."

Her history, trial, and execution, so beautifully and vividly described by Lamartine, we give as follows:—

Whilst Paris, France, the leaders and the armies of the factions were preparing to rend the republic to atoms, the shadow of a grand idea was flitting over the mind of a young girl, which was to disconcert events and men, by throwing the arm and the life of a female athwart the destiny of the Revolution. It would seem as though Providence deigned to mark out the greatness of the deed by the weakness of the hand, and took pleasure in contrasting two species of fanaticism in bodily conflict—the one beneath the hideous guise of popular vengeance, in the person of Marat; the other under the heavenly charm of love of country, in a Jeanne d'Arc of liberty; each, notwithstanding, ending, through their mistaken zeal, in murder, and thus unfortunately presenting themselves before posterity, not as an end, but as a means—not by the aspect, but the hand—not by the mind, but by blood!

In a large and thronged street which traverses the city of Caen, the capital of Normandy, at that time the focus of the Girondist insurrection, there stood at the bottom of a courtyard an ancient habitation, with grey walls, stained by the weather and dilapidated by time. This building was styled *le Grand Manoir*. A fountain with stone brim, covered with moss, occupied one angle of the courtyard. A narrow low door, whose fluted lintels uniting in an arch over the top, exposed the worn steps of a winding staircase which led to the upper story. Two windows, with their small octagon panes of glass held in leadwork, feebly lighted the staircase and the empty chambers. The misty daylight in this antique and obscure abode impressed on it the character of vagueness, mystery, and melancholy, which the human fancy likes to see spread as a shroud over the cradle of deep thoughts and the abodes of strongly imaginative minds. Here resided, at the commencement of 1793, a grand-daughter of the great French tragedy writer, Pierre Corneille. Poets and heroes are of the same race. There is between them no other difference than that which exists between idea and fact. The one does what the other conceives, but the thought is wholly the same. Women are naturally as enthusiastic as the one, and as courageous as the other. Poetry, heroism, and love inherit the same blood.

This house belonged to a poor woman, a widow, childless, aged, and infirm—a Madame de Bretteville. With her had lived for some years a young female relative, whom she had adopted and brought up, in order to comfort her old age and relieve her from utter isolation. This girl was then in her twenty-fourth year. Her serious but fine features, grave yet very beautiful, seemed to have received the imprint of this dull abode and sequestered existence. There was in her something not of this earth. The inhabitants of the district who saw her walking out with her aged aunt on Sundays in order to go to church, or caught a glimpse of her through the doorway, reading for hours at a time in the courtyard, seated in the sunshine at the brink o. the fountain, relate that their admiration of her was mingled with *prestige* and respect, arising from that strength of mind which, beaming forth, intimidates the vulgar eye; or that deep feeling of the soul imprinted on her features; or that presentiment of a tragic destiny which, anticipating the event, stamps its mark upon the brow.

This young creature was tall, without exceeding the usual height of the high statured and well proportioned women of Normandy. Natural grace and dignity, like the rhythm of poetry, displayed itself in her steps and action. The ardor of the south mingled itself in her complexion with the high color of the women of the north. Her hair seemed black when fastened in a large mass around her head, or arranged in clusters on each side of her brows. It seemed gold colored at the points of the tresses, like the ear of corn, deeper and more lustrous than the wheat-stalk in the sunlight. Her eyes, large and expanding almost to her temples, were of a color variable like the wave of ocean, which borrows its tint from the shadow or the day beam —blue when she reflected, almost black when called into animated play. Long eye-lashes, blacker than her hair, gave the appearance of great depth to her glance. Her nose, which united with her brow by an almost imperceptible curve, was slightly expanded near the middle. Her Grecian mouth displayed the well cut lips, whose expression, impossible to depict, fluctuated between tenderness and severity, equally formed to breathe love or patriotism.

The projecting chin, divided by a deep dimple, gave to the lower part of her face a character of masculine resolution which contrasted with the perfectly feminine contour of her lovely face. Her cheeks had the freshness of youth and the firm oval of health. She blushed or turned pale very suddenly. Her skin had the wholesome and marbled whiteness of perfect healthiness. Her chest, wide and somewhat thin, offered a bust of sculpture scarcely undulated by the characteristic contour of her sex. Her arms were full of muscle; her hands long, and her fingers taper. Her attire, conformable to the humbleness of her fortune and the retirement in which she dwelt, was simplicity itself. She relied on nature, and disdained every artifice or whim of fashion in her dress. Those who saw her in her youth describe her as always attired in a gown of dark cloth, cut like a riding habit, with a hat of grey felt, turned up at the sides with black riband, round and like those worn by women of rank at that period. The tone of her voice—that living echo which bespeaks the whole soul in a vibration of the air—left a deep and tender impression in the ear of those whom she addressed; and they spoke still of that tone, ten years after they had heard it, as of strange and unforgotten music ineffaceably imprinted on the memory. There were in this scale of the soul notes so sonorous and deep, that they said to hear was even more than to see her, and that her voice formed a portion of her beauty.

This young girl was named Charlotte Corday d'Armont. Although of noble blood, she was born in a cottage called le Ronceray, in the village of Ligneries, not far from d'Argentan. Misfortune had ushered her into life, which she was destined to quit by the scaffold.

Her father, François de Corday d'Armont, was one of those country gentlemen whose poverty made him almost on a level with the peasant. This nobility preserved nothing of its ancient elevation but a certain respect for the family name, and a vague hope of a return to fortune, which prevented him alike from lowering himself by his manner, or of raising himself by his labor. The land which such rural nobility cultivated in its small and inalienable domains nourished, without humiliating it by its indigence. Nobility and the soil seemed to be wedded in France, as aristocracy and the sea are wedded in Venice. M. de Corday united to this agricultural occupation a restlessness in politics, and literary tastes, then very common in this cultivated portion of the nobles of the population. He longed with all his soul for a coming revolution. He was wretched in his inaction and poverty. He had written some casual pamphlets against despotism and the law of primogeniture, and his productions were full of the feeling which was speedily to burst forth. He had a horror of superstition, the ardor of the newly springing philosophy, and the conviction of the necessity of a revolution; but either from lack of genius, restlessness of temperament, or the malevolence of fortune, which restrain the highest talents in oblivion, he could not make his way through events.

He pined in the obscurity of his petty fief of Ligneries, in the bosom of his yearly increasing family. Five children,—two sons and three daughters, of whom Charlotte was the second,—made him feel daily with more acuteness the stern and sad pressure of want. His wife, Jacqueline-Charlotte-Marie-de-Gonthier-des-Autiers, died, leaving her husband to her daughters, still young, but really bequeathing to her orphans that domestic tradition and daily inspiration which death carries off from children when it bereaves them of their mother.

Charlotte and her sisters lived on after this for some years at Ligneries, almost running wild, clothed in coarse cloth, like the young girls of Normandy, and, like them, working in the garden, making hay, gleaning and gathering the apples on the small estate of their father. At length necessity compelled M. de Corday to separate from his daughters, who, by favor of their nobility and their indigence, entered a monastery at Caen, of which Madame Belzunce was abbess. This abbey, whose vast cloisters and chapel of Roman architecture were built in 1066, by Matilda, wife of William the Conqueror, after having been deserted, degraded, and forgotten in its ruins, until 1730, was then magnificently restored; and at this day forms one of the finest hospitals in the kingdom, and one of the most splendid public buildings in the city of Caen.

Charlotte was then thirteen years of age. These convents were then really Christian abodes for women, who lived apart from the world, still hearing all its reports and sharing in all its movements. The monastic life, replete with pleasant employments and close friendships, for some time captivated the young girl. Her ardent soul and impassioned fancy threw her into that state of dreamy contemplation in which enthusiasts fancy they behold God,—a state which the careful watchfulness of a superior and the power of imitation so easily change in infancy into faith and devotional exercises. The iron disposition of Madame Roland herself would have warmed and softened in presence of this heavenly fire. Charlotte, more tender, yielded more easily. For some years she was a model of piety. She dreamed of ending her life—as yet hardly opened at its, first page, and of burying herself in this living tomb, where instead of death, she found repose, friendship, and happiness.

But the stronger were her feelings, the more rapidly did she penetrate and reach the extremity of her thoughts: she rapidly plumbed the depths of her childish faith, and contemplated beyond her domestic ideas others, fresh—luminous—sublime. She neither forsook God nor virtue, the two earliest passions of her soul, but she gave them other names—different shapes. Philosophy, which was then irradiating France with its lights, gained admittance, with the books then in vogue, through the gratings of nunneries. These were deeply studied in the seclusion of the cloister; and in opposition to monastic pettinesses, philosophy formed its most ardent adepts. The youth there, male and female, in the universal triumph of reason, saw their fetters broken, and adored their regained liberty.

Charlotte formed in the convent those affectionate predilections of infancy so like the relationships of the heart. Her friends were two young girls of noble houses, but of fortunes humble as her own—Mesdemoiselles de Faudoas and de Forbin. The abbess, Madame de Belzunce, and the assistant, Madame Doulcet de Pontécoulant, had distinguished Charlotte, and they admitted her into those somewhat mundane parties which custom permitted the abbesses to keep up with their relatives in the world, even in the seclusion of their convents.

At the period when monasteries were suppressed, Charlotte was nineteen years of age. The penury of her father's home had increased with time. Her two brothers in the king's service had emigrated; one of her sisters was dead, the other managed her father's poverty-stricken home at Argentan. Madame de Bretteville, the old aunt, received Charlotte into her house at Caen, though, like her family, she was poor, living in that obscurity and silence which hardly allowed the nearest neighbor to be aware of the existence and name of a poor widow. Her age and infirmities cast even a deeper gloom over her condition. Charlotte aided her in domestic duties, accompanying her aunt in the evenings to those meetings of the nobility which the fury of the people had not wholly destroyed, and where some remnants of the *ancien régime* were still tolerated in their attempts to console each other, and in their lamentations over the state of circumstances. Charlotte, respecting these regrets and superstitions of the past, never cast a word of reproach on them, but smiled to herself, whilst in her inmost soul she kept up the already kindled flame of different opinions—a flame which daily burnt more ardently.

Charlotte passed her days in the courtyard and garden, reading and musing. No one interfered or directed her in any way: her freedom, opinions, and studies are wholly unconstrained. The religious and political opinions of Madame de Bretteville were habits rather than convictions; and the republican sentiments of Charlotte's father had been more or less imbibed by every member of his family, inclining them all for the new ideas which had sprung up. Charlotte's age inclined her to the perusal of romances, which supplied visions ready drawn for unemployed minds. Her feelings led her to pursue works of philosophy, which transform the vague instincts of humanity into sublime theories of government; and historical productions, which convert theories into actions, and ideas into men.

She found this two-fold desire of her imagination and heart satisfied in Jean Jacques Rousseau, the philosopher of love, and the poet of politics; in Raynal, a fanatic of humanity; in Plutarch, a personification of history, who paints more than he relates, and imparts life to the events and characters of his heroes. These three works were incessantly in her hands, whilst from time to time she read *Heloise*, and works of that class. Yet, whilst her imagination was thus warmed, her mind lost none of its purity, nor her youth its chastity. Absorbed in the desire of loving and being loved, inspiring, and sometimes experiencing the first symptoms of love, her reserve, her dependence, and destitution always repressed the avowal of such feelings. Her love, thus restrained, changed not its nature but its ideal, and became a vague, yet sublime devotion to a dream of public happiness. The passion with which she would have been inspired for some one individual consumed her in her ardor for her country, and the desire of immolating herself to this had wholly possessed her—was her love or her virtue; and, however bloody was the sacrifice to be, she had resolved on its consummation.

She had reached that enthusiastic state of mind which is the suicide of happiness, not for the profit of glory or ambition, like Madame Roland, but for the sake of liberty and humanity, like Judith or Epicharis. She only awaited the occasion—it came, and she thought to seize it.

It was at this moment that the Girondists were struggling with daring courage and prodigious eloquence against their enemies in the Convention. The Jacobins only desired to wrest the republic from the Gironde, in order to precipitate France into a bloody anarchy. The convulsive throes of liberty, the hateful tyranny of the mob of Paris, substituted for the legal sovereignty of the nation, represented by its deputies; arbitrary imprisonments, the assassinations of September, the conspiracy of the 10th of March, the insurrection of the 30th and 31st of May, the expulsion and proscription of the purer portion of the Assembly, their scaffold in perspective, where liberty would ascend with them, the probity of Roland, the youth of Onfrede and Barbaroux, Isnard's cry of despair, Buzot's constancy, Pétion's integrity, from an idol become a victim, the martyrdom in the tribune of Lanjuinais, who only required that he might parallel Cicero's fate—that his tongue should be nailed to the rostrum; and finally, the eloquence of Vergniaud, that hope of good citizens, that remorse of froward ones, become suddenly mute, and leaving honest men to their discouragement, and the wicked to their infamy: in the place of these men, interesting or sublime, who appeared to defend in the breach the last ramparts of society, and the sacred hearth of every citizen, a Marat, the dregs and leprosy of the people, triumphing over the laws by sedition, crowned by impunity, carried into the tribune on the arms of the faubourgs, attaining the dictatorship of anarchy, spoliation, assassination, and threatening every species of independence, property, liberty, and life in the departments; all these convulsions, excesses, terrors, had deeply shaken the provinces of Normandy.

The presence in Calvados of the proscribed and fugitive deputies, appealing to liberty against oppression, and lighting up the hearths of the department in order to call up avengers for the country, had excited even to adoration the attachment of the city of Caen towards the Girondists, and execration against Marat, whose very name had become synonymous with crime.

What was desired in Normandy before the 10th of August was not so much the overthrow of the throne as an equalising constitution of the monarchy. The city of Rouen, capital of that province, was attached to the person of Louis XVI., and had offered him an asylum before his fall. The scaffold of that prince had saddened and humiliated the good citizens. The other cities of this part of France were rich, industrious, and agricultural. Peace and shipping were requisite to their prosperity, and a horror against the king's murderers, and a secret disposition to establish a *regime*, which should unite the assurances of a monarchy with the liberties of the republic, prevailed amongst them. Thence their enthusiasm for these Girondists, men of the constitution of 1791; thence, also, the hope which clung to their restoration and their vengeance. All patriotism was thus attacked, every virtue was thus sensibly assailed, all hope of real liberty died with them.

Charlotte Corday felt all these blows directed against her country concentrate themselves in anguish, despair, and daring in her already deeply stricken heart. She saw the loss of France, saw the victims, and believed she discerned the tyrant. She swore an inward oath, to avenge the one, punish the other, and save all. She pondered for many days over the vague determination of her heart, without clearly resolving on what deed her country required at her hands, which link of crime it was most urged to cut through. She considered things, men, circumstances, in order that her courage might not be fruitless, nor her blood spilled in vain.

The Girondists, Buzot, Salles. Pétion, Valady, Gorsas, Kervelegan, Mollevault, Barbaroux, Louvet, Giroux, Bussy, Bergoing, Lesage (d'Eure-et-Loir), Meihan, Henri Lariviere, Duchatel, had been for some time assembled at Caen, and occupied themselves with fomenting the general insurrection in the departments of the north and combining it with the republican insurrection of Brittany, in recruiting battalions of volunteers, and sending them to the army of Puisaye and Wimpfen, which was to march on Paris, and in keeping up, in their localities, the fire of indigna-

2

tion in the departments which were to consume their enemies. By rising against the omnipotence of Paris, and the dictatorship of the Convention, the youth of the departments believed they were rising against Marat only.

Danton and Robespierre, less conspicuous in the last efforts of the people against the Girondists, had in the eyes of the insurgents, neither importance nor authority over the people, nor the sanguinary delirium of Marat. They left the names of these two great partisans of the Montagne in the shade, in order not to damage the esteem in which these two popular and important persons were held by the Jacobins of the departments. The multitude was deceived, and saw tyranny and freedom in one man's hands only. Charlotte, amongst the rest, was so mistaken. The shadow of Marat darkened all the republic in her eyes.

The Girondists, whom the city of Caen had taken under its care, all lived together in the old palace of that city, whither the seat of the federalist government was removed, together with the insurrectional committee; and here were held assemblies of the people, where the citizens, and even the women, flocked in crowds in order to see and hear these first victims of anarchy, these last avengers of liberty. The names so long prevalent of Pétion, Buzot, Louvet, Barbaroux, pleaded more powerfully than their orations to the imaginations of Calvados. The vicissitudes of revolutions softened the spectators, and made them proud of speedily avenging such illustrious guests. They were overcome by the energetic accents of these persons, and pointed as they passed to Pétion, the king of Paris, to Barbaroux, hero of Marseilles, whose youth and beauty adorned eloquence, courage, and misfortunes; and they went about appealing to arms, and exciting sons, husbands, brothers, to enlist in their battalions. Charlotte Corday, surmounting the prejudices of her rank, and the timidity of her sex and age, ventured frequently to be present with some friend at these meetings, and was remarked for the silent enthusiasm which increased her feminine beauty, and which was only betrayed by her tears.

Louvet addressed inflammatory proclamations to the cities of the south:

"The forces of the department which are on the road to Paris," said he, "do not seek enemies to combat them: they go to fraternise with the Parisians; they go to support the tottering statue of liberty. Citizens! you who may see these friendly phalanxes pass through your roads, your towns, and your villages —fraternise with them. Do not suffer blood-thirsty monsters to establish themselves amongst you to arrest them on their march." These words produced thousands of volunteers. More than six thousand were already assembled in the town of Caen. On Sunday, the 7th of July, they were passed in review by the Girondist deputies and the authorities of Calvados, with all the requisite preparations to electrify their courage. The spontaneous assemblage rising, arms in hand, to go and die in avenging liberty for the insults of anarchy, recalled the patriotic insurrection of 1792; drawing to the frontiers all who desired to live no longer, if the country no longer existed. Charlotte Corday was present in a balcony at this enrolment and departure. The enthusiasm of these young citizens, abandoning their firesides to go and protect the violated hearth of the national representation, and brave cannon balls or the guillotine responded to her own. She even found it too cold. She felt indignant at the small number of enrolments which this review had added to the regiments and battalions of Wimpfen. There were not in fact on this day more than a score. This enthusiasm, it was said, was endeared to her by the mysterious but pure feeling which one of these volunteers, who thus tore themselves from their families, their love, and it might be from life, bore towards her. Charlotte Corday had not been able to remain insensible to this concealed adoration, but she immolated this attachment to one more sublime.

This young man was named Franquelin. He adored in silence the young female republican. He carried on a correspondence with her full of reserve and respect. She answered with the sad and tender reserve of a young girl who had no dowry but misfortune to bestow. She had given her portrait to the young volunteer, and permitted him to love her, at least through her image.

M. de Franquelin, borne away by the general impulse, and sure of obtaining a glance and approbation by arming himself in the cause of liberty, had enrolled himself in the battalion of Caen. Charlotte could not help trembling and growing pale on seeing this battalion defile to depart. Tears fell from her eyes. Pétion, who passed under the balcony, and who knew Carlotte, was astonished at this weakness, and thus addressed her: "Would you then be happy," said he to her, "if they did not depart?" The young maiden blushed, made no reply, and withdrew. Pétion had not comprehended this distress: the future revealed it to him. Young Franquelin, after the trial and execution of Charlotte Corday, death-stricken himself by the counter-blow of the axe which had decapitated her whom he adored, retired to a village in Normandy. There, alone with his mother, he lingered for some months, and died, requesting that the portrait and the letters of Charlotte Corday might be buried with him—that image and that secret repose in that coffin.

After the departure of the volunteers, Charlotte had but one thought: to anticipate their arrival in Paris, to spare their generous lives, and render patriotism useless, in delivering France from tyranny before them. This attachment, endured rather than tested, was one of the sorrows of her devotion, but was not the cause of it.

The true cause was her patriotism. A presentiment of terror already spread over France at this moment. The scaffold was erected in Paris. They spoke of speedily carrying it through all the republic. The power of La Montagne and Marat, if it triumphed, could only defend itself by the hand of the executioner. The monster, it was said, had already written the lists of proscription, and counted the number of heads which were necessary for his suspicions and his vengeance. Two thousand five hundred victims were marked out in Lyons, three thousand at Marseilles, twenty-eight thousand at Paris, and three hundred thousand in Brittany and Calvados. The name of Marat caused a shudder like the mention of death. To check such an effusion of blood, Charlotte desired to shed her own. The more she broke her ties on earth, the more agreeable would she be as the voluntary victim to the liberty which she desired to appease.

Such was the secret disposition of her mind, but Charlotte desired to see clearly before she struck the blow.

She could not better enlighten herself upon the state of Paris, upon men and matters, than through the Girondists, the parties interested in this cause. She wished to sound them without disclosing herself to them. She respected them sufficiently not to reveal a project which they might have possibly regarded as a crime, or prevented as a generous but rash act. She had the constancy to conceal from her friends the thought of sacrificing herself for their safety. She presented herself under specious pretexts at the Hôtel of Intendance, where the citizens who had business with them could approach the deputies. She saw Buzot, Pétion, and Louvet. She discoursed twice with Barbaroux. The conversation of a young, beautiful, and enthusiastic maiden with the youngest and the handsomest of the Girondists, under the guise of politics, was calculated to give rise to calumny, or at least to excite the smile of incredulity upon some lips. It was so at the first moment. Louvet, who afterwards wrote a hymn to the purity and glory of the young heroine, believed at first in one of those vulgar seductions of the senses with which he had embellished his notorious romance. Buzot, totally occupied with another image, hardly cast a glance upon Charlotte. Pétion, on crossing the public hall of the Intendance, where Charlotte awaited Barbaroux, kindly rallied her on her assiduity, and making allusion to the contrast between such a step and her birth, "Behold then," said he, "the beautiful aristocrat, who comes to see the republicans!" The young girl comprehended the smile, and the insinuation so wounding to her purity. She blushed, and, vexed afterwards at having done so, answered in a serious yet gentle tone, "Citizen Pétion, you judge me to-day without knowing me; one day you will know who I am."

In these audiences which she obtained of Barbaroux, and which she designedly prolonged, to feed herself, from his discourses, with the republicanism, the enthusiasm, and the projects of La Gironde, she assumed the humble part of a suppliant; she requested from the young Marseillais a letter of introduction from one of his colleagues in the Convention, which would introduce her to the minister of the interior.

She had, she said, claims to present to the government in favor of Mademoiselle de Forbin, her friend in infancy. Mademoiselle de Forbin had been induced to emigrate by her relatives, and was suffering poverty in Switzerland.

Barbaroux gave her a letter for Duperret, one of the seventy-three deputies of the Girondist party who were overlooked in the first proscription.

This letter of Barbaroux's, which afterwards led Duperret to the scaffold, did not contain a single word which could be imputed as criminal to the deputy who received it. Barbaroux confined himself to recommending a young female of Caen to the consideration and protection of Duperret. He announced to him a publication of their mutual friend, Salles, upon the constitution. Furnished with this letter and a passport which she had taken out some days before, for Argentan, Charlotte went to pay her farewell acknowledgements to Barbaroux. The sound of her voice struck Barbaroux with a presentiment which he could not then comprehend. "If we had known her design," said he at a later period, "and if we had been capable of a crime by such a hand, it was not Marat whom we should have pointed out for her vengeance."

The gaiety which Charlotte had always mingled with the gravity of her patriotic conversations vanished from her countenance on quitting for ever the dwelling of the Girondists. The last struggle between the thought and its execution was going on in her mind. She concealed this interior combat by careful and well-managed dissimulation. The gravity of her countenance alone, and some tears, ill concealed from the eyes of her relatives, revealed the voluntary agony of her self-immolation. Interrogated by her aunt: "I weep," said she, "over the misfortunes of my country, over those of my relatives, and over yours. Whilst Marat lives no one can be sure of a day's existence."

Madame de Bretteville remembered afterwards, that on entering Charlotte's chamber to awaken her, she found upon her bed an old Bible open at the Book of Judith, and in which she had read this verse, underlined with a pencil: "Judith went forth from the city, adorned with a marvellous beauty, which the Lord had bestowed on her to deliver Israel."

On the same day, Charlotte having gone out to make her preparations for departure she met in the street some citizens who were playing cards before the door. "You play," said she with an accent of bitter irony, "and the country is dying."

Her manner and speech testified the impatience and precipitation of a departure. She set out at length on the 7th July for Argentan. There she took her last adieu of her father and sister. She told them that she went to seek a refuge and existence in England against the Revolution and misery, and that she desired to receive the paternal benediction previous to this long separation. Her father approved of this decision.

On embracing her father and sister, she wept more over the past than for the future. She returned on the same day to

Caen. She there deceived the tenderness of her aunt by the same ruse which had deceived her father. She told her that she should soon set out for England, where some emigrant friends had prepared her an asylum and a lot which she could not hope for in her own country. This pretext concealed the sorrow of her adieux, and the various arrangements for her departure. She had privately arranged it for the morrow, the 9th of July, by the Paris diligence. Charlotte filled up these last hours in gratitude, attention, and tenderness towards that aunt to whom she owed such long and kind hospitality, and she provided through one of her friends for the old servant who had taken care of her in her youth. She ordered and paid in advance, at the tradespeople's shops in Caen, for some little presents of dresses and embroidery destined to be worn after her departure, by some youthful companions of her early days. She distributed her favorite books amongst the young persons of her acquaintance, and reserved none for herself but a volume of Plutarch, as if she did not desire to separate herself, in the crisis of her life, from the society of those great men with whom she had lived and wished to die. Finally, on the 9th of July, very early in the morning, she took under her arm a small bundle of the most requisite articles of apparel, embraced her aunt, and told her she was going to sketch the haymakers in the neigboring meadows. With a sheet of drawing paper in her hand, she went out to return no more. At the foot of the staircase she met the child of a poor laborer, named Robert, who lodged in the house, in the street. The child was accustomed to play in the court. She sometimes gave him little toys. "Here! Robert," said she to him, giving him the drawing-paper, which she no longer required to keep her in countenance: "that is for you; be a good boy and kiss me; you will never see me again." And she embraced the child, leaving a tear upon his cheek. That was the last tear on the threshold of the house of her youth. She had nothing left to give but her blood.

The freedom and harmlessness of her conversation in the carriage which conveyed her to Paris did not inspire her traveling companions with any other sentiment than that of admiration, good-will, and that natural curiosity which attaches itself to the name and fate of an unknown girl of dazzling youth and beauty. She continued to play during the first day with a little girl, whom chance had placed beside her in the carriage. Whether it were that her love for children overcame her pre-occupation of thought, or that she had already laid aside the burden of her trouble, and desired to enjoy these last hours of sport with innocence and with life.

The other travellers were Montagnards, who fled from the suspicion of federalism to Paris, and were profuse in imprecations against the Girondists and in adoration for Marat. Attracted by the graces of the young girl, they strove to draw from her her name, the object of her journey, and her address in Paris. Her loneliness at that age encouraged them to familiarities, which she repelled by the modesty of her manners, and the evasive brevity of her answers, which she was enabled to terminate by feigning sleep. A young man, who was more reserved, seduced by so much modesty and such charms, ventured to declare to her his respectful admiration. He implored her to authorise him to ask her hand of her relations. She turned this sudden love into kind railing and mirth. She promised the young man to let him know her name and her disposition in regard to himself at a later period. She charmed her fellow travellers to the end of the journey, by that delightful conduct from which all regretted to separate themselves.

She entered Paris on Thursday, 11th of July, at noon. She was conducted to the hotel which had been indicated to her at Caen, in the Rue des Vieux Augustins, No. 17, the Hôtel de la Providence. She retired to rest at five in the evening, and slept profoundly until the next day. Without a confidant, and without a witness, during those long hours of solitude and agitation, in a public house and amidst the noise of this capital whose magnitude and tumult absorb the ideas and trouble the senses, no one knows what passed in that mind, upon her awakening and recollecting the resolve which summoned her to execution. Who can measure the force of her thought, and the resistence of nature? The thought prevailed.

She arose, dressed herself in a simple but respectable gown, and went to Duperret's. The friend of Barbaroux was at the Convention. His daughters, in the absence of their father, received from the young stranger Barbaroux's letter of introduction. Duperret would not be home until evening.

Charlotte returned and passed the entire day in her chamber in reading, reflecting and in prayer. At six o'clock she returned again to Duperret's. The deputy was at table at supper with his family and friends. He rose and received her in his drawing-room, without a witness. Charlotte explained to him the service she expected from his courtesy, and begged him to conduct her to the minister of the interior, Garat, and to aid by his presence and credit the suit she had to urge. This request was but a pretext on her part to bring her into contact with one of these Girondists for whose cause she was about to sacrifice herself, and to derive from her discourse with him full information and proper indications, the better to assure her steps and her hand.

Duperret, pressed by time and recalled by his guests, told her he could not conduct her on that day to Garat's, but that he would call upon her at her residence on the following morning to accompany her to the offices. She left her name and address with Duperret, and made some steps as if about to withdraw, but as if overcome by the interest with which the honest countenance of this good man and the youth of his daughters had inspired her, "Permit me to advise you, Citizen Duperret:" said she, in a voice full of mystery and warning; "quit the Convention; you can do no more good there; go to Caen, and rejoin your colleagues and brothers." "My post is at Paris," replied the representative; "I will not leave it." "You are in error," replied Charlotte, with a significative and almost suppliant appeal. "Believe me," she added in a lower and more rapid voice; "fly, fly, before to-morrow night!" and she departed without awaiting an answer.

These words, the sense of which was only known to the stranger, were interpreted by Duperret as a simple allusion to the urgency of the perils which menaced those of his opinion in Paris. He went and reseated himself with his friends. He told them that a young female, with whom he had just discoursed, had, in her attitude and speech, something strange and mysterious, with which he was struck, and which commanded from him reserve and circumspection.

In the evening a decree of the Convention ordered seals to be put on the furniture of the deputies suspected of attachment to the twenty-one. Duperret was one of the number. He went, however, on the following day, the 12th, very early in the morning, to Charlotte at her lodging, and conducted her to Garat. Garat did not receive them. The minister could not grant an audience before eight o'clock in the evening This *contre-temps* appeared to discourage Duperret. He represented to the young girl, that his position as one suspected, and the measures taken against him on that very night, rendered his patronage henceforth more prejudicial than useful to his clients; that besides, she was not furnished with a power from Mademoiselle de Forbin to act in her name, and that in default of this formality his proceedings would be futile.

The stranger remonstrated but little, as a person who had no more need of the pretext with which she had colored her first steps, and who contented herself with the slightest argument to abandon her idea. Duperret left her at the door of the Hôtel de la Providence. She pretended to enter it. She went out immediately, and inquired, street by street, the way to the Palais Royal.

She entered the gardens, not a stranger who desired to satisfy her curiosity by the contemplation of monuments and public gardens, but as a traveller who had only one object in the city, and who did not desire to lose a step or a day. She sought with her eyes, under the galleries, for the shop of a cutler. She entered one; selected a poignard-knife with an ebony haft, paid three francs for it, concealed it under her handkerchief. and with slow steps returned to the garden, where she seated herself for a moment upon one of the stone benches abutting on the arcades.

She desired to make of this murder a solemn immolation, which should strike terror into the minds of the imitators of the tyrant. Her first idea had been to approach Marat, accost him, and sacrifice him in the Champ-de-Mars, at the great ceremony of the federation which was to take place on the 14th of July in commemoration of the triumph of liberty. The adjournment of this ceremony until the republic should suppress the Vendeans and rebels, deprived her of her theatre and victim. Her second idea was to strike Marat at the summit of the mountain, in the very midst of the Convention, beneath the eyes of his adorers and accomplices. Her hope in this case was that she herself should be immolated the next moment, and torn in pieces by the people, leaving no other trace or recollection than of two dead bodies and tyranny destroyed in its own blood. To bury her name in oblivion, and seek no recompense but in the act itself, asking her shame or renown but from her own conscience, God, and the good she could effect—such was to the last the single ambition of her mind. Shame! she would not have it for her family's sake. Renown! she desired not for herself. Glory! seemed to her a salary too commonplace, and unworthy of the disinterestness of her deed, and but calculated to deteriorate her virtue. However, the conversations she had had since her arrival in Paris, with Duperret and others informed her that Marat would not again appear in the Convention. Thus it was necessary to find the victim elsewhere, and to obtain access it was necessary to deceive him.

This she resolved on; yet was the dissimulation which was so foreign to the natural loyalty of her nature, which changed the dagger into a snare, courage into stratagem, and immolation into assassination,—the first remorse of her conscience, and her first punishment. Charlotte decided on striking the blow, but the means she was compelled to adopt cost her more than the deed itself. This she herself confessed. Conscience is just in the presence of posterity.

She returned to her chamber and wrote to Marat a billet, which she sent to the door of the friend of the people. "I have just arrived from Caen," she wrote. "Your love of country makes me presume that you will have pleasure in hearing of the unfortunate events of that portion of the republic. I shall present myself at your abode about one o'clock; have the goodness to receive me, and grant me a moment's conversation. I will put you in a position to be of great service to France."

Charlotte, relying on the effect of this note, went at the appointed hour to Marat's door, but could not obtain access to him. She then left with the portress a second note, more pressing and insidious than the former.

"I wrote to you this morning, Marat," she said; "did you have my letter? I cannot believe it, as they refuse me admittance to you. I hope that to-morrow you will grant me the interview I request. I repeat that I am just arrived from Caen, and have secrets to disclose to you most important for the safety of the republic. Besides, I am persecuted for the cause of liberty; I am unhappy, and that I am so should give me a claim on your patriotism."

Without awaiting his reply, Charlotte left her chamber at

seven o'clock P. M., clad with more than usual care in order, by a more studied appearance, to attract the persons about Marat. Her white gown was covered over the shoulders by a silk scarf, which, falling, over her bosom, fastened behind. Her hair was confined by a Normandy cap, the long lace of which played against her cheeks. A wide green silk riband was bound around her brows, and fastened her cap. Her hair fell loose down her back. No paleness of complexion, no wildness of gaze, no tremulousness of voice, revealed her deadly purpose. With this attractive aspect she knocked at Marat's door.

Marat inhabited the first floor of a dilapidated house in the Rue des Cordeliers, now Rue de l'Ecole de Médicine, No. 20. His apartment consisted of an ante-chamber and a writing room, looking out on a narrow courtyard, a small room containing his bath, a sleeping-room and dining-room looking on to the street. It was very meanly furnished. Numerous publications of Marat's were piled on the floor,—the newspapers of the day, still damp from the press, were scattered about on the chairs and tables, printers' lads going in and coming out incessantly, women employed in folding and addressing pamphlets and journals, the worn steps of the staircase, the ill-swept passages,—all attested the movement and disorder which surround a man much occupied, and the perpetual crowd of persons in the house of a journalist and leader of the people.

This abode displayed, as it were, the pride of poverty. It appeared as though its master, then all-powerful over the nation, was desirous of saying to his visitors when they contemplated his squalidness and his labor, "Look at the friend and model of the people! he has not cast off his abode, manners, or address."

This misery, though a display, was yet real. Marat's domestic arrangements were those of an humble artisan. A female, who controled his house affairs, was originally named Caterine Evrard, but was called Abertine Marat from the time the friend of the people gave her his name, taking her for his wife *one day in fine weather, in the face of open sunshine*, after the example of Jean-Jacques Rousseau. One servant aided this woman in her household duties. A messenger, named Laurent Basse, did the out door work, and when he had leisure, employed himself in the ante-chamber in packing up parcels of the papers and bills for the *friend of the people.*

The incessant activity of the writer had not relaxed in consequence of the lingering disease which was consuming him. The inflammatory action of his blood seemed to light up his mind. Now in his bed, now in his bath, he was perpetually writing, apostrophising, inveighing against his enemies, whilst exciting the Convention and the Cordeliers. Offended at the silence of the Assembly on the reception of his messages, he had recently addressed to it another letter, in which he threatened the Convention that he would be carried in his dying condition to the tribune, that he might shame the representatives with their cowardice, and dictate to them fresh murders. He left no repose either to himself or to others. Full of the presentiment of death, he only seemed to fear that his last hour, coming on too suddenly, would not leave him time to immolate sufficient criminals. More anxious to kill than to live, he hastened to send before him as many victims as possible, as so many hostages given by the knife to the completed revolution, which he desired to leave free from all enemies after his death. The terror which issued from Marat's house returned thither under another form—the unending dread of assassination. His companions and his intimate associates believed that they saw as many daggers raised against him as he raised over the heads of three hundred thousand citizens. Access to his house was forbidden, as it would be to the palace of tyranny. None were admitted to his presence but assured friends or denouncers strongly recommended, and who had submitted to interrogatories and severe examinations.

Charlotte was not aware of these obstacles, although she apprehended them. She alighted from the coach on the opposite side of the street, in front of Marat's residence. The day was on the wane, particularly in the quarters darkened by lofty houses and narrow streets. The portress at first refused to allow the young unknown to penetrate into the courtyard. She insisted, however, and ascended several stairs, regardless of the voice of the *concierge*. At these sounds, Marat's mistress half-opened the door, and refused to allow a female whom she did not know to enter. The confused sound of the altercation between these women, one of whom entreated that she might be allowed to speak to *the friend of the people*, whilst the other endeavored to close the door in her face, reached Marat's ears, who comprehended, by the few indistinct words that reached him, that the visitor was the stranger from whom he had received two notes during the day. In a loud and imperative voice he ordered that she should be admitted.

Abertine, either from jealousy or distrust, obeyed with much ill-will and grumbling. She showed the young girl into the small closet where Marat was, and left, as she quitted her, the door half open, that she might hear the lowest whisper or the smallest movement of the sick man.

The room was faintly lighted. Marat was in his bath, yet in this forced repose of his body, he allowed his mind no leisure. A plank, roughly planed, laid across the bath, was covered with papers, open letters, and half-written articles for his publication. He held in his right hand the pen which the arrival of the unknown female had suspended on its page. This was a letter to the Convention, to demand of it the judgment and proscription of the last Bourbons tolerated in France. Beside the bath, on a large block of oak, was a leaden inkstand, of the meanest fabric,—the foul source whence, for three years, had flowed so many delirious outpourings, so many denunciations, so much blood. Marat, covered in his bath with a cloth filthy with dirt and spotted with ink, had only his head, shoulders, the upper part of his chest, and his right arm out of the water. There was nothing in the features of this man to affect a woman's eye with tenderness, or give pause to a meditated blow. His matted hair, wrapped in a dirty handkerchief, with receding forehead, protruding eyes, prominent cheekbones, vast and sneering mouth, hairy chest, shrivelled limbs, and livid skin—such was Marat.

Charlotte took care not to look him in the face, for fear her countenance might betray the horror she felt at his sight. With downcast eyes, and her arms hanging motionless by her side, she stood close to the bath, awaiting until Marat should inquire as to the state of Normandy. She replied with brevity, giving to her replies the sense and tone likely to pacify the demagogue's wishes. He then asked the names of the deputies who had taken refuge at Caen. She gave them to him, and he wrote them down, and when he had concluded, said, in the voice of a man sure of his vengeance, "Well, before they are a week older, they shall have the guillotine!"

At these words, as if Charlotte's mind had awaited a last offence before it could resolve on striking the blow, she drew the knife from her bosom, and, with superhuman force, plunged it to the hilt in Marat's heart. She then drew the bloody weapon from the body of the victim, and let it fall at her feet. "Help, my dear,—help!" cried Marat, and then expired.

At this cry, Albertine, the maid servant, and Laurent Basse rushed into the apartment, and caught Marat's sinking head in their arms. Charlotte, motionless, and as if petrified at her crime, was standing behind the window curtain. The transparent material allowed her form to be easily distinguished. Laurent, taking up a chair, struck her a clumsy blow on the head, which knocked her to the floor, where Marat's mistress trampled her under foot in her rage. At the noise that ensued, and the cries of the two women, the inhabitants of the house hastened thither, neighbors and persons passing in the streets ascended the staircase and filled the room, the court-yard, and very speedily the whole quarter, demanding, with fierce exclamations that they would throw the assassin out to them, that they might avenge the dead—yet still warm—body of the people's idol. Soldiers and national guards entered, and order was, in some measure, re-established. Surgeons arrived, and endeavored to stanch the wound. The reddened water gave to the sanguinary democrat the appearance of having died in a bath of blood. It was a dead corpse that they lifted into bed.

Charlotte had risen from the floor without any assistance. Two soldiers held her with the arms crossed, as if in handcuffs, waiting until cords were brought to confine them. The file of bayonets which surrounded her could scarcely keep back the crowd which sought to rend her in pieces. Gesticulations, clenched fists, sticks, and brandished swords menaced her with a thousand deaths. Marat's concubine, escaping from the females who were consoling her, by turns uttered imprecations against Charlotte, and then burst into tears, or fainted. A fanatic Cordelier, named Langlois, a staymaker in the Rue Dauphine, had picked up the blood-stained knife, and made a funeral harangue over the victim. He interrupted his lamentations and eulogiums with revengeful gestures, in which he seemed to be perpetually thrusting the knife into the assassin's heart. Charlotte, who had made up her mind to any death that should follow, was, for a moment, fixed and petrified by this movement, these gestures, the hands and arms agitated so near to her, but was only affected by the piercing cries of Marat's mistress. Her countenance appeared to express towards this woman astonishment at not having thought that such a man could be loved, and regret at having been forced to pierce two hearts in order to reach one. Except the feeling of pity which the reproaches of Albertine for a moment impressed on her lips, no change was perceptible either in her features or complexion. Only, at the invectives of the orator, and the groans of the people at the loss of their idol, the bitter smile of contempt was visible on her features. "Poor people," she said, "you desire my death, whilst you owe me an altar for having freed you from a monster. Cast me to that infuriate mob," she said, afterwards, to the soldiery; "as they regret him, they are worthy to be my executioners." This remark, as a defiance to the fanaticism of the multitude, excited furious imprecations and fierce gesticulations. Guillard, the commissary of the section of the Théâtre Français, entered, escorted by a reinforcement of bayonets. He drew up the *procès verbal* of the murder, and had Charlotte conducted into Marat's dining room, to commence the interrogatory, where he wrote down her replies, which she gave calmly, clearly, and seriously, with a firm and resolute tone, in which the proud satisfaction at the act she had committed was alone perceptible. She made her confession as though it were praiseworthy. The report of the death of the "People's Friend" was spread abroad with the rapidity of an electric shock, by men running to and fro, full of excitement. All Paris was struck with stupor at the hearing of this deed. It seemed as though the republic was thunder-struck, and that dire events must spring from Marat's murder. Pale and trembling, several deputies entered the Convention, interrupting the business, and giving the first reports of the event. All refused to believe it, as they would refuse to give credit to a sacrilege. The commandant-general of the national guard, Henriot, came in and confirmed the news. "Yes," he said, "tremble, all of you. Marat has been assassinated by a young girl who rejoices at the blow she has struck. Look carefully after your own lives; the same peril threatens all. Mistrust green ribands, and let us swear to avenge the death of this great man!"

The deputies Maure, Chabot, Drouet, and Legendre, members of the committees of government, left the Chamber immediately and went to the spot. There they found the crowd increasing every moment, whilst Charlotte was replying to the interrogatories. They were overcome with surprise, at the sight of her youth and beauty, and at the calmness and firmness of her replies. Never had crime before presented such features to the eyes of men. She appeared so to alter it in their eyes that they felt a sympathy for her even in the very presence of her victim.

The *procès verbal* having finished, the deputies ordered that Charlotte should be conveyed to the Abbaye, the nearest prison. She entered the same hackney coach that had conveyed her thither. The Rue des Cordeliers was thronged with people, whose angry voices, frequently bursting out into vociferations and excess of rage, breathed vengeance, and made the transit difficult. Detachments of fusileers came up; the scarves of the commissaries, and the respect felt for the members of the Convention, kept back the mob, and cleared a way. At the moment when Charlotte, with her hands bound with cords, and supported by two national guards, crossed the threshold of the house to step into the coach, the people closed round the wheels with such gesticulations and groans that she felt as though her limbs were torn piece-meal by thousands of hands, and fainted. Returning to herself, she regretted that she still survived, yet she, with deep emotion, thanked those who had protected her from the brutalities of the crowd.

Chabot, Drouet, and Legendre followed her to the Abbaye, where she underwent a second examination, which lasted until very late. Legendre, proud of his revolutionary importance, and anxious to be thought also worthy to be a martyr to his patriotism, believed or feigned to believe that he recognised in Charlotte a young girl who had come to him on the previous evening in the dress of a nun, and whom he had sent away. "Citizen Legendre is mistaken," said Charlotte, with a smile, which disconcerted the deputy's pride. "I never before saw him. I do not esteem the life or death of such a man important to the safety of the republic."

She was searched, and in her pockets were found only the key of her trunk, her silver thimble, some implements of needle-work, a ball of cotton, two hundred francs in assignats and money, a gold watch, made at Caen, and her passport.

Beneath her neckerchief she still concealed the sheath of the knife with which she had stabbed Marat. "Do you recognise this knife?" she was asked. "Yes." "What led you to this crime?" "I saw," she replied, "civil war ready to rend France to atoms: persuaded that Marat was the principal cause of the perils and calamities of the land, I have sacrificed my life for his to save my country." "Mention the persons who urged you to this detestable crime, which you could not have conceived of yourself." "No one knew my intention. I deceived my aunt, with whom I lived, as to the object of my journey. I deceived my father similarly. Few persons visit my relations, and no one could have had the slightest suspicion of my idea." "Did you not quit the city of Caen with the decided resolution of assassinating Marat?" "That was my sole motive in quitting that city." "Where did you procure the weapon? What persons have you seen in Paris? What have you done since Thursday, the day of your arrival?"

To these questions she replied with the utmost sincerity, detailing every particular as to her arrival at Paris, and what she had done since. "Did you not attempt to escape after the murder?" "I should have gone out at the door if I had not been prevented." "Are you a single woman?" "I am." "Have you never had a lover?" "Never."

These answers, alternate, precise, proud, and disdainful, made the hearers reflect frequently on the power of the fanaticism which employed and strengthened so feeble a hand. They hoped to discover an instigator beneath this candor and beauty, and they found nought, save inspiration and intrepidity.

At the end of the examination, Chabot, disappointed at the result, devoured, with his eyes, the hair, the features, the whole person of the young girl. He fancied he perceived a folded paper pinned to the bosom of her dress, and extended his hand to take it. Charlotte had forgotten this paper, which contained an address to the French, drawn up by herself, and calling on them to punish tyrants and restore concord. She saw in the gesture and look of Chabot an insult to her modesty; she was unable to put out her hands, which were bound, but the horror and indignation she felt caused her to make so sudden and convulsive a spring backwards, that the string of her dress burst, and exposed her bosom. Quick as thought she stooped, and bent herself almost double to conceal her nudity from her judges. It was too late, and her chastity had to blush at the looks of man. Patriotism had not rendered these men cynical or insensible, and they appeared to suffer as much as Charlotte at this involuntary torture of her innocence. She entreated them to untie her hands, with which they complied, and Charlotte, turning round to the wall, arranged her dress. Advantage was taken of her hands being free to make her sign her replies. The cords had left blue marks on her arms, and when the guards were preparing to again bind her, she entreated to be allowed to put on her gloves, in order to save her unnecessary torture. The accent and gesture of the poor girl were so touching that Harmand turned aside to conceal his tears.

The following are the principal textual passages of this address to the French, which has been hitherto lost to history, and which has been communicated to us since the commencement of the publication of this work by the present possessor, M. Paillet. It is written in the hand of Charlotte Corday, in large bold characters, as though destined to be legible at some distance. The paper is folded in eight, and is pierced by the pin that fastened it to Charlotte's dress.

"*Address to Frenchmen friendly to the Laws and Peace.*

"How long, O unhappy Frenchmen! will you delight in trouble and division? Too long have the factious and villains substituted the interests of their ambition in the place of the general interest. Why, victims of their fury, should you destroy yourselves to establish the tyranny they desire on the ruins of France? Factions break out on every side; the Montagne triumphs by crime and oppression; a few monsters, bathed in our blood, lead these detestable plots. We are laboring at our own destruction with more zeal and energy than we ever employed in the conquest of liberty. O Frenchmen!—but a brief space, and nothing will remain but the recollection of your existence.

"Already the departments are indignantly marching on Paris. Already the fire of discord and civil war consumes the half of this vast empire; there is but one means of extinguishing it, but it must be promptly employed. Already that vilest of wretches, Marat, whose very name presents the image of every crime, by falling beneath an avenging steel, shakes the Montagne, and alarms Danton, Robespierre, and the other brigands, seated on this bloody throne, surrounded by the thunders which the avenging gods doubtless only suspend, in order to render their fall more terrible, and to deter all those who would seek to build their fortunes on the ruins of a deceived people.

"Frenchmen, you know your enemies.—Rise—march! Let the destruction of the Montagne leave nothing but brothers and friends. I know not if Heaven reserves for us a republican government, but a Montagnard can be given to us only in the excess of divine vengeance. O France! thy repose depends upon the execution of the laws. I do not infringe them by killing Marat. Condemned by the universe, he is beyond the pale of the law. What tribunal will condemn me? If I am guilty, so was Alcides when he destroyed the monsters.

"O my country! thy misfortunes rend my heart. I can only offer thee my life; and I thank Heaven that I am at liberty to dispose of it. No one will be a loser by my death. I will not imitate Paris (the murderer of Lepelletier de Saint Fargeau) by killing myself. I desire that my last sigh may be useful to my fellow-citizens—that my head, borne through Paris, may serve as a rallying point for all the friends of the laws; that the tottering Montagne should behold its destruction, written in my blood; that I may be their last victim, and that the universe may declare that I have merited well at the hands of humanity. And I declare that, if my conduct were viewed in another light, I should care but little.

> "'Qu'a l'univers surpris cette grande action
> Soit un objet d'horreur, ou d'admiration,
> Mon esprit, peu jaloux de vivre en la memoire,
> Ne considere point le reproche ou la gloire:
> Toujours independant et toujours citoyen,
> Mon devoir me suffit, tout le reste n'est rien.
> Allez ne songez, plus, qu'a sortir de l'esclavage!'"

"My parents and friends should not be molested. No one was acquainted with my plans. I join my baptismal register to this address, to show of what the weakest hand is capable, when aided by the most entire devotion. If I do not succeed in my enterprise, Frenchmen, I have shown you the way. You know your enemies. Arise—march! Strike them!"

On reading these verses written by the hand of the granddaughter of Corneille, we are at first led to believe that they are by her ancestor, and that she thus invoked the Roman patriotism of the great tragic author of her race. But this is not the case: they are in Voltaire's tragedy of "The Death of Cæsar."

The authenticity of this address is attested by a letter of Fouquier Tinville. This letter of the public accuser is directed to the Committee of General Safety of the Convention. We subjoin it: "Citizens, I forward to you the report of the examination of Charlotte Corday, and the two letters written by her in her confinement, one of which is addressed to Barbaroux. These letters are circulated in so mutilated a form that it will, perhaps, be necessary to print them in their present state; and if, citizens, after having read them, you think there is no obstacle to printing them, you will oblige me by informing me.

"I should observe, that I have just learned that this female assassin was the friend of Belzunce, a colonel, who was killed at Caen in an insurrection, and that since this period she has displayed an implacable hatred towards Marat; and that this hatred appears to have been re-kindled at the moment when Marat denounced Biron, the relation of Belzunce, and Barbaroux appears to have availed himself of the criminal feelings of this girl against Marat, to induce her to commit this horrible murder.

"FOUQUIER TINVILLE."

Charlotte Corday was placed in a cell and watched, even during the night, by two *gens d'armes*, spite of her repeated protestations against this profanation of her sex. The Committee of General Safety hastened her trial and sentence. She could hear in her cell the voices of the criers who hawked about the streets the account of the murder, and the shouts of the crowd, demanding the death of the assassin. Charlotte did not deem this voice of the people that of posterity; and through the horror she foresaw her apotheosis. With this feeling she wrote to the Committee of General Safety:—"As I have yet some moments to live, may I hope, citizens, that you will permit me to sit for my portrait, as I would fain leave this souvenir to my friends. Besides, as the likenesses of good citizens are carefully preserved, so curiosity sometimes seeks those of great criminals, in order to perpetuate their crime. If you grant my request, be so good as to send me a miniature painter. I renew my request to be allowed to sleep alone. I hear the account of the arrest of my accomplice, Fauchet, constantly cried in the streets. I never saw him but once from a window two years ago; I neither love nor esteem him, and he is the last man in the world to whom I would willingly have confided my project. If this declaration is of any service to him, I attest its truth."

The President of the revolutionary tribunal, Montanè, came on the next day, the 16th, to examine her. Touched by so much beauty and youth, and convinced of the sincerity of a fanaticism which almost absolved her in the eyes of human justice, he wished to save her life, and so framed his questions, and tacitly dictated the answers, as to induce the judges to look on them as the proof of madness rather than crime. But Charlotte frustrated his merciful attempt, and clung to her crime as though glorying in it. She was removed to the Conciergerie. Madame Richard, the wife of the gaoler, received her with the compassion inspired by this proximity of youth and the scaffold.

Thanks to the indulgence of her guardians, Charlotte obtained paper, pens, and solitude, of which she availed herself to write to Barbaroux a letter, in which she recounted all the events of her sojourn at Paris, in a style in which were mingled patriotism, mirth, and death-like sweetness and sorrow in the last cup of a farewell repast. After giving an almost facetious account of her journey to Paris in company with Montagnards, and of the sudden affection with which she had inspired a young passenger; "I did not know," she continues, "that the Committee of Public Safety had examined the passengers. I declared at first that I did not know them, in order to spare them the annoyance of an *interrogatoire;* and I followed on this occasion the maxim of my oracle Raynal, who says that you should not speak the truth to tyrants. It was through the lady who travelled with me that they learnt that I knew you, and that I had seen Duperret. You know his resolution; he told them the exact truth. Nothing can be alleged against him, but his firmness is a crime. I regretted, when too late, that I had spoke to him, and I endeavored to repair my error by persuading him to fly and rejoin you; but he was too resolute. Would you believe it, Fauchet is imprisoned as my accomplice! He, who was ignorant of my very existence! But they are not satisfied with having only a woman to offer to the manes of a great man. Pardon me, O men! The name of Marat dishonors your race. He was a ferocious beast, who was about to devour the remains of France by the fire of civil war; thank Heaven, he is not a Frenchman by birth! At my first examination Chabot had the air of a madman; Legendre wished to have it believed he had seen me at his house that morning. I, who never dreamed of this man. I do not think him likely to become the tyrant of his country; besides I cannot punish them all. I believe the last words of Marat have been printed; but I question if he uttered any. The last words he said to me were, after I had given him your names and those of the administrators of the department of Calvados, who are at Evreux, he told me to console myself, for he would have them all guillotined at Paris in a few days. These words decided his fate—though I confess that what entirely decided me was the courage with which our volunteers enrolled themselves on Sunday the 7th of July. You remember that I promised to make Pétion repent his unjust suspicions of my sentiments. I reflected how so many brave men were about to take the life of one man whose death (had their design succeeded) would have caused that of many excellent citizens—that this man was unworthy such an honor, and that the hand of a woman would suffice. I confess, I had recourse to a perfidious artifice to induce him to receive me. I intended originally to sacrifice him on the summit of the Montagne, but he no longer went to the Convention. All the Parisians are such good citizens, that they cannot comprehend how a useless woman, whose longest term of life would be good for nothing, can calmly sacrifice herself for her country. As I was really perfectly collected when I left Marat's house to go to the Abbaye, I was pained at the cries of some women. But those who save their country reck not what it costs them. May peace be established as speedily as I desire. This is a great preliminary. I enjoy this peace for the last two days. The happiness of my country is mine. A vivid imagination and a sensitive heart promised but a stormy life; and I pray those who regret me to consider this and rejoice at it. Amongst the moderns there are but few patriots who know how to immolate themselves for their country. All is egotism. What a wretched people to form a republic!"

The letter was interrupted here by the removal of the captive to the Conciergerie. She continued in the following terms:—"I had the idea yesterday of offering my portrait to the department of Calvados. The Committee of Public Safety has sent me no reply, and it is now too late. I must have a defender; that is the rule. I have chosen mine from the Montagne; and at one time thought of naming Robespierre or Chabot. To morrow, at eight o'clock, I am tried; and probably at twelve, to use the language of the Romans, I shall have lived. I know not how my last moments will be passed: it is the end that crowns the work. I have no need to affect insensibility; for up to this period I have not the least dread of death: I have never esteemed life save by its utility. Marat will not go to the Pantheon: he yet well deserved it. Remember the affair of Mademoiselle de Forbin, whose address in Switzerland I enclose, and tell her that I love her with all my heart. I am going to write to my father; but I shall say nothing to my other friends. I but ask from them to forget me speedily: their affection would dishonor my memory. Tell General Wimpfen that I believe I have aided him to gain more than one battle by facilitating the peace. Adieu, Citizen. The prisoners of the Conciergerie, far from insulting me, like the people in the streets, seem to pity me. Misfortune renders us compassionate: this is my last reflection."

Her letter to her father was brief, and written in a style rather of grief than mirth. "Pardon me for having disposed of my existence without your permission," said she. "I have avenged many innocent victims, and prevented many other disasters. The people, who will be disabused some day, will rejoice at their deliverance from a tyrant. If I sought to persuade you that I had gone to England, it was because I hoped to remain unknown. I hope that you will not be molested; but you have defenders at Caen. I have chosen Gustave Doulcet de Pontécoulant; but only for form's sake, as such a deed admits of no defence. Adieu, my dear papa; I pray of you to forget me, or rather to rejoice at my fate—the cause is noble. I embrace my sister, whom I love with all my heart. Do not forget this verse of Corneille,—

"'Le crime fait la honte et non pas l'échafaud!'*

"To-morrow, at eight o'clock, I am tried." This allusion to

---

*"The crime and not the scaffold causes shame!"

a verse of her ancestor, recalling to her father the pride of their name and the heroism of their race, seemed to place her action beneath the safeguard of the genius of her family. She guarded against the entrance of weakness or reproach into the heart of her father, by showing him the illustrator of Roman sentiments applauding her devotion beforehand.

The next morning, at eight o'clock, the *gens d'armes* conducted her to the revolutionary tribunal. The *salle* was situated above the vaults of the Conciergerie. A dark and steep stair, formed in the massive basement walls of the Palais de Justice, conducted the accused, and brought back the condemned criminals to the dungeons.

Before ascending, she arranged her hair and dress, to appear decently before death; then she said smilingly to the concierge, "Monsieur Richard, pray let my breakfast be ready on my return; my judges are doubtless pressed for time, and I wish to take my last meal with Madame Richard and yourself."

The hour fixed for the trial of Charlotte Corday was known in Paris the previous evening. Curiosity, horror, interrest and pity, had attracted an immense crowd. When she appeared, a murmur, as though of malediction, burst from this throng, but scarcely had she passed through them in the full blaze of her beauty, than this murmur of rage was changed into a shudder of interest and admiration. Her features, excited by the solemnity of the occasion, colored by emotion, troubled by the confusion of a young girl exposed to the regards of so many, ennobled by the very grandeur of a crime which she bore in her heart as a virtue, and her pride and modesty, gave her a charm mingled with terror, that troubled all eyes and all hearts, and her very judges seemed to be culprits in her presence. Men deemed they saw divine justice, or the antique Nemesis, substituting conscience for law, and appearing to demand from human justice, not to absolve, but to recognise her and tremble!

When she was seated on the bench of the prisoners, she was asked if she had a defender. She replied that a friend had undertaken this office, but not seeing him, she supposed his courage had failed him. The president then assigned to her the young Chauveau Lagarde, afterwards illustrious by his defence of the Queen, and already famous for his eloquence and courage in causes and times when the advocate shared the peril of his client. Chauvean Lagarde placed himself at the bar. Charlotte gazed on him, as though she feared lest, to save her life, her defender would abandon some part of her honor.

The widow of Marat wept whilst giving her evidence. Charlotte, moved by her grief, exclaimed, "Yes, yes,—'twas I that killed him." She then related the premeditation of the act for three months; her project of stabbing him in the Convention; and the *ruse* she had employed to obtain access to him. "I confess," said she, with humility, "that this means was unworthy of me, but it was necessary to appear to esteem this man in order to obtain access to him." "Who inspired you with this hatred of Marat?" she was asked. "I did not need the hatred of any one else," she replied. "My own was sufficient; besides, you always execute badly that which you have not devised yourself." "What did you hate in him?' "His crimes." "What did you hope to effect by killing him?" "Restore peace to my country." "Do you, then, think that you have assassinated all the Marats?" "Since he is dead, perhaps the others will tremble." The knife was shown her, that she might recognize it. She pushed it from her with a gesture of disgust. "Yes," replied she; "I recognize it." "What person did you visit at Caen?" "Very few; I saw Laure, a municipal officer, and the Curé of Saint Jean." "Did you confess to a conforming or non-juring priest?" "Neither one nor the other." "Since when had you formed this design?" "Since the 31st of May, when the deputies of the people were arrested. I have killed one man to save a hundred thousand. I was a republican long before the Revolution." Fauchet was confronted with her. "I only know Fauchet by sight," said she, disdainfully. "I look on him as a man devoid of principles; and I despise him." The accuser reproached her with having dealt the fatal stroke downwards, in order to render it more certain, and observed that she must doubtless have been well exercised in crime. At this suggestion, which destroyed all her ideas, by assimilating her to professed murderers, she uttered a cry of horror. "Oh, the monster!" exclaimed she. "He takes me for an assassin!"

Fouquier Tinville summed up, and demanded that sentence of death should be passed.

Her defender rose. "The accused," said he, "confesses her

crime, she avows its long premeditation, and gives the most overwhelming details. Citizens, this is her whole defence. This imperturbable calm and entire forgetfulness of self, which reveals no remorse in presence of death,—this calm and this forgetfulness, sublime in one point of view, is not natural: they can only be explained by the excitement of political fanaticism, which placed the poignard in her hand. It is for you to decide what weight so stern a fanaticism should have in the balance of justice. I leave all to your consciences."

The jury unanimously sentenced her to die. She heard their verdict unmoved; and the president having asked her if she had anything to say relative to the punishment inflicted on her, she made no reply; but, turning to her defender,—"Monsieur," said she, "you have defended me as I wished to be defended: I thank you: I owe you a proof of my gratitude and esteem, and I offer you one worthy of you. These gentlemen (pointing to the judges) have just declared my property confiscated; I owe something in the prison, and I bequeath to you the payment of this debt."

During the examination she perceived a painter engaged in taking her likeness; without interrupting the examination, she smilingly turned towards the artist, in order that he might the better see her features. She thought of immortality, and already sat for her portrait, to immortality.

Behind the painter stood a young man, whose fair hair, blue eyes, and pale complexion, marked him for a native from the north. His eyes were rivetted on the prisoner; and at each reply he shuddered and changed color. He seemed to drink in her words, and to associate himself by gesture, attitude, and enthusiasm, with the sentiments she expressed. Unable frequently to repress his emotion, he drew to himself, by involuntary exclamations, the attention of the audience and of Charlotte Corday. At the moment when the president passed sentence of death, the young man half rose from his seat, with the gesture of a man who protests from the bottom of his heart, and then sank back, as though his strength had failed him. Charlotte, insensible to her own fate, perceived this movement, and comprehended that, at the moment when all on earth abandoned her, a kindred spirit attached itself to hers, and that amidst this hostile or indifferent throng she possessed an unknown friend, and she thanked him with a look.

This young stranger was Adam Lux, a German republican, sent to Paris by the revolutionists of Mayence, to concert the movements of Germany with those of France, in the common cause of human reason and the liberty of the people. His eye followed Charlotte until she disappeared amidst the *gens d'armes* beneath the arch of the stairs. His thoughts never quitted her.

On her return to the Conciergerie, which was so soon to yield her up to the scaffold, Charlotte Corday smiled on her companions in prison, who had arranged themselves in the corridors and courts to see her pass. She said to the concierge—"I had hoped that we should breakfast together once more, but the judges detained me so long that you must forgive me for having broken my word." The executioner arrived; she requested him to allow her time to finish a letter, which was neither the outpouring of weakness or regret, but the last act of wounded friendship—addressing an eternal reproach to the cowardly spirit which had abandoned her.

It was addressed to Doulcet de Pontécoulant, whom she had seen at her aunt's, and on whom she believed she had called in vain to be her defender. The letter was as follows;—"Doulcet de Pontécoulant is a coward, to have refused to defend me when it was so easy. He who undertook it performed his task with all possible dignity, and I shall retain a grateful recollection of him to my last moments." Her indignation was unjust; the young Pontécoulant, who was absent from Paris, had not received her letter: his generosity and courage were a sufficient guarantee that he would have accepted the office; and Charlotte bore an error and an injustice to the scaffold.

The artist who had sketched Charlotte's likeness at the tribunal, was M. Hauer, a painter, and officer of the national guard of the section of the Théâtre Française. On her return to the prison, she requested the concierge to allow him to finish his work, and on his arrival Charlotte thanked him for the interest he appeared to take in her, and quietly sat to him, as though whilst she permitted him to transmit her form and features to posterity, she also charged him to hand down her mind and her patriotism to unborn generations. She conversed with M. Hauer on his profession, the events of the day, and the peace of mind she felt after the execution of her design; she also spoke of her young friends at Caen, and requested him to paint a miniature from the portrait, and send it to her family.

Suddenly a gentle knock was heard at the door, and the executioner entered. Charlotte, turning round, perceived the scissors and red chemise he carried over his arm. "What! already," exclaimed she, turning pale. Then recovering her composure, and glancing at the unfinished portrait, "Monsieur," said she, to the artist, "I know not how to thank you for the trouble you have taken; I have only this to offer you. Keep it in memory of your kindness and my gratitude." As she spoke, she took the scissors from the executioner, and severing a lock of her long fair hair, gave it to M. Hauer.

This portrait, interrupted by death, is still in the possession of the family of M. Hauer. The head only was painted, and the bust merely sketched. But the painter, who watched the preparations for the scaffold, was so struck with the sinister splendor added by the red chemise to the beauty of his model, that after Charlotte's death, he painted her in this costume.

A priest, sent by the public accuser, presented himself to offer the last consolations of religion. "Thank," said she to him, "those who have had the attention to send you, but I need not your ministry. The blood I have spilt, and my own which I am about to shed, are the only sacrifices I can offer the Eternal." The executioner then cut off her hair, bound her hands, and put on the *chemise des condamnés.* "This," said she, "is the toilette of death, arranged by somewhat rude hands, but it leads to immortality."

She collected her long hair, looked at it for the last time, and gave it to Madame Richard. As she mounted the fatal cart, a violent storm broke over Paris, but the lightning and rain did not disperse the crowd who blocked up the squares, the bridges, and the streets along which she passed. Hordes of women, or rather furies, followed her with the fiercest imprecations; but, insensible to these insults, she gazed on the populace with eyes beaming with serenity and compassion.

The sky cleared up, and the rain which wetted her to the skin, displayed the exquisite symmetry of her form, like those of a woman leaving the bath. Her hands bound behind her back, obliged her to hold up her head, and this forced rigidity of the muscles gave more fixity to her attitude, and set off the outlines of her figure. The rays of the setting sun fell on her head; and her complexion, heightened by the red chemise, seemed of an unearthly brilliancy. Robespierre, Danton, and Camille Desmoulins, had placed themselves on her passage, to gaze on her; for all those who anticipated assassination were curious to study in her features the expression of that fanaticism which might threaten them on the morrow. She resembled celestial vengeance appeased and transfigured, and from time to time she seemed to seek a glance of intelligence on which her eye could rest. Adam Lux awaited the cart at the entrance of the Rue St. Honoré, and followed it to the foot of the scaffold. "He engraved in his heart," to quote his own words, "this unutterable sweetness amidst the barbarous outcries of the crowd, that look so gentle, yet penetrating,—these vivid flashes that broke forth like burning ideas from these bright eyes, in which spoke a soul as intrepid as tender. Charming eyes, which should have melted a stone."

Thus an enthusiastic and unearthly attachment accompanied her, without her knowledge to the very scaffold, and prepared to follow her, in hope of an eternal reunion. The cart stopped, and Charlotte, at the sight of the fatal instrument, turned pale, but, soon recovering herself, ascended the scaffold with as light and rapid a step as the long chemise and her pinioned arms permitted. When the executioner, to bare her neck, removed the handkerchief that covered her bosom, this insult to her modesty moved her more than her impending death; then, turning to the guillotine, she placed herself under the axe. The heavy blade fell, and her head rolled on the scaffold. One of the assistants, named Legros, took it in his hand and struck it on the cheek. It is said that a deep crimson suffusion overspread the face, as though dignity and modesty had for an instant lasted longer even than life.

Such was the death of Marat; such were the life and death of Charlotte Corday. In the face of murder history dares not praise, and in the face of heroism, dares not condemn her. The appreciation of such an act places us in the terrible alternative of blaming virtue or applauding assassination. Like the painter who, despairing of rendering the expression of a mingled sentiment, cast a veil over the face of the figure, we must leave this mystery to be debated in the abysses of the human heart. There are deeds of which men are no judges, and which mount, without appeal direct to the tribunal of God.

There are in human actions so strange a mixture of weakness and strength, pure intent and culpable means, error and truth, murder and martyrdom, that we know not whether to term them crime or virtue. The culpable devotion of Charlotte Corday is amongst those acts which admiration and horror would leave eternally in doubt, did not morality reprove them. Had we to find for this sublime liberatrix to her country, and generous murderess of a tyrant, a name which should at once convey the enthusiasm of our feelings towards her and the severity of our judgment on her action, we would coin a phrase combining the extreme of admiration and horror, and term her the Angel of Assassination.

A few days afterwards Adam Lux published the "Apology of Charlotte Corday," and associated himself with her deed, in order to share her martyrdom. Arrested and sent to the Abbaye, he exclaimed, as he entered the prison, "I shall die, then for her." He perished soon after, saluting as the altar of liberty and love, the scaffold which the blood of his model had hallowed. The heroism of Charlotte was sung by the poet André Chénier, who was himself so soon to die for that common fatherland of all great souls—pure liberty.

"Whose is this tomb?" sings the German poet, Klopstock. "It is the tomb of Charlotte. Let us gather flowers, and scatter them over her ashes, for she is dead for her country. No, no, gather nothing; let us seek a weeping willow, and plant it o'er her tomb, for she is dead for her country. No, no, plant nothing; but weep, and let your tears be blood, for she is dead in vain for her country!" Vergniaud, on learning, in his dungeon, of the crime, trial, and death of Charlotte, exclaimed, "She destroys us, but she teaches us how to die."

HENRY AND JOHN SHEARES.

THEIR TRIAL, CONVICTION AND EXECUTION FOR HIGH TREASON IN IRELAND IN 1798.—SKETCH OF THE PATRIOTS.—FULL ACCOUNT OF THEIR TRIAL AT DUBLIN.—THE PRISONERS PROSECUTED BY ATTORNEY-GENERAL TOLER, AFTERWARDS THE NOTORIOUS LORD NORBURY.—THE ELOQUENT SPEECHES OF JOHN PHILPOT CURRAN AND LORD PLUNKETT IN DEFENCE OF THE PRISONERS.—TOUCHING LETTERS OF JOHN SHEARES TO HIS MOTHER AND SISTER PREVIOUS TO THE EXECUTION.—THE FINAL SCENE.—HARROWING INCIDENTS AT THE SCAFFOLD.—EXTRAORDINARY APPEARANCE OF THE BODIES ON BEING VIEWED SOME YEARS AFTER IN THE VAULTS OF ST. MICHAN'S CHURCH, DUBLIN, &c. &c.

Henry and John Sheares were sons of a Cork Banker, well educated and well connected, both barristers, and at the time of the trial, Henry was forty-five years old, and married a second wife, by whom he had a large family. John was thirty-two, a man of fine feeling and vigorous intellect. They were men of very unequal characters. Henry, the eldest, was amiable, changeful, and weak; John, the youngest, fiery and firm, and of much greater abilities. Both had been to France, were present at the taking of the Bastille, and John, who was thoroughly republican, witnessed the downfall of the French monarchy, quenched in the blood of Louis XVI., and was seen, after his return to Ireland, to exhibit with delight a handkerchief stained with the royal blood of the unhappy king.

Henry's property was £1,200 a year, which he encumbered; John's £3,000, on which he lived after lending his brother money; Miss Steel, to whom John was engaged to be married, says he "bought nothing but books." They resided in Bagott street (now No. 130), Dublin, and there Henry was arrested. John was arrested at Surgeon Lawless's, in French street. They had been United Irishmen from 1793, and John was a frequent chairman, and apparently a man of weight in "The Union." He contributed to "THE PRESS," was peculiarly active with his brother in pushing the organization in Cork, and became one of the executive. After the arrests of others of the Patriots at Bond's in March, 1798, the Sheareses stepped into the dangerous posts and shared the same fate in ten days after; their betrayal, arrest and conviction, was brought about through a Captain Armstrong, who was the spy selected for the occasion.

This John Warnford Armstrong was a man of good family, a Captain in the Kings County Militia. He resided near the town of Moat, at a place called Ballycumber, where he died a few years ago; he was in receipt of a pension from the British Government, the price of the Sheares' blood, up to his decease; then stationed at Loughlinstown Camp, between Dublin and Bray. On the 10th of May, 1798, he went to the store of Byrne, a bookseller, in Grafton street, a notorious member of the United Irish Society. He was in the habit of bringing there the books current among the republicans, and Byrne (a feeble but not treacherous man) was absurd enough to introduce him to Henry Sheares at Armstrong's own request. Henry declined communication, and went away, but John (who had before noticed Armstrong in the store) soon came in, was introduced, and plunged headlong into communication with the spy. Frequent interviews followed. The means of taking the Castle Island-bridge Barracks and Loughlinstown Camp were constant topics. On the twentieth of May [Sunday] he dined at Bagott street, on John's invitation. The notorious Castlereigh encouraged and instructed Armstrong in his treacherous movements. At this meeting John informed Armstrong on part of the executive, that he was to command the Kings County forces, and discussed many raw but important projects. Armstrong had thus formed the acquaintance to get the brothers in his clutches. On the twenty-first of May they were taken prisoners.

On their arrest a rough draft of a proclamation written by John Sheares, was found in the writing desk of Henry. The latter knew nothing of it. It was paraded in the front of the prosecution, Captain Armstrong being the main force of the attack. Speaking of him, Thomas Davis said, "This frightful wretch had sought the acquaintance of the Sheareses—made it—encouraged their projects—assisted them with military hints—professed tender love for them—mixed with their family—and used to dandle Henry Sheares' children. We hear the technical monster denies this little fact, though he admits all the rest. He shared their hospitality—urged on their schemes—came to condole with them in prison—and then assassinated them with his oath!"

THE TRIAL.

On the 26th of June, Chief Justice Lord Carleton, Baron George and Justices Crookshank, Chamberlain and Daly,—opened the Special Commission. After the grand juries for Dublin city and county were sworn, they were addressed by Lord Carleton; and their numerous prisoners arraigned.

Two bills were found against Samuel Nelson, Michael Byrne, Henry and John Sheares, John McCann, and Oliver Bond.

In those days the court assigned the counsel for the prisoner, a concession granted by the 5th of George III., an act introduced by the father of the Sheares, when a member of the Irish Parliament. Prior to that act, no person on a charge of treason was entitled to the benefit of counsel.

The prosecution was conducted by the Attorney-General Right Hon. John Arthur Wolfe, the Solicitor-General, John Toler (afterwards Lord Norbury), and the other counsel for the crown Mr. Prime Sergeant Fitzgerald with Messrs. Saurin, O'Grady, Mayne, Webber and Ridgway.

The counsel for Henry Sheares were Mr. John Philfort Curran and Mr. William Conyngham Plunkett; counsel for John Sheares, Messrs. Curran and McNally, assisted by Messrs. Orr and Finlay.

On the 4th of July, 1798, Lord Carleton, Baron Smith and George and Justices Crookshank and Daly sat; and Henry and John Sheares being put to the bar, their indictment for High Treason was read by the clerk of the crown. The first count stated sixteen overt acts. The second count was for associating as United Irishmen, &c.

Mr. McNally objected after some delay, that John Decluzeau, one of the grand jurors, who found the bills, was an alien, not naturalized, and filed a plea in court. The crown replied, and Curran supported the plea as follows:—

My lords, we have looked over this replication, and we find that the gentlemen concerned for the crown have thought proper to plead in three ways. The subject matter of our plea in abatement came very recently to our knowledge. To suppose that an alien had been upon the grand jury finding a bill of indictment involving the duty of allegiance was a rare thing; the suspicion of it came late to our knowledge. It would have been our duty to be prepared, had we known it in time; but as we did not, and as it is a plea of great novelty, we hope the court will not think it unreasonable to give us time till to-morrow to answer this pleading.

The court over-ruled the application.

Mr. Curran—My lords, before we rejoin, it may be prudent to consider, whether this replication should not be *quashed*. There are three distinct matters in the replication, and they are repugnant to one another. One is, that the juror is *not an alien;* the second and third contain averments that he *is an alien.* Clearly, in civil cases, a party cannot plead double matter, without the leave of the court; even the statute which gives that benefit, does not admit it without a special motion, in order that the court may see whether the pleas can stand together. But even that holds only in civil cases, and by the authority of an act of parliament. Therefore, your lordships will consider, whether a replication of this kind, consisting of three parts, contradictory and repugnant, ought to be answered.

Lord Carleton—In civil cases, certainly, the right of pleading double arises from the act of parliament. As to the objection you now make, you must avail yourself of it in some other way. We will not quash the replication upon motion.

A rejoinder and demurrer of insufficiency were then filed on the part of the prisoners.

Mr. Curran—My lords, it is my duty to suggest such reasons as occur to me in support of the demurrer filed here on the part of the prisoners. My lords, the law of this country has declared that in order to the conviction of any man, not only of any charge of the higher species of criminal offences, but of any criminal charge whatsoever, he must be convicted upon the finding of two juries; first, of the grand jury, who determine upon the guilt in one point of view; and, secondly, by the corroborative finding of the petty jury, who establish that guilt in a more direct manner; and it is the law of this country, that the jurors who shall so find, whether upon the grand, or whether upon the petty inquest, shall be *probi et legales homines omni exceptione majores.* They must be open to no legal objection of personal incompetence. They must be capable of having freehold property; and, in order to have freehold property, they must not be open to the objection of being born under the jurisdiction of a foreign prince, or owing allegiance to any foreign power. Because the law of this country, and, indeed, the law of every country in Europe, has thought it an indispensable precaution, to trust no man with the weight or influence which territorial possession may give him, contrary to that allegiance which ought to flow from every man having property in the country.

This observation is emphatically forcible in every branch of the criminal law; but in the law of treason, it was a degree of force and cogency that fails in every inferior class of offence, because the very point to be inquired into in treason, is the nature of allegiance.

The general nature of allegiance may be pretty clear to every man. Every man, however unlearned he may be, can easily acquire such a notion of allegiance, whether natural and born with him, or whether it be temporary, and contracted by emigration into another country, he may acquire a vague, untechnical idea of allegiance, for his immediate personal conduct.

But I am warranted in saying, that the constitution does not suppose, that any foreigner has any direct idea of allegiance, but what he owes to his original prince. The constitution supposes, and takes for granted, that no foreigner has such an idea of our peculiar and precise allegiance, as qualifies him to act as a juror, where that is the question to be inquired into: and I found myself upon this known principle, that though the benignity of the English law has in many cases, where strangers are tried, given a jury half composed of foreigners and half natives, that benefit is denied to any man accused of treason, for the reason I have stated; because, says Sir W. Blackstone, "aliens are very improper judges of the breach of allegiance." A foreigner is a most improper judge of what the allegiance is which binds an English subject to his constitution. And, therefore, upon that idea of utter incompetency in a stranger, is every foreigner directly removed and repelled from the possibility of exercising a function that he is supposed utterly unable to discharge.

If one Frenchman shall be suffered to find a bill of indictment between our Lord the King and his subjects, by a parity of reasoning, may twenty-three men of the same descent be put into the box, with authority to find a bill of indictment. By the same reason that the court may communicate with one man, whose language they do not know, may they communicate with twenty-three natives of twenty-three different countries and languages.

How far do I mean to carry this? Thus far: that every statute, or means by which allegiance may be shaken off, and any kind of benefit or privilege conferred upon an emigrating foreigner, is for ever to be considered by a court of justice with relation to that natural incompetency to perform certain trusts, which is taken for granted, and established by the law of England. I urge it with this idea, that whether the privilege is conferred by letters patent, making the foreigner a denizen, or whether by act of parliament, making him as a native subject, the letters patent, or act of parliament, should be construed *secundum subjectam materiam;* and a court of justice will take care, that no privilege be supposed to be granted, incompatible with the original situation of the party to whom, or the constitution of the country in which, it is conferred.

Therefore, my lords, my clients have pleaded, that the bill of indictment to which they have been called upon to answer, has been found, among others, by a foreigner, born under a foreign allegiance, and incapable of exercising the right of a juror, upon the grand, or the petty inquest. That is the substance of the plea in abatement. The counsel for the crown have replied, and we have demurred to the second and third parts of the replication.

My lords, I take it to be a rule of law, not now to be questioned, that there is a distinction in our statute laws; some are of a public, some of a private nature.

That part of the legislative edict which is considered as of a public nature, is supposed to be recorded in the breasts of the King's judges. As the King's judges, you are the depositories and the records of the public law of the country.

But wherever a private indulgence is granted, or a mere personal privilege conferred, the King's judges are not the depositories of such laws, though enacted with the same publicity; you are not the repositories of deeds or titles which give men franchises or estates, nor of those statutes which ease a man of a disability, or grant him a privilege. With regard to the individual to whom they relate, they are mere private acts, muniments, or deeds, call them by what name you please; they are to be shown as private deeds, to such courts as it may be thought necessary to bring them forward. Therefore, if there be any act of parliament, by which a man is enabled to say he has shaken off the disability which prevented him from intermeddling in the political or judicial arrangement of the country; if he says he is no longer to be considered as an alien, he must show that act specially to the court in his pleading. The particular authority, whether by letters of denization, or act of parliament, must be set forth, that the court may judge of them, that if it be by act of parliament, the court may see whether he comes within the provisions of the act. This replication does no such thing.

The second and the third parts were intended to be founded upon the statute of Charles II., and also, I suppose, upon the subsequent statute, made to give it perpetuity, with certain additional requisites. The statute of Charles recites, that the kingdom was wasted by the unfortunate troubles of that time; and that trade had decreased, for want of merchants. After thus stating generally the grievances which had afflicted the trade and population of the country, and the necessity of encouraging emigration from abroad, it goes on and says, that strangers may be induced to transport themselves and families, to replenish the country, if they may be made partakers of the advantages and free exercise of their trades, without interruption and disturbance.

The grievance was the scarcity of men; the remedy was the encouragement of foreigners to transport themselves: and the encouragement given was such a degree of protection, as was necessary to the full exercises of their trades, in dealing, buying, and selling, and enjoying the fullest extent of personal security. Therefore, it enacts, that all foreigners, of the Protestant religion, and all merchants, &c., who shall, within the *term of seven years*, transport themselves to this country, shall be deemed and reputed natural-born subjects, and *may implead and be impleaded, and prosecute and defend suits.*

The intention was to give them protection for the purposes for which they were encouraged to come here; and therefore the statute, instead of saying generally they shall be subjects *to all intents and purposes*, specifically enumerates the privileges they shall enjoy. If the legislature intended to make them subjects *to all intents and purposes*, it had nothing more to do than say so. But not having meant any such thing, the statute is confined to the enumeration of the mere hospitable rights and privileges to be granted to such foreigners as come here for special purposes. It states, that he may implead, and shall be answered unto, that he may prosecute and defend suits. Why go on and tell a man, who is *to all intents and purposes* a natural-born subject, that he may implead and bring actions? I say, it is to all intents and purposes absurd and preposterous. If *all* privileges be granted in the first instance, why mention *particular* parts afterwards? A man would be esteemed absurd, who by his grant gave a thing under a general description, and afterwards granted the particular parts. What would be thought of a man who gave another his horse, and then said to the grantee, "I also give you liberty to ride him when and where you please?"

What was the case here? The government of Ireland said, we want men of skill and industry, we invite you to come over, our intention is, that if you be Protestants, you shall be protected: but you are not to be judges, or legislators, or kings. We make an act of parliament, giving you protection and encouragement to follow the trades for your knowledge in which we invite you; you are to exercise your trade as a natural-born subject. How? With full power to make a bargain and enforce it: we invest you with the same power, and you shall have the same benefit, as if you were appealing to your own natural form of public justice; you shall be here as a Frenchman in Paris, buying selling the commodities appertaining to your trade.

Look at another clause in the act of parliament, which is said to make a legislator of this man, or a juror, to pass upon the life and death of a fellow-subject,—no, not a fellow-subject, but a stranger. It says, "you may purchase an estate, and you may enjoy it, without being a trustee for the crown." Why was that necessary, if he were a subject *to all intents and purposes?*

This statute had continuance for the period of seven years only: that is, it limited the time in which a foreigner might avail himself of its benefits to seven years. The statute 4 George I. revives it, and makes it perpetual. I trust I may say, that whenever an act of parliament is made, giving perpetuity to a former act, no greater force or operation can be given to the latter, than would have been given to the former, had it been declared perpetual at the time of its enactment. An act of that kind is merely to cure the defect of continuance; therefore, it does no more than is necessary to that end. Then how will it stand? Thus: that any man, who, within seven years after the passing of the act of Charles II. performing the requisities there mentioned, shall have the privileges thereby granted for ever thereafter. The court would assume the office of legislation, not of construction, if they inferred or supplied by intendment, a longer period than seven years; there is nothing in the subsequent act, changing the term of seven years limited in the former; it is not competent to a court of justice to alter or extend the operation of a statute by the introduction of clauses not to be found in it. It is the business of the legislature to enact laws, of the court to expound them.

It is worthy of observation, my lords, that this subsequent statute has annexed certain explicit conditions to be performed by the person who is to take the benefit of the preceding act; for it is provided, that no person shall have the benefit of the former act, unless he take the several oaths appointed to be taken by the latter; among which, is the oath against the Pretender, which is not stated in the replication.

There is a circumstance in the latter act, which, with regard to the argument, is extremely strong, to show, that the legislature did not intend to grant the universal franchise and privilege to all intents and purposes. It revives every part of the former, save that part exempting aliens from the payment of excise. Will it be contended, that an alien should be considered as a natural-born subject *to all intents and purposes*, and yet be exempt from the payment of excise? It is absurd, and impossible.

Put it in another point of view. What is an act of naturalization? It is an encroachment upon the common law rights, which every man born in this country has in it; those rights are encroached upon and taken away by a stranger. The statute therefore should be construed with the rigour of a penal law. The court, to be sure, will see, that the stranger has the full benefit intended for him by the statute; but they will not give him any privilege inconsistent with the rights of the natural-born subjects, or incompatible with the fundamental principles of the constitution into which he is admitted; and I found myself upon this, that after declaring that he shall be considered as a natural born subject, the act states such privileges only as are necessary to the exercise of trade and the enjoyment of property.

Therefore, it comes back to the observation just now made. Is not any man pleading a statute of naturalization, by which he claims to be considered as a natural-born subject, bound to set forth a compliance with all the requisites pointed out by that statute? He is made a native to a certain extent, upon complying with certain conditions; is he not bound to state that compliance? Here he has not stated them. But I go farther; I say, that every condition mentioned in the statute of Charles, should be set forth in the second part of the replication; that he came with an intent of settling; that he brought his family and his stock; that he took the oaths before the proper magistrates; and after a minute statement of every fact, he should state the additional oath required by the statute George I.

But, my lords, a great question remains behind to be decided upon. I know of no case upon it. I do not pretend to say, that the industry of other men may not have discovered a case. But I would not be surprised, if no such case could be found; if since the history of the administration of justice in all its forms in England, a stranger had not been found intruding himself into its concerns; if through the entire history of our courts of justice, an instance was not to be found, of the folly of a stranger interfering upon so awful a subject, as the breach of allegiance between a subject and his king.

My lords, I beg leave upon this part to say, that it would be a most formidable thing, if a court of justice would pronounce a determination big with danger, if they said that an alien may find a bill of indictment involving the doctrine of allegiance. It is permitting him to intermeddle in a business of which he cannot be supposed to have any knowledge. Shall a subject of the Irish crown be charged with a breach of his allegiance upon the saying of a German, an Italian, a Frenchman or a Spaniard? Can any man suppose any thing more monstrous or absurd, than that of a stranger being competent to form an opinion upon the subject? I would not form a supposition upon it. At a time when the generals, the admirals, and the captains of France are endeavoring to pour their armies upon us, shall we permit their petty detachments to attack us in judicial hostility? Shall we sit inactive, and see their skirmishers take off our fellow-subjects by explosion in a jury room?

When did this man come into the country? Is the raft upon which he floated now in court? What has he said upon the back of the bill? What understanding had he of it? If he can write more than his own name, and had wrote *ignoramus* upon the back of the indictment, he might have written truly; he might say, he knew nothing of the matter.

He says he is naturalized; I am glad of it; you are welcome to Ireland, sir; you shall have all the privileges of a stranger, independent of the invitation by which you came; if you sell, you shall recover the price of your wares, you shall enforce the contract; if you purchase an estate, you shall transmit it to your children, if you have any, if not, your devisee shall have it. But you must know, that in this constitution, there are laws binding upon the court as strongly as upon you; the statute itself which confers the privileges you enjoy, makes you incapable of discharging offices. Why? Because they go to the fundamentals of the constitution, and belong only to those men who have an interest in that constitution transmitted to them from their ancestors.

Therefore, my lords, the foreigner must be content; he shall be kept apart from the judicial functions; in the extensive words of the act of parliament, he shall be kept from "all places of trust whatsoever." If the act had been silent in that part, the court would notwithstanding be bound to say, that, it did not confer the power of filling the high department of the state. The alien would still be incapable of sitting in either house of parliament, he would be incapable of advising with the king, or holding any place of constitutional trust whatever. What! shall it be said, there is no trust in the office of a grand juror? I do not speak or think lightly of the sacred office confided to your lordships of administering justice between the crown and the subject, or between subject and subject: I do not compare the office of a grand juror to that. But, in the name of God, with regard to the issues of life and death, with regard to the consequences of imputed or established criminality, what difference is there, in the importance of the constitution, between the juror who brings in a verdict, and the judge who pronounces upon that verdict the sentence of the law? Shall it be said, that the former is no place of trust? What is the place of trust meant by the statute? It is not merely giving a thing to another, or depositing for safe custody, it means *constitutional trust*, the trust of executing given departments, in which the highest confidence must be reposed in the man appointed to perform them. It means not the trust of keeping a paltry chattel, it means the awful trust of keeping the secrets of the state, and of the king.

Look at the weight of the obligation imposed upon the

juror; look at the enormous extent of the danger, if he violate or disregard it. At a time like the present, a time of war, what is the trust to be confided to the conscience of a Frenchman? But I am speaking of the lives of my clients, and I do not choose, even here to state the terms of the trust, lest I might furnish as many hints of mischief, as I am anxious to furnish arguments of defence. But shall a Frenchman, at this moment, be entrusted with those secrets upon which your sitting upon that bench may eventually depend. What is the inquiry to be made? Having been a pedlar in the country, is he to have the selling of the country, if he be inclined to do so? Is he to have confided to him the secrets of the state? He *may* remember to have had a *first* allegiance, that he has sworn to it: he might find civilians to aid his perfidious logic, and to tell him, that a secret communicated to him by the humanity of the country which received him, might be disclosed to the older and better matured allegiance sworn to a former power! He might give up the prefidious use of his conscience to the integrity of the older title. Shall the power of calling upon an Irishman to take his trial before an Irish judge, before "the country," be left to the broken speech, the *lingua Franca*, of a stranger coming among you and saying, I was naturalised by act of parliament, and I cannot carry on my trade without dealing in the blood of your citizens.

He holds up your statute as his protection, and flings it against your liberty, claiming the right of exercising a judicial function, feeling at the same time, the honest love for an older title to allegiance. It is a love which every man ought to feel, and which every subject of this country would feel if he left this country to-morrow, and went to spend his last hour among the Hottentots of Africa. I do trust in God, there is not a man who hears me, who does not feel, that he would carry with him to the remotest part of the globe, the old ties which bound him to his original friends, his country, and his king: I do as the advocate of my clients, of my country—as the advocate for you, my lords, whose elevation prevents you from the possibility of having advocates for yourselves,—for your children, stand up and rely upon it, that this act of parliament has been confined to a limited operation. It was enacted for a limited purpose, and will not allow this meddling stranger to pass upon the life, fame or fortune of the gentlemen at the bar,—of me, their advocate,—of you their judges,—or of any man in the nation.

My lords, you deny him no advantage that strangers ought to have. By extending the statute, you take away the right from a native of the country, and you transfer one to an intermeddling stranger. I do not mean to use him with disrespect; he may be a respectable and worthy man; but whatever he may be, I do with humble reliance upon the justice of the court, deprecate the idea of communicating to him that high, awful, and tremendous privilege of passing upon life, of expounding the law in cases of treason; it being a fundamental maxim that strangers will, most improperly, be called upon to judge of breaches of allegiance between a subject and his sovereign.

The counsel for the crown replied and contended that by the 14th and 15th of Chas. II. chap. 23, for the encouragement of foreigners of the Protestant religion settling as colonists in Ireland, aliens, having taken the oaths of supremacy and allegiance in being of the Protestant religion were to be reputed as lieges, free and natural subjects of his Majesty's Kingdom in all respects, construction and purposes, as if they had been born in the Kingdom of Ireland.

The Court overruled the objection.

Affidavits were then put in on part of the prisoners stating that material witnesses, without the benefit of whose testimony the prisoners could not go to trial, were to be summoned from distant parts of the Kingdom, and a postponement of their trials was prayed for on these grounds. The witnesses named by John Sheares were Sir Joseph Hoare, Sir Richard Kellet, Sir Patrick O'Connor, Rev. Mr. Lee, Rev. Mr. Stowell, Mr. Henry and Edward Hoare, Esq., and the Earl of Cork and Orrery. Some of these gentlemen were the intimate friends of the father of the prisoners. The Rev. Mr. Lee was the tutor of the younger prisoner.

The Solicitor-General urgently opposed the postponement, as the public he said were waiting the event of it with anxious expectation, and though he would not wish to accelerate it, yet he felt the disposal of it was of great importance.

Lord Carleton, however, acceded to the application, and the trial was postponed to 12th July following.

In the interim, Arthur Wolfe, (subsequently Lord Kilwarden) was elevated to the Bench, and Toler became Attorney-General, and acted in that capacity at the trial; Mr. Stewart being made Solicitor-General.

SPECIAL COMMISSION,

Dublin, July, 1798.

Before Lord CARLETON, Barons SMITH and GEORGE, and Justices CROOKSHANK and DALY.

On July, 12 1798, the trial was regularly commenced, at the desire of John Sheares. Mr. Ponsonby was assigned as one of his counsel in the place of Mr. Curran, in order that each prisoner should have four counsel between them.

The Clerk of the Crown then called over the panel of Jurors, when the following Jury, composed of men of high respectability, and compared with the ordinary Juries of this frightful period, was one that the prisoners might have thought an honest and impartial one.

Sir Thomas Lighton, *Foreman*, Robert Shaw, Price Blackwood, John Stewart, George Palmer, Henry Woodward, Richard Sayers, John Farrange, Cornelius Gantier, William Sparrow, Charles Bingham, and John Ferns.

Some of these were intimate friends of Curran; the last mentioned gentleman, one of his convivial associates. It was to this intimacy Curran alluded at the commencement of his speech, when in referring to the atrocious statement of the Attorney-General, that the public mind required to be appeased by the speedy disposal of this case.

The traversers' counsel were John Philpot Curran, Mr. Plunket, Mr. McNally, and Mr. George Ponsonby, with Mr. Armstrong Fitzgerald as agent.

Mr. Webber opened the pleadings, and Toler as Attorney-General stated the case for the prosecution to the Jury. This speech, says Dr. Madden, was one of the most rancorous, and so far as concerned Henry Sheares, one of the most unjustifiable speeches that was ever pronounced by a public prosecutor. Not only facts were distorted, circumstances favorable to the prisoner suppressed, but statements were boldly made, utterly at variance with the evidence he had to adduce on the part of the prosecution.

He commenced his speech by describing the prisoners as "gentlemen of that profession to which he belonged, and to which he was bound by every tie of affection, regard, and gratitude that can bind a man of honorable feelings." A little further he designates them "as men of considerable talents and learning in the law." And in a subsequent sentence, he says:—"The prisoners were not persons such as had been seen too frequently on the circuits which they had attended as barristers; men of a low rank in life, unlettered, unacquainted with the excellence of the law under which they lived; nor were they men, whose ignorance, at the same time that it exposed them to being made the wretched instruments of seduction, rendered them rather objects of pity than punishment. No! the gentlemen of the jury would find, in the course of the trial, that the prisoners were no strangers to literary pursuits, or to the exercise of talents." He then proceeded to preface his vituperation against the prisoners, with a declaration of the pain enforced on him by his duty as a public prosecutor on such an occasion. He said: "There was not a man who knew him in private life, that did not know it weighed heavily upon him." There was not a man living acquainted with the character of the learned gentleman, who knew that a feeling of compunction in the discharge of any duty, however awful, ever weighed one jot on his mind.

"But mistaken lenity," added Mr. Toler, "to atrocious delinquents is at all times '*crudelis misericordia*' with respect to the public. A banditti of men associated under the denomination of United Irishmen, imported French principles, and improved on them; the pen and tongue of every revolutionary ruffian was put in requisition,—these were the principles and doctrines which approached us like plague, pestilence and famine, and were the dreadful presagers and forerunners of battle, murder and sudden death." He says it would be illiberal to overbear men in the situation of the prisoners with the language of insult;" and he then proceeds to denominate them assassins and cowards as well as traitors. In alluding to the paper written by John Sheares, he asks, "who can read the bloody scroll, and not pronounce upon the intentions and imagination of the heart which composed it?"—and whilst he thus beheld it, he thought he had in full and palpable form before him, the sanguinary author penning it, with his bloody dagger in one hand, and pointing in triumph to the revolutionary tribunal and guillotine with the other. I admire the wisdom of the laws of those countries, which put traitors and cowards in the same class as public criminals; and I am free to say, that the man who is a traitor or coward enough, not to take that unequivocal part which becomes him at such a time as this, deserves the severest punishment, and the execration of his country." With this observation, and a remark that there was not a single line of the paper in question, the effect of which was not

> "But to teach
> Bloody instruction, which, being taught, returns
> To plague the inventor."

* * * * he committed the case of the prisoners to God and his country, without being able so far to preserve the common decency of his office as crown prosecutor, as to conclude his laborious effort to establish the guilt of the prisoners, with the ordinary form of recommendation to the jury, of giving the accused the benefit of any doubt that might be favorable to them in the evidence adduced against them."

The first witness called for the prosecution, was Alderman Alexander, who proved "that he found in John's open desk, in Bagott's street, the following paper. (The words in *italics* were interlined; those between the crochets were struck across with the pen.)

"IRISHMEN,

["Your country is free; all those monsters who usurped its government to oppress its people are in our hands, except such as have]

"Your country is free and you are about to be avenged [already] that vile government which has so long and so cruelly oppressed you is no more; some of its most atrocious monsters have already paid the forfeit of their lives, and the rest are in our hands [waiting their fate.] The national flag, *the sacred green*, is at this moment flying over the ruins of despotism, and that capitol which a few hours past [was the scene] witnessed the debauchery, [the machinations] plots and crimes of your tyrants, is now the citadel of triumphant patriotism *and virtue*. Arise, then, united sons of Ireland; arise like a great and powerful people determined to [live] be free or die; arm yourselves by every means in your power, and rush like lions on your foes; consider, that [in disarming your enemy] for every enemy you disarm, you arm a friend, and thus become doubly powerful; in the cause of liberty, inaction is cowardice, and the coward shall forfeit the property he has not the courage to protect. Let his arms be seized and transferred to those gallant [patriots] *spirits* who want, and will use them; yes, Irishmen, we swear by that eternal justice, in whose cause you fight, that the brave patriot, who survives the present glorious struggle, and the family of him who has fallen, or shall fall hereafter in it, shall receive from the hands of a grateful nation an ample recompense out of [those funds] that property which the crimes of our enemies [shall] have forfeited into its hands, and his name [too] shall be inscribed on the national record of Irish revolution, as a glorious example to all posterity; *but we likewise swear to punish robbery with death and infamy.*

"We also swear that we will never sheathe the sword until every [person] being in the country, is restored to those equal rights, which the God of nature has given to all men; until an order of things shall be established, in which no superiority shall be acknowledged among the citizens of Erin, but that [which] of virtue and talent [shall entitle to.]

"[As for those degenerate wretches who turn their swords against their native country, the national vengeance awaits them. Let them find no quarter unless they shall prove their repentance by speedily deserting, exchanging from the standard of slavery, for that of freedom, under which their former errors may be buried, and they may share the glory and advantages that are due to the patriot bands of Ireland.]

"Many of the military feel the love of liberty glow within their breasts, and have [already to] joined the national standard; receive [those] with open arms, such as shall follow so glorious an example, they can render signal service to the cause of freedom, and shall be rewarded according to their deserts: but for the wretch who turns his sword against his country, let the national vengeance be visited on him, let him find no quarter, two other crimes demand——

"Rouse all the energies of your souls; call forth all the merit and abilities which a vicious government consigned to obscurity, and under the conduct of your chosen leaders march with a steady step to victory; heed not the glare of [a mercenary] hired soldiery, or *aristocratic yeomanry*, they cannot stand the vigorous shock of freemen, [close with them man to man, and let them see what vigor the cause of freedom can.] Their trappings and their arms will soon be yours, and the detested government of England to which we vow eternal hatred, shall learn that the treasures [she it] *they* exhaust on [their mercenary] its accoutered slaves for the purpose of butchering Irishmen, shall but further enable us to learn to turn their swords on its devoted head.

Attack them in every direction by day and by night; avail yourselves of the natural advantages of your country, which are innumerable, *and with which you are better acquainted than they;* where you cannot oppose them in full force, constantly harrass their rear and their flanks; cut off their provisions, and magazines, and prevent them as much as possible from uniting their forces; but whatever moment you cannot [pass him] devote to fighting for your country, be [devoted to] passed in learning how to fight for it, or preparing the means of war; for war, war alone, must occupy every mind and every hand in Ireland until its long oppressed soil be purged of all its enemies.

Vengeance, Irishmen, vengeance on your oppressors. Remember what thousands of your dearest friends have perished by their [murders, cruel plots,] *merciless orders;* remember their burnings, their rackings, their torturing, their military massacres, and their legal murders. Remember Orr.

Mr. Dwyer, Secretary to the Attorney-general, was the next witness called, who proved that he was intimately acquainted by professional intercourse with both the Sheares, knew their handwriting, and the proclamation was the handwriting of John, and also proved to the documents as being in the handwriting of Henry.

Cross examined: Both of these gentlemen are of unblemished character as men of honor and integrity. I come here reluctantly to testify in this case.

The Crown next called as a witness *Captain John W. Armstrong,* who was examined by Mr. Sawrin; the witness detailed his meeting with the Sheareses, his conversation with them; that John had undertaken to find what United men were in Armstrong's regiment; that the witness entreated secrecy on John's part,—that he called on the brothers at their house at 4 o'clock, P. M., on the 10th of May, and there discussed the taking of the camp at Leighlinstown; he also met them on the evenings of the 11th and 12th, and dined with him on Sunday, when after dinner John wrote down many names of officers and men, including Captain Crofton, Lieutenant Wilkinson, &c., who could be relied on. A return of the number organized and armed men in the different counties was also written on the same paper. This paper was produced in Court, and proven to be found on the person of John at the time of his arrest. That when the prisoners were taken to the guard room of the castle, and while there in custody, Armstrong called on John, expressed his apparent surprise and concern at seeing the prisoner there, inquired if there was any danger of the prisoner, or if the government had any charge against him—offered his services in the most friendly manner. The prisoner expressed his gratification for his friendly visit and attention; he also remarked that all he feared was that a certain paper had been found in his desk; that if it was, he would certainly be committed, and recommended the witness to withdraw immediately from the room, lest any injurious suspicion might attach upon him, if seen in conversation with him, the prisoner; and requested the witness to call on his family and pacify their fears, which he promised to do, and departed.

Armstrong's cross-examination by Mr. Curran was very searching, terse and bitter.

The leading features of the cross-examination are as follows:

Witness first became acquainted with the Sheares at Byrne's book-store in Grafton street; subsequently visited at their house in Bagot street; dined with the family; had a conversation about politics after dinner; don't remember of speaking in harsh terms of the government, the chancellor or the Speaker of the House; might have done so; am a captain in the Kings County Militia; after making the acquaintance of the prisoners was not in active service, nor until after their arrest; was not allowed to join my own regiment, which was then in service some distance from Dublin. This was by prohibition from Lord Castelreagh. I was desirous to get in active service, and volunteered and obtained the command of the Grenadier company of the Londonderry Militia. I was one of the few who escaped with life at the unfortunate battle of Slievebrury Mountain, where Colonel Walpole was killed and his party discomfitted. I was wounded at this place in the engagement on the 4th of June; this was a fortnight after my last interview with the

Sheares and six weeks prior to this trial; our party caught three of the peasants; one of them I had hanged for refusing to give information, the other was shot, and the third was suspended, taken down and ordered twenty-five lashes. When he received eight, he cried out that he would give information; we then made a guide of him.

Mr. Curran.—Which did you make a guide of?

Armstrong, (jocularly).— The one that was neither shot or hanged.

Mr. Curran —When you dined at the house of the traversers did you not caress the children of Henry, and take them in your arms?

Armstrong.—I did not. I don't remember.

Q. Do you believe in the existence of a deity, and a future state of rewards and punishments.

A. I have always professed that belief, and have never denied the obligation of an oath. I have never said "that if no person could be found to cut off the head of the King of England, that I would do it." I have never declared "that the works of Paine contained my creed." Was instructed by Lord Castelreagh to dine with the prisoners, and extract if possible, all their secrets.

This concluded the case for the prosecution.

An application for adjournment on the part of the prisoners was then made, but in vain. Counsel were desired to proceed with the defence, when

Mr. G. Ponsonby opened on the part of John Sheares, and commented severely on the law of high treason in Ireland, where one witness was sufficient to convict, and that witness in this case being a spy and informer, whereas the law of England required two witnesses in order to secure conviction. He animadverted with great severity on Captain Armstrong's testimony, and said of him: "I know not how you will be inclined to appreciate the conduct of a man who gets into the confidence of another for the purpose of acquiring a knowledge of matters he could not otherwise obtain, and make use of that knowledge against the life of a person from whom he obtained it!—and yet, if we believe him, he did this. I pass no opinion on such conduct, I leave that for you to do; but this I will say, that if I were a juryman, I would not be quick to convict upon the evidence of a man who acknowledged that he became the friend of another for the purpose of betraying the friendship and taking away the life of that friend."

On the conclusion of Mr. Ponsonby's address, Mr. Plunket followed in behalf of Henry, in a very able and luminous argument, and after speaking to the points of law in the case, he continued the argument as follows:

My Lords and Gentlemen:

A very few observations remain in point of fact. What I have hitherto said applies to both the prisoners, so far as respects the law of the case. But with regard to the facts, I must trouble you, upon the case of Mr. Henry Sheares, much less indeed than I would otherwise do, if I was not to be followed by a very able advocate, who will speak to the evidence.

With regard to Mr. Henry Sheares, the evidence against him rests upon the testimony of Captain Armstrong alone. As to the law stated by Mr. Ponsonby, of two witnesses being necessary, I will not give any positive opinion upon it. I do not pretend to say whether the statute in England enacted a new law, or only declared the old. There are great authorities, who say it is only a declaratory statute—among others, Lord Coke says, two witnesses were necessary by the common law. If he be right, we are entitled to the benefit of the common law, and will claim it. But I throw that out of the case—not concluded indeed; but supposing that, in point of law, the testimony of one witness is sufficient to convict, I beg leave to observe upon the nature of that testimony; which kind of story it is which fell from the lips of the witness—how far it is natural or probable, or entitled to credit, merits your consideration, when compared with your observance upon life and manners. That so rash and indiscreet a confidence should be reposed in this stripling, without any previous acquaintance of himself, his life, or manners—without any pledge of secrecy—but rashly and suddenly, as if he had fallen in love with him upon first interview—is matter for your conjecture. How far it was an honorable ministry, is for your judgment.

In the case of a common informer, his evidence is weighed with caution. Every circumstance throwing a doubt upon it is to be attended to. If the testimony exceeds the common rules of life and course of experience, the jury are cautious in admitting it. But this is not the case of a common informer. It is not the case of an accomplice, who repents his crime. That might be the fate of an honorable mind. A man may be involved in the guilt of conspiring or treason, and retrieve himself nobly by making an atonement to his country and his God, by a fair and full confession of the crime. But that is not the case here. This is the case of a man going for the purpose of creating and producing guilt, that he might make discovery of it. Does it not appear that the conception of the guilt was entertained in the mind, if not fomented by the witness. You are to consider the different motives and movements of the human heart, and how wavering dispositions may be taken advantage of, and urged on by dexterous persuasion to a conduct which the seduced may abhor. You are not now trying whether the prisoner be a man of strong frame—of firm nerves and mind, capable of resisting allurements of guilt and temptation to vice. But you are to try whether the evidence has satisfied you that he has been guilty of treason.

Suppose now the evidence to be true: would it not shake the mind of an ordinary man, not of the most strong and firm disposition, if he saw an officer of the camp making declarations hostile to government—making a sacrifice of his situation, saying, "I will betray the camp which I am appointed to guard"—if he goes and persecutes another with his volunteering treason, fastens upon him in the streets, follows him abroad, and haunts him at his house; I say, are you surprised at seeing the other listen for a moment to the temptation, when he perceives that the man whose more immediate duty it is to resist the treason, has adopted it? I say this, supposing for a moment that the evidence is true; I will show you presently it is not.

Was it the part of an honest man to seek repeated interviews —to follow the other to his house and into the bosom of his family, until at last he lodged him in a jail? Did he know the prisoners before?—was he acquainted with their lives and characters? No; but, seized with a sudden zeal of turning informer against them, he insinuates himself into their acquaintance. I can conceive the zeal of an honest mind in the moment of mistaken enthusiasm to be led into an act of vice to save his country. I can conceive an exertion of Roman virtue flinging morals into the gulf as a sacrifice to patriotism. But what a life must there have been to claim praise for that act of enthusiastic ardour? There must have been a life of religious feelings, of continued virtue, and disinterested, honorable views. In such a case you can, by exerting your imagination, account for an act of perfidy to save the country. But does this witness stand in that point of view? No, gentlemen, by his own confession he is convicted, and we shall show by a crowd of witnesses, whose characters are above imputation, that he does not believe in the existence of God, or a future state of rewards and punishments—that he is a notorious republican, and devoid of the principles of loyalty. Hear his own account. Was he a man of decided loyalty—attached to his king and country? No; he confessed he had been in the habit of reading Paine's pamphlets—his *Rights of Man* and his *Age of Reason*—his creed was founded upon these, and he drinks republicanism as a toast—and this man, the companion of Byrne, and who had been foolishly democratic, engages in conference with Mr. Sheares, and enters upon the new office of informer for the good of his country! It is surprising that between the violence of republicanism and the zeal of an informer for the crown, the mean proportion of virtuous patriotism could not be found! The friend of Mr. Patrick Byrne—the drinker of republican toasts, suddenly becomes a spy for the good of his country! You see, gentlemen, the evidence which has been laid before you. Is there any one fact brought forward, except the naked testimony of this informer, to fasten guilt upon Mr. Henry Sheares? He has chosen his time of interview with great discretion; no person has been present at the conversations, but the prisoners, who cannot give evidence for each other. Has the person who introduced them been brought forward, or the sergeant of the militia? They are in the power of the crown; or did the counsel for the prosecution conceive this witness to be so immaculate, that he could not be impeached, and not necessary to be supported? Why not produce Connors? He is in the barrack. Why not produce Byrne? He is in prison. Why not produce Fannan? Why not produce any one to give steadiness to the tottering evidence of this man?

Gentlemen, as to the proclamation which has been commented upon, it is not in the handwriting of the prisoner, Mr. Henry Sheares. It was not in his possession; he knew nothing of it; he had an opportunity of destroying it, if he chose, or knew of it. Whatever the effect of it may be, as applying to the other prisoner, I meddle not with it. But I do not think it affects the other, and most certainly, gentlemen, the court will tell you, that this evidence is not to weigh a feather upon your minds in determining the case of one man, to whom it does not apply, although it may be thought to have some relation to another. It is an unpublished, blotted, and unfinished paper. The mere circumstance of that blotted paper being found in the house of Mr. Henry Sheares, where Mr. John Sheares resorted—not received by Mr. Henry Sheares, not acknowledged by him; on the contrary, from the evidence you must infer he knew nothing about it—cannot weigh with you, nor affect his life. Is it proved that Mr. Henry Sheares did any act—corrupted any man, or frequented any society, or took any political step, beyond the mere coloring which Captain Armstrong gives to the conversation between them? And how is that, with regard to Mr. Henry Sheares? Did he appear eager to gain proselytes? At the first interview, Mr. Henry Sheares declined to say anything; he departed, and did not return that day. Did that show an eagerness to gain a proselyte? He deserted Captain Armstrong, is hunted and persecuted by him; he infests the society of his wife and children—still no act is done; it rests in conversation; not a single act done; no men corrupted; no societies frequented, arms taken up, or furnished to others; no act countenancing rebellion, or hostility to the crown.

Gentlemen, we will prove by a crowd of witnesses that this gentleman, Mr. Henry Sheares, has been unconnected with and unconcerned in politics, devoted to pursuits of a different nature, to literature, to science, and attention to private affairs; enjoying the society of an amiable wife and children, beyond whose company he sought no pleasure. You certainly are not to be influenced by humanity. But your verdict must be founded in justice and in truth. You cannot suppose that a man in possession of every comfort and enjoyment, with a wife and six children, would voluntarily engage in treason; would rashly confide his life, his fortune and his family to the stripling of an informer, whom he never before beheld. Gentlemen, I have troubled you too long. I now conclude, and with a firm hope, I trust my client to your hands.

Mr. McNally urged a variety of law points, but with little effect upon the tribunal before whom he appeared, when

The first witness called for the defence was

Thomas Drought.—Am well acquainted with Captain Armstrong; he has spoken to me in regard to the engagement at Slievebury Mountain, and the number there killed; he told me they had caught two or three (peasants) at a distance; that he was hanged for refusing to give information, another I believe was suspended, and Captain Armstrong said he cut him down, but one was hanged outright. We both agreed that it was not a good way to make him confess; he said that on his (Armstrong's) suggestion the fellow that was suspended had the rope round his neck; I'm not sure which was ordered twenty-five lashes, and when he received eight he cried out with vociferation, that he would give information; he then let him down and said the person who was hanged could have given the same information, though he suffered himself to be hanged; I asked how he could possibly reconcile it to himself to deprive these wretches of life, without even the form of a trial; he acknowledged they did so; I asked him whether he expected any punishment for it, and although he might not expect it from Government, yet there was an All-powerful Being who would punish him; he said, "you know my opinion long ago upon the subject." The witness further deposed that he had known Armstrong from his infancy; he had frequently heard him utter atheistical expressions; he spoke of the state of the soul after death "as an eternal sleep," and told witness "he had left the Somersetshire Militia on account of his democratic principles."

Lieutenant Shervington of the Forty-first regiment, deposed that "he was a nephew by marriage of Captain Armstrong, and had known him since his childhood. When in Lord Coke's regiment in England, had conversations with him. Did not think his principles exactly such as a military man's should be. Had a conversation with him at his agent's, Mr. Mulholland; talked of various things, among others of the French Revolution, and he said he did not wish for kingly government. *He said, that if there was not another executioner in the kingdom for George III. but himself, he would be one, and piqued himself upon being so. I told him he was a d——d fellow, and ought to give up his commission, and go over to France.* He had met him in Byrne's, the bookseller's, in Grafton street; he handed him a book, saying, 'Read this, it is my creed;' he (the witness) found it was 'Paine's Rights of Man;' he thrust it into the fire, and said, he (Captain Armstrong) should be served so." The witness further deposed that "he did not know the Messrs. Sheares, and never had seen them until that day. That he would not have come forward to give evidence on this trial, but had been summoned, 'and would not have appeared for one hundred guineas.' That on meeting with Captain Clibborn, he had said, 'he was sorry to hear that John Armstrong was finding out the secrets of men, in order to dis cover them, and being told it was a different thing, that the Sheares wanted to seduce the soldiers, he had said, d——n him, he should have run them through the body."

Mr. Bride, a barrister, deposed to his having been acquainted with Armstrong; recollected having been, within the last six or eight months, in company with him, at the chambers of a Mr. Brown, in college, and heard him (Armstrong) express an opinion slighting the obligation of an oath.

Mr. Graydon, a barrister, deposed that he had known Armstrong, had heard him express republican opinions "in a very violent and unqualified manner." "He uniformly expressed opinions of that kind."

Mr. Boardman, a barrister, deposed that he had known the brothers for seven or eight years. So far as he could collect their political principles from any conversation he had had with them, he thought them anxious to bring about a parliamentary reform and Catholic emancipation. They went no farther as well as he could recollect. Three months before he had met Mr. John Sheares in company, and he had expressed sentiments of similar import. Mr. John Sheares, interrupting the witness, said, "I wish to remind Mr. Boardman whether I did not regret that reform had not taken place, as the best mode to prevent revolution, which would take place if not prevented by reform." Mr. Boardman replied, "I do not recollect that Mr. Sheares made use of expressions to that effect."

Mr. Edward Hoare deposed, that he "had known Henry and John Sheares a great many years, and their father before them. Their political opinions were very much alike as to men and measures."

Mr. St. Leger, a barrister,— had known the brothers since he was six years old; John Sheares had been his school-fellow;

during the whole of their acquaintance, his opinion as to their general character was, 'it was the very best that he could conceive any man to possess.'"

Mr. Thomas Casey, a barrrister, deposed that "he has been long acquainted with both brothers, and most particularly with John. Their general moral character was as good and as high as that of any men he had ever known. With regard to Mr. John Sheares, he had lived with him a long time, and during that time he never had an occasion to do otherwise than admire, esteem, and respect him, and that was for a period of eighteen months during which they lived together." He was asked if he considered the Sheares' were men who were likely to encourage murder and bloodshed? He replied, "With regard to Mr. Henry Sheares, I do not conceive it possible; with regard to Mr. John Sheares, if it be possible, I do conceive there must have been as great revolution in his mind, as any that ever took place upon the face of the earth. And I do recollect, about two years ago or upwards, that I did hear John Sheares, in as warm a manner as I ever heard him speak truth to me upon any occasion, say that he would be the first to take up arms against a foreign enemy, and the last to lay them down." Being asked by the counsel for the crown if he did not confine what he had said to their moral character, the witness replied, "I mean it to the full extent of what I have said. I speak of their moral character, and as to their political also, as far forth as my words can reach. At the assizes of Cork, we had some conversation; John Sheares and myself talked about the politics of the day, upon which he differed. He spoke with confidence to me, as two men intimately acquainted might do in conversation, and the opinions he expressed were against a revolution and a foreign enemy." The counsel for the crown asked the witness if the conversation would not have terminated, had Mr. Sheares intimated a contrary opinion? The following reply was made by Counselor Casey: "I do not know that it would, for I should have endeavored to persuade him to be of my opinion, which is full and entirely contrarient. I would not give him up while I had a hope of him, nor till I had a solid reason for the contrary (opinion)."

This closed the evidence for the defence; it was then past midnight; the trial had already occupied fifteen hours, when Mr. Curran, like every one around him, judge, jury and advocates, was exhausted with fatigue. He was racked by the contests and the excitement of a day in which he had to resist the royal blood-hounds, to cross-examine a demon, and gaze on the Sheares—the one trembling for his brother, the other for himself. He was literally worn out with fatigue after sixteen hours of anxiety, in a crowded court, in the midst of a red-hot summer.

He then rose and said,

My Lords :—

Before I address you or the jury, I would wish to make one preliminary observation; it may be an observation only, it may be a request: for myself I am indifferent, but I feel I am now unequal to the duty—I am sinking under the weight of it. We all know the character of the jury; the interval of their separation must be short, if it should be deemed necessary to separate them. I protest I have sunk under this trial. If I must go on, the court must bear with me, the jury may also bear with me: I will go on until I sink. But after a sitting of sixteen hours, with only twenty minutes' interval, in these times, I should hope it would not be thought an obtrusive request, to hope for a few hours' interval for repose, or rather for recollection.

Lord Carleton—What say you, Mr. Attorney-General?

Mr. Attorney-General—My Lords, I feel such public inconvenience from adjourning cases of this kind, that I cannot consent. The counsel for the prisoners cannot be more exhausted than those for the prosecution. If they do not choose to speak to the evidence, we shall give up our right to speak, and leave the matter to the court altogether. They have had two speeches already [Mr. Ponsonby and Mr. Plunkett had spoken], and leaving them unreplied to is a great concession.

Lord Carleton—We would be glad to accommodate as much as possible. I am as much exhausted as any other; but we think it better to go on.

Mr. Curran then rose and addressed the jury on behalf of the prisoners, as follows :—

Gentlemen of the jury, it seems that much has been conceded to us. God help us! I do not know what has been conceded to me, if so insignificant a person may have extorted the remark. Perhaps it is a concession, that I rise in such a state of mind and body, of collapse and deprivation, as to feel but a little spark of indignation raised by the remark, that much has been conceded to the counsel for the prisoner; much has been conceded to the prisoners! Almighty and merciful God, who lookest down upon us, what are the times to which we are reserved, when we are told, that much has been conceded to prisoners who are put upon their trial at a moment like this, of more darkness and night of the human intellect, than a darkness of the natural period of twenty-four hours; that public convenience cannot spare a respite of a few hours to those who are accused of their lives, and that much has been conceded to the advocate, almost exhausted in the poor remark which he has endeavored to make upon it. My countrymen, I do pray you, by the awful duty which you owe your country, by that sacred duty which you owe your character (and I know how you feel it), I do obtest you, by the Almighty God, to have mercy upon my client, to save him, not from guilt, but from the baseness of his accuser, and the pressure of the treatment under which I am sinking. With what spirit did you leave your habitations this day? with what state of mind and heart did you come here from your families? with what sentiments did you leave your children, to do an act of great public importance, to pledge yourselves at the throne of eternal justice, by the awful and solemn obligation of an oath, to do perfect, cool, impartial and steady justice, between the accuser and accused? Have you come abroad under the idea, that public fury is clamorous for blood? that you are put there under the mere formality or memorial of death, and ought to gratify that fury, with the blood for which it seems to thirst? If you are, I have known some of you, more than one, or two, or three, in some of those situations, where the human heart speaks its honest sentiments. I think I ought to know you well, you ought to know me, and there are some of you, who ought to listen to what so obscure an individual may say, not altogether without some degree of personal confidence and respect. I will not solicit your attention by paying the greatest compliment which man can pay to man; but I say, I hold you in regard as being worthy of it; I will speak such language as I would not stoop to hold, if I did not think you worthy of it.

Gentlemen, I will not be afraid of beginning with what some may think I should avoid, the disastrous picture which you must have met on your way to this court. A more artful advocate might endeavor to play with you, in supposing you to possess a degree of pity and feeling beyond that of any other human being. But I, gentlemen, am not afraid of beginning by warning you against those prejudices which all must possess; by speaking strongly against them; by striking upon the string, if not strong enough to snap it, will wake it into vibration. Unless you make an exertion beyond the power almost of men to make, you are not fit to try this cause. You may preside at such an execution as the witness would extol himself for—at the sentence flowing from a very short inquiry into reason; but you are not fit to discharge the awful trust of honest men, coming into the box, indifferent as they stand unsworn, to pronounce a verdict of death and infamy, or of existence and of honor. You have only the interval between this and pronouncing your verdict to reflect, and the other interval when you are resigning up your last breath, between your verdict and your grave, when you may lament that you did not as you ought.

Do you think I want to flatter your passions? I would scorn myself for it. I want to address your reason, to call upon your consciences, to remind you of your oaths, and the consequence of that verdict, which upon the law and the fact, you must give between the accuser and the accused. Part of what I shall say must of necessity be addressed to the court, for it is matter of law: but upon this subject, every observation in point of law is so inseparably blended with the fact, that I cannot pretend to say, that I discharge your attention, gentlemen, even when I address the court. On the contrary, I shall the more desire your attention, not so much that you shall understand what I shall say, as what the court shall say. Gentlemen, this indictment is founded upon the statute 25th Edward III.

The statute itself begins with a melancholy observation on the proneness to deterioration which has been found in all countries unfortunately to take place in their criminal law, particularly in the law respecting high treason. The statute begins with reciting, that in the uncertainty of adjudications, it became difficult to know what was treason, and what was not; and to remove further difficulty, it professes to declare all species of treason, that should thereafter be so considered; and by thus regulating the law, to secure the state and the constitution, and the persons of those interested in the executive departments of the government, from the common acts of violence that might be used in their destruction. The first three clauses of the statute seem to have gone a great way indeed upon the subject; because the object of the provision was to protect the person, and I beg of you to understand what I mean by person, I mean the *natural person;* I mean no figure of speech, not the monarch in the abstract, but the natural man. The first clause was made without the smallest relation to the executive power, but solely to the natural body and person. The words are, "when a man doth compass or imagine the death of the King, or of our lady his Queen, or of their eldest son and heir, and thereof be, upon sufficient proof, attainted of open deed by men of his condition, he shall be a traitor." This I say relates only to the natural person of the King The son and heir of the King is mentioned in the same manner, but he has no power; and therefore a compassing his death, must mean the death of his natural person, and so must it be in the case of the King. To conceive the purpose of destroying a common subject, was once a felony of death, and that was expressed in the same language, compassing and imagining the death of the subject. It was thought right to dismiss that severe rigor of the law in the case of the subject, but it was thought right to continue it in the case of the King, in contradistinction to all the subjects within the realm. The statute, after describing the persons, describes what shall be evidence of that high and abominable guilt: it must appear by open deed; the intention of the guilty heart must be proved by evidence of the open deed committed towards the accomplishment of the design. Perhaps in the hurry of speaking, perhaps from the mistakes of reporters, sometimes from one, and sometimes from the other, judges are too often made to say, that such or such an overt act is, if proved to have been committed, ground upon which the jury must find the party guilty of the accusation. I must deny the position, not only in the reason of the thing, but I am fortified by the ablest writers upon the law of treason. In the reason of the thing, because the design entertained, and act done, are matters for the jury. Whether a party compassed the King's death or not, is matter for the jury: and therefore if a certain fact be proved, it is nonsense to say, that such a conclusion *must* follow; because a conclusion of law would then be pronounced by the jury, not by the court.

I am warranted in this by the writers cited by Mr. Justice Foster; and therefore, gentlemen, upon the first count in the indictment, you are to decide a plain matter of fact, 1st, whether the prisoner did compass and imagine the death of the King? and whether there be any act proved, or apparent means taken, which he resorted to for the perpetration of the crime? Upon this subject, many observations have already been made before me. I will take the liberty of making one; I do not know whether it has been made before. Even in a case where the overt act stated has of its own nature gone to the person of the King, still it is left to the jury to decide, whether it was done with the criminal purpose alleged, or not. In Russell's case, there was an overt act of a conspiracy to seize the guards; the natural consequence threatened from an act of gross violence so immediately approaching the King's person, might fairly be said to affect his life; but still it was left to the jury to decide, whether that was done for the purpose of compassing the King's death. I mention this, because I think it a strong answer to those kind of expressions, which in bad times fall from the mouths of prosecutors, neither law nor poetry, but sometimes half metaphysical. Laws may be enacted in the spirit of sound policy, and supported by superior reason; but when only half considered, and their provisions half enumerated, they become the plague of the government. and the grave of principle. It is that kind of refinement and cant which overwhelmed the law of treason, and brought it to a metaphysical death; the laws are made to pass through a contorted understanding, vibratory and confused, and, therefore, after a small interval from the first enactment of any law in Great Britain, the dreams of fancy get around, and the law is lost in the mass of absurd comment. Hence it was that the statute gave its awful declarations to those glossaries; so that if any case arise, apparently within the statute, they were not to indulge themselves in conjecture, but refer to the standard, and abide by the law as marked out for them. Therefore, I say, that the issue for the jury here is to decide in the words of the statute, whether the prisoners did compass the death of the King; and whether they can say, upon their oaths, that there is any overt act proved in evidence manifesting an intention of injury to the natural person of the King? I know that the semblance of authority may be used to contradict me: if any man can reconcile himself to the miserable toil of poring over the records of guilt he will find them marked, not in black, but in red, the blood of the unfortunate, leaving the marks of folly, barbarity and tyranny. But I am glad that men, who in some situations appear not to have had the pulse of honest compassion, have made sober reflections in the hour of political disgrace. Such has been the fate of Lord Coke, who, in the triumph of insolence and power, pursued a conduct which, in the hour of calm retreat, he regretted in the language of sorrow and disappointment. He then held a language which I willingly repeat, "that a conspiracy to levy war, was no act of compassing the murder of the King." There he spoke the language of law and of good sense; for a man shall not be charged with one crime, and convicted of another. It is a narrow and a cruel policy, to make a conspiracy to levy war an act of compassing the King's death; because it is a separate and distinct offence; because it is calling upon the honest affections of the heart, and creating those pathetical effusions, which confound all distinct principles of law, a grievance not to be borne in a state where the laws ought to be certain. This reasoning is founded upon the momentary supposition that the evidence is true; for you are to recollect the quarter from whence it comes; there has been an attempt by precipitate confession, to transfer guilt to innocence, in order to escape the punishment of the law. Here, gentlemen, there is evidence of levying war, which act, it is said, tends to the death of the King: that is a constructive treason, calculated as a trap for the loyalty of a jury; therefore you should set bounds to proceedings of that kind; for it is an abuse of the law, to make one class of offence, sufficiently punished already, evidence of another. Every court, and every jury should set themselves against crimes, when they come to determine upon distinct and specified guilt: they are not to encourage a confusion of crimes, by disregarding the distinction of punishments; nor show the effusion of their loyalty, by an effusion of blood. I cannot but say, that when cases of this kind have been under judgment in Westminster Hall, there was some kind of natural reason to excuse this confusion in the reports—the propriety of making the person of the King secure. A war immediately adjoining the precincts of the palace, a riot in London might endanger the life of the King; but can the same law prevail in every part of the British empire? It may be an overt act of compassing the King's death to levy war in Great Britain; but can it be so in Jamaica, in the Bahama isles, or in Corsica, when it was annexed to the British empire? Suppose at that time a man had been indicted there for compassing the King's death, and the evidence was, that he intended to transfer the dominion of the island to the Genoese, or the French, what would you say if you were told that was an act by which he intended to murder the King? By seizing Corsica, he was to murder the King? How can there be any immediate attempt upon the King's life, by such a proceeding? It is not possible, and therefore no such consequence can be probably inferred; and therefore I call upon you to listen to the court with respect, but I also call upon you to listen to common sense, and consider, whether the conspiring to raise war can in this country be an overt act of compassing the King's death in this country? I will go further: if the statute of Edward III. had been conceived to make a conspiracy to levy war an overt act of compassing the King's death, it would be unnecessary to make it penal by any subsequent statute; and yet subsequent statutes were enacted for that purpose; which I consider an unanswerable argument that it was not considered as coming within the purview of the clause against compassing the King's death.

Now, gentlemen, you will be pleased to consider what was the evidence brought forward to support this indictment. I do not think it necessary to exhaust your attention, by stating at large the evidence given by Captain Armstrong. He gives an account which we shall have occasion to examine, with regard to its credibility. He stated his introduction, first to Henry Sheares, afterwards to his brother; and he stated a conversation which you do not forget, so strange has it been! But in the whole course of his evidence, so far from making any observation, or saying a word in connexion with the power at war with the King, he expressly said, that the insurrection, by whomsoever prepared, or by what infatuation encouraged, was to be a home exertion, independent of any foreign interference whatever. And therefore I am warranted in saying, that such an insurrection does not come within the first clause of the statute. It cannot come within the second, of adhering to the King's enemies; because that means his foreign enemies; and here, so far from any intercourse with them, they were totally disregarded.

Adhering to the King's enemies means co-operating with them, sending them provisions, or intelligence, or supplying them with arms. But I venture to say, that there has not been any one case deciding that any act can be an adherence to a foreign enemy, which was not calculated for the advantage of that enemy. In the case of Jackson, Hensey, and Lord Preston, the parties had gone as far as they could in giving assistance. So it was in Quigley's. But in addition to this, I must repeat, that it is utterly unnecessary the law should be otherwise; for levying war is, of itself, a crime; therefore it is unnecessary, by a strained construction, to say, that levying war, or conspiring to levy war, should come within any other clause equally penal, but not so descriptive.

But, gentlemen, suppose I am mistaken in both points of my argument; suppose the prisoners (if the evidence were true) did compass the King's death, and adhere to the King's enemies; what are you to found your verdict upon? Upon your oaths: What are they to be founded upon? Upon the oath of the witness: and what is that founded upon? Upon this, and this only, that he does believe that there is an eternal God, an intelligent supreme existence, capable of inflicting eternal punishment for offences, or conferring eternal compensation upon man, after he has passed the boundary of the grave! But where the witness believes he is possessed of a perishing soul, and that there is nothing upon which punishment or reward can be exerted, he proceeds regardless of the number of his offences, and undisturbed by the terrors of exhausted fancy, which might save you from the fear, that your verdict is founded upon perjury. I suppose he imagines that the body is actuated by some kind of animal machinery. I know not in what language to describe his notions. Suppose his opinion of the beautiful system framed by the Almighty hand to be, that it is all folly and blindness, compared to the manner in which he considers himself to have been created; or his abominable heart conceives its ideas; or his tongue communicates his notions. Suppose him, I say, to think so, what is perjury to him? He needs no creed, if he thinks his miserable body can take eternal refuge in the grave, and the last puff of his nostrils can send his soul into annihilation! He laughs at the idea of eternal justice, and tells you that the grave into which he sinks as a log, forms an entrenchment against the throne of God, and the vengeance of exasperated justice!

Do you not feel, my fellow-countrymen, a sort of anticipated consolation, in reflecting, that Religion—which gave us comfort in our early days, enabled us to sustain the stroke of affliction, and endeared us to one another,—when we see our friends sinking into the earth, fills us with expectation that we rise again; that we but sleep for a while, to wake forever? But what kind of communion can you hold, what interchange expect, what confidence place, in that abject slave, that condemned, despaired of wretch, who acts under the idea that he is only the folly of a moment, that he cannot step beyond the threshold of the grave, that that which is an object of terror to the best, and of hope to the confiding, is to him contempt, or despair?

Bear with me, my countrymen; I feel my heart run away with me—the worst men only can be cool. What is the law of this country? If the witness does not believe in God, or a future state, you cannot swear him. What swear him upon? Is it upon the book, or the leaf? You might as well swear him by a bramble, or a coin. The ceremony of kissing is only the external symbol, by which man seals himself to the precept, and says, "May God so help me, as I swear the truth." He is then attached to the divinity, upon the condition of telling truth; and he expects mercy from heaven, as he performs his undertaking. But the infidel!—By what can you catch his soul, or by what can you hold it? You repulse him from giving evidence; for he has no conscience, no hope to cheer him, no punishment to dread!

What is the evidence touching that unfortunate young man? What said his own relation, Mr. Shervington? He had talked to him freely, had known him long. What kind of character did he give of him? Paine was his creed and his philosophy He had drawn his maxims of politics from the vulgar and furious anarchy broached by Mr. Paine. His ideas of religion were adopted from the vulgar maxims of the same man, the scandal of inquiry, the blasphemer of his God as of his King He bears testimony against himself, that he submitted to the undertaking of reading both his abominable tracts, that abominable abomination of all abominations, Paine's "Age of

Reason," professing to teach mankind, by acknowledging that he did not learn himself! working upon debauched and narrow understandings. Why not swear the witness upon the vulgar maxims of that base fellow, that wretched outlaw and fugitive from his country and his God? Is it not lamentable to see a man laboring under an incurable disease, and fond of his own blotches?

"Do you wish" says he, "to know my sentiments with regard to politics? I have learned them from Paine! I do not love a King, and if no other executioner could be found, I would myself plunge a dagger into the heart of George III., because he is a King, and because he is my King. I swear by the sacred missal of Paine, I would think it a meritorious thing to plunge a dagger into his heart, to whom I had devoted a soul, which Mr. Paine says I have not to lend." Is this the casual effusion of a giddy young man, not considering the meaning of what he said? If it were said among a parcel of boarding-school misses, where he might think he was giving specimens of his courage by nobly denying religion, there might be some excuse. There is a latitude assumed upon some such occasions. A little blasphemy and a little obscenity passes for wit in some companies. But recollect it was not to a little miss, whom he wished to astonish, that he mentioned these sentiments; but a kinsman, a man of boiling loyalty. I confess I did not approve of his conduct in the abstract, talking of running a man through the body; but I admired the honest boldness of the soldier who expressed his indignation in such warm language. If Mr. Shervington swore true, Captain Armstrong must be a foresworn witness; it comes to that simple point. You cannot put it upon other ground. I put it to your good sense, I am not playing with your understandings, I am putting foot to foot, and credit to credit. One or other of the two must be perjured; which of them is it? If you disbelieve Captain Armstrong, can you find a verdict of blood upon his evidence?

Gentlemen, I go further: I know your horror of crime—your warmth of loyalty. They are among the reasons why I respect and regard you. I ask you, then, will you reject such a witness? or would you dismiss the friend you regarded, or the child you loved, upon the evidence of such a witness? Suppose him to tell his own story:—"I went to your friend, or your child—I addressed myself in the garb of friendship—in the smile of confidence, I courted confidence, in order to betray it—I traduced you, spoke all the evil I could against you, to inflame him—I told him, your father does not love you." If he went to you, and told you all this—that he inflamed your child, and abused you to your friend, and said, "I come now to increase it, by the horror of superadded cruelty," would you dismiss from your love and affection the child or the friend you had loved for years? You would not prejudge them. You would examine the consistency of the man's story—you would listen to it with doubt, and receive it with hesitation.

Says Captain Armstrong—"Byrne was my bookseller; from him I bought my little study of blasphemy and obscenity, with which I amused myself." "Shall I introduce Mr. Sheares to you?"—not saying which. What is done then? He thought it was not right till he saw Captain Clibborn. Has he stated any reason why he supposed Mr. Sheares had any wish at all to be introduced to him?—any reason for supposing that Byrne's principles were of that kind?—or any reason, why he imagined the intercourse was to lead to anything improper? It is most material that, he says, he never spoke to Byrne upon political subjects; therefore, he knew nothing of Byrne's principles, nor Byrne of his. But the proposal was made and he was so alarmed, that he would not give an answer till he saw his Captain. Is not this incredible?

There is one circumstance which made an impression upon my mind: that he assumed the part of a public informer, and, in the first instance, came to the field with pledgets and bandages; he was scarcely off the table, when a witness came to his credit. It is the first time that I saw a witness taking fright at his own credit, and sending up a person to justify his character.

Consider how he has fortified it: he told it all to Captain Clibborn! He saw him every evening when he returned, like a bee, with his thighs loaded with evidence. What is the defence? That the witness is unworthy of belief. My clients say, their lives are not to be touched by such a man; he is found to be an informer—he marks the victim! You know the world too well, not to know that every falsehood is reduced to a certain degree of malleability by an alloy of truth. Such stories as these are not pure and simple falsehood: look at your Oateses, your Bedloes, and Dugdales!

I am disposed to believe as shocking as it is, that this witness had the heart, when he was surrounded by the little progeny of my client—when he was sitting in the mansion in which he was hospitably entertained—when he saw the old mother supported by the piety of her son, and the children basking in the parental fondness of the father—that he saw the scene, and smiled at it; contemplated the havoc he was to make, consigning them to the storms of a miserable world, without having an anchorage in the kindness of a father! Can such horror exist, and not waken the rooted vengeance of an eternal God? But it cannot reach this man beyond the grave. Therefore, I uphold him here. I can imagine it, gentlemen, because, when the mind becomes destitute of the principles of morality and religion, all within the miserable being is left a black and desolate waste, never cheered by the rays of tenderness and humanity. When the belief of eternal justice is gone from the soul of man, horror and execution may set up their abode. I can believe that the witness—with what view, I cannot say—with what hope, I cannot conjecture—you may—did meditate the consigning of these two men to death, their children to beggary and reproach, abusing the hospitality with which he was received, that he might afterwards come here and crown his work, having obtained the little spark of truth by which his mass of falsehood was to be animated.

I have talked of the inconsistency of the story. Do you believe it, gentlemen? The case of my client is, that the witness is perjured; and you are appealed to, in the name of that ever-living God, whom you revere, but whom he despiseth, to consider, that there is something to save him from the baseness of such an accuser.

But I go back to the testimony; I may wander from it, but it is my duty to stay with it. Says he: "Byrne makes an important application—I was not accustomed to it; I never spoke to him, and yet he, with whom I had no connexion, introduces me to Sheares—this is a *true brother*." You see, gentlemen, I state this truly—he never talked to Byrne about politics. How could Byrne know his principles? By inspiration? He was to know the edition of the man, as he knew the edition of books. "You may repose all confidence." I ask not is this true; but I say it can be nothing else than false. I do not ask you to say it is doubtful; it is a case of blood, of life or death; and you are to add to the terrors of a painful death, the desolation of a family—overwhelming the aged with sorrow, and the young with infamy. Gentlemen, I should disdain to reason with you; I am pinning your minds down to one point, to show you to demonstration, that nothing can save your minds from the evidence of such perjury; not because you may think it may be false, but because it is impossible it can be true. I put into one of the scales of justice that execrable perjury, and I put into the other, the life, the fame, the fortune, the children of my client. Let not the balance tremble as you hold it; and, as you hold it now, so may the balance of eternal justice be held for you.

But is it upon his inconsistency only I call upon you to reject him? I call in aid the evidence of his own kinsman, Mr. Shervington, and Mr. Drought; the evidence of Mr. Bride and Mr. Graydon. Before you can believe Armstrong, you must believe that all those are perjured. What are his temptations to perjury? The hope of bribery and reward. And he did go up with his sheets of paper in his hand: here is one, it speaks treason—here is another, the accused grows paler—here is a third, it opens another vein. Had Shervington any temptation of that kind? No; let not the honest and genuine soldier lose the credit of it. He has paid a great compliment to the proud integrity of the King, his master, when he did venture, at a time like this, to give evidence, "I would not have come for one hundred guineas." I could not refuse the effusion of my heart, and exclaiming, may the blessings of God pour upon you, and may you never want a hundred guineas!

There is another circumstance. I think I saw it strike your attention, my lords; it was the horrid tale of the three servants whom he met upon the road. They had no connexion with the rebels; if they had, they were open to a summary proceeding. He hangs up one, shoots a second, and administers torture to the body of the third, in order to make him give evidence. Why, my lords, did you feel nothing stir within you? Our adjudications had condemned the application of torture for the extraction of evidence. When a wild and furious assassin had made a deadly attempt upon a life of much public consequence, it was proposed to put him to the torture, in order to discover his accomplices. I scarcely know whether to admire most the awful and impressive lesson given by Felton, or the doctrine stated by the judges of the land. "No," said he, "put me not to the torture; for in the extravagance of my pain, I may be brought to accuse yourselves." What say the judges? "It is not allowable by the law and constitution of England, to inflict torture upon any man, or to extract evidence under the coercion of personal sufferings." Apply that to this case: if the unfortunate man did himself dread the application of such an engine for the extraction of evidence, let it be an excuse for his degradation, that he sought to void the pain of body by public infamy. But there is another observation more applicable :—Says Mr. Drought, "Had you no feeling, or do you think you will escape future vengeance?" "Oh, sir, I thought you knew my ideas too well, to talk in that way." Merciful God! Do you think it is upon the evidence of such a man that you ought to consign a fellow-subject to death? He who would hang up a miserable peasant, to gratify caprice, could laugh at remonstrance, and say, "You know my ideas of futurity."

If he thought so little of murdering a fellow-creature, without trial and without ceremony, what kind of compunction can he feel within himself, when you are made the instruments of his savage barbarity? He kills a miserable wretch, looking, perhaps, for bread for his children, and who falls, unaccused, uncondemned. What compunction can he feel at sacrificing other victims, when he considers death as eternal sleep, and the darkness of annihilation. These victims are at this moment led out to public execution; he has marked them for the grave—he will not bewail the object of his own work: they are passing through the vale of death, while he is dozing over the expectancy of annihilation.

Gentlemen, I am too weak to follow the line of observation I had marked out; but I trust I am warranted in saying, that if you weigh the evidence, the balance will be in favor of the prisoners.

But there is another topic, or two, to which I must solicit your attention. If I had been stronger, in a common case, I would not have said so much; weak as I am here, I must say more.

It may be said that the parole evidence may be put out of the case; attribute the conduct of Armstrong to folly, or passion, or whatever else you please, you may safely repose upon the written evidence. This calls for an observation or two. As to Mr. Henry Sheares, that written evidence, even if the handwriting were fully proved, does not apply to him. I do not say it was not admissible. The writings of Sidney found in his closet were read, justly, according to some; but I do not wish to consider that now. But I say, the evidence of Mr. Dwyer has not satisfactorily established the hand-writing of John. I do not say it is not proved to a certain extent; but it is proved in the very slightest manner that you ever saw paper proved: it is barely evidence to go to you; and the witness might be mistaken.

An unpublished writing cannot be an overt act of treason; so it is laid down expressly by Hale and Foster. A number of cases have occurred, and decisions have been pronounced, asserting, that writings are not overt acts, for want of publication; but if they plainly relate to an overt act proved, they may be left to the jury for their consideration. But here it has no reference to the overt act laid; it could not be intended for publication until after the unfortunate event of revolution had taken place; and therefore, it could not be designed to create insurrection. Gentlemen, I am not counsel for Mr. John Sheares, but I would be guilty of cruelty, if I did not make another observation. This might be an idle composition, or the translation of idle absurdity from the papers of another country. The manner in which it was found leads me to think that the more probable. A writing designed for such an event as charged, would hardly be left in a writing-box, unlocked, in a room near the hall-door. The manner of its finding also shows two things: that Henry Sheares knew nothing of it, for he had an opportunity of destroying it, as Alderman Alexander said he had; and further, that he could not have imagined his brother had such a design; and it is impossible, if the paper had been designed for such purposes, that it would not be communicated to him.

There is a point to which I will beseech the attention of your lordships. I know your humanity, and it will not be applied merely because I am exhausted or fatigued. You have only one witness to any overt act of treason. There is no decision upon the point in this country. Jackson's case was the first; Lord Clonmel made allusion to the point; but a jury ought not to find guilty upon the testimony of a single witness.

It is the opinion of Foster, that by the common law one witness, if believed, was sufficient. Lord Coke's opinion is, that two were necessary: they are great names; no man looks upon the works of Foster with more veneration than myself, and I would not compare him with the depreciated credit of Coke; I would rather leave Lord Coke to the character which Foster gives him; that he was one of the ablest lawyers, independent of some particulars, that ever existed in England. In the wild extravagance, heat, and cruel reign of the Tudors, such doctrines of treason had gone abroad, as drenched the kingdom with blood. By the construction of crown lawyers, and the shameful complaisance of juries, many sacrifices had been made, and therefore, it was necessary to prune away these excesses, by the statute of Edward VI., and, therefore, there is every reason to imagine, from the history of the times, that Lord Coke was right in saying, not by new statute, but by the common law, confirmed and redeemed by declaratory acts, the trials were regulated.

A law of Philip and Mary was afterwards enacted; some think it was a repeal of the statute of Edward VI.—some think not. I mention this diversity of opinions, with this view, that in this country, upon a new point of that kind, the weight of criminal prosecution will turn the scale in favor of the prisoner, and that the court will be of opinion, that the statute 7th Wm. III. did not enact any new thing, unknown to the common law, but redeemed it from abuse. What was the state of England? The king had been declared to have abdicated the throne; prosecutions, temporizing juries, and the arbitrary construction of judges, condemned to the scaffold those who were to protect the crown, men who knew, and after the destruction of the cottage, the palace was endangered. It was not, then, the enactment of any thing new; it was founded on the caution of the times, and derived from the maxims of the constitution. I know the peevishness with which Burnet observed upon that statute; he is reprehended in a modest manner by Foster; but what says Blackstone, of great authority, of the clearest head and the profoundest reading? He agrees with Montesquieu, the French philosopher:—

"In cases of treason, there is the accused's oath of allegiance to counterpoise the information of a single witness; and that may perhaps be one reason why the law requires a *double* testimony to convict him: though the principal reason undoubtedly is, to secure the subject from being sacrificed to fictitious conspiracies, which have been the engines of profligate and crafty politicians in all ages."

Gentlemen, I do not pretend to say, that you are bound by an English act of parliament. You may condemn upon the testimony of a single witness. You, to be sure, are too proud to listen to the wisdom of an English law! Illustrious independents! You may murder under the semblance of judicial forms, because you are proud of your blessed independence! You pronounce that to be legally done which would be murder in England, because you are proud! You may imbrue your hands in blood, because you are too proud to be bound by a foreign act of parliament; and when you are to look for what is to save you from the abuse of arbitrary power, you will not avail yourself of it, because it is a foreign act of parliament! Is that the independence of an Irish jury? Do I see the heart of any Englishman move, when I say to him, "Thou servile Briton, you cannot condemn upon the perjury of a single witness, because you are held in by the cogency of an act of parliament."

If power seeks to make victims by judicial means, an act of parliament would save you from the perjury of abominable malice. Talk not of proud slavery to law, but lament that you are bound by the integrity and irresistible strength of right reason; and at the next step bewail, that the all-powerful author of nature has bound himself in the illustrious servitude of his attributes, which prevent him from thinking what is not true, or doing what is not just. Go, then, and enjoy your independence. At the other side of the water, your verdict upon the testimony of a single witness would be murder. But here you can murder without reproach, because there is no act of parliament to bind you to the ties of social life, and save the accused from the breath of a perjured informer. In England, a jury could not pronounce conviction upon the testimony of the purest man, if he stood alone; and yet, what comparison can that case bear with a blighted and marred informer, where every word is proved to be perjury, and every word turns back upon his soul?

I am reasoning for your country and your children. Let me

not reason in vain. I am not playing the advocate; you know I am not—your conscience tells you I am not. I put this case to the Bench: The statute 7 Henry III. does not bind this country by its legislative cogency; and will you declare positively, and without doubt, that it is not common law, the enactment of a new one? Will you say it has no weight to influence the conduct of a jury, from the authority of a great and exalted nation—the only nation in Europe where liberty has seated herself? Do not imagine, that the man who praises liberty is singing an idle song; for a moment, it may be the song of a bird in his cage—I know it may. But you are now standing upon an awful isthmus, a little neck of land, where liberty has found a seat. Look about you—look at the state of the country—the tribunals that dire necessity has introduced. Look at this dawn of law, admitting the functions of a jury; I feel a comfort—methinks I see the venerable forms of Holt and Hale looking down upon us, attesting its continuance. Is it your opinion that bloody verdicts are necessary—that blood enough has not been shed—that the bonds of society are not to be drawn close again, nor the scattered fragments of our strength bound together, to make them of force, but they are to be left in that scattered state, in which every little child may break them to pieces? You will do more towards tranquilizing the country, by a verdict of mercy. Guard yourselves against the sanguinary excess of prejudice or revenge; and though you think there is a great call of public justice, let no unmerited victim fall.

Gentlemen, I have tired you—I durst not relax. The danger of my client is from the hectic of the moment, which you have fortitude, I trust, to withstand. In that belief I leave him to you; and as you deal justice and mercy, so may you find it; and I hope that the happy compensation of an honest discharge of your duty may not be deferred till a future existence, which this witness Armstrong does not expect, but that you may speedily enjoy the benefits you will have conferred upon your country.

Mr. Prime-Sergeant replied in a long and not candid speech.

Mr. Henry Sheares—My lord, I wish to say a word.

Lord Carleton—It is not regular after the counsel for the

crown have closed. I asked you at the proper time, you then declined. However, go on.

Mr. Henry Sheares—My lord, after the able and eloquent defence which has been made for me by my counsel, it would ill become me to add anything to it. But there is one part of it which appears to me not to have been sufficiently dwelt upon. It is respecting that paper. I protest most solemnly, my lords, I knew nothing of it; to know of it, and leave it where is was when the magistrate came, was a folly so glaring, that I cannot be supposed to have been guilty of it. When the Alderman rapped at the door, I asked, what was the matter? After he was admitted, he said he wanted my papers; I told him there they were. My lords, is it possible, I could commit myself and all I hold dear, by so egregious an act of folly? Having the dearest sources of happiness around me, should I sacrifice them and myself, by leaving such a document in an open writing-box.

My lords, I beg your lordships' pardon. I thank you for this indulgence: it would be irregular for me to expatiate further. The evidence of Captain Armstrong is one of the most ingenious and maliciously fabricated stories, with respect to me, I ever heard of. My lords, I should think, I could not be legally implicated by any paper found in that way.

Lord Carleton charged elaborately, reading the evidence thoroughly, and Justice Crookshank and Baron Smith concurred.

The following is substantially his lordship's charge:

CHARGE TO THE JURY.

After laying down the law of treason, and adverting to the question raised by the counsel of the prisoners, as to the sufficiency of the evidence of one witness in cases of treason, to convict the accused, he said:

"It has been argued, that in treason two witnesses are necessary here; that they were necessary by the common law of England, and that the common law being the same in both countries, two witnesses are necessary here. That the common law is the same in both countries, I admit; but as to the point of two witnesses being necessary in treason in this kingdom, with the concurrence of the bench and the opinion of several judges of this country, given in some of the late cases here, I avow that two witnesses are not necessary. They are necessary in England by a statute, which does not prevail to the same extent here. It is very true that Lord Coke was of a different opinion, as to the common law of England: however, Lord Hale and Mr. Justice Forster say it was the received opinion that Lord Coke was wrong."

His lordship then proceeded to comment on the evidence of Alderman Alexander with respect to the proclamation found in the house of the prisoners. He said: "it was found in a writing-box which lay upon a table, open and unlocked, and that it did not appear evident whose property that writing-box was, or to which of the prisoners the house belonged."

Here Mr. John Sheares interposed, saying: "I beg your lordship's pardon, it was in my writing-box that paper was found."

His lordship observed: "I cannot call upon the prisoner for any admission of this kind, and I wish the paper may be determined by the evidence alone. It does not appear by express evidence, which of the prisoners was to be deemed as having it in his possession; as against John, who had written it, it is of more weight than against Henry; but as against the latter, it is of weight as being the act of one of the conspirators, in possession of the nature and objects of the conspiracy; nevertheless, as to him, leaving the discussion open as to the extent of his guilt, gentlemen, this paper wants one circumstance of additional strength, in not being published; but notwithstanding, it is very powerfully operative in the cause, as corroborative of the other evidence, and as making the intention of the party whom it is to affect."

With respect to the evidence of Armstrong, he said: "His testimony is sought to be impeached, by showing that he does not believe in a Supreme Being, and in a future state of rewards and punishments. He has sworn that he does believe in a Supreme Being, and in a future state of rewards and punishments; though it has been sworn he declared the contrary." His lordship left it to the jury, "whether he had made those declarations which had been imputed to him, seriously, and communicating his real opinions (for he had been described as giddy and inconsiderate in his expression), or not," observing that "the evidence of Captain Clibborn supported and fortified his testimony, and that on several parts of his testimony, the papers establish his credit in a very strong manner."

His lordship concluded by observing, that "if the jury were satisfied with regard to the first count, that the facts had been established against both prisoners, they would find them both guilty; and if they entertained any rational doubt, not merely a capricious doubt, but the doubt that might be entertained by sensible men, then in a capital case like this, they would lean to mercy."

The jury were to determine whether the communication made to Armstrong, by John Sheares, of the pressure of events preventing their waiting any longer for French assistance, implied the purpose of opening rebellion by the seizure of the camp, city and privy council, expecting at a later period the assistance of the French, and that the rising was acted on, with a view to aid the foreign enemy; that intent was absolutely necessary, and the jury must be satisfied of this intent.

The jury asked for the papers, which, with the prisoners' consent, were taken to the jury room. They then retired for seventeen minutes, and brought in a verdict, finding both the prisoners GUILTY.

As soon as the verdict was pronounced, the prisoners clasped each other in their arms.

It being now near eight o'clock on Friday morning, the court adjourned to three o'clock.

When the court met in the afternoon, the Attorney-General moved that the prisoners be brought up for judgment. Mr. M'Nally tried to make a point, on the want of venue for the "war" alleged in the indictment. The point was at once set aside, as at best only affecting one count, and then the prisoners were brought up.

The Clerk of the Crown read the indictment, and asked them what they had to say, why judgment of death and execution should not be awarded against them, according to law.

Mr. Henry Sheares—My lord, as I had no notion of dying such a death as I am about to meet, I have only to ask your lordship for sufficient time to prepare myself and family for it. I have a wife and six children, and hope your humanity will allow me some reasonable time to settle my affairs, and make a provision for them. (*Here he was so overwhelmed with tears that he could not proceed.*)

Mr. John Sheares—My lord, I wish to say a few words before the sentence is pronounced, because there is a weight pressing upon my heart much greater than that of the sentence which is to come from the court. There has been, my lord, a weight pressing upon my mind, from the first moment I heard the indictment read upon which I was tried; but that weight has been more peculiarly and heavily pressing upon my heart, when I found the accusation in the indictment enforced and supported upon the trial; and that weight would be left insupportable, if it were not for this opportunity of discharging it. It should be insupportable since a verdict of my country has stamped that evidence as well founded.

Do not think, my lords, that I am about to make a declaration against the verdict of the jury, or the persons concerned in the trial; I am only about to call to your recollection a part of the charge, which my soul shudders at; and if I had not this opportunity of renouncing it before your lordships and this auditory, no courage would be sufficient to support me. The accusation, my lords, to which I allude, is one of the blackest kind, and peculiarly painful, because it appears to have been founded upon my own act and deed, and to be given under my own hand. The accusation of which I speak, while I linger here yet a moment, is, "that of holding out to the people of Ireland a direction to give no quarter to the troops fighting for its defence." My lords, let me say this, and if there be any acquaintances in this crowded court, I will not say my intimate friends, but acquaintances, who do not know that what I say is truth, I should be reputed the wretch which I am not; I say, if any acquaintance of mine can believe, that I can utter a recommendation of giving no quarter to a yielding and unoffending foe, it is not the death that I am about suffer which I deserve —no punishment could be adequate to such a crime. My lords, I can not only acquit my soul of such an intention, but I declare in the presence of that God, before whom I must shortly appear, that the favorite doctrine of my heart was, *that no human being should suffer death, but where absolute necessity required it.*

My lords, I feel a consolation in making this declaration,

which nothing else could afford me; because it is not only a justification of myself, but where I am sealing my life with that breath. which cannot be suspected of falsehood, what I say may make some impression on the minds of men not holding the same doctrine. I declare to God, I know no crime but assassination, which can eclipse or equal that of which I am accused. I discern no shade of guilt between that, and taking away the life of a foe, by putting a bayonet to his breast, when he is yielding and surrendering. I do request the bench to believe that of me, I do request my country to believe that of me, I am sure God will think that of me.

Now, my lords, I have another favor to ask of the court: my country has decided that I am guilty, and the law says that I shall suffer: it sees that I am ready to suffer.

But, my lords, I have a favor to request of the court, that does not relate to myself. My lords, I have a brother whom I have ever loved dearer than myself; but it is not from any affection from him alone that I am induced to make the request. He is a man, and therefore I hope, prepared to die, if he stood as I do, though I do not stand unconnected, but he stands more dearly connected. In short, my lords, to spare your feelings and my own, I do not pray that I should not die; but, that the husband, the father, the brother, and the son, all comprised in one person, holding these relations, dearer in life to him, than to any other man I know, for such a man I do not pray a pardon, for that is not in the power of the court, but I pray a respite for such time as the court in its humanity and discretion shall think proper. You have heard, my lords, that his private affairs require arrangement. I have yet a farther room for asking; if immediately both of us be taken off, an aged and revered mother, a dear sister, and the most affectionate wife that ever lived, and six children, will be left without protection, or provision of any kind. When I address myself to your lordships, it is with the knowledge you will have of all the sons of our aged mother being gone. Two have perished in the service of the King; one very recently. I only request, that, disposing of me with what swiftness either the public mind or justice requires, a respite may be given to my brother, and that the family may acquire strength to bear it all. That is all I wish; I shall remember it to my last breath, and I will offer up my prayers for you to that Being, who has endued us all with a sensibility to feel. This is all I have to ask. I have nothing more to say.

Lord Carleton then proceeded to pass sentence of death in a feeling manner, as follows:

In the awful duty imposed upon me, no man can be more sensibly affected than I am, because I knew the very valuable and respectable father and mother from whom you are both descended; I knew and revered their virtues. One of them, happily for himself, is now no more; the other, for whom I have the highest personal respect, probably, by the events of this day may be hastened into futurity. It does not rest with me, after the conviction which has taken place, to hold out mercy; that is for another place; and I am afraid, in the present situation of public affairs, it will be difficult to grant even that indulgence which you, John Sheares, so pathetically request for your brother. With respect to one object of your soliciting time for your brother, unfortunately, it could be of no use, because by the attainder he will forfeit all his property, real and personal; nothing to be settled will remain.

"It cannot be too much lamented, that two gentlemen well educated, of good birth, respectable descent, and considerable talents, should be involved in a conspiracy, that might have spread desolation over the Kingdom, and brought us all to ruin. This country has enjoyed as much freedom and security in the possession of everything that was dear and valuable, as was consistent with a staple and effectual government, where a part of our natural liberty is taken away in order to secure the rest; his majesty has been celebrated for his mild and gracious reign, as a strict observer and protector of our laws, our rights, and our religion. His reign has been a continued series of liberal concession to the people of this country, calling upon them to make a suitable return of fidelity, attachment, and allegiance. The conspiracy in which you have been involved, proposed as one of the means of effecting its object, to invite a foreign enemy into this kingdom, and to subject this country to foreign yoke; the conspiracy had been remarkable for the system, perseverance, and art with which it has been conducted, and for the wide diffusion of its principles. Other revolutions have had for their object a change of monarchy, or an alteration of the constitution. But this consoiracy proposed the de, struction of the higher orders of the state, and an almost general massacre. Those who formed this system, so artfully carried on, endeavored to make the people of the country bad *men*, and thereby to make them more likely to become bad *subjects*. The conspiracy of which you have been convicted, had for its object the destruction of the monarchy and of the constitution, and to substitute anarchy, the worst of all tyrannies, in their place; and as far as we can collect from the intelligence received upon the subject, to annihilate all religion and morality, without having any substitute, save the unrestrained licentiousness of profligacy and vice; and this was done when a foreign enemy had threatened to invade this country—had denounced its destruction, and had avowed an intention to erase its name from the list of nations.

When you meditate the destruction of our laws, religion, and constitution, it is suprising you were not checked and restrained in the attempt by the danger attending yourselves; or by adverting to the extensive mischiefs which must have necessarily ensued.

Let me with great earnestness and charity request you to reflect upon the enormity of your guilt, and that you will call to your minds that effusion of human blood which has already taken place, and that incalculable mischief which may follow a deliberate system of massacre and devastation. I could wish that the manifesto read in evidence against you had contained nothing sanguinary; but recollect, that in that manifesto it was declared that no person should be spared who did not join the rebellion prior to the attack."

Mr. John Sheares.—I beg pardon, my lord, that was the evidence of Captain Armstrong—it is not part of the paper.

Lord Carleton.—"I have not the paper here; but that evidence was given against you. It now falls to my lot, and I never felt more pain than I do upon the present occasion, to pronounce that sentence which the law has provided against persons committing crimes of such magnitude as aim at the destruction of society. It is a sentence of great horror, but such as the wisdom of our ancestors ordained as a guard round the person of the king, and as a fence about that noble constitution which was acquired by our ancestors, and which I trust, we will transmit unimpaired to posterity, in order to hold out terror to those who are disposed to do ill, and to afford protection to the loyal part of the country."

His lordship then pronounced sentence, that they be executed on the following day.

Mr. Attorney-General.—"My lord, I could with great sincerity, allow any indulgence of time, if the country could by possibility admit of it. But, my lords, I have a great duty to discharge, and must pray that execution may be done to-morrow."

Court.—"Be it so."

The prisoners were then removed.

LETTERS OF JOHN SHEARES TO HIS MOTHER AND SISTER PREVIOUS TO HIS EXECUTION.

In the interval between the 10th and 14th of July, the following most painfully affecting letters were written by John Sheares to his mother and sister:

"KILMAINHAM PRISON, July 10th, '98.

"*To Julia Sheares.*

"The troublesome scene of life, my ever dear Julia, is nearly closed and the hand that now traces these lines, will, in a day or two, be no longer capable of communicating to a beloved and affectionate family, the sentiments of his heart. A painful task yet awaits me,—I do not allude to my trial, nor to my execution. These, were it not for the consciousness I feel of the misery you all will suffer on my account, would be trivial, in comparison with the pain I endure at addressing you for the last time. You have been kind to me, Julia, beyond example; your solicitude for my welfare has been unremitting, nor did it leave you a moment's happiness, as a wayward fate seems, from the earliest moment of my life, to have presided over my days. I will not recapitulate the instances of a perverse destiny, that seems to have marked me out as the instrument of destruction to all I loved.

Robert and Christopher, dear valued brothers; if it be true that the human mind survives the body, I shall shortly join you, and learn for what wise purpose Heaven thought fit to select me as your destroyer. My mother too! O, God! my tender, my revered mother! I see her torn locks—her broken heart—her corpse! Heavenly Author of the universe, what have I done to deserve this misery?

"I must forbear these thoughts as much as possible, or I must forbear to write. My time comes on the day after to-morrow, and the event is unequivocal. You must summon up all the resolution of your soul, my dear, dear Julia—if there be a chance of snatching my afflicted mother from the grave, that chance must arise from your exertions—my darling Sally, too, will aid you—she will for a while suspend her joy at the restoration of her husband to her arms; for of his escape I have no more doubt, than I have of my conviction and its consequences. All, all of you, forget your individual griefs and joys and unite to save the best of parents from the grave,—stand between her and despair,—if she will speak of me, sooth her with every assurance calculated to carry consolation to her heart. Tell her that my death, though nominally ignominious, should not light up a blush in her face; that she knew me incapable of a dishonorable action, or thought; that I died in full possession of the esteem of all those who knew me intimately; that justice will yet be done to my memory, and my fate be mentioned, rather with pride than shame, by my friends and relations. Yes, my dear sister, if I did not expect the arrival of this justice to my memory, I should indeed be afflicted at the nominal ignominy of my death, lest it may injure your welfare and wound the feelings of my family. But above all things, tell her that at my own request, I was attended in my latest moments, by that excellent and pious man, Dr. Dobbin, and that my last prayer was offered up for her. While I feared for Harry's life, hell itself could have no tortures for the guilty, beyond what I have endured.

"I picture you all, a helpless, unprotected group of females, left to the miseries of your own feelings, and to the insults of a callous insensible world. Sally, too, stripped of a husband, on whom she so tenderly doats, and his children of their father, and all by my cursed intervention, by my residence with them. Yet, Heaven is my witness, how assiduously I sought to keep aloof in any of my political concerns from him, and would have entirely succeeded in doing so, if it had not been for the art of the villain Armstrong, and Harry's own incaution. My efforts, however, have kept him clear of any of those matters, that have involved me in destruction. When

Sally has got him back to her arms, and that I (who caused his danger and her unhappiness) shall be no more, she will cease to think of me with reproach,—this I trust she will do—she ought—for she herself could never have done more for his salvation, than I endeavored to do. But the scene is changed, I am no longer that frantic thing I was, while his danger appeared imminent. A calm sorrow for the suffering that awaits you on my account, and a heartfelt regret at being obliged to quit your loved society for ever, has succeeded. Yet, all this will soon have an end, and will comfort. I already anticipate the moment, when your subsiding grief gives you back to the enjoyment of each other. Still, my dearest Julia, even when I shall be no more, your prayers on my account are not likely to cease. You remember, I am sure you do, your kind promise of protection to my poor unfortunate little Louisa? I make no doubt but her mother will give her up to your care without reluctance, yet how to impose this new anxiety on you I know not. But of this I will say nothing; I know your heart, and never could resist the goodness, with which it insisted on easing mine, by burdening itself. What to recommend relative to her, I cannot resolve. Harry did once desire me to take her into his house, but I had a thousand objections to that plan then, some of which still remain; one material one is, that she would soon learn from servants and others, how different her situation there was, from that of the other children, and her young mind would very early feel that chilling inferiority and degradation, that lead to a debasement of principle, and ultimately to mean and unworthy actions. No—a great many reasons concur, to decide me against that measure. She should be put to some school, where more care is taken of health than education, and where the only attention to morals, consists in good honest example. Apropos, she was at a Mrs. Duggan's, at Bray, to whom I yet owe ten guineas for her, and which I request of my dear mother to pay for me, when convenient; I do not owe any more on her account, to any one whatever. I likewise owe a note of hand for about thirteen pounds, or guineas, to a man in Capel street, whom the Fleming's know. I cannot mention the names of these friends without emotions of gratitude and tenderness, not to be expressed; never cease to assure them that I preserve the recollection of their goodness, though the instances of it are so many, and I shall feel it to the last moment; this debt they will be obliged to pay, if not discharged by my mother, as they passed their word for it. You will therefore mention it to my poor afflicted mother. Great God! how have I stripped her and you; but I have stripped you of happiness, and should not talk of money. I owe a few guineas to the worthy Charles Corghlan, of Cork; and about two, to Cole, the shoemaker, on Ormond Quay; to H. Fleming's tailor, also, for a suit of black clothes, and I believe some small balance of an account to H. Fleming himself. This is all at present I recollect. Good night, Julia; I am going to rest, with a heart, thank God! free from the consciousness of intentional offence, and from any wish tainted with personal resentment, I seek my bed with pleasure, because in it, I so often fancy myself in the full possession of that domestic happiness, which I always regarded as the first of human enjoyments. Pray Heaven, I dream of you all night.

"J. S."

"KILMAINHAM PRISON.—Wednesday night, July 11, 1798.

"The troublesome scene of life is nearly closed; and the hand that now traces these lines, in a short time will be no longer capable of communicating to a beloved family the sentiments of his heart.

"It is now eleven o'clock, and I have only time to address my beloved Julia in a short, eternal farewell. Thou sacred Power!—whatever be thy name and nature—who has created us the frail and imperfect creatures that we are, hear the ardent prayer of one now on the eve of a most awful change. If thy Divine Providence can be affected by mortal supplication, hear and grant, I most humbly beseech thee, the last wishes of a heart that has ever adored thy greatness and thy goodness. Let peace and happiness once more visit the bosom of my beloved family. Let a mild grief succeed the miseries they have endured; and, when an affectionate tear is generously shed over the dust of him who caused their misfortunes, let all their ensuing days glide on in union and domestic harmony. Enlighten my beloved brother: to him and his invaluable wife grant the undisturbed enjoyment of their mutual love; and, as they advance, let their attachment increase. Let my Julia, my feeling, my too feeling Julia, experience that consolation which she has so often imparted to others; let her soul repose at length in the consummation of all the wishes of her excellent heart; let her taste that happiness her virtues have so well merited. For my other sisters, provide those comforts their situation requires. To my mother—O, Eternal Power! what gift shall I wish for this matchless parent? Restore her to that peace which I have unfortunately torn from her: let her forget me in the ceaseless affections of my sisters, and in their prosperity; let her taste that happiness which is best suited to her affectionate heart; and, when at length she is called home let her find, in everlasting bliss, the due reward of a life of suffering virtue.

"Adieu, my dear Julia! My light is just out. The approach of darkness is like that of death, since both alike require me to say farewell! farewell, for ever! O, my dear family, farewell!—Farewell, for ever!

"J. S."

The night before his execution the following letter was written to his mother. That letter, short as it is, to "his dear, dear, his injured, his beloved mother," might have satisfied the vindictive feelings of his most obdurate enemy, had he known the mortal pangs that must have exceeded all former agonies of mind of his unfortunate adversary, which that last farewell to a fond mother from a favorite child must have cost the writer. This letter bears the simple superscription,—"My Mother."

"My dear, injured, perhaps expiring mother, hear a son's, —an unworthy son's—last request: grant to my beloved sister Sally, that portion of your generosity bestowed on me, else she is penniless; but why urge this?—you know her worth; she is generosity itself. Farewell, my dear, dear (mother), my injured, my adored mother. Oh! Sally, I hear your curses; they are just! Julia, beloved Julia—farewell for ever.

"JOHN SHEARES.

"Send poor little Jane to the Swetes, with her dying father's request that they will let her be partaker with her sister of their bounty, from which alone she can hope for support. If they should be ——— enough to reject her, need I suggest to my adored mother the appropriation of whatever fragment, however small, may by chance be within her gift. But I know that my harpy talons have seized on all. Once more, and forever, adieu, thou best and most beloved of parents."

THE EXECUTION.

At twelve o'clock, the time appointed for the execution, "when the sheriffs arrived, the prisoners entreated them to be the bearers of a supplication to government for a short respite, in consideration of which, they offered to make the most useful discoveries. This message being carried to the castle, Government being already possessed of complete information of everything which the Sheares could discover, refused to grant the respite. Upon this refusal, a new supplication was made, in the most abject terms, entreating a respite until Monday, for at least one of them. Of this message, the sheriffs were humane enough to be also the bearers, but returned with a second refusal. At this repeated disappointment, the prisoners were most dreadfully shaken; but upon being directed to prepare for death, made a sudden and short effort by mutual encouragement to rouse themselves. In the interval between the reply to their last message and the execution, the clerical gentleman who attended, continued to exhort them to full repentance and disclosure of their crimes. Henry declared that his object was reform, and that he never had intended to excite indiscriminate massacre. John made the same declaration. While the executioner was fixing the rope, he by some awkwardness roughly pressed the neck of Henry, who exclaimed, "do you intend to strangle me before my time?" They requested that they might not continue long exposed to the gaze of the multitude; and having each an halter fixed round his neck, and a cap drawn over his face, holding each other's hands, they tottered out upon the platform in front of the prison. *In making the rope fast within, John Sheares was hauled up to the block of the tackle,* and continued nearly a minute suspended alone, before the platform fell. It did fall, and instantly both were suspended. After hanging about twenty minutes, they were, at a quarter past three o'clock, let down into the street, when the hangmen separated their heads from their bodies, and taking the heads severally up, proclaimed, 'Behold the head of a traitor!' In the evening, the trunks and heads were taken away in two shells, provided by a respectable gentleman unhappily connected with one of the brothers."

It was the cruel custom of those times, to make the extreme rigor of the law as terrible as possible to its victims. Their friends were seldom permitted to see them. Whoever has perused the life of Lord Edward Fitzgerald, will have noticed the obstacles thrown in the way of the immediate members of his lordship's family, to obtain a private interview with the dying man, and the rigor of the regulation being only relaxed by the exertions in their behalf of the most powerful influence, when the noble being was in the agony of death.

In the case of the Sheares, no member of their family was allowed to see them.

Another account of the execution states that on Saturday, at midnight, they were conducted from their cells to the room adjoining the place of execution. There, as they had done in the dock, when their doom was sealed, they clasped each other in their arms, and for some minutes the unfortunate Henry seemed utterly stupefied and appalled at the frightful spectacle before him. He rallied sufficiently to disclaim the sanguinary intentions imputed to him, as John had done, and while still clinging to the latter, he was pushed out on the platform, hand-in-hand with his brother No violence was requisite to bring the other victim to the saffold; his only fears were for that dear brother, whose death he reproached himself of being the cause of. The last words of John Sheares were—"I forgive the world as I expect to be forgiven." In life and death they were indeed united brothers.

After the mutilation of their bodies (that remnant of the judicial barbarism of former times), had afforded the requisite satisfaction to offended justice, their remains were borne to the same place of burial, and deposited in one of the vaults of St. Michan's church.

A small party of the Dublin Loyal Cavalry attended as a guard at the execution. The number of spectators was incalculable.

The unnecessary cruelties inflicted by the executioner on both brothers, previously to their being launched into eternity, —but especially the barbarity practiced on the younger, as detailed in the preceding account, which is given by those most hostile to them, there is too much reason to believe, were not to be ascribed to the "awkwardness," which is assigned as a reason for part of the unnecessary violence practiced on the elder brother. The amount of violence done to the other, forty-four years after the event, remains still visible on the face and head of John Sheares.

EXTRAORDINARY APPEARANCE OF THE BODIES AFTER INTERMENT.

In the church-yard of St. Michan's, the remains of some of their former friends and associates are interred—those of Bond and of Dr. William Jackson, whose funeral the Sheares had attended in 1795, and who, for so doing, had incurred the displeasure of Lord Fitzgibbon.

There is some peculiarity in the soil of this place of burial, as well as in the atmosphere of the vaults beneath the church of St. Michan's, the tendency of which is to resist decomposition, and to keep the dead bodies, especially those deposited in the vaults, in a state of preservation the most extraordinary known in any country, with the exception of a cemetery in the Island of Sicily, where the same process of embalming, naturally effected, has gone on for centuries.

Bodies, which have been interred for upwards of a century, in St Michan's, are still to be seen in the vaults, in a state of preservation as perfect as that of the exsiccated mummies of the humbler classes of the Egyptians, which were preserved by a less expensive process of embalming than that used for persons of distinction

In this dry and shrivelled state, the integuments remain perfect, the features preserve their character, the hair undergoes no alteration, and the limbs even, in some degree, retain their shape.

"One of these bodies," Mr. Madden, in his *United Irishmen*, speaking of this singular phenomenon, continues to say—"whose antiquity is of ancient date, for the tenants of European sepulchres, is still existing in the same vault in which the Sheares' remains are interred: the remains are those of a person, in former time renowned for piety—a member of a religious community—of the name of Crookshank, some sixty or seventy years ago, the wonder-working effects produced by this good lady's remains, used to bring vast numbers of visitants to her tomb—till the spirit of whiskey unfortunately mingled a little too much with the spirit of veneration for the virtues of the nun, and the rudiments of a fine "pattern" were spoiled by the intervention of the authorities. Poor Miss Crookshank's relics, from that period till about the year 1816, when I first saw them, were visited only by curious boys and scientific gentlemen. In the month of February in the present year, after a lapse of twenty-six years, I found the remains of the nun removed from the place where they were originally deposited, as likewise those of John and Henry Sheares, and deposited in what is called the Parish Vault. Up to the time of the removal, which took place about five or six years ago, the remains continued, I was informed, in the same perfect state in which they have been long known to exist. But the exposure to the air, consequent to the removal of her remains, and those of the Sheares on the same occasion, had proved injurious to them, and to the latter especially.

When I first saw the remains of the Sheares, about twenty-six years ago, I was accompanied to St. Michan's by a school-fellow, of the name of Blake. When I visited the place in the month of January last, the same companion was with me likewise on that occasion. I found the remains of the Sheares in a state of dissolution. The features were no longer discernible; the coffins even had mouldered away, after the exposure to the external air, on their removal from an adjoining vault. On examining the head of the body described as that of John Sheares, I was surprised to find the head was that of a person extremely aged, the sutures entirely obliterated, and the alveolar processes quite worn down. I said to the Sexton, "This is not the head of John Sheares; he replied, "that it could be no other."

For some days subsequently to this visit to the place of interment of the Sheares, the circumstances connected with it were uppermost in my mind, and were spoken of to several persons. At length, I received a communication from a gentleman well known in the city of Dublin, which removed all doubt as to the correctness of the opinion I had expressed with respect to the head shown with the remains of John Sheares.

This gentleman informed me that, when a mere boy, about twenty years ago, he went with some other lads of his own age, to see the remains of the Sheares. The idea had come into his mind, to take away the head of John Sheares, whom he had often heard spoken of with enthusiasm by one of his companions, a young fellow of rather democratic opinions—and, it was added, of the Roman Catholic religion—[my informant was of neither one nor the other]. He took a boy with him into the vault, whom he had seen in the church-yard, and promised to reward him if he carried away the head unperceived.

The head was attached to the body by a strip of the integuments of the back part of the neck. The boy was supplied with a penknife, and the head was removed and carried home to the person's house, where it had remained for the last twenty years. This gentleman told me he had often regretted taking it; and as he knew that I was interested in matters appertaining to the Sheares, I might have it. I willingly accepted the offer, on condition of doing with it what might seem best to me, and it was sent to me the day following. It was in the state precisely in which I had seen it twenty-six years ago, as perfect as any New Zealand or Egyptian head of the inferior class of mummies. The head was finely formed, but the expression of the face—that of the most frightful agony. The mark of very violent injuries, done during life to the right eye and nose, were particularly apparent; the very indentation round the neck, from the pressure of the rope, was visible; and there was no injury to the cervical vertebræ occasioned by any instrument—in fact, the head had not been entirely separated from the body at the time of execution.

The marks of violence on the face, there can be little doubt, were occasioned by the barbarous act committed by the executioner, before he was launched into eternity, as described in a Cork paper. The circumstance of the head having been found attached to the body at the time of its removal, is connected with a matter somewhat singular. I may observe, that the head thus slightly attached to the trunk, was seen by Mr. William H. Curran, about twenty-one years ago. John Sheares, after sentence was pronounced on him, in order to prevent or put some difficulty in the way of the executioner holding up his head pursuant to the sentence, after execution, had his hair cut close, and the act had the effect he intended; for though the barbarous ceremony of cutting through the neck was performed, the head was not separated from the body. Barrington saw the executioner holding up the head of his friend (Henry) on his arrival, but he makes no mention of the same being done with John's.

The hair on the head, as it was when sent to me, was of a light brown color; and was cut, or rather clipped, extremely short.

In the latter end of January, 1842, having obtained the necessary permission from the clergyman of St. Michan's church, the remains of the Sheares were placed in coffins of lead, and the best Irish oak that could be procured for them, in the presence of one who had been in his young days a member of the same society to which they belonged, and of two other individuals.

The head of which I have spoken was placed with the remains of John Sheares, a plaster cast of it having been previously taken, which is now in the possession of Mr. Donovan, a London phrenologist.

The two coffins were laid side by side, and so far, I trust, the possibility is prevented of their remains being disturbed in future.

The remains of Mr. Samuel Rosborough, a man once of some notoriety in Dublin; and likewise those of the nun, Miss Crookshank, semi-canonized nearly a century ago in the minds of thousands of her—Catholic—fellow citizens, are deposited in the same vault of Henry and John Sheares.

THE BURNING OF THE SHEAS

TERRIBLE AGRARIAN OUTRAGE COMMITTED IN IRELAND IN 1821.—EIGHTEEN HUMAN BEINGS BURNED TO DEATH IN THEIR OWN HOUSE.—A CHILD BORN IN THE FLAMES.—SINGULAR CIRCUMSTANCES ATTENDING THE DETECTION OF THE CULPRITS.—AN EYE-WITNESS TO THE SCENE KEEPS THE SECRET SIXTEEN MONTHS.—THE TRIAL AND EXECUTION OF THE FIENDS WHO COMMITTED THE MURDER.—RICHARD LALOR SHIEL'S* GRAPHIC HISTORY OF THE TRAGEDY, AND SPEECH AT CLONMEL IN RELATION THERETO, &C. &C.

In Ireland very many murders have been committed, growing out of the horrible tyranny of the landlord, and their grinding oppression over the poor tenants, who by rents, tythes, taxes and English statutes, were and are reduced to a state inferior to that of abject slavery. The misfortunes of this long-suffering people are familiar to every reader of history. These misfortunes can be traced in letters of blood. Yet nothing could justify or palliate the horrible barbarities which were perpetrated under the goading and maddening despotism exercised over them. In the catalogue of these crimes, the "burning of the Sheas" stands foremost as the bloodiest record in the book of crime. This tragic affair is so well told in "Sketches Legal and Political," by the late Richard Lalor Shiel, edited by M. W. Savage, and published in London in 1855, that we transcribe it almost *literatim.* These sketches were written by Mr. Shiel for one of the magazines of the day, and it was not known for some time who the author was.

"The assizes of Clonmel (Ireland), held there in 1828, presented a dreadful miscellany of the most barbarous crimes, most of which were of an insurrectionary character, and re-

* The same sketches were edited by Dr. Shelton McKensie, and published in New York some years ago.

quired the exercise of the strongest powers of the law. The presiding justice was Judge Burton, who seemed to recoil in dismay from the calendar, which numbered not less than three hundred and eighty prisoners. The government felt that it was necessary to do their utmost in order to repress so alarming a growth of crime; and with a view to the production of effect, and in order to give the administration of justice more impressiveness, deemed it advisable to send Mr. Sergeant Blackburne, as special Counsel for the crown. He accordingly arrived in Clonmel at the beginning of the assizes; and as he enjoyed no ordinary reputation, his mission had the desired effect, by drawing the general attention to the cases which he conducted.

"Upon the first day of his appearance, he availed himself of the right of the crown to address the jury (although that privilege at that time was denied to the prisoner against whom the speech was directed), in order to present a picture of the general condition of the country. The county Tipperary was almost in a state of insurrection. Armed bands of peasants traversed the country in open day, and put to death in face of the law whoever presumed to violate the code of regulations which they had arbitrarily imposed, under authority of their invisible chieftain, Captain Rock. During the assizes themselves, two murders were committed, and Mr. Lanigan, the land-agent of Lord Landaff, was fired at by a party of armed men. The evils by which the county was actually afflicted were in themselves sufficiently alarming, without looking into ulterior results; but it was impossible not to reflect upon the consequences which might ensue from the political and moral state of a famished and ferocious population, provided with arms, regularly organized, and acting upon systematic principles of insubordination.

"Independently of the general aspect of the country, which opened such a wide field to a powerful speaker, the individual case in which he addressed the jury was one of the most appalling that can be imagined, and attended with circumstances of strangeness as well as atrocity, which furnished an occasion for the noblest oratory. Eighteen individuals had been burnt alive in one of the dark and lonely glens of the Mountain of Slievenamaun, and the chief perpetrator of that terrible deed stood in all the ghastliness of guilt at the bar. The court-house was filled to suffocation, by persons of all classes; and the vast asembly, together with the leading aristocracy of that opulent county, included in all likelihood some of the brother-incendiaries of the villain who was brought at last to a tardy justice. The deepest silence prevailed. The judge himself, however, from his judicial experience disastrously familiar with scenes of this kind, seemed to be awe-struck by the consciousness of the important consequences of the trial, and weighed down by the magnitude of the crimes over the investigation of which he was condemned to preside. While the oath was administered to each of the jury, every eye was rivetted upon the individual who held the sacred volume in his hand. While he pressed the word of God to his lips, his countenance was closely watched, and it was easy to perceive upon the faces of the twelve men, upon whose concurrent voices the life of their fellow-creature was to depend, a strong solicitude, amounting almost to an expression of fear, at the hazard which they were about to incur by a conviction."

This jury was impanelled for the trial of William Gorman, to which I have already referred, for "the burning of the Sheas." It is by that title that the terrible crime in which so many immolators and so many victims are involved, is habitually designated; and whenever a man expatiates upon the atrocities which disgrace the country, and upon the conflagrations by which its character is blackened, he refers as to a leading illustration, to "the burning of the Sheas."

I shall not readily forget the impression which was produced upon me, on my first passing near the spot in which that dreadful incident took place, when some of its details were narrated by one of my fellow-travellers, in descending the narrow defile of Glenbower. The remains of the habitation in which the eighteen human beings were committed together to the flames, are not visible from the road that winds at the foot of the mountain on which it was situated; but the dark and gloomy glen in which the deed was done can be pierced by the eye, when the mists that hang upon the lofty ridge do not envelop it· and it is always with awe, which is not a little assisted by the loneliness and dreariness of the scene, that the traveller turns his eyes toward that dismal valley, to which his attention is directed by the habitual exclamation which I had never failed to hear: "There is the place where the Sheas were burnt!" I had an opportunity, in consequence of having attended two trials connected with that frightful event, of learning the circumstances by which it was attended.

Upon the morning of the 20th of November, 1821, the remains of the house of Patrick Shea, a respectable farmer, who held a considerable quantity of land at the foot of the mountain of Slievenamaun, exhibited an appalling spectacle. It had been consumed by fire on the preceding night; and a large concourse of people (the intelligence of the conflagration having been rapidly diffused through the neighboring glens) assembled to look upon the ruins. Of the thatched roof which had first received the fire, a few smoking rafters were all that remained. The walls had given way, and stood gaping in rents, through which, on approaching them, the eye caught a glimpse of the dreadful effects of the devouring element. The door was burnt to its hinges; and, on arriving at the threshold, as awful a scene offered itself to the spectator as is recorded in the annals of terror. The bodies of sixteen human beings of both sexes lay together in a mass of corpses. The door having been closed when the flames broke out, the inhabitants precipitated themselves toward it, and in all likelihood mutually counteracted their efforts to burst into the open air. The house being a small one, every individual in it had an opportunity of rushing toward the entrance, where they were gathered by hope, and perished in despair. Here they lay piled upon each other. Those who were uppermost were burnt to the bones, while the wretches who were stretched beneath them were partially consumed. One of the spectators, the uncle of a young woman, Catherine Mullaly, who perished in the flames, described the scene with a terrible particularity. With an expression of horror which six years had not effaced, he said, when examined as a witness, that the melted flesh ran from the heap of carcasses in black streams along the floor.

But terrible as this sight must have been, there was another still more appalling. The young woman, whom I have already mentioned, Catherine Mullaly, resided in the house, and had been not very long before married. She had advanced a considerable period in pregnancy, and her child, which was born in the flames in a premature labor, made the eighteenth victim.

I shall never forget the answer given by her uncle at the trial; when he was asked how many had perished, he answered that there were seventeen: but that if the child that was dropped, (that was his phrase) in the fire was counted, the whole would make eighteen. His unfortunate niece was delivered of her offspring in the midst of the flame. She was not found among the mass of carcasses at the door. There were sixteen wretches assembled there, but, on advancing farther into the house in a corner of the room, lay the body of this unhappy young creature, and that condition in which her child was discovered accounted for her separation from the group of the dead. A tub of water lay on the ground beside her. In it she had placed the infant of which she had been jnst delivered while the fires were raging about her, in the hope of preserving it; and in preserving its limbs she had succeeded, for the body was perfect with the exception of the head, which was held above the water, and which was burned away. Near this tub she was found, with the skeleton of the arm with which she had held her child hanging over it! It will be supposed that the whole of this spectacle excited a feeling of dismay among the spectators; but they were actuated by a variety of sentiments. Most of them had learned caution and silence, which are among the characteristies of the Irish peasantry, and, whatever were their feelings, deemed it advisable to gaze on without a comment; and there were not wanting individuals who, folding their arms, and looking on the awful retribution, whispered sternly to each other that "William Gorman was at last revenged!"

When information of this dreadful event reached Dublin, it produced, as it was natura to expect, a very great sensation. It was at first believed that "the burning of the Sheas" was the result of that confederacy by which the peasantry had regulated the taking of lands; and that as the previous tenant, one William Gorman, had been ejected by the Sheas, against the will of the people, the house had been set on fire. But it was asked, "what object could there be in destroying so many individuals who were innocent of all crime, and were mere laborers and servants in the employment of the occupying farmer?" This reflection, and a wish to rescue the national character from the disgrace of so wanton an atrocity, gradually induced a surmise that the fire had been accidental: and this conjecture was confirmed by the fact that, notwithstanding a large reward had been offered for the discovery of the incendiaries, no information was given to the Government. At length, however, the fatal truth was disclosed, and it was ascertained that the conflagration was the result of a plot executed by a considerable band of men, and that the whole population in the neighborhood were well aware both of the project and of its execution. The first clew to this abominable transaction was given by a woman of the name of Mary Kelly.

This female had been a person of dissolute life, and had married a servant, who, having relinquished his employment, some time after his marriage, established, with the assistance of his wife, what is commonly called a *shebeen-house*, in the vicinity of the Sheas, at the foot of Slievenamaun. It was a kind of mountain-brothel, or rather combined the exercise of a variety of trades, which, in the subdivision of labor that takes place in towns, are generally practised apart. Her husband stated that he sold spirits without license; provided board and lodging to any passengers who thought it expedient to take up their abode with him; and that if a young man and woman had any wish to be left alone in his hospitable and accommodating mansion at a late hour at night, he and his wife did not think it genteel to meddle with their discourse. It will be thought singular that, in so wild and desolate a district, in the midst of solitary glens and moors, such conveniences should exist; but they are not unfrequent; and one often meets these traces of civilization in parts of the country which carry no other evidence of refinement!

Mary Kelly appears to have superintended and conducted this establishment; her husband merely giving it the sanction of wedlock, and joining in the licentious conviviality which took place under his auspices. But although his wife had, upon her own admission, been of profligate habits, until time had transmuted her, by the ordinary process, from a harlot to a procuress, yet she does not appear to have been utterly devoid of all virtuous sentiment; and, indeed, the scene which she had witnessed was of such a nature as to awaken any remnant of conscience, which often, in the midst of depravity, is found to linger behind.

A peasant of the name of William Gorman, at whose trial Sergeant Blackburne conducted the prosecution, had originally held the house where the Sheas resided. He was their under-tenant, and held the lowest place in those numerous gradations of tenure into which almost every field is divided and subdivided; for the Sheas were not middle-men in the strict sense of the word, but stood themselves at a great distance from the head-proprietor of the estate, although they were the immediate landlords of Gorman. The more remote the head-landlord, the heavier the weight with which oppression falls on the occupier of the soil. The owner of the fee presses his lessee; the latter comes down upon the tenant, who derives from him, who, in his turn, crushes his own immediate serf; and if, which often happens in this long concatenation of vassalage, there are many other interventions of estate, the occupier of the soil is in proportion made to suffer; and is, to use the expression of Lord Clare, "ground to powder," in this complicated system of exaction! William Gorman was dealt with most severely. He was distrained, sued in the superior courts, processed by civil bill—in short, the whole machinery of the law was put into action against him. Driven from his home, deprived of his few fields, without covert or shelter, he made an appeal to the league of peasants with whom he was associated; and, as the Sheas had infringed upon their statutes, it was determined that they should die, and that an exemplary and appalling vengeance should be taken of them.

I saw William Gorman at the bar of the court in which he was condemned. He heard the whole detail of the atrocities of which he had been the primary agent. He was evidently most solicitous for the preservation of life; yet the expression of anxiety which disturbed his ghastly features occasionally gave way to the exulting consciousness of his revenge; and, as he heard the narration of his own delinquencies, so far from intimating contrition or remorse, a savage joy flashed over his face; his eyes were lighted up with a fire as lurid as that which he had kindled in the habitation of his enemies; his hand, which had previously quivered, and manifested, in the irregular movement of his fingers, the workings of deep anxiety, became, for a moment, clinched; and when the groans of his victims were described, his white teeth, which were unusually prominent, were bared to the gums; and, though he had drained the cup of vengeance to the dregs, still he seemed to smack his lips, and to lick the blood with which his injuries had been redressed!

This man had the vindictive feelings of a savage; but, while his barbarities admit of no sort of extenuation, they still were not without a motive. His co-partners in villany, however, who arranged and conducted the enterprise, had no instigation of personal vengeance, toward the oppressors of William Gorman. At their head was a bold and sagacious ruffian, whose name was Maher. It was determined that their plot should be carried into execution on Monday, the 20th of November. On the preceding Saturday, Maher went to Mary Kelly's house, and retired to a recess in it, where he employed himself in melting lead, and fusing it into balls. He was supposed to be a paramour of Mary Kelly (though she strenuously denied it), and she was certainly familiar with him. She had heard (indeed, it was known through the whole of that wild vicinage) that it was intended to inflict summary justice upon the Sheas; and being well aware that Maher was likely to dip his hands in any bloody business which was to go on, and observing his occupation, which he did not seek to hide from her, she taxed him with his "slaughterous thoughts," and having some good instincts left, begged him not to take life away. Maher answered with equivocation.

During this colloquy, Catherine Mullaly, a cousin of Mary Kelly, came into the house. Maher was well-acquainted with her, and had the rude gallantry which is common among the Irish pe santry. She resided as a servant with the Sheas. Maher believed that there were arms in the Sheas' possession, and knew that there were a number of persons living in the house, with a view to their defence. The extent, however, of their means of self-protection the murderers had not ascertained, and it was important to learn the fact, in order that they might adapt to circumstances their mode of attack. It is probable, that, if there had been no weapons in the house, the conspirators would have burst open the door, dragged the Sheas out, and put them to death, and would have spared the more unoffending victims: but having discovered that there were firearms in abundance, they considered the burning of the house as a measure of self-defence, independently of the impression which a massacre upon a large scale would be likely to produce. Maher, therefore, sought to ascertain the state of defence from Catherine Mullaly, and entered into conversation with her in the tone of mixed joke and gibe, of which the lower orders, who delight in repartee, are exceedingly fond. The young woman was pleased with his attentions, and in the innocence of her heart, not having any suspicion of his intent, gradually disclosed to him that there was a quantity of arms in the house. Maher, on her departure put on her cloak, and bade her farewell in the tone of friendship. Mary Kelly, who knew him well, and guessed at his objecct, the moment Catherine Mullaly was gone (for she did not dare to speak in her presence) implored Maher, whatever he might intend, not to harm Caterine Mullaly.

She extorted a promise from him to that effect, on which she relied for the moment, and they separated; Maher with his balls, and Mary Kelly with the undertaking for the life of Catherine Mullaly, in which she placed so mistaken a confidence. After some reflection, however, her alarm for the safety of her relative, to whom she was much attached, revived, and during the next day her suspicions were increased by the notes of preparation which she observed between Maher and his confederates. However, she did not venture to speak; for, to use her own phrase, "a word would have been as much as her life was worth;" still a terrible inquietude preyed upon her, and, as if actuated by some mysterious impulse, upon Monday night, when her husband, to whom she never communicated her apprehensions, was asleep, she silently rose from bed, and having huddled on his coat, left her cabin, though it was near midnight, and advanced cautiously and slowly along the hedges, until she made her way to near Maher's house. She stopped, and heard the voices of men engaged in discussion, which lasted some time; at length the door opened — she hid herself behind some brambles, and bending down, in order to avoid detection, which would have been death, she marked the murderers as they came forth. They issued from Maher's house in arms, and walked in a sort of array, advancing in file. Eight of them she knew; and, as she alleged, distinctly recognized them by their voices and looks. One of them carried two pieces of turf, lighted at the extremities, and kept the fires alive with his breath.

They passed her without observation and proceeded upon their dreadful destination. Trembling and terror-struck, but still impelled to pursue them, she followed on from hedge to hedge, until they got beyond her; and perceiving that they proceeded toward the house of the Sheas, she stopped at a spot from which the house was visible, and by which the murderers, after executing their diabolical purpose, afterward returned. Here she remained in terrible anticipation, and her conjecture was speedily verified. A fire suddenly appeared in the roof of Shea's bouse; the wind high, it rose rapidly into a flame, and the whole was speedily in a blaze. It cast round the rocky glen a frightful splendor, and furnished, in its extensive diffusion of light, the means of beholding all that took place close to the burning cottage, in which shrieks and cries for mercy began to be heard. The murderers had secured the door; and having prevented all possibility of escape, stood in groups about the house, and gazed on the progress of the conflagration. So far from being moved to pity, they answered the invocations of their victims with yells of ferocious laughter. They set up a war-whoop of exultation, and in token of triumph, discharged their guns and blunderbusses to celebrate their achievement. There was an occasional pause in their shouts: nothing then was heard but the crackling of the flames, that shed far and wide their desolate illumination; and the spectatress of this dreadful scene, though at some distance from it, declared that, in the temporary abatement of the wind, and the cessation of its gusts, she could at intervals hear the deep groans of the dying, and the gulps of agony with which their tortures were concluding.

But the fiends by whom these infernal fires were kindled, soon reiterated their cries of exultation, and discharged their guns again. The report of their firearms, which was taken up by the echoes of the mountain, produced a result which they had not anticipated. On the opposite side of a hill which adjoined the house, there resided a man of the name of Philip Dillon, who was a friend of the Sheas. Hearing the discharge of guns, and suspecting what had taken place, he summoned as many as he could gather together, and proceeded at their head across the hill, in order, if possible to save the Sheas. They advanced toward the house, but arrived too late: neither had they courage to attack the murderers, who at once drew up before the flames to meet them. Philip Dillon, indeed, defied them to come on, but they declined his challenge, and waited his attack, which, as his numbers were inferior, he thought it prudent not to make. Both parties stood looking at each other, and in the meanwhile the house continued to blaze. The groans were heard for a little time, until they grew fainter and fainter; and at length all was silent.

Although the arrival of Philip Dillon did not contribute to save any of the sufferers, still it was the means of convicting William Gorman, by affording a corroboration to the testimony of Mary Kelly. John Butler, a boy, who was in the employment of Philip Dillon, and accompanied him to the burning-house, was the brother of one of the servants of the Sheas. Notwithstanding he could not give any assistance to his brother, yet his anxiety to discover the murderers inducd him to approach nearer than his companions to the flames, when, by the fire which they had kindled, Butler had an opportunity of identifying William Gorman, against whom he gave his testimony, and thus sustained the evidence of Mary Kelly.

All was now over—the roof had fallen in, and the ruins of the cottage were become a sepulchre. Gorman and Maher, with their associates, left the scene of their atrocities, and returned by the same path by which they had arrived. Another eye, however, besides that of God, was upon them. They passed a second time near the place where Mary Kelly lay concealed; again she cowered at their approach; and, as they went by, had a second opportunity of identifying them. Here a circumstance took place which is, perhaps, more utterly detestable than any other which I have yet recorded. The conversation of the murderers turned upon the doings of the night, and William Gorman amused the party by mimicking the groans of the dying, and mocking the agonies which he had inflicted.

The morning now began to break, and Mary Kelly, haggard, affrighted, and laden with the dreadful knowledge of what had taken place, returned to her home. Well aware, however, of the consequences of any disclosure, she did not utter a syllable to her husband, or to her son, upon the subject; and although examined next day before a magistrate, who conjectured, from the ill fame of her house, that she must have had some cognizance of what had taken place, she declared herself to be innocent of all knowledge. John Butler, too, who had witnessed the death of his brother, immediately proceeded to the house of his mother, Alicia Butler, an old woman, who was produced as a witness for the crown; he awoke her from sleep, and told her that her son had been burned alive. Her maternal feelings burst into an exclamation of horror upon first hearing this dreadful intelligence; but instead of immediately proceeding to a magistrate, she enjoined her son not to speak on the subject, lest she herself, and all her family, should suffer the same fate.

For sixteen months, no information whatever was communicated to Government. Mary Kelly was still silent, and did not dare to reproach Maher with the murder of Catherine Mullaly, for whose life she had made a stipulation. She did not even venture to look in the face of the murderer, although, when he visited at her house, which he continued to do, she could not help shuddering at his presence. Still the deeds which she had seen were inlaid and burned in dreadful colors in her mind. The recollection of the frightful spectacle never left her. She became almost incapable of sleep; and, haunted by images of horror, used in the dead of night to rise from her bed, and wander over the lonely glen in which she had seen such sights; and although one would have supposed that she would have instinctively fled from the spot, she felt herself drawn by a kind of attraction to the ruins of Shea's habitation, where she was accustomed to remain till the morning broke, and then return wild and wan to her home. She stated when examined in private previous to the trial in which she gave her evidence, that she was pursued by the spectre of her unfortunate kinswomen, and that whenever she lay down in her bed, she thought of the "burning," and felt as if Catherine Mullaly was lying beside her, holding her child, "as black as a coal in her arms." At length her conscience got the better of her apprehensions, and in confession she revealed her secret to a priest, who prevailed upon her to give information, which, after a struggle, she communicated to Captain Despard, a justice of the peace for the county of Tipperary.

Such were the incidents which accompanied the perpetration of a crime, than which it is difficult to imagine one more enormous. To do the people justice, immediately after the conviction and execution of William Gorman, they appeared to feel the greatest horror at his guilt; and of that sentiment a Roman Catholic assembly, held during the assizes, afforded a strong proof. The assizes had gathered an immense concourse of the lower orders from all parts of the country, and Mr. Sheil, conceiving that a favorable opportunity had presented itself for giving a salutary admonition to the people, and believing that his advice would be fully as likely to produce an impression as the declamation of Mr. Sergeant Blackburne, used his influence in procuring a public meeting to be summoned. A vast multitude thronged to the place of assembly; and I am bestowing no sort of encomium upon Mr. Sheil, when I say that his speech produced a great deal of effect upon the peasantry, for the bare statement of the facts which appeared in evidence in the course of the assizes, would have been sufficient to awaken deep emotions wherever the instincts of humanity were not utterly extinguished. As Mr. Sheil's address contained a summary of the principal cases in which Sergeant Blackburne was engaged, and he dwelt especially upon that of Mathew Hogan, which was attended by many afflicting circumstances, I shall close this article by a citation from the concluding passages of that gentleman's speech. "The recollection," he continued, "of what I have seen and heard during the present assizes, is enough to freeze the blood. Well might Judge Burton, who is a good and tender-hearted man—well might he say, with tears in his eyes, that he had not in the course of his judicial experience beheld so frightful a mass of enormities as the calendar presented. How deep a stain have those misdeeds left upon the character of your country, and what efforts should not be made by every man of ordinary humanity, to arrest the progress of villany, which is rolling a torrent of blood, and bearing down all the restraints of law, morality, and religion, before it. Look, for example, at the murder of the Sheas, and tell me if there be anything in the records of horror by which that accursed deed has been excelled? The unborn child, the little innocent who had never lifted its innocent hands, or breathed the air of heaven—the little child in its mother's womb . . . I do not wonder that the tears which flow down the cheeks of many a rude face about me should bear attestation to your horror of that detestable atrocity. But I am wrong in saying that the child who perished in the flames was not born. Its mother was delivered in the midst of the flames. Merciful God! Born in fire! Sent into the world in the midst of a furnace! transferred from the womb to the flames that raged round the agonies of an expiring mother! There are other mothers who hear me. This vast assembly contains women, doomed by the primeval malediction to the groans of child-birth, which can not be suppressed on the bed of down, into which the rack of maternal agony still finds its way. But say, you will know it best, you who are of the same sex as Catherine Mullaly, what must have been the throes with which she brought forth her unfortunate offspring, and felt her infant consumed by the fires with which she was surrounded! We can but lift up our hands to the God of justice, and ask him why has he invested us with the same forms as the demons who perpetrated that unexampled murder! And why did they commit it?—by virtue of a horrible league by which they were associated together, not only against their enemy, but against human nature and the God who made it!—for they were bound together—they were sworn in the name of their Creator, and they invoked Heaven to sanctify a deed which they were confederated to perpetrate by a sacrament of Hell. Although accompanied by circumstance of inferior terror, the recent assassination of Barry belongs to the same class of guilt. A body of men at the close of the day enter a peaceful habitation, on the Sabbath, and regardless of the cry of a frantic woman, who, grasping one of the murderers, desired him 'to think of God, and of the blessed night, and to spare the father of her eight children!' dragged him forth, and when he, 'offered to give up the ground tilled and untilled if they gave him his life,' answered him with a yell of ferocious irony, and telling him 'he should have ground enough,' plunged their bayonets into his heart! An awful spectacle was presented on the trial of the wretched men who were convicted of the assassination. At one extremity of the bar there stood a boy, with a blooming face and with down on his cheek, and at the other an old man in the close of life, with wild haggard look, a deeply furrowed countenance, and a head covered with hoary and dishevelled hair. In describing the frightful scene it is consoling to find that you share with me in the unqualified detestation which I have expressed; and, indeed, I am convinced that it is unnecessary to address to you any observation on the subject.

"But, my good friends, I must call your attention to another trial. I mean that of the Hogans, which affords a melancholy lesson. That trial was connected with the insane practice which exists among you, of avenging the accidental affronts offered to individuals, by enlisting whole clans in the quarrel, and waging an actual war, which is carried on by sanguinary battles. I am very far from saying that the deaths which occur in these barbarous feuds are to be compared with the guilt of preconcerted assassination, but that they are accompanied with deep criminality there can be no question: the system, too, which produces them, is as much marked with absurdity as it is deserving of condemnation. In this county, if a man chances to receive a blow, instead of going to a magistrate to swear informations, he lodges a complaint with his clan, which enters into a compact to avenge the insult—a reaction is produced, and an equally extensive confederacy is formed on the other side. All this results from an indisposition to resort to the law for protection; for among you it is a point of honor to avoid magistrates, and to reject all the legitimate means provided for your redress. The battle fought between the Hickeys and the Hogans, in which not less than five hundred men were engaged, presents in a strong light the consequences of this most strange and preposterous system. Some of the Hickey party were slain in the field, and four of the Hogans were tried for their murder:—they were found guilty of manslaughter—three of them are married and have families, and from their wives and children are condemned to separate forever. In my mind, these unhappy men have been doomed to a fate still more disastrous than those who have perished on the scaffold. In the calamity which has befallen Matthew Hogan every man in court felt a sympathy. With the exception of his having made himself a party in the cause of his clan, he had always conducted himself with propriety. His landlord felt for him not only an interest, but a strong regard, and exerted himself to the utmost in his behalf. He never took a part in deeds of nocturnal villany. He does not bear the dagger and the torch; honest, industrious, and of a mild and kindly nature, he enjoyed the good will of every man who was acquainted with him. His circumstances in the world were not only comparatively good, but when taken in reference to his condition in society, were almost opulent; and he rather resembled an English yeoman than an Irish peasant. His appearance at the bar was in a high degree moving and impressive—tall, athletic, and even noble in his stature, with a face finely formed, and wholly free from any ferocity of expression, he attracted every eye, and excited, even among his prosecutors, a feeling of commiseration. He formed a remarkable contrast with the ordinary class of culprits who are arraigned in our public tribunals. So far from having guilt and depravity stamped with want upon him, the prevailing character of his countenance was indication of gentleness and humanity. This man was convicted of manslaughter; and when he heard the sentence of transportation for life, all color fled from his cheek, his lips became dry and ashy, his hand shook, and his eyes were the more painful to look at from their being incapable of tears. Most of you consider transportation a light evil, and so it is, to those who have no ties to fasten them to their country. I can well imagine that a deportation from this island, which for most of its inhabitants is a miserable one, is to many a change greatly for the better. Although it is to a certain extent, painful to be torn from the place with which our first recollections are associated, and the Irish people have strong local attachments, and are fond of the place of their birth, and of their fathers' graves—yet the fine sky, the genial climate, and the deep and abundant soil of New Holland, afford many compensations. But there can be none for Matthew Hogan:—He is in the prime of life, was a prosperous farmer:—he has a young and amiable wife, who has borne him children; but, alas!

> "'Nor wife, nor children, more shall behold,
> Nor friends, nor sacred home."

He must leave his country forever—he must part from all that he loves, and from all by whom he is beloved, and his heart will burst in the separation. On Monday next he will see his family for the last time. What a victim do you behold, in that unfortunate man, of the spirit of turbulence which rages among you! Matthew Hogan will feel his misfortune with more deep intensity, because he is naturally a sensitive and susceptible man. He was proved to have saved the life of one of his antagonists in the very hottest fury of the combat, from motives of generous commiseration. One of his own kindred, in speaking to me of his fate, said, 'he would feel it the more because' (to use the poor man's vernacular pronunciation) 'he was so *tinder*.' This unhappy sensibility will produce a more painful laceration of the heart than others would experience, when he bids his infants and their mother farewell forever. The prison of this town will present on Monday next a very affecting spectacle. Before he ascends the vehicle which is to convey him for transportation to Cork, he will be allowed to take leave of his family. His wife will cling with a breaking heart to his bosom; and while her arms are folded round his neck, while she sobs in the agony of a virtuous anguish on his breast, his children, who used to climb his knees in playful emulation for his caresses, his little orphans, for they are doomed to orphanage in their father's lifetime——— I will not go on with this distressing picture: your own emotions (for there are many fathers and husbands here) will complete it. But the sufferings of poor Hogan will not end at the threshold of his prison:—He will be conveyed in a vessel, freighted with affliction, across the ocean, and will be set on the lonely and distant land, from which he will return no more. Others, who will have accompanied him, will soon forget their country, and devote themselves to those useful and active pursuits for which the colony affords a field, and which will render them happier, by making them better men. But the thoughts of home will still press upon the mind of Matthew Hogan, and adhere with a deadly tenacity to his heart. He will mope about, in the vacant heedlessness of deep and settled sorrow; he will have no incentive to exertion, for he will have bidden farewell to hope. The instruments of labor will hang idly in his hands; he will go through his task without a consciousness of what he is doing: or if he thinks at all while he turns up the earth, he will think of the little garden beside his native cottage, which it was more a delight than a toil to till. Thus his day will go by, and at its close his only consolation will be to stand on the seashore, and fixing his eyes in that direction in which he will have been taught that his country lies—if not in the language, he will at least exclaim in the sentiments which have been so simply and so pathetically expressed in the Song of Exile:—

"'Erin, my country! though sad and forsaken,
In dreams I revisit thy sea-beaten shore;
But alas! in a far foreign land I awaken,
And sigh for the friends that can meet me no more.'"

THE MURDER OF HELEN JEWETT.

SKETCH OF THE EVENTFUL LIFE AND CAREER OF THE MURDERED WOMAN.—HER INTRIGUES IN PORTLAND, BOSTON, NEW-YORK AND OTHER PLACES.—CAPTIVATING POWERS OF THE BEAUTIFUL CYPRIAN.—HER MEETING WITH RICHARD P. ROBINSON.—ACCOUNT OF THEIR MUTUAL CAREER.—THE MURDER.—TRIAL OF ROBINSON.—FULL REPORT OF THE EVIDENCE.—PUBLIC EXCITEMENT.—ACQUITTAL, &C.

Probably no case has ever been tried in this country which caused more excitement at the time than that of Richard P. Robinson, for the murder of the beautiful, yet erring, Helen Jewett. The circumstances surrounding this brutal assassination were of the most romantic character, while the parties mixed up in the affair represented many of the most wealthy and respectable families of the metropolis, some of whom are living at the present day.

The beautiful unfortunate whose life paid the forfeit of her erring existence, was widely known throughout the country. Her intrigues and elegant person were the theme of many a tongue. Her name was whispered among the fast and fashionable society of the country. In the ball-room, the promenade, the bar-rooms, and all the public resorts of Boston, Portland, New-York and other places where her star shone out for the time being, she was criticised and talked of by thousands.

The proper name of Helen Jewett was Dorcas Dyon. She was born in Augusta, in the State of Maine, in the month of June, 1813. Her parents were Welsh, having emigrated to the United States a short time prior to the birth of their daughter. They were humble people, the father being a mechanic, and the mother, in order to help the family along, tookin sewing. The first love of Helen Jewett (as we shall call her) was said to be a lad named Sumner, when the girl was only eleven years of age. Her parents becoming aware of the unholy intimacy, Sumner had to fly the country, and took to a sea-faring life. This first intrigue of Helen was, however, kept secret from all, with the exception of the two families of the boy and girl.

Among the playmates of Helen Jewett were the children of

Judge Weston, a wealthy resident of the neighborhood. In consequence of this connection Helen became acquainted with the Judge, who at once took a great liking to the vivacious and beautiful child, and adopted her into his family. She was sent to school and received a liberal education, becoming as accomplished as she was handsome. During the years which passed under the roof of Judge Weston, Helen's conduct was most exemplary. She was now sixteen, and a more beautiful girl could scarcely be conceived. Her form was graceful and voluptuous, her eyes flashing with ardent fire, while her movements bespoke the well-bred lady. Walking one evening through the groves which surrounded the palatial residence of Judge Weston, she was suddenly confronted by Sumner, who had returned from a voyage to China. From that moment her fate was sealed—she was lost irrevocably. Meetings frequently took place between the parties, until at last the details of her shame reached the astonished ear of her good patron. She was cast into the world unfriended and alone (her parents having previously died, and Sumner called off suddenly to rejoin his vessel).

Helen now turned her steps to Portland, with the intention of seeking employment. Here she was engaged by a Mrs. Brown, who told her that she desired to employ her for the purpose of sewing for the family. But instead of being engaged for this laudable employment, Helen was ushered into a brothel, and again fell. Here she became acquainted with a gentleman of means, who took her out of the brothel after but a few days' stay, and hired for her accommodation a magnificent residence. She reigned the Queen of this establishment for several months, when one day in looking over the papers she saw an account of the arrival of Sumner from sea. She wrote to him, asking him to call and see her that evening. He did so. Benson (the gentleman to whose generosity Helen owed her sumptuous living, and who actually had made arrangements to marry her), discovered the pair in each other's arms. A separation took place, and Helen next wended her way to Boston. A short time previous to her departure from Portland, however, Sumner, her first love, died of consumption, a disease contracted from the perilous duties of his profession. The girl felt this blow keenly, and to the day of her death remembered Sumner with thoughts of the deepest affection.

On arriving in Boston, she wandered through the streets until she fell fainting in the public thoroughfare, and was picked up by some negroes and brought to their shanty. It happened that those negroes were a band of thieves, and the poor girl was robbed of everything she possessed. A descent was made upon the house and the whole party brought up in the police court. Here a wealthy gentleman of the city being present in court, took compassion on Helen, and brought her to his residence, where she was nursed until her health was entirely restored. In Boston the fair one became entangled in numerous intrigues. Among others she engaged the affections of a wealthy broker, who had completed all arrangements for the nuptial ceremony, when an anonymous letter conveyed to the astonished gentleman the previous career of Helen.

The girl next steered her course for New York, and arrived in the Empire city in the middle of winter, 1832. Her career in New York was as chequered and extraordinary as in any other of the large cities, where she had reigned with so much lustre as the "Queen of the Pave." She entered several of the "most fashionable" houses of disrepute in the city, walked Broadway in the afternoons, shone resplendent nightly at the theatres, when "Helen Jewett" became the chief topic of conversation at the Club rooms of the fast young men, and throughout the city generally where such topics were received and canvassed.

It was while residing at one of those dens of infamy, that Helen Jewett became acquainted with Richard P. Robinson. This young man was born in Connecticut of a highly respectable family. He possessed a handsome exterior, pleasing manners and very passionate disposition. At the age of fourteen he came to New York in search of fame and fortune, when he was employed in a dry-goods store by a relative. Even at this early age he plunged into all the licentious excesses of a gay metropolis. Quarrelling with his first employer, he was taken into the establishment of Mr. Joseph Hoxie, No. 100 Maiden Lane, where he remained up to the date of his arrest for the horrible crime with which he was charged. At the houses of ill-repute and throughout metropolitan society generally, he was known by the name of "Frank Rivers."

The first time that Robinson and Helen Jewett met was while both were perambulating Broadway. The handsome youth and the dashing female exchanged glances and passed on. They next met at the Park Theatre and after this Robinson became a regular visitor at the residence of his fair innamorata. Helen loved with a fiery passion the handsome Robinson, while he, for a time, retuned the burning ardor of her attachment. But he soon tired of her company and sought that of other women. Maddening jealousy seized upon Helen, and she followed him to his haunts, upbraiding him for his desertion of her. A rumor had reached her that Robinson was paying his addresses to a relative of his employers with a view to matrimony. She wrote a letter, threatening to expose him and hinting at a knowledge which she had of some dangerous crimes committed by Robinson. Then it is stated, the resolution was formed to murder the poor girl.

Much has been said and written as to the guilt or innocence of Robinson, who was acquitted when brought up for trial. It is not for us, as compilers of this volume, to say whether or not Richard P. Robinson murdered in cold blood Helen Jewett. Public opinon was divided upon the question at the time. We will say, however, that the majority of those who lived at that date and who were most intimate with the details, asserted positively that Richard P. Robinson was the villain who took away the life of Helen Jewett.

On the night of the murder—the 10th of April, 1836—Helen

resided at the house of Mrs. Rosina Townsend, No. 41 Thomas St., We will detail the murder, as related by one of the chroniclers of that period, who laid the deed at the door of Robinson.

A biography of Helen Jewett and Richard P. Robinson, was written at the time, from which we extract the following account of the murder. We commence the extract from where Robinson arrived at the door of the house in Thomas Street.

"Twice he impatiently rang the bell, and at the second summons came the landlady to the door. The cautious Rosina, however, did not open the door, merely because there was a summons of impatience on the outside. That was not her mode of doing business, and she was the more careful of her rule on this occasion, as her furniture and conscience had recently suffered from the irruption of some riotous characters, whom one of her girls had incautiously let in. Moreover Helen had cautioned her not to let in Bill Easy, if he came, as she had discarded him altogether, and as she expected Robinson himself. Mrs. Townsend, therefore, under this combination of restrictive influences, inquired through the pannel who was there, and being answered that the visitor was for Helen, and recognizing the voice to be other than Bill Easy's, she let the comer in. It was then that she recognized the person in the cloak to be Richard P. Robinson, and telling him to wait a moment, went to the parlor door to inform Helen that her lover had come.

"Robinson answered not a word in reply to the landlady, but pulled his hat over his eyes to hide his face from the light, and drawing up his cloak for the same purpose, hurried through the entry to the stairs. As he passed the parlor door, he turned upon his heel for a moment, as if he would wait for Helen to come out. While he paused, and while Mrs. Townsend's head was in the front room, Emma French and Maria Stevens glided by him, and the latter whispered in his ears, 'Some one has been before you, Frank. Helen has just come down stairs.' Robinson did not raise his head, or give other token that he heard the words, and as the speaker glided off, he turned to go up stairs, by no means shaken, by his information, from his original intentions. At this moment, Helen issued from the parlor, and catching him by the cloak, exclaimed, loud enough for Mrs. Townsend to hear, 'Ah, my dear Frank, how glad I am you have come.' Robinson made no reply, and they both went up stairs together.

"The nature of the circumstances, and the terrible character of the tragedy which transpired within that room, will not allow us to pursue the same course in relation to it, which we have followed in regard to the less important portions of our narrative. A writer who knows that at a certain time two persons met together to buy and sell a horse (or to do any other special act), and that the horse was bought and sold, and for a certain price, may, without violation of any rule of propriety or credit, imagine for his readers, if such a course will relieve the heaviness of his narrative, what the buyer and seller probably said to each other, in the making of the bargain Nothing is disturbed by such a course; the great fact is preserved and the method, instead of condemning the matter as mere fiction, is only an enlargement of the ornament, not a whit more extravagent or out of place, than the use of those beautiful flowers which rhetoric flings upon the severest task for the writer's temporary compensation and repose. With matters, however, of superior importance, and of times when every pulsation of circumstances and point of detail may be the pivot of a great conclusion, this license must be dropped, and the historian must content himself with such rigid data, as the proven elements alone afford.

"It was between nine and ten o'clock on the night of the tenth of April, 1836, when Richard P. Robinson and Helen Jewett retired to their chamber at the house No. 41 Thomas street. For an hour, neither of them issued from the room (except Helen, who once ran down for a moment, to receive a pair of shoes), but at eleven Helen, all languid and in her dishabille, came to the head of the stairs and called for a bottle of champagne. She proposed to wait and take the salver of wine and glasses from Rosina at the head of the stairs, probably at Robinson's desire to prevent Mrs. Townsend from coming in the room; but it so happened, that the demand for wine had been very great at No. 41 Thomas street, and that Mrs. T. was obliged to descend into the cellar. This occasioned a loss of considerable time, during which Helen's patience gave out; so when Mrs. Townsend went upstairs with the salver. she found she was obliged to knock for admittance. Helen opened the door at her summons, and as the mistress of the house handed in the tray, she saw Robinson lying on the bed, with his head on his arm, and his face turned to the wall. The foot of the bed stood towards the door, and being without curtains, and of the low kind known as French bedstead, it exposed the whole surface of the couch to any person standing at the entrance of the room. Helen, perceiving that the presence and position of her lover had been observed, asked the landlady, in the way of courtesy, if she would not come in and join her in a glass; but alas for her, the landlady refused, and when the door closed upon her, this poor creature virtually bade good night to the rest of the world forever. With the departure of Mrs. Townsend, she looked her last upon a human face, save that of the demon on the bed, if this might so be called.

Gradually all the inmates of that house of sinful luxury retired, and with the rest, the beautiful Augustan, still as blooming to the eye as when she left her home, sought the soft repose of sleep. At one o'clock everything was hushed within that palace of passions. At two, or perhaps a little after, Maria Stevens, who laid directly opposite the room of Helen, and who was kept wakeful by disturbances which to her were not unusual, heard in the opposite chamb r the sound of a heavy blow, which, though it did not resound, seemed to shudder in the floor. It was followed by a long and heavy moan, so pitiful, that, enemy as she was to Helen, the event made disturbance at Maria's heart, and inspired her with a compassionate desire to know more. After whispering silence to her companion, she got up out of bed, and listened at the door; but nothing further followed, save two or three broken sobs, which her strange experience told her might proceed from a very ordinary cause. Presently, as she was about returning to her couch, she heard the door of Helen's chamber softly open and as softly close again, and in the next moment a person left it for the stairs. Turning the door-knob gently, she pulled it suddenly open, and saw a person going down. He was wrapped in a cloak, and bore in his hand a small glass-globe lamp, while something which he held within his mantle seemed to engage the other arm. He was going swiftly but stealthily down. Miss Stevens would have followed, and was about stepping forth to do so, when the person with whom she was resident that night, reached forth his hand and caught her clothes, and with an exclamation at her folly, told her to close her door and come to bed. Maria Stevens then returned, and hearing nothing further from the brunette's chamber, soon fell asleep.

"At three o'clock or thereabouts, there came a knock at the front door which roused Mrs. Townsend, and she was obliged to let a person in. Before retiring to bed again, however, she was a little surprised at perceiving a lamp burning in the parlor in the rear. Such a thing being unusual, she went to see about it, and there perceived upon a marble table, the glass lamp which belonged to Helen Jewett's room. At the same moment Mrs. Townsend discovered that the back door was open, and the bar which fastened it stood by its side. Supposing that some person was in the yard who would soon return within the house, she returned to her own chamber, and waited some ten minutes, when hearing no one come in, she went to the rear again, and having called "who's there" twice without avail, put up the bar and went upstairs to Helen's room. She found it on the latch, but as she pushed it open, a dense volume of offensive and stupifying smoke rushing out drove her back. Retiring over to Miss Stevens' room, the terrified landlady beat against her door, and roused the house. First came out Maria, and leading the way she plunged into the burning chamber. Twice were she and Mrs. Townsend driven back by the stifling torrents, but the vent at length threw up the smoke into flame, and there before their eyes, with her transparent forehead half divided with a butcher's stroke, and her silver skin burnt to a cinder where it was not laced with blood, lay all that was left of the mortal remains of the unfortunate Dorcas Doyen."

Robinson was arrested next day and lodged in jail. A coroner's inquest, held upon the body of deceased, laid the crime at the door of Richard P. Robinson, and he was formally held for trial.

The utmost excitement prevailed throughout the city, and the press took sides for and against the alleged murderer.

THE TRIAL.

On June 2nd, 1836, the trial was commenced in the Court of Oyer and Terminer, before Judge Edwards and Aldermen Benson, Banks, Ingraham and Randall.

Messrs. Ogden Hoffman, Price and Hugh Maxwell appeared for the prisoner, and District Attorney Phœnix for the prosecution.

The New York *Transcript* of that date, thus describes the scene at the opening of the trial.

The doors of the large court room were thrown open at precisely ten o'clock, and immediately thereafter the immense multitude which had collected in the avenues, passages and round the city hall, (despite the extremely wet and boisterous weather), rushed in and literally jammed every nook and corner. Notwithstanding the dense and closely packed mass of human beings that were congregated together, the arrangements for the free and uninterrupted ingress of the reporters, witnesses, members of the bar, &c., were excellently planned—to the great credit of the police magistrates, and the active and indefatigable exertions of high sheriff Hays.

Soon after the judges took their seats, the prisoner was brought into court by Mr. Lyons, the principal keeper of Bellevue prison, followed by his counsel—Messrs. Hoffman, Price and Maxwell—and a train of relatives and friends. He walked to the place assigned to him with a firm and steady step, occasionally glaring round at the forest of heads around him with a calm, composed and even cheerful look. The inner bar was thronged with members of the legal profession and gentlemen connected with the press—publishers, pamphleteers, editors and reporters: of the latter there were not less than twenty—several of them being from distant and adjacent cities and towns.

The Court having been opened in the usual form by Mr. Bedell, the crier, Mr. Maxwell arose in his seat and stated as counsel for the prisoner, that he was not aware that there was any circumstances which would prevent the trial being immediately proceeded with as far as the defence was concerned, and Mr. Phœnix (the district attorney), replied that he was ready to go on with the prosecution.

Previous to the panel of jurors being gone over (which was done by Henry Meigs, Esq., the clerk of the court, at the request of Mr. Hoffman), the names of the witnesses for the prosecution were called over at the instance of the District Attorney, and there being but one, a Mr. Masterson, absent, the judges ordered the prisoner to be placed at the bar for arraignment.

Mr. Meigs (the clerk), then said to the prisoner, "Richard P. Robinson, stand up and hold up your right hand." The prisoner rose as desired, and he listened to the arraignment with an unquivering lip and an unblanched cheek. His appearance generally was much better, and more free from embarrassment and anxiety than on the first occasion of his being brought to court, and submitted to the keen and searching gaze of perhaps three thousand strangers. He was dressed as on his first arraignment in a new suit of blue, and for a cause that will appear during the progress of the trial, he wore a wig—curly and of light hair. During the empannelling of the jury—which occupied a considerable time—he stood up erect, holding in his hands a blue cloth cap which he has been accustomed to wear—occasionally dangling it, as if heedlessly about.

After considerable delay a jury was found, when the clerk proceeded to read the indictment, charging the prisoner, Richard P. Robinson with wilful and deliberate murder of Helen Jewett, on the 10th of April, 1836. The indictment contained but one count, and during its reading the prisoner's countenance underwent no change—not a feature faltered—not a muscle was agitated.

At this stage the court took a recess for half an hour, the jury being placed in charge of eight police officers, who were sworn in the usual form for that purpose; the jury were compelled to remain in custody of these officers until the close of the trial.

At the expiration of the recess the court resumed its sitting, but for some time the proceedings were suspended in consequence of the bustle and confusion that took place among the crowd—now increased to an overwhelming mass—each strenuously striving to obtain a standing or sitting place.

As soon as order was restored, the District Attorney opened the case for the prosecution in a very impressive and elegant address, in the course of which he detailed to them all the facts that he intended subsequently to prove in evidence for the prosecution, and upon which he relied for the conviction of the prisoner at the bar. He dwelt briefly but emphatically upon the enormity of the offence with which the prisoner stood charged—characterising the circumstances as the most atrocious and diabolical that had ever been presented to a jury in this or any other country—not only in reference to the murder itself, but also in relation to the aggravated crime of arson which was connected with it. He said that although the evidence against the prisoner was almost exclusively circumstantial, yet it was of so strong, clear and conclusive a character as to render the situation of the unfortunate accused a most perilous and awful one.

At the conclusion of the learned gentleman's address, he called upon the stand as the first witness for the prosecution,

Rosina Townsend, who, after being sworn, deposed as follows:—I was acquainted with Helen Jewett. The last time that I saw Helen Jewett alive was on Saturday night, the 9th of April last. It was about eleven o'clock in the night, or it might be about a quarter past eleven. I then knew the prisoner at the bar. He was known to me by the name of "Frank Rivers" and by no other name. Helen Jewett was a resident and boarded in my house at the time. She had been a resident and boarder in my house precisely three weeks on the 8th of April last. I cannot exactly recollect the number of times that I had seen the prisoner at my house before the 9th of April; but as near as I can recollect I think I had seen him there six or seven times. I was at one time called upon by Helen Jewett to notice Frank Rivers (as he was called) particularly. I did at that time notice him particularly. This was on the second or third night after Helen Jewett came to live with me. I saw the prisoner at the bar on the night that Helen Jewett was murdered. A person knocked at my hall-door; I went to the door and asked who was there? This was about nine o'clock, or it might have been as late as half-past nine. When I asked who was there—the door was still locked—I asked a second time the same question. The person outside then either said is Helen Jewett or Miss Jewett (I cannot say which) within,—that he wanted to see her. Upon getting an answer to my second inquiry I then opened the door. The reason I did not open the door to the first answer as well as to the second was that I wished to ascertain who was the person making the inquiry if possible by his voice. The reason that I wished to ascertain this was that Miss Jewett had requested me in the course of the evening not to admit a certain young man who went by the name of Bill Easy to se her if he should happen to come there. There was a young man who went by the name of Bill Easy in the habit of visiting Hellen Jewett at my house. His particular nights for visiting her were on a Saturday night; he had previously visited her on each Saturday night since she had been at my house. The reason that Helen Jewett assigned to me for not wishing to see Bill Easy on that night was that she then expected Frank Rivers to visit her.

[At this stage of the proceedings a rush was made among the crowd and one of the officers brought up a young man for contempt of court. Judge Edwards explained to him the penalty to a breach of the peace and reprimanded him for his misconduct. On condition however of his promising not to offend again in like manner he was suffered to go his way unpunished.]

The examination of the witness was then resumed:—When I endeavored to ascertain who was the person at the door from his voice, I did not positively know that the person outside was Frank Rivers, but I positively knew that it was not Bill Easy's voice. I mean by Frank Rivers Mr. Robinson—the prisoner at the bar.

When I opened the door, I discovered that it was Frank Rivers or Mr. Robinson who was there. He wore a dark cloth cloak, but I cannot say exactly of what color it was. When I opened the door he stood close against the casement by the door post. There was a lamp light in the entry, and the light of this when I first observed him stand against the casement fell right upon his face. I am certain from this circumstance that the person I have reference to was no other than the prisoner at the bar. He entered the hall, and as soon as he entered he raised his cloak so as nearly to conceal his face. He did not say a word when he came into the entry, nor did I say anything to him. He went on before me towards the parlor door which stood at the end of the passage, and I followed close behind him. The parlor door stood upon a jar; I went and pushed it open and called for Helen. Helen was then sitting in the parlor nearly opposite the door. When I called Helen I told her that Frank had come. When I told her this he had turned the entry to go up stairs. There are two stairs in that house—which is a double house—one being on the left and the other on the right of the entry—both leading to the same platform or landing. Frank went up the right stairs, Helen Jewett's room was in the second story, back room at the west side of the house, the door of which is nearly opposite the landing of the right stairs. Immediately on Frank's going up stairs, Helen Jewett came out of the parlor and followed him up. When she came out of the parlor she took hold of Robinson's cloak, and said:—"my dear Frank, I am glad you have come." The stairs up which Robinson went, turned about half way up to the second story, and he had reached the first landing when she caught hold of his cloak. Helen remained up stairs a considerable time, and the next time that I saw her was about eleven o'clock, as near as I can recollect. In the interim she, I believe, came down stairs once to receive a boot which a shoe-maker brought home for her—it having been sent to him to repair. She came down into the hall but I did not see her. About eleven o'clock, Helen came to the head of the stairs, being then in her night dress, and asked me to get for her a bottle of champagne. She said that if I would hand it to her she would not trouble me to carry it up stairs. I went to the cupboard where I generally kept my wine, but I found that there was none there, and having to go into the cellar for some, I told Helen that as she was in her night gown she had better not wait—that I could take it up; I did shortly afterwards take it up together with two wine glasses—champagne glasses. When I took it up Helen opened the door of the bed-room, and asked me to walk in and take a glass of wine; I took the wine and glasses up stairs on a waiter. I declined to go into the room and did not go in, but the door was opened sufficiently wide for the admission of the tray or waiter, so that I could see who was in the room and nearly everything in it; I stood immediately before the door, and the door opened inside towards the wall; I could see who was on the bed in the room; it was a French bed stead, and there were no curtains round it. There was a person then lying upon the bed; that person was Robinson; I am perfectly sure of this. He was lying on the bed with his head upon his elbow inclining a little to the left. The bed was by the side of the wall, immediately opposite the door at which I stood and against which the door opened. The foot of the bed faced the door and was about five feet from the door, and from the place where I stood; I distinctly saw the side face of the person who was on the bed, and I cannot be mistaken that the person I noticed there with his head resting on his elbow was the prisoner at the bar. He had in his other hand a paper or a book which he was reading, I cannot tell which—something of the kind. There was a candle in the room which I think when I was up there, stood on one of the pillows or a little table which stood by the head of the bed,—I cannot tell which. After this I immediately went down stairs. That was the last that I saw of the prisoner at the bar on that night. At the time that I saw the prisoner lying upon the bed in the way I describe, I saw something about his head which peculiarly struck my attention. His hair was extremely thin on the back part of his head where it was parted; it was on the upper part of his head directly at the back; I never have had an opportunity to observe that fact since that time.

I have mentioned the circumstance once or twice since; I believe once to Mrs. Gallagher and once to Mr. Brink. I cannot recollect when it was that I mentioned this, but I think it was on the nineteenth of April, when my furniture was sold. When I told it to Mr. Brink, I asked him if Robinson's hair did not bear such an appearance as I have described. On the night that Helen Jewett was murdered I retired to bed about a quarter past twelve o'clock. I had a clock in my house which stood in my bed-room on the mantel-piece. I looked at the clock on that night before I retired. Twelve o'clock was my usual hour for shutting up the house. I had made that my rule, but on that night it was quarter past twelve. My bed-room was the front room on the first floor, on the right hand side of the hall as you enter the house. That is on the opposite of the entry directly fronting my bed room. After I got to bed and got asleep I was partially awoke by some person knocking at my door, but I did not awake sufficiently to know at what time this was. I don't know how long I had been asleep. The person who knocked at the door asked me to let him out, and I answered him in this way—"Get your woman." I remained in bed. After I so remained and had given the answer I have stated, I went to sleep. About three o'clock, I think, I was awoke again by some person knocking at the street door. I cannot tell how long it was between the knocking that I heard at the street door and the knocking at my door, as I went to sleep in the intervening time. I let the person in who came at three o'clock; I know that person; I had a light in my room by which I let that person in; after letting that person in, I discovered a light in my parlor; that was an unusual occurrence in my house at such a time of the night; the parlor that I speak of runs across in the entry the full width of the house in the rear; on discovering the light it induced me to go into the parlor, and on going there I found a lamp lying burning on the marble table; it was a small glass-globe lamp, with a square bottom; I had but two lamps of that description in the house: those two lamps were generally used one in the room of Maria Stevens, and the other in the room of Helen Jewett; Maria Stevens' room was immediately adjoining that of Helen Jewett; those lamps were not used in any other rooms; when I went into the parlor and discovered the lamp of which I have spoken, I found that the back door was open; the back door was ordinarily fastened with a bar, so that any person inside the house could open it without difficulty and without a key; when I discovered this I went into my room and staid there five or ten minutes—perhaps more—partly in a doze; at the end of this time I recollected that I had not heard any person come in, and I went a second time into the parlor, and opened the back door a little wider than it was, and called out "who's there?" I so called out twice, and receiving no answer, I put the bar up, and secured the door; I then went up stairs and came to Maria Stevens' door first. I tried it, and found it fast. I then went to Helen's door, tried it, and found it on the latch; I shoved it, opened it, and smoke rushed out in torrents. I then ran to Miss Caroline Stewart's room, which was directly opposite Helen Jewett's, knocked at the door, told her Helen's room was on fire, and begged her to get up. By knocking at Miss Stewart's door I alarmed the whole house; I cannot exactly say who came out of their room first, but it appeared to me that all the girls came on to the platform at one time. Miss Stevens and myself attempted to get into the room to get to Helen Jewett's bed, but at first we were not enabled to do so. Miss Stevens first reached the bed; the bed was on fire; we found the bed-clothes all consumed; they seemed to be all burnt without blazing. I don't know whether I then called the watch or whether somebody else called them; three watchmen came in first, and I think afterwards four others. One side of Helen Jewett's body was burnt;

when I first saw her she was lying nearly on her back, with her left side very much burnt, and a large gash on the side of her head; I don't recollect that either Miss Stevens or myself saw the body until the watchmen came. When Miss Stevens first got to the bed, she brought some of the ashes of the burnt clothes, and remarked that they must all be burnt up.

[The witness here asked for a glass of water, which was given to her, after which the same glass with some water was handed to one of the jurors, and he declined drinking from it, and asked the officer for another glass, which was given to him.]

Examination resumed:—When I saw Helen Jewett after giving the alarm she was quite dead; I don't know that during the time Helen Jewett lived at my house that she had a quarrel with any person living there, nor that there was any dispute or ill-feeling between her and any person that visited there or any person or persons.

Cross examined by Mr. Maxwell:— I am 39 years of age; I am a married woman; my husband is not, that I know of, dead; it is eleven years since I heard of him. I was married at Castleton, N Y. I was never in New York before my marriage: I came to New York in 1825; previous to that time my husband left me at Cincinnati, Ohio, and went away with another woman; I came after that to New York; I never, at any time, lived at the South; I never lived at Charleston or Savannah; my parents lived at Castleton when I was married; after my husband left I went to my father's house, and remained there three or four weeks, when I came to New York; I came to New York in September 1825, and went to live in Duane St.; then I took in sewing and continued to do so until December, when my head became so affected that my sight was injured, and I applied to Dr David L. Rogers, who operated upon me and inserted an issue in my arm; after I recovered I went to live as a chambermaid at the house of Mr Beekman in Greenwich Street. I remained there but a few weeks and then went to live at a house kept by a woman named Maria Piercy; this was a house of assignation: I remained there I think until April, 1826, and since then up to the present time, I have either been a boarder at or the keeper of a house of prostitution. Helen Jewett once lived with me before she came to me at the house No. 41 Thomas St. in March last; I think it was in 1833; I don't remember that I had a quarrel with her at that time or with any other person in relation to her. I think it there ever had been any difficulty or quarrel between us I should now recollect it. I know a person who is called English Charley. I never had a quarrel with him in reference to his visiting Helen Jewett at my house. I never had any suspicions of his visiting her. The six or seven times that I have spoken of as having seen Robinson at my house during the three weeks that Helen Jewett was there occurred the last time that she lived at my house prior to the 9th of April; he generally came in the night time, but once he came on a Saturday afternoon; he was there on the Thursday night before the Saturday when Helen was murdered. He was once in my room in company with Helen Jewett and three Southern gentlemen. Robinson was known generally as Frank Rivers at my house, and was so known by many persons who came there. *There were two visitors at my house who called themselves Frank Rivers,* the prisoner at the bar being one of them.

[On the witness stating this, there was very great confusion in the Court, hissing and clapping of hands, evidently from the friends and partizans of the unfortunate prisoner. The court directed the officers to bring all persons to the bar who acted so indecorously, and this order produced immediate silence.]

Examination resumed—On the occasion when I was called by Helen Jewett to take particular notice of Frank Rivers (Robinson) she wished me to look at him and say whether he or Bill Easy was the handsomest. I am not positive that the person who spoke to me from outside the door on the night of the ninth of April, on my first answering the knock, was Robinson, nor was I very positive that it was his voice when I received the second answer—but I knew that it was not Bill Easy's voice. Bill Easy is a little taller in person than Robinson. I do not recollect that I have given any different statement. I don't know whether or not I mentioned Bill Easy's name in my examination at the police office. When I first saw Robinson he was standing by the casement at the door. The lamp was near the stairway, in the entry, and my back was towards it. I do not think that because I was between Robinson and the lamp it would prevent me seeing Robinson's face, or prevent the light shining upon it when he came in. I know that it could not so prevent my seeing him, and that it did not, as the lamp (a globe lamp) hung very high from the ceiling, and when I opened the door I stepped a little aside. The lamp was more than six feet in the entry-way from the door; Robinson, or Frank Rivers, as I then knew him, was in the habit of lifting his cloak up to his face, as if to conceal it, when he came to my house. I don't know what his object was, and I never thought anything particularly about it; his doing so, therefore, on the ninth of April, did not excite my suspicion of anything. On that night (the night of the murder) when he came in in the manner I have described, a girl named Emma French, who lived at my house, was standing at the room door in the passage-way. She, I have no doubt, saw him as plainly and as well as I did. When she took hold of his cloak and said to him "My dear Frank, I am glad to see you," I was in the entry near my room. Shortly after I admitted Mr. Rivers (Robinson) and he had gone up stairs, I retired to my sleeping room. That was about nine or half-past nine o'clock. I was in and out of the room several times before Helen Jewett called for a bottle of champagne. It was about eleven o'clock when the champagne was called for. In the interim I had been busy in admitting persons in and letting persons out of my house. I admitted all the persons that came into the house after Mr. Robinson came in. No person was admitted on that night after eight o'clock that I did not admit myself; before eight o'clock other persons attended the door, and some persons might have been in the house that I knew nothing of, and whom I had never seen before. I had not drank any wine or liquor that night, nor was there any drank in my room. All the liquor or wine that was had in my house that night beside the champagne that Helen had, was a bottle of champagne in the parlor, which I did not partake of. On the night of the murder I had a person in the room with me. I know him. He came about eleven o'clock, and I let him in. He was in my room when Helen Jewett called for the champagne. He was not in bed then, nor was I, nor had I then been. He remained in that room the whole night. There was but one bed in the room. He was in the same bed with me, and he was awakened at the same time with me by the knocking at the door at three o'clock in the morning. I don't know that he asked who the person was that knocked at the door. I don't think he did. I know who the person was that came in at that hour. Robinson wore a cloth cap on the night of the murder. When I saw Robinson in Helen Jewett's room, he was laid on his stomach, with the bed-clothes nearly up to the shoulders. I cannot say what it was that he was reading. I cannot say whether the candle was on the pillow or on the round table near the head of the bed. He was laid on the front side of the bed. I did not see his full face—only his side face. I do not think that he changed his position in the bed while I remained at the door. The singular appearance that I remarked on the back of Robinson's head was, it was nearly or entirely bald, and I noticed it because I thought I would mention it to Helen on the following morning. I did not mention it to any person on the following morning, nor, that I know of, at the police office. I did not do this because I was so much agitated by the murder that I forgot many things that did not occur to me till afterwards. There were six men in my house on the night that the murder took place. I admitted the whole of them after eight o'clock in the evening. I did not personally know them all; I knew some of them. I had ten girls in my house on that night. When the alarm was given, the gentlemen who were in the house made their escape from the front door, in which I had left the key when I let in the second party of watchmen who came. I think that Mr. Palmer was the first watchman who arrived at the house. I do not know that any other watchmen came there before him. It was my wish that no person should leave the house until an examination into the occurrence of the murder. I was so much agitated that I can scarcely say what took place on the horrible discovery of the murder being made. I don't remember that when the watchmen first came into the house there were two men in their shirt-sleeves standing near my door. I don't know, and never heard, that the watchmen, on going up stairs, found a man partially dressed, near the door of Helen Jewett's room. All the men in the house made their escape from thence before the coroner came there to hold an inquest. In the course of a week it is probable that from eighty to one hundred persons visited the different girls at my house. The majority of the visitors at my place are entire strangers to me. On some weeks I would have considerably more visitors than others. From my peculiar situation of life I have of course been frequently subjected to rude and brutal treatment from ruffians and others.

[Mr. Maxwell here stated, that for the present he should suspend a further cross-examination of the witness, until a future period: and begged she would remain in the vicinity of the court to be ready to come in when called upon. Previous, however, to the witness leaving the stand, she was examined by one of the jurors as follows.]

Juror—Did you see the prisoner at the coroner's inquest, or at the police office, and if you did, had he his hat on when you saw him?

Witness.—I saw him when he was brought to my house, No. 41 Thomas street, by the officers, but he then had his hat on. I don't remember whether he had his hat on or off at the police office.

Mr. Hoffman—Now don't you remember, madam, that when you were before the grand jury, you sat near Robinson, who then had his hat off, and that you had then an opportunity of seeing the remarkable place, as you call it upon his head?

Witness—Now I recollect, I think that I did.

Mr. Hoffman—I thought so, madam.

Mr. Hoffman—Did you ever think before that time of mentioning anything in reference to the remarkable discovery of yours?

Witness—Yes: I think that several days previous to that, I mentioned it to Mr. Brink.

Mr. Hoffman—Have you not, madam, seen an account of Robinson wearing a wig in one of the papers, and did not this fact lead to make the statements to Mr. Brink and Mrs Gallagher, that you say you have done?

Witness—I saw something in the *Transcript* or *Sun*—I forget which, but that did not lead me to mention the fact I have related; I had mentioned it before.

[The witness after giving this testimony left the stand, and she was led out of Court by Mr. police officer Welch. It was nearly half past eight o'clock when her testimony was closed.]

Dr. David L. Rodgers was then called for the prosecution, and examined by Mr. Phenix. He merely deposed to the examination of the body of Helen Jewett after the murder, and pronounced the wounds on her head to be the cause of death. He said the principal wound fractured the skull, compressing the bones upon the brain, and that the body bore every appearance of its having made no movement after the fatal blow, and that death consequently must have been instantaneous.

[The hatchet found in the rear of Mrs. Townsend's was here

shown the witness, and he said it was such a weapon as he had supposed had been used by the murderer, and that he doubted not that that it had been the instrument of death.]

Richard Eldridge, examined by Mr. Phenix—I am a watchman. On Sunday morning the 10th of April, about four o'clock I was in Thomas street, and went into the house of Mrs. Townsend: I had some conversation with Mrs. Townsend in relation to what had taken place there, and in consequence of what she said to me, I went to search in the yard and about the premises to see if I could find anything there; she said to me that when it was daylight, perhaps I might find something in the yard which would lead to some discovery. In a yard next to Mrs. Townsend's, belonging to a lot on Hudson street, I found a hatchet and a cloak (the hatchet was produced, and it was the same that Doctor Rodgers testified to as having been likely to produce such wounds and gashes as were discovered on the head of the deceased). The witness continued:—The cloak was found in the yard adjoining Mrs. Townsend's house, about two or three yards from the railing in the rear of the lots in Hudson and Duane streets.

Cross-examined by Mr. Maxwell—I had some talk with Mrs. Townsend before I went into the yard. I also had some talk with Mr. Palmer, a watchman, I think it was one of the watchmen who first made a proposition to go out into the yard. When I got into the yard I took my own course in searching. Mrs. Townsend did not tell me where to go: I went towards the south-west corner of the yard, and there I perceived, about six inches at the other side of the railing, the hatchet which has been produced. The fence between Mrs. Townsend's yard and the yard belonging to the house in Hudson street is about nine feet high, and in some places twelve feet. The cloak was about fifteen feet from the fence of Mrs. Townsend's yard in the yard belonging to the lot in Hudson street, and about half way across the yard between the rear of a lot in Duane street, and the rear of Mrs. Townsend's premises. The cloak could not have been dropped in the place where it was found by a person climbing over the fence, nor do I think a person could have thrown it so far from Mrs. Townsend's yard. There is no place for a person to get away that I know of from the garden in the rear of the Duane street lot: when I first discovered the cloak I did not see that it had any string attached to it. I gave the cloak to some one belonging to Mrs. Townsend's house, and saw it about two hours afterwards before the coroner's inquest. It was then that my attention was drawn to a stain in the cloak. When I found the axe, I did not observe that there was any blood upon it. The axe and cloak were both deposited in a back room on the first floor of the house immediately under the room in which the body was lying. When I put them into this room I locked the door and, I think, I fastened the shutter so that nobody could get to them. It was a small door that I locked. The key was a common one; I don't know that there were two doors to that room; I cannot see myself, how any person could have got away from the rear of Mrs. Townsend's by way of Hudson street or Duane street, without getting through the halls of the houses built upon the lots.

By Mr. Phenix—There were a number of alleys both on Duane and Thomas streets, by which a person probably might by climbing over a number of fences escape from the rear of Mrs. Townsend's house. Mrs. Townsend was I believe the only one who saw me lock up the cloak and hatchet in the room down stairs; I remained in the house until the coroner held an inquest, after I had deposited these articles in the room, but not in such a situation that I could not see whether any person went in there with another key. I cannot say in what particular way I deposited these articles.

By Mr. Morris, for the prosecution:—I had the hatchet in my hand a second time at the coroner's inquest; it was handed to me by the coroner or some one connected with him; he asked me to examine it and say if it was the one I had found in the yard; to the best of my knowledge, I think I told him it was. When he asked me if I thought a spot he pointed out on it was blood, I think I said I thought it was rust; I did not, until they were pointed out to me at the coroner's inquest, observe either the string on the hatchet or the string upon the cloak. Whilst I and Mr. Palmer were looking about the yard, some of the girls in the house came out to us. When I first took up the axe or hatchet it was wet and covered with dew or moisture, as if it had lain there some time. In addition to the wet on the hatchet, there was some earth on the blade, and some on the handle.

By a Juror—I did not see the hatchet until I got within about six inches of it, and after a good deal of walking about.

Some of the girls were looking out in the yard at the time I found it.

By Mr. Morris—I think it was improbable, though not entirely impossible, that the hatchet mght have been thrown to the place where I found it by some of the girls who were standing about the yard. I should be inclined to think, however, that such a thing could have been done. If it had, I think we might have been hurt.

[It being now near ten o'clock, Judge Edwards suggested to his associate judges that the court be adjourned until ten o'clock next morning, and it was adjourned accordingly until that hour, the jury remaining in custody of the officers who were sworn to attend them.]

SECOND DAY.

Scarcely ever in the annals of criminal prosecutions, in any country on the globe, has there been witnessed such a scene of tumult and confusion as took place at the opening of the court the next morning, on the trial being resumed. As early as seven o'clock in the morning, regardless of the wet and stormy weather, vast crowds of persons began to assemble in the vicinity of the City Hall, and at a little past eight o'clock, when the high constable arrived with his posse of officers, not less than from five to six thousand persons were packed together in one impenetrable and solid mass. At the hour appointed for the opening of the court, so alarming was the confusion and excitement among the immense assemblage, that before the judges ventured to take their seats, they sent a requisition to the sheriff, ordering him to require the attendance of his deputies, together with thirty additional constables and officers. Until the arrival of this force, it was impossible to obtain anything like order or tranquility, and even then the disorder which prevailed was truly frightful and appalling. At length the uproar became so violent, and of so aggravated a character, that it was at one time apprehended that it would be necessary to summon the aid of the military, and the mayor was sent for and advised with as to the best mode of action. During the period occupied by these proceedings, no attempt was made to proceed with the trial of the prisoner, and all business was suspended. After a brief consultation between the mayor, the police magistrates and the judges of the court, it was determined to clear the court-room of every person except those who were within the bar, consisting exclusively of gentlemen connected with the pre s, the counsel engaged in the trial, and members of the legal profession. With great difficulty,—and only with the most strenuous exertions on the part of the police officers, marshals, constables and sheriff's deputies—the object was ultimately accomplished. By this time it was past twelve o clock, when the jury entered their box, and the judges took their seats. Robinson took his position in the same place that he sat in on Thursday, close to the jury box, and immediately behind him as on the previous day, were his late employer, Mr. Joseph Hoxie, the prisoner's venerable and respectable father from Durham, Conn., and also his brother-in-law, the husband of his eldest sister.

Previous to the trial being resumed, the Court gave direction to the several officers in attendance to readmit as many of the persons outside as could conveniently take seats ; and in an instant almost a thousand persons were in the court-room, the doors immediately being closed upon them to prevent a crowd or riot.

The case for the prosecution was then resumed by Mr Phenix calling upon the stand—

William Schureman, who, being sworn, was examined by Mr. Phenix, and deposed as follows—I am the coroner for the City and County of New York. On the tenth of April last I was called to the house No. 41 Thomas street—to the house of Mrs. Townsend—to hold an inquest upon the body of a female who had been murdered. It was very soon after daylight when I was called to the house. I was at the house when a cloak was found in one of the yards in the rear. That cloak was handed to me in the yard of the house in Thomas street by a watchman who found it on the other side of the fence, in a yard in the rear of Hudson Street. I saw him coming over the fence with it. I was nearly in the rear of the yard when I received it from the watchman. [The cloak was here produced, and the witness positively identified it as being the same cloak which was found by the watchman.] Witness continued—The string now attached to the cloak was attached to it when it was found, and from certain circumstances and conversation which then took place between me and some of the persons in the house, I was induced to notice it particularly. I saw the string attached to the cloak before it was taken into Mrs. Townsend's house, and shortly after I received it from the watchman. After I perceived the string I gave the cloak into the hands of either one of the police officers or one of the watchmen—I cannot positively say which. I don't know what the person did with the cloak after I handed it to him. I went on to empannel the jury. There was a hatchet also found in the rear of the house. [The hatchet was here produced, and the witness identified it as being the same one as found.] I think the hatchet was found shortly after the cloak, but I am not certain of this. When the hatchet was handed to me, I looked at it, but did not discover anything at that time very particular upon it. It was wet as if with dew; at that time I did not perceive a string upon the hatchet—I mean when it was handed to me in the yard. I did not observe the string upon the hatchet until it was brought to me a second time before the jury I think it was handed to me by Mr Brink and he called my attention to it; then myself, in company with some of the jurors, compared the string upon the cloak and the string upon the hatchet, and they were similar in all respects the string appeared to be new, and to have been recently cut off.

By the Judge—It was about daylight when the cloak and hatchet were first handed to me, and it was two or three hours afterwards—between nine and half past nine—when I again saw them, they were then shown before the jury who were on the inquest. I won't be certain, but I think Mr. Brink brought the hatchet and cloak before the jury—it was one of the officers, at all events.

Cross-examined by Mr. Maxwell—I do not know Mr. Eldridge the watchman, that I know of. I remember that there was one person at the house by that name. When I first arrived at Mrs. Townsend's house there were several officers and watchmen there, but I cannot say how many. If Mr. Eldridge is the man who took the axe up, he must be mistaken if he says he had it in his possession half an hour before he handed it to any one. I do not think that the person who found it had it in his hand more than a minute before he gave it to me. I did not notice any blood on the hatchet, but it had a reddish appearance the same that it has now. I gave particular direction, when I handed the hatchet and cloak to a person to keep until I empannelled a jury, to be sure to keep them safe. I gave this injunction more particularly in relation to the string that was upon the cloak, as I understood from some of the persons in the house that a person had been there who wore a cloak. I did not then notice or know anything about the string upon the hatchet, and my directions therefore had not such particular reference to it. With the exception of the string being more dirty now than it was at the inquest, it has every appearance now that it had then. I cannot say whether it is any longer or shorter now than it was then. Neither the cloak nor the hatchet were found, to the best of my belief, until after I got to the house. I don't recollect that I made a proposition to go and make a search in the yard. I think Mr. Palmer first made the proposition,—and that he first went into the yard—but I am not certain. I do not recollect that I had any conversation Mrs. Townsend on the subject of making a search in the yard.

By a Juror—When I first saw the string I cannot say whether there was any appearance of its being damp. It did not appear to be dirty or muddy. The morning was a dull morning. It was after daylight when the hatchet was found, and when it was handed to me. It strikes me that if the string had been upon the hatchet when it was first found, it would have attracted my attention, and I should have observed it. The string, however, might possibly have been there, and I might not have seen it.

By the Judge—The string might have possibly been on the hatchet. My attention was drawn to the string on the cloak before I saw the hatchet, and it is now, on reflection, my impression that if the string had been on the hatchet when it was found I should have noticed it in connection with the circumstance.

By Mr. Morris—My attention was called to the tassel of the cloak, particularly before the cloak was examined, and in looking for the tassel I found the string; I was induced to look for the tassel from some conversation that I had with some person in the house, respecting the tassel of a cloak.

By the Judge—When I first saw the string of the cloak it appeared to me to have been severed with a jerk or broken off, not cut. My impression at the time was, that it was not cut.

By Mr. Hoffman—When the cloak was found in the yard, I wrapped it up and my attention was then first attracted to the tassel.

By Mr Price—It was my intention to have the hatchet and cloak deposited in some safe place; from the circumstance of the hatchet having been found in the yard, it was my impression that the horrible murder was committed with it; I ordered them to be kept together, thinking that they might be jointly identified; the string notwithstanding this, might have then been on the hatchet and I not notice it; *it is possible* that some of the persons to whom I gave the cloak, having the string then attached to it, might have tried the hatchet to the string, and subsequently broken it off.

By Judge Edwards—On examining the string upon the cloak now, it appears to me shorter than it was when I first noticed it; I may however, be mistaken; I am now under the impression that the string was longer than it is now; I had no impression when I saw the string at the inquest, that it had been altered, that it was either shorter or longer than it was when I first saw it in the yard; I am now more certain that the string is shorter than when I first saw it; I did not measure the string, nor was it measured at any time that I know of; I don't think that the string was as much longer on the cloak as it would be with the addition of the piece on the hatchet; I think if it had been as much larger I should have observed it, but I am not positive.

By Mr. Morris, for the prosecution—When I first saw the string on the cloak, I did not notice it so very minutely as to know its dimensions atall, and until I saw the string on the hatchet before the coroner's jury, I did not attach much importance to it. When I speak of my impression about the string being shorter now than it was before, I have reference both to when I first saw it in the yard, and to when it was brought before the coroner's inquest.

George W. Noble, examined for the prosecution by Mr. Morris—I am an assistant captain of the watch. I remember that on the morning of the tenth of April information was brought to me at the watchhouse in the park that a murder had been committed in Thomas street. I immediately started off there, having with me three or four watchmen. I think Eldridge was in the company We arrived at Mrs. Townsend's house before daylight, and before the hatchet and cloak were found. We were in the house nearly an hour and a-half before these articles were found. When they were found I was in the room where Helen Jewett was laid. I heard a noise in the yard, and saw a man jump over the fence, and say "Here's the cloak now." I immediately went down stairs, and a number of my men were there. They said to me, "We've found a cloak." When I got into the yard both the cloak and hatchet were found. I saw the hatchet and examined it myself. I examined it before it was taken into the house with the cloak. I saw the string upon the cloak before it was taken into the house.

[The cloak was here produced, and the witness identified it as the same that he then saw. He also identified the hatchet which was shown to him.]

By a juror—I had both the hatchet and cloak in my hand.

By Mr. Morris—I saw the string on the hatchet as it is now upon it, in the yard, before it was taken into the house, and directly after it was found. I did not compare the string upon the hatchet and the string upon the cloak, but Mr. Brink, the officer, did in my presence. He examined and compared them, and he concluded as I did that they were both alike. The hatchet and cloak were given in charge to one of my men, and they were taken into one of the back rooms of the house, and laid in a recess in the northwest corner of the room. I did not observe the hatchet in the room, but I believe it was wrapped up in the cloak. I cannot say whether the door of the room was locked. There were watchmen about the place all the time. I was at the house until past twelve o'clock, and until the coroner held an inquest upon the body of the murdered female. I did not stop in the house all the time. I went with Mr. Brink to Maiden Lane and Pearl street in a carriage. We went to those places to try to find out who was the perpetrator of the deed. I was with Mr. Brink at the time the arrest of the accused (Mr. Robinson) was made. We found him in Dey street, between Broadway and Greenwich street. This was about seven o'clock on Sunday morning.

Cross-examined by Mr. Maxwell—When I got to the house in Thomas street the coroner was not there. I was there full three quarters of an hour as I suppose, before he came there; we had not discovered the cloak or hatchet before the coroner came. I was in the yard when the coroner received the cloak and hatchet; they were not both received by the coroner at the same time, but not more than a moment intervener. The coroner was in the yard all the time that we were in the yard (myself and Brink); the coroner had the cloak and hatchet about five minutes before he handed them to be put away; I don't know whether the coroner was standing close by Brink and me when Brink made the comparison between the string on the cloak and the string on the hatchet; when he did make the comparison, I considered it to be an important fact; Brink considered it to be an important fact. I did not communicate it to the coroner, nor did Brink that I know of. I heard the men say "there's the cloak, we've found the cloak," or "there's a cloak, we've found a cloak." I am not certain which. When I was in Helen Jewett's room there were several persons round there; none of the girls said anything to us about going to search the yard; there were several of them in the house; it is possible that some persons might have gone into the room where the cloak and hatchet were while Brink and I went out in the carriage to Maiden Lane; it is possible that some person might have entered during that time, and got possession for a time of the cloak and hatchet; Brink and I found no difficulty in ascertaining where Robinson was; we found him at his boarding-house. When we inquired for him we were shown up to his bedroom, and we entered it. Brink told him that he wanted him to get up and dress himself, and go to the police-office. He did so without making any objection, merely inquiring what we wanted him for; he accompanied us in the carriage to the house in Thomas street.

By Mr. Morris:—We did not observe anything particular in Robinson's clothes when he was dressing himself. We did observe something particular however, when we got him to the house in Thomas street. It was on the right side of the right leg below the knee, and on the left side near the hip. I took it to be lime, but that it was lime I cannot positively say, as I did not taste or smell it. When we went up to Robinson's bedroom, there was a young man with him. It was that gentleman who got up and opened the door. Robinson was then asleep, and he (his bedroom companion), shook him to awake him. They slept in the same bed together, Robinson in the front and his companion at the back.

By the Judge—I did not observe whether Robinson's eyes

were closed or not. He jumped up very quick after we got in. The girl who showed us up stairs knocked at the door. I cannot say how loud she knocked at the door. When he jumped out of bed, we merely told him that we wanted to see him, and he instantly dressed himself. It was in the entry that he asked us what we wanted with him, and that Brink told him that he wanted him at the police office.

By Mr. Morris—After the young man opened the door, Brink and I went directly into the room. The young man got over Robinson when he jumped into bed again. After we got into the room I could not swear whether Robinson was awake or asleep. The young man touched him and shook him and he immediately got up. The young man dressed himself shortly after Robinson did, and accompanied us to Thomas street in the carriage. As Robinson was going out of the room with us, the young man said to him, "Do you want me to go with you?" and Robinson replied:—"You may go if you've a mind to." He was then in bed, and he jumped up, dressed himself and accompanied us. When Mr. Brink and I brought Robinson out of his room, something was said to him in the entry about a cloak. We were in the hall nearer the front door than the room door, when the cloak was mentioned. Only Brink, Robinson and myself were then present. Mr. Brink asked him if he ever wore a blue cloth cloak, or if he was the owner of a blue cloth cloak—I forget which, but I think it was if he ever wore a blue cloth cloak. He said no; but he said he had an old camblet cloak that hung up in the bedroom. Brink and he talked about cloaks three or four times over:—they were talking about cloaks 3 or 4 minutes. The fence round Mrs. Townsend's yard in the rear was of board and rather high than otherwise. The rear fence is nine or ten feet high, and the fence at the south west corner is full as high. The fence all round the yard is whitewashed. There is a stable adjoining the fence on the west side, and pickets are put up on the fence on that side. A person in getting over that fence into the yard would I think necessarily whiten his trowsers; but it would of course depend upon the manner he got over.

By Mr. Maxwell, for the prisoner—While the conversation took place between Brink and Robinson in the entry, the young man who slept in the same room with him, was dressing himhimself. The bed room door was only partially open, and I don t know whether or not, the young man could hear what was said with Robinson about the cloak. The conversation was not in a low tone. I distinctly remember now, that Robinson positively denied that he was ever the owner of a blue cloth cloak. I cannot be mistaken in this.

Denis Brink, police officer, examined by Mr. Phenix for the prosecution—I was at the house of Mrs. Townsend, in Thomas street, on the morning of the tenth of April. I am one of the police officers of this city. I went to Mrs. Townsend's house about half past four on the morning of the tenth of April. It was before daylight. I was there when the cloak and hatchet were found. My first information and knowledge of the finding of the cloak and hatchet was after daylight. The coroner was in the yard when they were found. Mr. Eldridge, the watchman, handed the cloak and hatchet to the coroner. I had both the cloak and hatchet in my hand before they were taken into the house. [The cloak and hatchet were here shown to and identified by the witness.] I know the cloak from the tassel particularly. The string that now appears upon this cloak was in the yard before it was taken into the house. It was fastened to the end of the cloak. I had the hatchet in my hand before it went into the house. I saw a string upon the handle of the hatchet. I compared the string on the handle of the hatchet with the string that was fastened to the cord of the cloak. It appeared as though it had been cut apart with a scissors or knife. I am not positive in whose possession they were given after they were taken out of the yard, but I think it was to one of the watchmen. It was between daylight and sunrise when the hatchet and cloak were found. I saw the string on both the cloak and hatchet not more than two minutes after they were found. After they were given into the possession of the watchman I did not again see them until they were brought before the coroner's inquest, perhaps two or three hours after. There was not a particle of difference between the strings on the hatchet and cloak when I first saw them in the yard, and when I saw them at the coroner's inquest. I went with Mr. Noble, the assistant captain of the watch, to arrest the prisoner.

[Mr. Phenix here asked the witness how he came to suspect Robinson, but the question was objected to by Mr. Maxwell, and it was withdrawn.]

Examination continued—Mr. Noble and I went to the house No. 42 Dey street. I rang the bell. The servant came to the door, and I asked her if Mr. Robinson was within. She said yes, and led me up to his bed-room. I think she knocked at the door. It was on a jar when we reached it, and when she knocked I called out "Is Mr. Robinson within?" and he (Robinson) immediately answered and said, "Yes, that's my name." I then said to him, "I want to speak to you, I wish you would get up." He then got up and put on his pantaloons. I did not then discover anything particular in relation to his dress. I discovered something white, but I did not think anything of it at that time. That afterwards turned out to be lime. I asked him as soon as he got dressed to walk out with me into the hall—that I wanted to speak to him. He went with me into the hall, and I then asked him if he had a blue cloth cloak, or a cloak of any kind. I asked him afterwards if he had a blue cloth cloak, or if he had worn one. His answer was no, that he had never had a cloth cloak. He then remarked that he had an old camlet cloak, which was then hanging in his bed-room, at the same time pointing to it and saying "There it is." When he pointed to his cloak we were standing in the hall near his room door. I then told him that I wanted him to go with me to the Hall or to the police office — I am not certain which. Before we started off together, he asked my consent to let his room-mate go with him, which I gave; and his room-mate did go with us, getting dressed and ready in a very few minutes. We came up Broadway to Duane, and from Duane into Chapel on our way to Thomas street. After we got into the house in Thomas street I saw the whitewash again on Robinson's pantaloons. It did not occur to me until I saw the whitewash on the fence to take particular notice of it. The whitewash was partly in front and partly on the side of the right leg of the pantaloons. I did not at any time examine the pantaloons particularly. When I first went into Mrs. Townsend's yard in the morning, I observed a little saw bench standing close to the southeast corner of the fence, which struck me that a person might have used for getting over the fence. A person by using that might have got over the fence with less difficulty than without its assistance.

[It being now after three o'clock, the Court took a recess for half an hour.]

Shortly after the appointed time for reassembling after the recess, the judges and jury came into Court, and took their respective seats.

The examination of Mr. Brink was resumed for the prosecution, examined by Mr. Phenix—I obtained some articles from the room of Mr. Robinson. In the first place, I obtained a miniature; after which I brought away his trunks and bureau, containing a great number of articles. I examined the trunk and bureau previous to taking them to the police office. I examined the trunks and bureau for the purpose of finding some letters, but did not find any. I found the miniature in the bureau at his lodgings, on Sunday afternoon, after his arrest.

[The miniature was here exhibited to the witness, and he identified it as the one he had found at the prisoner's lodgings.]

Examination continued—Upon finding the miniature, I took possession of it, took it to the police office, and gave it to Mr. Justice Lowndes. I believe it was a likeness of Mr. Robinson. I did not at the same time bring away any other article. I merely locked the trunks and bureau and brought away the keys, which I gave to Mr. Lowndes. The trunks and bureau were afterwards brought to the police office. I was not present when they were unlocked and opened there. I did not, after that, visit Helen Jewett's room, and take some things away from there. I was present in Helen Jewett's room when Mr. Tompkins, or some other officer, came there, and took away some books, and some other articles which I don't recollect. They took them, I believe, to the police office.

Cross-examined by Mr. Maxwell—I have been an officer nine or ten years. I have known Rosina Townsend three years. I am not particularly familiar there. I was not particularly acquainted with the locality of the premises previous to the murder of Helen Jewett. I have never, prior to that time, been in the upper part of the house. I knew Helen Jewett. Have seen her at Mrs. Townsend's. Never visited her there especially. Never visited Helen Jewett elsewhere. Have been several times in Mrs. Townsend's house. Have gone there officially. Have had processes against persons in the house—sometimes against servants, and sometimes against the girls in the house. I never particularly knew whether Mrs. Townsend was a woman of wealth. I have been at Mrs.

Townsend's house when I have not had any processes. Sometimes she would send for me when she had been threatened by rioters there. Never saw rioters at the house, nor did I ev see a riot there. I was there about two months before the murder of Helen Jewett. Never played cards at Mrs. Townsend's house, nor did I ever see any cards played there. Never served a police warrant upon anybody in Mrs. Townsend's house on the complaint of Helen Jewett. I have, I think, on one occasion, seen Helen Jewett before the Grand Jury. I was in Court this morning when Mr. Noble gave his testimony. Have said that when I went to Mr. Robinson's house I told him to get up, that I wanted a word with him. The reason of my asking him to walk into the entry was in the first place to charge him directly with the murder of Helen Jewett—but I afterwards changed my mind, and began to ask him about the cloak. On my oath, my object was not to get him to say something to me out of the hearing of his room companion. I could have charged him with the murder, or spoken to him about the cloak in the bedroom as well as outside. I cannot say why I did not take this course. It was a notion of mine, I suppose. When I spoke to him about the cloak, I asked him if he had a blue cloth cloak. He said no—had never had one. He then told me about the camlet cloak, and pointed to it as I have before stated. I think what I tell you now as to what Robinson said when I spoke to him about the cloak is the same as stated when examined before the recess, and in all that I stated. I now recollect he swore he told me he had never worn a cloth cloak. I again swear that he did tell me he never had a cloak.

[At this stage of the examination Sheriff Hillyer and Lowndes, and Mr. A. M. C. Smith brought in one of a large gang of men whom he had arrested while making a disturbance outside the gates of the City Hall. The Judge ordered him to be taken to the police office for disposal by the magistrate.]

The cross-examination of Mr. Brink was continued by Mr. Maxwell—I intended to convey to the jury the fact that Robinson not only told me he had not a cloth cloak, such as I described, but also that he had never worn a cloth cloak — I mean a blue black cloth cloak. He did not tell me that he had such a cloak belonging to any other person. I knew a person named Gray. He did not say anything about a cloak of that person's. That was an after transaction, and not connected with Robinson. I cannot tell the reason why I did not communicate to the coroner the important fact of the strings on the cloak and the hatcnet bearing a resemblance to each other. I considered myself as acting under the coroner, and not as superior to him. The second time I saw the hatchet and cloak was when they were exhibited at the coroner's inquest. When I first saw the white mark upon Robinson's pantaloons, I did not feel it nor attempt to dust it. I did not attach sufficient importance to it at first, nor did I think much about it. There was considerable whitewash on the fence of the yard; it was thickly laid on. I believe I mentioned the fact at the coroner's inquest, before the coroner's jury. I solemnly assert on my oath I did not say a word to Robinson at his lodging-rooms, or at Mrs. Townsend's, about the white on his trowsers; and I also solemnly avow that he never told me it was paint. I never had any conversation with him on the subject. I have never received any money, goods, wares, or merchandise from Mrs. Townsend, except on one or two occasions, my regular fees for the service of processcs. I never served any process on Mrs. Townsend; but I have served processes upon persons in her house, for which perhaps she has paid the money. I have received no other money from her. I now remember that she has paid me some money, as also some other officers, for attending her sale. She paid us five dollars per day each. I bought a clock at the sale. I bought it for thirty dollars. I never paid any money for it myself, but I believe Mr. Welsh, who was also an officer in attendance at the sale, settled for it when he settled with the auctioneer and Mrs. Townsend for our services. The clock is now at my house. I forget now how much money I gave Welsh to pay the balance due upon the clock. I did give him some money for that purpose—I think fifteen or twenty dollars. Welsh bought some articles at the sale, but I don't know what they were. I don't know what he paid for them. I don't know whether Helen Jewett had any money when she was murdered. I don't know that she was remarkable in her sphere of life for having splendid jewelry, chains and dresses. When I reached Helen Jewett's room after the murder, I did not find any money or jewels. I was not told where she kept her money. I did not find any notes or coins. I believe that Mr. Welsh found a small box in her room, containing little coins.

By Mr. Price—There was considerable whitewash on the fence in Mrs. Townsend's yard. I did not notice any whitewash on the cloak, except a little on the tassels. A person could have got over the fence without getting any whitewash on the cloak. A person might have thrown the cloak over the fence, and then got over.

Mr. Price—Now I want you to say to this jury, whether in all your conversations with the prisoner, from the period of his being examined before the Police, you noticed anything in his conduct, manner or deportment, that led you to suspect him to be guilty of murder?

Witness—I must say he acted very curiously, very differently from any prisoner that I ever had before.

Mr. Price—How did he act?

Witness—Why, he did not appear alarmed at all. I must say, however, when I told him in the coach, before getting to Rosina Townsend's house, of the accusation made against him, he changed color. That is all I know of by which he acted curiously.

Mr. Price—Did you not swear, sir, before the grand jury, you observed nothing in his conduct to lead you to suppose that he had been guilty?

Witness—I do not remember swearing any such thing. I do not believe that I did.

Mr. Price—Very well, sir. We will wait and see whether you did or did not when we get the grand jury here as witnesses.

Mr. Hoffman—Now, Mr. Brink, you and I have been public officers together, and I may ask you a few questions with a little more freedom than usual. Did you ever receive any money from Mrs. Townsend for speaking to the District-Attorney in er favor?

Witness—I don't think that I ever did.

Mr. Hoffman—Did you ever receive any money from Helen Jewett?

Witness—Never.

Mr. Hoffman—Did you not know that Helen Jewett prosecuted a man named Bryd, and that Bryd afterwards turned round and proseuted Mrs. Berry, the keeper of a house of prostitution in Duane street?

Witness—I remember something of the kind.

Mr. Hoffman—Did you not receive money for acting in behalf of Mrs. Berry on that occasion?

Witness—I have received some money from Mrs. Berry sometimes. I cannot tell exactly what for or how much—perhaps a dollar or so at a time.

Mr. Hoffman—Did you never receive any money for going to the District-Attorney in relation to an indictment that was pending against Mrs. Townsend, to intercede with him in her behalf?

Witness—I never did, that I recollect.

Mr. Hoffman—Who was the District-Attorney at that time?

Witness—Mr. Hoffman was—you were, sir.

Mr. Hoffman—Did you ever receive any money for endeavoring to get a prosecution settled in the Court of Sessions, that was pending against two prostitutes?

Witness—I do not recollect that I ever did. I think I should recollect such a circumstance if I had done it.

Mr. Hoffman—Do you recollect on any other occasion having received money from prostitutes, or the keepers of prostitutes, and if you do, state what occasion it was, and how much money you received?

Witness—I do not recollect ever having done anything of the kind.

Mr. Morris—The gentleman appears to be very anxious on this subject. I will endeavor to satisfy him about the prostitution case.

Mr. Hoffman—If my learned friend does not wish me to proceed with the examination, I will forego it.

Witness examined by Mr. Morris—I did receive money from a gentleman for arranging a difference between two prostitutes, where one had torn the clothes of the other.

Mr. Morris—Who was that gentleman?

Mr. Hoffman—I object to the gentleman's name being disclosed; although of course if the gentleman persists in it, he can have an answer.

Mr. Phenix—If the gentleman does not persist in his mode of cross-examination, I shall not persist in mine.

Mr. Hoffman—Never mind, I will drop it.

Mr. Schureman, recalled for the defence, and examined by Mr. Maxwell—I did not see or hear of any comparison of the string on the cloak with a string on the hatchet by Mr. Brink or Mr. Noble. I was and still am under the impression that the hatchet was handed to me immediately after it was found by the watchman. I may, however, be mistaken. I did not particularly observe any white marks on the prisoner's trousers. I think he wore pantaloons of a light brown color. I have expressed it as a somewhat singular circumstance, that neither Brink nor Noble mentioned to me in especial manner about their comparing the strings on the hatchet and the cloak.

Charles Tyrrell called for the prosecution, and examined by Mr. Phenix—I know the prisoner at the bar; I boarded at the same house with him in Dey street. On the Saturday night, previous to the morning on which Helen Jewett was murdered, I walked up Beekman street with the prisoner as far as the brick church; it was between eight and nine o'clock at night. He then wore a dark colored cloth cloak with velvet collar and facings, and I think he had a cap on.

[The cloak was produced, and it was one of such a description as was represented by the witness.]

Examination continued—I left him at the corner of Beekman and Nassau streets, and he went towards the park. He told me that he was going to the Clinton hotel, but to my certain knowledge he did not go in there. I have heard from him that he was acquainted with Helen Jewett, and I have frequently heard boarders in the house banter him about Helen—but I don't know positively what Helen they meant.

Cross examined, by Mr. Maxwell—I saw Robinson put on the cloth cloak before he left the house. [The witness here put the cloak on and showed how he did it.] If there had been a hatchet attached to the cloak, I should certainly have seen it. I also had an opportunity of seeing the inside of the cloak before he left me in Beekman street. He pulled it open in such a manner, that had the hatchet been there I could most probably have seen it. On that evening before he left the house he was very cheerful, and had been joking with some of the boarders in the house. In the course of his talk in Beekman street, he told me that he was on that day nineteen years of age, and spoke of the circumstance with evident emotion of pleasure.

By Mr. Phenix—Before the occasion of which I have spoken, I have seen Robinson wear a cloth cloak similar to the one which he wore on that night. When he put it on he took it either off the bed or out of his trunk. He was in the habit of keeping it in his trunk.

Elizabeth Salters, examined by Mr. Phenix, for the prosecution—I know the prisoner. I knew him before Helen Jewett was killed. I knew him for about seven weeks before that occurrence; I knew him at Mrs. Townsend's during that time. He used to come and see me there. He generally wore a cloak when he came there in the night time. It was a dark cloak made of cloth. He had to it a black silk corded tassel. On one occasion I discovered something deficient as regards one of the ornaments of the cloak. One of the tassels was off. The tassels were of long silk braid. One of the tassels that was broken off and sewed on again, was of long narrow braid. I discovered this about two weeks before Miss Jewett came to the house. I was at Mrs. Townsend's on the morning that the murder was committed. I was there when the cloak was found. I made a statement in reference to one of the tassels of the cloak, before the cloak was exhibited to me. [The cloak found back of Mrs. Townsend's yard, was here exhibited to the witness, and she positively identified it as the one that Robinson alias Frank Rivers used to wear.]

The examination was continued—I never knew the prisoner before the murder by any other name than that of Frank Rivers. There was another young man who called himself Frank Rivers who used to come to the house with the prisoner. They said that they were cousins. Helen Jewett lived at Mrs. Townsend's three weeks before she was murdered. I knew her before she came there, she was a favorite among all the girls, and I never knew or heard of her having a quarrel with any one in the house, or out of it. On the night of the murder, I was in the house. At a late hour, towards the morning, there was a person called to see me. At the time the alarm of the fire and murder was given, the person was in my room. He came in a quarter of an hour before I heard the alarm. I expected him there on that night. He was undressed at the time of the alarm was given. I did not hear him come into the house; I did not hear him until he was in my room. I recollect hearing a person calling for a bottle of champagne after I went to bed. It was Helen Jewett called for the champagne. I went to bed about half past ten o'clock. It was about half an hour afterwards when the wine was called for, I had a conversation with Robinson about the tassel that was broken off the cloak. He said it was broken off during a sleigh ride. The conversation took place about two weeks before Helen Jewett's death. He happened to speak about the tassel because I had it in my head.

Cross examined by Mr. Maxwell—I have talked with Mrs. Townsend about the murder to-day; I also spoke to her about it, and to several other persons on the day of the murder. On the morning of April 10th. when the cloak was brought into Mrs. Townsend's, I did not pretend to swear to the cloak, but only to the tassel. Don't know that there is anything very peculiar in the sewing of the tassel on the cloak. I expect that the tassel torn off in the same manner as the one on the cloak exhibited, must necessarily be sewn on the same way. I was in bed when I heard Helen Jewett calling for a bottle of champagne. My room was immediately opposite to Helen Jewett's room. Could not hear everything, or indeed anything that took place in Helen Jewett's room, unless it was loud. Was nineteen years of age in April last. Before I went to live at Mrs. Townsend's I lived at my mother's house. Have been away from my mother's house upwards of two years. Have lived the greater part of that time at Mrs. Townsend's. Before I went to live there, I lived at a house kept by Mrs. Brown. Cannot say how many persons came to Mrs. Townsend's on the night of the murder. There were several persons in the parlor, but cannot say how many, nor who they were. Did not see any person attempt to leave the house on the morning of the murder. Heard Mrs. Townsend say that a person attempted to leave the place and that she had prevented him. Do not know that Helen Jewett knew that Robinson visited me prior to coming to Mrs. Townsend's to see her. The other Frank Rivers came to see me. They have both been in my room at the same time. They used sometimes to dress a good deal alike. When the alarm of the murder was given, I ran out of my room. I did not dress before coming out. Saw several men there. Cannot say how many; was too much frightened. Did not see any of the men attempting to get away. They did get away,

I believe, when the doors were opened to let the watchmen in. Did not see a person at Helen Jewett's room when the alarm was given, who subsequently got away. Did not hear Mrs. Townsend speak of such an occurrence. Saw Helen Jewett bureau examined on the morning of the murder. She had a gold watch and chain and ear rings. Saw Mrs. Townsend have the watch and chain on the morning of the murder. Was present when Frank Rivers came in on Saturday night to see Helen. We were in the parlor when he came in, and she told us that her dear Frank had come. Did not see him when he came, and don't know how he was dressed. The other Frank Rivers used occasionally to visit Helen Jewett. Mrs. Townsend told me some day last week of the particular bald mark which she had observed on Mr. Robinson's head. She told me it was a curious bald place on the crown of his head. Before she told me this never knew anything of it. I have more than once seen the prisoner with his clothes off, and so exposed that I should think I could have observed the place upon his head about which Mrs. Townsend spoke. I never to my knowledge did see any such place. Heard of a person's visiting Helen Jewett regularly every Saturday night, but never saw him.

By Mr. Morris—The name of the person was, I believe, Bill Easy, or at all events, that was the name by which he was known.

By Mr. Hoffman—There was no ill-feeling between Helen Jewett and me, because of Frank Rivers leaving me to visit her. I never said anything to her about his visiting me. I thought that she had most right to him, as I understood from her that she had known him intimately for a long time.

James Wells, examined by Mr. Phenix for the prosecution—I am a porter in the employ of Mr. Joseph Hoxie. I have been in such employment since last June. There was a hatchet in the store; I was accustomed to use it for the purpose of splitting up wood. The last time that I recollect seeing the hatchet in our store, was on the Wednesday before the murder was said to be committed. Richard P. Robinson was in the employment of Mr. Hoxie in the same store in which the hatchet was. I used to open the store in the morning. The first time that I missed the hatchet was on the Monday after the murder. I then wanted it and looked for it, but could not find it. Sometimes I wanted it for opening boxes, and I wanted it on that morning for that purpose. Had not heard of the murder when I missed the hatchet; did not make any particular inquiries about it.

[The hatchet found in the rear of Mrs. Townsend's house was here positively sworn to by the witness, as being the hatchet that belonged to Mr. Hoxie.]

Cross-examined by Mr. Maxwell—The hatchet was used in different parts of Mr. Hoxie's premises, and sometimes in the street for opening boxes. On the Saturday afternoon before the murder Robinson was engaged in the store up to half-past five o'clock. Have always considered him to be a kind and amiable young man. Have seen him day after day without his hat, and never observed that he had any particular mark at the back of his head; never saw any baldness at the back of his head. Know the axe from the dark marks that are upon it, and from its being blunted in a particular way. There was never any blood upon it that I observed. On the Saturday before the murder we had part of our store painted white, and some of the upright pillars or supporters of the cellar whitewashed. I remember that Mr. Hoxie got some of his clothes rubbed with paint.

By Mr. Morris—I do not know that the prisoner's clothes in any part were painted.

Emma French, examined by Mr. Phenix for the prosecution—Lived at the house of Mrs. Townsend sixteen months. Boarded there at the time of Helen Jewett's death. Know a person named Frank Rivers—he never visited me. Have seen him at Mrs. Townsend's four or five times. Knew of his being there on the night of Helen Jewett's murder; he wore a hat and cloak. My room was on the lower floor, in front, opposite Mrs. Townsend's room. Saw Frank Rivers come in between nine and ten o'clock on the night of the murder; was standing at my room door in the entry when he came in. The reason that I was at the room door is that I expected some one on that night. He did not come into my room; he went directly through the passage. Saw him enter the recess towards the stairs. Saw Helen Jewett on that night, about half an hour before he came, and she said in my presence that her "dear Frank was coming." About eleven o'clock on that night saw Helen Jewett. At that time Frank Rivers was there. Helen came down stairs to get a boot that the shoemaker had brought. Previous to that night had spoken with the prisoner at the bar. Had seen him in Mrs. Salters' room. When he came in on the night of the murder did not hear him speak. Mrs. Townsend let him in. Before she did so, she twice asked "who's there?" It was between nine and ten o'clock when she let him in. The lamp in the entry was at that time lighted. It hung near the foot of the stairs. The light was so clear that I could see any person that entered distinctly.

Cross-examined by Mr. Maxwell—Have been all day in the Grand Jury room. Mrs. Townsend has also been there all day. We were all waiting there yesterday. Mrs. Townsend told us she had been examined in the court yesterday. She did not tell us particularly what she said, or what the lawyers asked her. There were two Frank Rivers visited Mrs. Townsend's house. Sometimes I have seen them dressed alike, except their cloaks. Robinson wore a cloth cloak, and the other Rivers wore a Boston wrapper. I have seen both Frank Rivers in Miss Salters' room. Mrs. Townsend never said anything to me about being able to see a person in the entry by the lamp. The person Mrs. Townsend let into the house did not say a word. When he came in he put his cloak up to his face, so I could only see his forehead and eyes. I thought from what I then saw of him that it was the prisoner at the bar, but I cannot now swear that it was he that I saw. I can not say why, if it was he on that night, he wished to cover his face, as I had seen him several times previously. When Helen came down, about eleven o'clock, to receive the boot from the shoemaker, she was in full dress, the same as she had been all the evening. With the exception of a bottle of champagne that Helen Jewett had, only know of one bottle of champagne being drunk in Mrs. Townsend's house on that night. It was drunk in the parlor. Did not have any more in Mrs. Townsend's room on the night of the murder; nor was I awake, until Mrs. Townsend came down stairs crying out fire. Did not see two men in the passage, half dressed, when the alarm was given; am positive of this. Saw the watchmen come in. Cannot tell how many came in, or hardly what took place, as I was much frightened. Did not hear a man say, to one of the watchmen, "Don't take me, I'm not the person that was in that room." Saw some gentlemen try to leave the house, and in great confusion. Some of them were undressed. A great number of strangers used to come to Mrs. Townsend's house in the course of a week. Cannot say how many there were there on the night of the murder. Live at Miss Brown's, in Grand street, now. It is a house similar to Mrs. Townsend's. Cannot say how many strangers I have had to see me in the course of a week. Sometimes I had several. Have, whilst there, let persons out of my room before daylight. When I did so, I was compelled to go to Mrs. Townsend's room, to get the key, that being a rule of the house, as I understood. It was the custom of the girls to go to her room and ask for the key when they wished to let any one out of the house after the door was locked for the night.

Denis Brink, recalled for the prosecution—I looked into the trunks and bureau that were brought from Robinson's room, and did not find a cloth cloak in them, nor did I find one in his room. I believe the coroner took possession of the letters that were found in Helen Jewett's room.

Mr. Eldridge, the watchman, recalled by Mr. Hoffman, for the defence—When the cloak was found, it was not in a heap; it was spread out two-thirds of its length—probably about three feet.

[It being now nine o'clock, the Judge ordered the Court to be adjourned until ten o'clock the next day, and it was adjourned accordingly. The Jury were placed in the mean time under the charge of eight police officers and constables.]

THIRD DAY.

The excellent arrangements that were made the previous day by Sheriff Hillyer and Lowndes, and High Constable Hayes, and their deputies and assistants, fortunately prevented a repetition of the tumult, disorder, and violence, which interrupted the progress of the proceedings in this most extraordinary trial on the two preceding days.

Shortly after teh o'clock, the doors of the great court room were opened for the ingress of members of the bar, reporters and witnesses. All the entry gates of the hall were closed, and attended by various constables and officers, and business in all other tribunals of the hall was suspended in consequence of the excitement amongst the multitude, who, notwithstanding the bars to their admittance to the court room, and the still damp and wretched weather, still densely congregated in the vicinity of the hall.

Immediately on the court being opened in the usual form, and the ordinary proclamation being made, the prisoner was brought to the bar, attended as before, by his counsel, and Mr. Joseph Hoxie, his relatives and friends. He bore the same firm, calm, and composed appearance that he has even done since the discovery of the horrid murder of the unfortunate Helen Jewett, even when gazing upon her mangled and bloody corpse, when before the coroner's inquest. The proceedings were resumed by Mr. Phenix calling as a witness for the prosecution, a colored girl named

Sarah Dunscombe, who, on being sworn, was examined by Mr. Phenix, and deposed as follows :—I was acquainted with Helen Jewett; was employed by her shortly before her death; was employed by her to do her work in the morning, and dress her in the evening. Used to go in the morning to clean her room up, and in the evening about half past five o'clock to assist in dressing her. Was employed by Helen Jewett all the time that she was in Mrs. Townsend's house, and a short time previous at Mrs. Cunningham's, in Franklin street; saw a miniature in Miss Jewett's when I worked for her. Saw it in her possession on the Friday morning before her death. On Friday morning, Helen Jewett went out, and she placed the miniature in my possession to clean and dust the frame. After I had done this, I put it in the drawer—Miss Helen's drawer—the drawer of the bureau. Did not set the miniature after putting it in Helen's drawer. It was the miniature of a male. Have seen the miniature at the police office. [The miniature taken from Robinson's trunk by Mr. Brink on the 10th of April was here shown to the witness, and she identified it as being the same which she had seen in Helen Jewett's room.]

Cross-examined by Mr. Maxwell—My mother lives at No. 188 Franklin street; she takes in work; I used to go to Miss Jewett's room between eight and nine o'clock. I went pretty punctually every morning, and did not perhaps vary any more than five or ten minutes any morning. I was with Miss Jewett on Saturday afternoon about half past five o'clock, as near as I can recollect. It was on the morning of Friday that I saw Helen Jewett's miniature; I think it was about half past seven o'clock when I left Miss Jewett, on Saturday evening. I went to my mother's when I left Miss Jewett. I know it was half past seven o'clock when I left Miss Jewett, because after I left her I went into the grocery to inquire what time it was,—having after that to go an errand down town for my mother. She had not finished dressing when I left the house. There was a fire in the room on that night. I made the fire. I took up some wood from the cellar for that purpose. Took up three piece of wood. It was small wood; the wood was not split. Don t know whether it was hickory wood or not. There was a carpet on the floor. The end of the bed was not near the fire place. The fire was lighted when I left the house; know it was half past five when I went to the house on Saturday night, because I inquired as I was going to the corner of Franklin and Hudson streets; when I went to Helen's room at half past five o'clock, there was a gentleman in the room with her; did not see the face of that gentleman; did not hear her call that gentleman by any name; heard her say, when he was sitting on a chair with his knee on the bed, "Frank." Did not hear her add anything but Frank. After being in the room about ten minutes, went for a pitcher of water, and when I returned the gentleman was gone; fetched the wood from the cellar to make the fire, while he was there. [Mr. Maxwell here read the witness' deposition as given at the police office to compare it with her present testimony. It did not differ materially in fact, except that she left Helen Jewett's room on the Saturday night, and that she took the young man who was in the room when she went there to be Robinson, the prisoner at the bar. In her deposition, however, she swore that she only supposed it to be Robinson, from his figure, and that she did not see his face, as Helen was sitting upon his knee at the time he was there.]

Witness continued, examined alternately by Messrs. Maxwell and Hoffman—If I swore positively, at the police office, that I thought the young man whom I saw in Miss Jewett's room on Saturday night was Robinson, I said so without meaning it, and while I was frightened, and I therefore hope to be excused; I cannot say but I am frightened now; I was never before brought up for the purpose of swearing. Mrs. Townsend has never, at any time, told me what I ought to say. Might have said that I thought the young man who was with Miss Jewett was Mr. Robinson, from his dress and figure, and the color of his hair; but, if I did, it was because I was frightened as I had no reason to speak positively to any one; I have never spoken to any one but my mother about this, and she told me to tell nothing but the truth. Have not spoken to any girls, officer, or any body else respecting the affair. The gentleman that I saw on the Thursday previous to the murder at Helen Jewett's room I think was Mr. Robinson. Cannot be mistaken in him. Think that the gentleman that I saw with Helen on Saturday night was dressed in black; am certain that he had not white pantaloons on.

Joseph Hoxie, Jr., examined by Mr. Morris, for the prosecution—Am a nephew to Mr. Joseph Hoxie of Broadway and Maiden Lane. Am in Mr. Hoxie's employ. Am in the same store that the prisoner was in. Think that I can identify his handwriting. [Mr. Morris here showed the witness a letter and asked him if that was in the handwriting of the prisoner.]

Witness—after looking at the letter—It does bear some resemblance to the prisoner's handwriting, but I cannot swear positively that it is. I am acquainted with his handwriting only in some measure. Have been in my uncle's employ eight months. Cannot say exactly how long, Robinson has been in his employ. He was there before I went to live with my uncle. He was a sort of general clerk in my uncle's employ; and sometimes he kept the books. He began to keep the books after the partner of Mr. Hoxie went away. Francis P. Robinson, a cousin of the prisoner, was the partner. The duty of the book-keeper is not only to keep the books but to copy letters. Have seen the prisoner, (Richard P. Robinson), in the act of copying letters. Soon after Mr. Hoxie's partner left, Mr. Somerindyke was engaged as book-keeper for my uncle.

Mr. Maxwell—I object to the gentleman going on with the witness' examination to prove the handwriting of the prisoner—he being incompetent to prove it from the fact of being only measurably acquainted with it.

Mr. Morris—I submit to the Court whether I have not a right to know the extent of the measure by which the judgment or opinion of the witness, as to his knowledge of the prisoner's handwriting, is guided.

Judge Edwards ruled in favor of Mr. Maxwell's objection.

Mr. Morris (to the witness)—Are you acquainted with the prisoner's handwriting from having seen him write?

Witness—Don't think I am sufficiently acquainted with his handwriting to be able to swear positively to it.

Cross-examined by Mr. Maxwell—Saw Robinson (the prisoner) on the Saturday afternoon preceding the murder. Saw him at the store between three and four o'clock. Don't recollect seeing him in the morning. It was just before dinner on Saturday afternoon that I saw the prisoner.

By Mr. Morris—There were three clerks in my uncle's store —Mr. Newton Gilbert, Mr. P. F. Robinson and myself—and Mr. Somerindyke, the bookkeeper. Mr. Gilbert was the principal clerk. He used to keep one key of the store, and the partner (James Wells) the other. It was his (Mr. Gilbert's) business to lock up the store at night. Mr. Robinson (the prisoner) has, on some occasions, had charge of the key. Can not recollect when. He has had charge of the key when Mr. Gilbert was there. Mr. Gilbert, I think, took charge of the key for some time previous to the night of the murder—perhaps two or three weeks. Know positively that this was the case. Cannot tell how I know this. Did not see the key given to Mr. Gilbert. It is only my impression that Mr. Gilbert had the key for two or three weeks prior to the murder. Sometimes Mr. Gilbert had it, and sometimes the prisoner at the bar had it. I believe Mr. Gilbert lives in Chambers street. He is not a married man; he is single.

William Van Nest, examined by Mr. Morris for the prosecution—I am a public porter. Know Mr. Robinson, the prisoner. Remember on one occasion delivering a letter to him. Went to the store of Mr. Hoxie, No. 101 Maiden lane. Asked if Richard P. Robinson was within; did not know him by name at that time. As I went in at the door a young man passed me. Found out by inquiring at the store it was Robinson, the prisoner, who had just gone out. I went into the street, and spoke to him in front of the store; told him I had a letter for him which I was directed to give him. Don't know that I told him who the letter was from. Think I showed him the letter, but am not certain. He told me to pass through the store, and leave the letter on a beam. I thought he meant in the privy. Went through the store into the yard, but, thinking Robinson's conduct very strange, did not leave the letter, and passed through the store, and went and did a job with my cart. On returning to my stand at the corner of Maiden lane and Pearl street, the prisoner came up to me and asked me what I had done with the letter. Told him I had it still in my possession, because I was expressly directed to give it to him. Did give it to him, and he gave me two shillings. I reside at 28 Thomas street. Heard of the murder of Helen Jewett about seven or eight o'clock on the morning of April 10th. Soon after hearing of the murder, I went to the house where the corpse was lying, and saw the corpse. When I first saw it, I did not think I had seen the person of the corpse before. On seeing the corpse a second time, on Monday morning, I thought I had seen the corpse, I mean, the person of the corpse, before. Had seen her before in Cedar street. It was she who gave me the letter to take to Richard P. Robinson, the prisoner at the bar.

Mr. Price objected to the counsel for the prosecution proving a correspondence between the prisoner and the deceased by showing that prior to her death she had written letters to the prisoner. The learned gentleman argued that the only manner in which such correspondence should be proven, according to the strict rules of law, was first to establish the fact that the prisoner had written letters to her (the deceased), as every man living was liable to receive letters from any prostitute who thought proper to address him. The Court ruled in favor of the argument, and the examination of the witness on this subject was discontinued.

Edward Strong, examined by Mr. Morris, for the prosecution—I do not know Mr. Robinson. Know Helen Jewett; saw her twice in the street on the Saturday prior to her murder—once in the morning, and once in the afternoon. Was in Helen Jewett's room at Mrs. Townsend's house between five and six o'clock on the afternoon of Saturday, the ninth of April, on the day previous to the murder. A black girl came into the room when I was there, on the Saturday afternoon. She brought in some clean clothes, a pitcher of water, and some wood, whilst I was there. I sat on a chair near the end of the bed, which is close by a window, the greater part of the time. When I saw Helen walking in the street in the afternoon there was another girl walking with her. Saw Helen go into the house Went into the house at the same time that she did. Think that it was between five and six o'clock when I went into the house with her.

By the Judge—Part of the time that I was there, I sat on chair near the bed, with my head leaning on the bed; do not recollect that she mentioned my name or any other name on that night.

Mr. Morris—Did she mention the name of any person that was coming there on that night?

Mr. Hoffman objected to any answer being made to this, and it was withdrawn.

The witness was not crose-examined.

Samuel Van Nest, examined by Mr. Morris, for the prosecution—I am a porter. Am stationed in Cedar street opposite No. 1. Know Mr. Robinson, prisoner at the bar; have known him about a year. Knew Helen Jewett. Knew her for about a year. Have carried papers at different times from Mr. Robinson, directed to Helen Jewett. They were folded and sealed as letters, and had every appearance of being letters.

By the Judge—Although the letters were directed with the name and number, he would sometimes mention Helen Jewett's name, and tell me to deliver them to her.

[Mr. Morris here handed some letters to the witness that he might identify them as being the same that he had taken to Helen Jewett, but Mr. Maxwell objected to their being identified in this manner, as it was not yet proof that they were letters. For all the court and jury know, said the learned counsel, they might be mere blanks inside. The court ruled that Mr. Morris had a right to present the letters to the witness in the manner he was about to do.]

Witness (after looking at the letters)—I cannot positively swear to the identity of the letters now shown to me, although I have very little doubt but that they are the same as I carried to Helen Jewett from Mr. Robinson. Only carried one letter to her in Thomas street. The most of the letters I carried to her from him were directed to Mrs. Berry's, in Duane street, where she then lived. On one or two occasions, I took back letters to Mr. Robinson from Helen Jewett. Did this when he told me to wait for an answer Have carried bundles or packages in the shape of books from Mr. Robinson to Helen Jewett. Don't remember ever carrying any from her to him. Don t know that I could possibly identify any of the letters that I have taken from Helen Jewett to the prisoner.

Oliver M. Lowndes, police magistrate, examined by Mr. Phenix, for the prosecution—Have examined the premises of No. 41 Thomas street. Know where the cloak and hatchet were found, but think it would be difficult to explain the precise position without a diagram. Understood the cloak to have been found in the rear of a lot fronting on Hudson street. The fence in the rear of two lots on Hudson street is so dilapidated between the privies, that a person could easily get into Hudson street from the rear of the house 41 Thomas street. A person could not escape without going through houses. There were no alleys into Hudson street. There are alleys, or were alleys, running from the rear of those lots into Duane and Chapel streets. The lot just in the rear of No. 41 Thomas street is surrounded by a very high fence. There was an alley east of the rear of Mrs. Townsend's house, running into Duane street, by which a person could without difficulty escape. A watch and chain, and some rings, were exhibited to me by the coroner as having been obtained by him from Helen Jewett's room. He also took some letters and papers from her room, and I, on going there, also found some papers and letters, which I brought to the police office. Was on one occasion at the house, No. 41 Thomas street, in company with Mr. Lawrence (the mayor) when the lamp in the entry of the house was lit. Did not make any experiments to see whether the lights reflected in a person's face coming in, or not. I believe Mr. Tompkins, police officer, and Mr. Hunt, one of the city marshals, made such an experiment. Never went to Mr. Robinson's room. Was at the police office when the bureau and trunks of Mr. Robinson were brought there. There was a little pocket wallet found in one of his trunks. Examined the wallet to see what it contained.

[The wallet was handed to the witness, and he identified it as being the one he found in the bureau. It contained papers—bank bills of exchange to a large amount—belonging to Mr. Hoxie.]

Mr. Maxwell cross-examined the witness at great length, in reference to the exact situation of the premises in Thomas street, and the adjacent buildings, in the course of which a diagram was exhibited and explained, but no material fact was elicited favorable to the prisoner.

At the close of this examination, Mr. Phenix, at the solicitation of the gentlemen of the jury, rose and stated to the court that it was now apparent that the trial of the prisoner at the bar was yet likely to occupy one or more days beyond the period it had already progressed, and that if any arrangement or order could be made for the accommodation of the jury on the Sunday which would intervene — consistent with the established usages in criminal prosecutions, the law of the land, and just administration of public justice,—he and his associate counsel for the prosecution, as also the counsel for the prisoner would gladly accede to it. Each, or most of the gentlemen, said the learned counsel, had perhaps some domestic duty to attend to, which he was anxious to fulfil, and if they could be permitted, with officers to attend them, to visit their families on Sunday they would be glad. Mr. Price cited the instance of the jury empannelled in the case of Mr. Jennings, who was murdered in Orange county, the trial of which occupied seventeen days, during which occasion the jury were permitted on two or three occasions to visit their families.

The court said that they would take time to consider as to what would be the best and proper means of acting with reference to the jury.

Elizabeth Salters, recalled by Mr. Phenix for the prosecution—Was in the room of Helen Jewett shortly after her murdered body was discovered. Found between the bed post and pillow a silk handkerchief. Should know it if I saw it again.

[A handkerchief was here produced by the learned counsel, and identified by the witness, as being the same which she found under the pillow of Helen Jewett's bed.]

Examination continued—The other person who called himself Frank Rivers, was in Mrs. Townsend's house on the night of the murder He was in the lower part of the house; he was there between nine and ten o'clock; he was not there a great while; there was another person with him; he talked to me when he was there; there was a gentleman in the parlor who came out and talked to him; don't know who that person was. He remained in the entry all the time he was there The other person also remained there with him, and they went away together The next time I saw him was on the Sunday morning after the murder He came to the house in company with the prisoner at the bar and the officers Brink and Newbolt The young man I speak of was the other Frank Rivers. When they were first brought in, I cannot recollect what time it was. I have not since discovered the real name of the other Frank Rivers.

[Mr. Phenix here asked if Mr. Tew was in court, and a young man by that name rose from among the witnesses. The witness immediately recognized him as the other young man who went by the name of Frank Rivers.]

By Mr. Hoffman—When the other Frank Rivers (Mr. Tew) left the house, I let him out. Mrs. Townsend was then down stairs, or in the parlor. I think it was about ten o'clock when I let him out. I cannot say exactly how long he was there.

By Mr. Morris—He was dressed in a Boston wrapper.

Mary Gallagher, examined by Mr. Phenix for the prosecution—I was at Mrs. Townsend's house in Thomas street on the morning the murder was committed. Saw the prisoner at the bar there. Had never seen him before. Asked him what induced him to commit so cruel and barbarous an act. He replied, "Do you think I would blast my brilliant prospects by so ridiculous an act? I am a young man of only nineteen years of age yesterday, with most brilliant prospects." My answer was, "My dear boy, God grant that you may prove innocent." "Why," said he, "there's another man's handkerchief under the pillow, with his name full upon it." He then added, "I am not afraid that I shall be convicted." My answer was, "But, my dear boy, your cloak has been found on the other side of the fence." I then again said to him, "God grant that you may prove innocent, for the sake of your poor mother." Then asked him if he had seen what an awful state she (Helen Jewett) was in, with her head split open, and burnt almost to a crisp. He said, "No, they won't let me see her." I said, "If you could see, if you committed the act, I am sure your heart would break." At that time Mr. Brink came up and struck me on the shoulder, saying, "We allow no person to speak to the prisoner." I begged his pardon, and sat down. He further said, "We don't allow any person to speak to induce him to say anything to convict himself." I said I had no intention of the kind.

Cross-examined by Mr. Maxwell—Reside at No. 122 Chapel street; have no husband; keep house. It was in the afternoon, before dinner, when I went to Mrs. Townsend's house in Thomas street. It was towards the middle of the day when I had the conversation spoken of with the prisoner at the bar. When he spoke to me about there being another man's handkerchief under the pillow, I did not know that a handkerchief had been discovered under the pillow. Did not ask any one to go and see if there was a handkerchief in the situation in which he had described. I am very confident that the conversation I have mentioned did take place between me and Robinson, and no other. There were several persons in the room when the conversation took place. Mrs. Townsend was in the room,—Mr. Newbolt, some of the female boarders in the house, and other persons. We spoke together in a loud tone, and all the persons in the room might have heard it, for all that I know. I had never been in Mrs. Townsend's house more than three times prior to the murder—twice in the daytime, and once at night. It is two winters since I was there in the night time. Put my arms round Mr. Robinson's neck when I first spoke to him, and felt more favorable to him than otherwise. Went to Mrs. Townsend's in the daytime to converse with her about some men who had stoned a number of houses.

George B. Marston, examined by Mr. Phenix for the prosecution—Knew Helen Jewett; visited her at Mrs. Townsend's; assumed while there the name of Bill Easy. Know how the handkerchief spoken of got into Helen Jewett's room. Took it there several days before her death for her to mark my name upon it. When I took it there she asked me if the colors were fast; I mean, if they would not fade. I bought it for a first-rate English handkerchief. I reside in Cliff street; was at home on the night of the murder, after eight o'clock. After marking my handkerchief Helen washed it, and the colors washed out; she bought me another and marked it, and kept the one that I bought, as she said, for a duster. I had no particular nights to go to see Helen, except on Saturday nights. Believe I went to see her every Saturday night that she was in the house, except the one on which she was murdered. Was there two or three times of a Saturday night. The name of the person who kept the boarding house at which I live in Cliff street is Mrs. Morrison. It was at 80 Cliff street. I was not in Mrs. Townsend's house on the Saturday of the murder at all, neither day nor night.

Cross-examined by Mr. Maxwell—As far as I know, Helen Jewett was very fond of being employed at her needle. She was fond of obliging persons. Previous to washing my handkerchief, she made some shirts for me. I don't know that she ever mended any. Independent of sewing things for me, I believe she did similar favors for other persons. Have seen other clothes there. Have left things with her to be mended and fixed.

By Mr. Phenix—I do not positively know that Helen Jewett ever fixed or mended any articles or garments for any other person but myself; have seen her have ear and finger rings, buckles, (some very handsome), a gold watch and chain, &c. I have seen her have more than one ring on every finger. When I speak of buckles, I mean waist buckles. Don't know positively what articles of jewelry Helen had shortly before her death; knew her about eight months before her death; have seen her in possession of the jewelry of which I speak both before and after she went to Mrs. Townsend's; among her buckles was a large cameo one; she had full six rings, I think, while at Mrs. Townsend's—amongst them, two emerald ones. I was with Helen on the Friday night before her murder; was with her only fifteen or twenty minutes; don't know in what part of her room Helen kept my handkerchief.

By Mr. Maxwell—Helen was one of the most splendidly dressed women that went to the third tier of the theatre. She had a variety of dresses,—very valuable ones. I have seen her sometimes, when full dressed, wear a great number of ornaments; sometimes, however, she would dress without using such ornaments. I don't know that, although she had very rich and splendid dresses and jewelry, that they were more splendid and valuable than those possessed by other females of a similar description. On the Friday night, when I went to see Helen, it was about nine o'clock. Don't recollect who let me in. A great number of persons used to visit Mrs. Townsend's house; I have heard her house called the City hotel; I have never heard it called the Kentucky house, or the Alabama house. I was not at the house on the Sunday morning that the murder was discovered.

By Mr. Morris—I don't know that Helen Jewett ever had a bracelet.

[At the conclusion of the witness's examination, the Court took a recess for half an hour.]

About half an hour after the expiration of the recess, the Court resumed its sitting, and Judge Edwards thereupon informed the jury that the court had duly considered the application made, on their behalf, by the District Attorney, but that it could not, consistently with its duty, permit them to leave the custody of the officers, or the immediate vicinity of the city hall, until the close of the trial. The learned Judge then desired the sheriff to summon twelve officers to attend the jury next day (Sunday), so that the latter might have every accomodation that could be afforded to them.

Joseph Hoxie, Senr., was examined by Mr. Morris, and deposed as follows:—I know the prisoner. I have known him five years. He was in my employ at the time the transaction took place. He had been in my employ two years on the 11th of March preceding. When he first came here, he came to me in the capacity of an under clerk. He had been in a store previous to coming to live with me—in the store of Mr. James Robinson. James Robinson did not afterwards become my partner. I was pretty well acquainted with Robinson's qualifications as a clerk when he first came to me.

[Mr. Morris asked the witness upon what terms and conditions of salary the prisoner entered his employ. Mr. Maxwell objected to the question. Mr. Morris replied that in consultation with the district attorney, they had thought this question important. The learned gentleman then conferred privately with the Court, stating the object of his interrogatory, after which he sat down without resuming the question.]

Examination continued—The prisoner was promoted to be assistant book-keeper, and afterwards general out door clerk. About one year previous to the 18th January last, he was promoted to be assistant book-keeper, but I am not positive as to the time. In this capacity, he copied letters for me. I have seen him write.

Mr. Morris—Did you become acquainted with his hand writing from seeing him write.

Witness—I do not exactly understand the import of the question. I have seen him write frequently?

Mr. Morris repeated his question, and explained, and the witness then said that he was acquainted with prisoner's handwriting.

Mr. Morris then handed to the witness a MS. book (being the private diary of Robinson), and asked him if that was in the handwriting of the prisoner. The witness replied:—"I dare not swear it is—there is a considerable variety of hands in the book itself."

Mr. Morris—Can you see any part of the book where you can identify the prisoner's handwriting.

Witness—Some parts of the book look something like the character of his handwriting; I have little opportunity of judging of any part of his writing except from what I have seen in my books, and that is a plain business-hand character —unlike what I see generally in the book. On looking carefully over the book, I cannot see any writing that I would venture to swear positively to be his. I would not like to swear positively to the handwriting of any man in the world, and if the Court please I will state my reasons.

Mr. Morris—Is it because you would not like to swear to the handwriting of any man in the world, that you do not choose to swear to the handwriting in that book?

Witness—No, sir, that is only one of my reasons; there are some parts of the book where there is writing that I believe to be the prisoner's, but I shall hesitate to swear to it positively.

Mr. Morris—Please, sir, point out such parts as you believe to be his.

Witness—If I say even that I believe the parts to be his, I should qualify my assertion by stating that I was in doubt whether the handwriting was his, or that of another person in my employ, or whose handwriting is very similar to what I see throughout the book.

Mr. Morris—What person do you mean, sir?

Witness—Mr. Francis P. Robinson.

Mr. Morris—Is he in New York, sir?

Witness—He is not; he is in Europe.

Mr. Morris—When did he go to Europe?

Witness—On the 26th of Feburary last.

Mr. Morris—Look at the latter part of the book, sir, and at the dates, and see, after the date of which you speak, whether you find any handwriting that you believe to be the writing of the prisoner.

Mr. Maxwell objected to this course of the examination as illegal, and as not being within the ordinary rule of evidence.

Mr. Phenix replied, and after a brief technical discussion, Judge Edwards decided that it was quite proper to ask of the witness his belief as to the handwriting of the prisoner, and that his belief on the subject was admissible testimony.

Mr. Morris then handed the book or journal to the witness,

and asked him to mark with a pencil such pages in it as he believed to be in the handwriting of the prisoner at the bar.

The witness then took the book and marked a great number of pages, after which it was handed to the Counsel for the prosecution.

Mr. Morris then handed to the witness a number of letters that were found in the room of Helen Jewett, bearing the name of Richard P. Robinson, and which were sent by him to the deceased either by messengers or through the post office. Out of fifteen of the letters of the description then exhibited to the witness, he only expressed his belief that one of them was in the handwriting of the prisoner.

Frederick W. Gourgous, examined by Mr. Phenix, for the prosecution—I am a clerk in the employ of Dr. Chabert, the Fire King. He keeps an apothecary's store. Was in the store of Dr. Chabert on the Saturday evening preceding the murder of Helen Jewett.

Mr. Phenix—Did you know the prisoner at the bar,—Robinson?

Witness—Not by that name, sir. Knew him by the name of Douglas.

Mr. Phenix—Are you certain that he is the person?

Witness—Am not very positive, but think he is. It is some time since I saw him before that day. I believe the prisoner at the bar, to the best of my knowledge, is the same person who called himself by name Douglas. I think I have seen him four or five times in Mr. Chabert's store. Have seen him in the back room of the store. Never saw him write in the back room. Remember on one occasion he called at the store and wished to procure of me some poison; believe this was a day or two before I heard of the murder. There was another person in the store at the time. The name of the person was Francis Meyers. The poison that he asked for was arsenic. He said that he wanted it for the purpose of killing rats. We did not sell any to him. We are not in the habit of selling it to anybody.

Cross-examined by Mr. Maxwell—Have been in the employ of the Fire King four years. The store is 324 Broadway. We do a great deal of business, and a number of persons are frequently in the store. Had seen the prisoner several times in the house before the murder. The last time that I saw him there was on the Saturday night before the murder. We are always in the habit of refusing to sell arsenic to strangers and others. It was after dark when he called to buy the arsenic. We have frequent applicatious in the course of a year for arsenic for killing rats. It is a very common thing. I have mentioned this circumstance before to Mr. Lowndes. I forget exactly how long it is since I mentioned this to Mr. Lowndes. My memory is bad, but not very bad. I think I mentioned this circumstanee to Mr. Lowndes about two weeks after the young man came to purchase the arsenic. I did not go to Mr. Lowndes to tell him the circumstance; he came to me I did not mention it to any one except to Mr. Chabert. I did not mention to Mr. Lowndes after Robinson was arrested for the murder that a person of the name of Douglas had been to our store to buy some poison. The first time that I saw Mr. Robinson, the prisoner at the bar, knowing him to be Mr. Robinson, was in this court. I knew him before as Mr. Douglas. One or two persons in the court pointed him out to me as Mr. Robinson.

[The witness was here requested by the counsel to point out to him any gentleman who informed him that the prisoner was Mr. Robinson, and he pointed out two persons from among the spectators,—a Mr. Rockway, and a Mr. Trowbridge.]

The cross-examination of the witness was continued—I did not know the prisoner at the bar as Mr. Robinson, until he was pointed out to me in the court. I know Mr. Brink. Mr. Brink did not point him out to me. We have frequently had prostitutes in our store and office, the same as I expect every other apothecary in this city has. There is a private office attached to the store, and I have seen females in there frequently. I have not seen more there since the murder of Helen Jewett than before.

By Mr. Phenix (handing a paper to the witness)—This paper is in my hand-writing. It was given by me to the prisoner. It is a receipt for money paid by him to Dr. Chabert. The person to whom I gave that paper is the same person who called to buy the arsenic.

By Mr. Maxwell—I meant to say, when I said that I did not know the prisoner, and asked persons where he was, that I did not know where he was seated.

[Mr. Maxwell here cross-examined the witness so rigidly that he became completely confounded. The counsel closed with some impassioned remarks, which led to loud plaudits from the audience. The judge put a stop to the uproar, however, and the counsel took his seat.]

By Mr. Phenix—I mind just now that the first time I knew prisoner by the name of Robinson was in the court; but I know that the person I knew as Douglas is Robinson. Knew this from Mr. Chabert.

By Mr. Maxwell—There were no persons but Mr. Meyers and myself in Doctor Chabert's when the arsenic was called for.

Newton Gilbert, examined by Mr. Morris, for the prosecution—Know the prisoner. Have known him two years. Have seen him write. Think I can tell his handwriting.

[The diary of the prisoner was here shown the witness, and he was asked if it, or any part of it, was in the handwriting of the prisoner.]

The witness continued—Do not believe it is all in his handwriting; do not think it is. It resembles it very much.

[After carefully looking over the leaves of the journal one by one, the witness deposed that he thought some of them were in the handwriting of the prisoner; and he marked twelve pages with a pencil which he believed to be so. The remainder of the pages he could not, he said, unequivocally recognize to be in the prisoner's handwriting, although he said they resembled it very much. The witness identified a part of the title page of the journal as being in the handwriting of the prisoner, namely, the words:—"New York, June, 1834." The counsel then showed the witness seventeen letters bearing the prisoner's signature addressed to Helen Jewett, nine of which he could not identify as being in the handwriting of the prisoner, but he swore to eight of them as being so.]

Examination of the witness continued—I have on one occasion, I think, seen the witness wear a cloth cloak; it was about the latter part of February last, or the beginning of March; I cannot give a description of the cloak more than any other gentleman's. I met him in the day time at the corner of John and Gold streets, when he wore such a cloak.

This witness was not cross-examined.

Dr. Walker was called upon the stand as a witness for the prosecution, but before he was sworn, the district-attorney requested him to stand down, and he called

Elizabeth Stewart, who, being sworn, deposed as follows:— I have seen the prisoner at the bar; the first time I ever saw him was in August last, in Reed street; I kept the house in Reed street that he visited; he came to see me about a room that he wanted. [The District-Attorney was about to ask for whom he wanted the room, when Mr. Price objected to the question, and the Court sustained the objection. The District-Attorney then stated that the principal object of his asking the question, was to prove that the prisoner at that time went by the very name which the clerk of Dr. Chabert knew him by. Mr. Price objected to this description of evidence as inadmissible and illegal, and stated the circumstances of the prisoner attempting to obtain poison for the purpose of killing Helen Jewett, or any other woman, was not proper evidence under this indictment,—in which the date, the hour, the weapon, and death were specifically charged—and therefore any evidence in corroboration of it could not be received. The Court took the same view as to the admissibility of the evidence as was expressed by the learned gentleman (Mr. Price), and Judge Edwards decided that the objection was well taken and well provided.]

The witnes was not cross-examined, and no other question being asked of her by the counsel for the prosecution, she left the court.

Mr. Morris, under the direction of the district-attorney, now offered to read the letters of the prisoner to Helen Jewett which had been proved to be in his handwriting, and admitted in evidence.

Mr. Hoffman rose to object to their being read, and he made his objection in a brief and energetic address to the court, in the course of which he was anticipated by the District-Attorney who withdrew his proposition, on the ground that he had himself some doubt as to the legality of their admission as testimony for the prosecution, against the accused.

The District-Attorney then said that, at this stage of the proceedings, he should rest the prosecution, and then the counsel for the prisoner consulted together; soon after which the defence was opened by Mr. Ogden Hoffman in one of those brilliant effusions, which in the course of his long and extensive practice, justly acquired for him an imperishable celebrity. He detailed in the course of his address the course which the counsel for the prisoner would pursue in conducting the defence of their client, and spoke with keen and cutting severity of the reputation and character of the witnesses who had been produced for the prosecution. He dwelt at considerable length upon the disadvantages under which the prisoner labored in not being able, from his comparatively obscure situation in life, to produce witnesses to prove where he was on the night of the murder, and mentioned in illustration of this, the fact that although he (the prisoner), was eating oysters and taking wine at a certain refectory in this city, as late as eleven o'clock on the night of the murder, yet from his not being known, as public men generally were, (wherever they go) by the persons who were present, he was unable to avail himself of their testimony, as they could not again identify or recognize him.

The learned Counsel then adverted, in emphatic terms, to the course that had been adopted by certain New York papers, in reference to the accused, taking advantage of the most minute and trifling circumstances to turn the tide of public prejudice against him. In proof of this, he pointed directly to an unfair paragraph which had appeared in the *Sun* in relation to the prisoner, having had his head shaved since he had been in prison,—and paid a tribute to the papers which had not resorted—for profit or effect—to such mean subterfuges, as honorable and worthy exceptions to the culpable conduct of some conductors of newspapers in the city. In conclusion, the learned gentleman stated, that he and his associate counsel should rely greatly for the complete exculpation of their client by proving by the testimony of a highly respectable tradesman a positive *Alibi*, showing that the prisoner up to past ten o'clock, on the night of the 9th of April last (the night of the murder), was smoking cigars in a grocery store in this city, situated full a mile and a half from the house of Rosina Townsend, in Thomas street. After finishing his opening address (the peroration of which was loudly applauded by the spectators and persons generally in the court room), the learned counsel called as the first witness for the defence:—

Robert Furlong, who, on being sworn, was examined by Mr. Hoffman, and deposed as follows—Keep a grocery store at the corner of Nassau and Liberty streets. Keep a family grocery store. It is about twenty feet wide and sixteen feet deep.

Have kept there twelve months; and before that I kept at the corner of Liberty and Nassau street. Have been a grocer twenty-five years. Am now thirty-three years of age, and have been in the business with Miles Hitchcock the time I have mentioned. Was brought up by Miles Hitchcock. Know the prisoner at the bar by sight. He has often been in my store to buy segars. Always thought that he was a clerk in the neighborhood. Never knew his name or occupation. I heard an account of the murder of Helen Jewett read from the newspaper by a boy in my store. This was on the Monday morning after the murder. The prisoner was in my store the Saturday night previous to the murder. He came there, as near as I can say, about half-past nine o'clock. He bought at the store a bundle of segars, containing twenty-five. After he bought the segars, he lighted one, and took a seat on a barrel, and smoked there until ten o'clock. When the clock struck ten, that gentleman (the prisoner) took out his watch and looked at it. He said that his watch, which was a small silver lepine, was one minute past ten o'clock. I also took out my watch, which I had regulated on that day by Mr. Harold, of Nassau street, and compared my watch with his. When the clock struck, my partner said, "There's ten o'clock, and it is time to shut up." That was our usual time, and the porter went out to put up the shutters. Before he shut up, he brought into the store out of the street a number of barrels that were standing there. Robinson remained seated in the store until he did this, smoking all the time, and by the time the porter got the store closed, he had nearly got through the second segar. When we got completely shut up, Mr. Robinson remarked to me that he was encroaching on my time. I replied, "O, no, not at all; I shall remain at the store until the boy returns." When Mr. Robinson first came into the store, my partner was asleep, and he remained dozing, with his head laid back, and his mouth wide open, until Mr. Robinson, in a jocular manner, knocked the ashes off his second segar upon his face, which awoke him. He woke just before the clock struck. He then wore a dark colored frock coat and cap. Before he went away, he stood a short time on the stoop, and afterwards said, "I believe I'll go home; I'm tired," and then bade me good-night. It must have been full ten or fifteen minutes after ten when he left my store. I should think it to be a full mile from my store to Thomas street. I cannot be mistaken in what I have stated as to the prisoner's being at my store on Saturday night, and at the time and the hour that I have mentioned. When I first heard the murder read on the Monday morning after the murder, I did not think very much about it, the woman being one of those characters that so often appear in the papers. It was about Wednesday following before I thought anything about Mr. Robinson, and learning then that he was one of Mr. Hoxie's clerks in Maiden lane, and not having seen of him for two or three days, I had the curiosity to pass by that store, but did not see him within. I still felt certain that it must be he, and went up to the Bellevue, knowing the keeper, to see him. I cannot say positively what day of the week this was. It was about a fortnight after the murder. My porter boards in my house. I am a married man. I live with my wife. My porter remains at my house on Sunday, and on the Sunday of the murder he informed me of the circumstances in relation to it that he had heard. As soon as I saw him at Bellevue I recognized him as being the same person that I saw in my store on the Saturday night to which I had reference. He also recognized me, and called me by name. Told him I was sorry to see him in that situation, but that justice would be done him. I am now positive that the prisoner here is the person who was in my store on the ninth of April. I cannot be mistaken in this. Am not related to the prisoner, nor to any of his connections, in any way, even in the most distant manner. It was my intention to have gone out of the city with my wife, and should have done so, if you (Mr. Hoffman) had not called upon me for the purpose of appearing as witness in the trial, and in justice to Mr. Robinson.

Cross-examined by Mr. Phenix—I did not positively know that the prisoner was a clerk; I only supposed, from his youth, that he could not be an employer. He had been in my store frequently before the Saturday night of which I have spoken. I cannot say precisely how many times, but perhaps twenty times within a month or so. He has often lighted segars in my store, and sometimes he has stopped to smoke there ten or fifteen minutes. He made several remarks while he remained in the store on the Saturday night. Remember some remarks that he made about the weather, about its being unpleasant. I was reading the paper on that night nearly the whole time that he was there—the *New York Evening Post.* It did not rain on that night, but it was damp. I know that it was damp, because I remember the watchman coming up to me, just as I was leaving the store, and saying to me, "I've brought my coat with me to-night. It appears as if we were going to have a storm." I think that when the prisoner was in my store on Saturday night he wore dark clothes entirely—coat, vest, and pantaloons. I did not know that the prisoner was a clerk in Mr. Hoxie's until I saw him at Bellevue. I began to think, from what I had read in the papers, the person arrested for the murder must be the young man I had seen at my store. I began to think this the man after reading a minute description of him in one of the papers. I forget which of the penny papers it was. It gave a description of his person, his stature, his dress, and general appearance, that exactly agreed with the young man who came to my store. I remember meeting you, at the prison, and asking your permission to see Robinson ; I did then state to you that I did not know young Robinson, and that I wished very much to find out whether I could identify him. Had been there to see him before that, and had seen him, and the time that I met you there I went up with an order to see him from Mr. Hoxie, but they would not let me in, as they said the order was from a Whig, and I therefore asked you for an order. Some weeks might have elapsed from the time I first went to see him, and the time I met you. Mr. Burnham, one of the keepers, was present when I first went there, and I told him that my object in wishing to see Robinson was mere curiosity, to ascertain whether or not I knew him. Mr. Burnham went up with me to the cell, and he called him out. When he came out, I said to Mr. Burnham, "Now let us see whether he will speak to me," and as soon as he came up to me he shook hands and said, "How d'ye do, Mr. Furlong." The second time I went to see Mr. Robinson at Bellevue, Mr. Lyons accompanied me to his cell, and told me I could not say anything to him without his being present. I told him I did not wish to say anything, that I merely wished to have a good look at the prisoner, in the event of my being brought up as a witness, so that I could not be mistaken in him. Was not in Robinson's company three minutes at the second time I went to see him. I merely asked him how he was, and he said very well. Mr. Burnham told me that if I knew the facts that I said I did, I ought to communicate them to the prisoner's counsel. Subsequent to this, Mr. Hoxie's clerk called upon me, and requested me to go and see the gentleman. I did see him, and told him the whole story. No one ever told me that my testimony would be very material in this case. I did not know that I should be called upon as a witness until lately. Did not know it until just as I was going out of town, and then Mr. Hoffman requested me to remain in the city, saying that I should be wanted. Afterwards received a subpœna to attend this trial. I don't vary being in my store of an evening, perhaps once a month.

By Mr. Price—From the time that I saw Mr. Robinson at my store on the Saturday night, I have no doubt in my mind up to the present time, that he is the person who was there; I am positive of it.

By Mr. Maxwell [holding up a lepine watch, which he took from Robinson's desk]—Have no doubt that is the watch that Robinson showed me on Saturday night, when he was at my store. I remember that in comparing his watch with mine, I remarked, from its thickness, that it was a shad.

Joseph Hoxie, Sr., recalled by Mr. Maxwell—The watch now presented is one that I have known the prisoner to wear several months. I think I can positively identify it, although there are no particular marks upon it. I bought the watch for him myself.

Mr. Furlong, recalled by Mr. Morris—The person from whom I had the order to go to Bellevue the second time, was Mr. Hoxie. I presented it to Mr. Lyons, and he threw it away, saying it was from a Whig, and that the fellow who wrote it, had nothing to do with them; that he had no power there.

By Mr. Morris—I think Mr. Lyons was in jest when he made this remark. Indeed, I feel assured that he was in jest, as he treated me in a very polite and gentlemanly manner afterwards.

[It being now near ten o'clock, Mr. Price suggested the propriety of adjourning before any other witnesses were called, and the court complied with the suggestion of the gentleman, by ordering the court to be adjourned until eleven o'clock on Monday morning, when the defence of the prisoner would be resumed.]

Each day's progress in this interesting trial seemed but to increase the interest and excitement which existed in the public mind since its commencement, and the gates of the City Hall were again surrounded on Monday by a dense and anxious multitude.

The proceedings were resumed by Mr. Hoffman's calling upon the stand as a witness for the defence

Peter Collyer, who being sworn, deposed as follows—I am a watchman; belong to the city watch, and first district, under Captain Hall. Was on duty on the night of the murder. Was on my post between Franklin and Chapel streets on that night. I heard the alarm rap from the house in Thomas street; proceeded down Chapel street from Franklin, and I enquired of some persons who were in the street where the alarm came from. Think I was the fifth man who got to the house. Remained at the house until daylight. Saw Rosina Townsend, that night, the keeper of the house. Had some conversation with her. Conversed with her so as to endeavor to find out who committed the murder. Asked her if she knew the person who was in the room on that night with Miss Jewett. She told me that she knew him by the name of Frank Rivers. Asked her if she thought that that was his right name, and she told me that she did not know whether it was or not. I then asked her if she knew him in case she should see him, and she said she would not by daylight. She went on to say that he had not visited the house more than four or five times, and that when he came he wore a cap, and covered his face with a cloak, so that she would not be able to recognize him if she saw him, or that she had no opportunity of seeing his face, and should not know him if she met him in the street. This was said in the presence of some of the girls. I presume that every girl in the house was in the room at the time. There were six or seven there. She said that he went upstairs into Helen Jewett's room. Understood her that there was a bottle of champagne called for, which she (Mrs. Townsend) carried up. Asked her if she had an opportunity of seeing him when she took the wine up, and she said that she had not, as Helen took the wine from her at the door, and she immediately afterwards came down stairs. She did not say where he was, whether in bed or not. Then asked the girls who were sitting round, collectively and individually, if any of them knew the young man. With the exception of one, they all replied that they did not.

Cross-examined by Mr. Phenix—There were other men in the room besides myself when the conversation took place—Mr. Secor and Mr. Lane. She did not say that she saw any person in Helen Jewett's room. This conversation was loud enough for all persons in the room to have heard it—or, at all events, I think so. She said she let a person in that answered to the name of Frank Rivers. I did not understand her that it was in the entry that he put his cloak up to his face. I understood her that he always came in the door with his cloak up to his face, and that this was the way he always came. She did state that she did not see his face, and that she could not swear positively that it was him. The purpose of making the inquiries that I did make, was to detect the murderer. I enquired of her where this Frank Rivers lived. Her answer was that she did not know. One person present, I think it was Miss Stevens, who occupied a room adjoining Helen Jewett's (at the south-east corner of the house), stated that she knew him. Miss Stevens stated that he attended a dry goods store in Pearl street, a few doors from Chatham, and that if it was a week day, she could find him in a few minutes. Miss Stevens did not give me his name, nor any other person. They all said that they did not know him by any other name than Frank Rivers. Upon getting this information, I went in company with Mr. Lane, a watchman, for Mr. Brink. We went to his house and called him up, and he came after us. I did not know Mrs. Townsend before this. I was not in court when she testified. I have not seen her since to my knowledge. This is not the first time of my being in court. Came into court on Friday. Only knew that the person I spoke to was Mrs. Townsend because she appeared to be mistress of the house, and the girls in the house called her by that name. She did not say a word about the lamp having been lit in the entry when she let Frank Rivers in. If she said anything on the subject, I must have heard it. In the course of the conversation, she might have said other things that I do not now recollect. I am positive that she did not say that she saw Frank Rivers' face by the light of the lamp when she let him in. She did not say anything about seeing a person in the room when she let him in; she did not say a word about the door swinging open towards the wall when she took the champagne up. She did not say anything as regards the light in the room, or where it

13

was standing. I did not hear her say that she saw a light standing in the back room at three o'clock in the morning, but she said that she saw a light standing in the entry ; I cannot be mistaken about that. I am as certain that she said that as I am of any other fact that I have sworn to. She said that she found the back door on the jar. She said that the light in the entry was a round lamp—that there were but two in the house—one belonging to Miss Stevens' room and the other to Miss Jewett's room. She went on to say what she did when she discovered that the back door was open. She stated that when she first observed the light, she did not go immediately down to see about it, but a few minutes afterwards she went to see about it, and she thought that some of the girls had gone into the yard. She then went down in a short time, opened the door, and called to see if any person was in the yard ; she called two or three times and got no answer ; she then took a light and went up stairs to Maria Stewart's door, which she found locked. From there she went to Helen Jewett's room, and opened the door, when the smoke burst out upon her face. I did not go with Mr. Brink in pursuit of the prisoner ; Mr. Noble, I believe went. I saw them go off. To my knowledge there were no other watchmen there. Lane and Seers were present when I had the conversation with Mrs. Townsend. At the time I had a conversation with Mrs. Townsend, Mr. Lane also had some coversation with her. Mr. Lane, Mr. Palmer, Mr. Carter and myself, all went, I think, into the house together ; when I first went into the house, I found Mrs. Townsend standing on the platform of the stairs, up stairs near Helen Jewett's door. When we got to the house we found the watchmen there—Gardner, Van Norden and Hall. Mr. Van Norden let me in ; the fire was not quite extinguished when we got to the house, but it was not blazing. All the watchmen had something to say to Mrs. Townsend when they first went in, but I don't know what any of them said in particular. Talked principally about the persons that had been there the night before, with Helen Jewett. I heard Mr. Lane ask Mrs. Townsend some questions about the person who was in the house the night before. I did not pay particular attention to what he said to her. Don't know whether any other watchman asked her any questions. Some part of what she told me, she told me without putting any questions to her. After our conversation finished, I went into another room. After I had heard the conversation I have spoken of, I communicated it to a number of watchmen in the watch house. I mentioned it to Mr. Secor, Mr. Garland, Mr. Jagger, and Mr. Griffin, I told all these persons that Mrs. Townsend had represented to me that she did not see Frank Rivers' face when he came into the house. Don't recollect that I told these persons, or any of them, that she informed me there was a light standing in the entry. Don't know that I stated to any of them that she came down and found the door open. I think that I told them all that she had stated to me with the exception of the lamp being in the entry, and the door being open. Mrs. Townsend told me when she spoke about the lamp being in the entry, that it was by the back door on the floor. I can't be positive that she said so, but I understood her to say so. Have had no communication with the prisoner's counsel about what I could testify in relation to this affair, except with Mr. Maxwell this morning. Now, I recollect, I think I had some similar conversation with Mr. Hoffman on Friday. I told those gentlemen what I have told here, right off, and without being interrogated by them; I think I have told more here than I told them.

By Mr. Maxwell—I am a charcoal inspector as well as a watchman; have lived in New York twelve years; have been a city watchman since October last; have had no conversation with Mr. Hoxie, Mr. Robinson, Senr., (the father of the prisoner), or any other of his friends or relations, in relation to this affair, and I have no other motive under heaven in coming here to testify than to speak the whole truth. The room in which Maria Stevens slept was only divided from Helen Jewett's room by a thin partition of lath and plaster. [Mr. Maxwell here asked Mr. Phenix if he had Maria Stevens in attendance among his list of witnesses for the prosecution. Mr. Phenix replied that she was dead, that on the morning of the murder she caught a severe cold which resulted in her breaking a blood-vessel; and that she died a few days since. In stating this Mr. Phenix remarked that had she lived she would have been a most important witness for the prosecution.] Examination of witness continued by Mr. Maxwell—Maria Stevens, the girl now said to be dead, is the girl who informed me that she knew who Frank Rivers was, and where he lived. She said that on one occasion she had played at cards with him.

Rosina Townsend recalled by Mr. Maxwell—I know a colored girl named Sarah Dunscombe. That girl told me I think that Frank Rivers had been in Helen Jewett's room on the Thursday preceding the murder. I do not believe that I said positively that Frank Rivers (Robinson), was at my house on the Thursday preceding the murder; think that I said it was on the Wednesday or Thursday preceding. If Sarah Dunscombe said that it was Thursday I should be inclined to believe her, although I am not governed in anything that I say by her opinions or statements. I repeat that I think the prisoner was at my house on the Thursday preceding the murder, but I am not certain. It might be on the Wednesday preceding. Maria Stevens room was adjoining Helen Jewett's. Maria Stevens died on Wednesday week last, I think it was. She died at the house of Mrs. Gallagher, the female who has been examined as a witness in this case.

Mr. Maxwell here asked the witness if she knew or had heard of any man having committed suicide since the murder who was in her house on the night of the murder?

Mr. Phenix objected to the question, but the court overruled the objection.

Mr. Maxwell then repeated the question, and the witness answered that she never heard of such a suicide.

By Mr. Phenix—I mentioned the circumstance of the white mark at the back of the prisoner's head before I saw any account in one of the newspapers of his having his head shaved while in prison. I did read such an account in one of the papers. Prior to seeing that publication, I mentioned the circumstance to you (Mr. Phenix) and Mr. Morrill. Mentioned it at Mr. Morrill's office. Saw a watch and chain and ruby ring that were found in Helen Jewett's room. I connot exactly say who took possession of them. I think one of the watchmen brought them to me, and I think I afterwards delivered them to one of the officers of justice; think it was the coroner. Know of nothing else found in Helen's room except her books and clothing. A box of things was afterwards brought to me that I understood to belong to Helen Jewett, to be taken care of. Did not tell any watchman, nor any other person on the morning of the tenth of April that I did not see the face of Frank Rivers when I let him in. Don't know that I know a watchman named Collyer. Did not to my knowledge state anything to any watchman or any other person in relation to the murder, different from what I stated on my direct examination. Did not tell any watchman that I found a lamp lit in the entry standing upon the floor near the back door.

By M . Price—I do not recollect that I had any conversation with any watchman. I do not recollect that any watchman interrogated me at all on that morning, until after the coroner's inquest. The coroner's inquest did not sit until past nine o'clock. I am almost positive that I did not converse with any watchman on that morning. I called them in to assist in extinguishing the fire. Last Thursday, Friday, and Saturday, I spent the principal part of my time in the grand jury-room in the building across the park. I was in company with the ladies there,—Miss Salter, Miss French, Miss Johns, Miss Caroline Stewart, Miss Elliott, and Miss Brown. The colored girl, Sarah Duncombe, was also with us. During those three days no one came to us except one person on one evening to converse with us about the trial. I know that Miss Salter and Miss French have been examined, because they spoke of it when they returned from the court. They have spoken a great deal about what passed in the court, but I took very little notice of what they said. Have heard Sarah Dunscombe say she thought Frank Rivers was the person who was with Helen Jewett on Thursday. The girls and I have dined together every day except one during the progress of this trial. Since Sarah Dunscome left my house, until the commencement of this trial, I have not seen her.

By Mr. Phenix—I have been requested not to hold conversation with any one in reference to this affair, and I have invariably observed the injunction, and when the girls have spoken to me, I begged them not to do so. All the girls who were in my house at the time of the murder remained there until the Monday following.

Oliver M. Lowndes, police magistrate, examined by Mr. Hoffman—I conducted the examination of witness, in conjunction with the coroner, at the coroner's inquest held upon the body of Helen Jewett. Rosina Townsend and Sarah Dunscombe were present at the examination. Rosina Townsend stated in her examination, in reference to the voice which she heard at the door on the Saturday night, that she knew it to be Robinson's, on receiving the second answer. If she had not known it to be his, she said, she would have opened the window to see who it was, before opening the door. I do not recollect that on that occasion, she said a word about Bill Easy's voice, or even mentioned his name. I am very well satisfied that in some of my conversations with Rosina Townsend, she stated that she believed that Robinson was at her house on the Thursday night preceding the murder. I am not certain that she stated this under oath. Not a word was said by her about the bald place on Robinson's head. She stated that Robinson was lying in bed when she went up with the champagne, on his side, with his book a little raised on his elbow. I think she stated that there were two lights in the room, a lamp on the mantle piece, and a candle by which he was reading. I remember that you, (Mr. Hoffman) asked her if the light was between her and Robinson when she was at the room door, but I forget the reply. She stated that when she took up the champagne, she remained but a few moments—but she had no business to remain there. She said that the door went back against the wall, and she had refused to go out of the room as she did not think that she had any business to remain there. Sarah Dunscombe in her examination, stated that Robinson was with Miss Jewett on the Thursday preceding the murder, and I understood Mrs. Townsend in her examination, as confirming her statement. Sarah Dunscombe described a person being with Helen Jewett on Saturday evening, (the night of the murder,) between five and six o'clock. That person, it appeared, turned out to be Mr. Strong, who has been examined as witness here, but from the positiveness with which Sarah stated that it was Robinson, I was at first led to believe that it was him. She said that the person she referred to sat in Helen Jewett's room, upon a chair near the bed, with Helen Jewett upon his knee, and that his position was such, that she could not see his full face. Sarah stated that on Friday morning Helen Jewett showed her a portrait, and asked her if it was not a good likeness of the person who was there on the evening previous, (Thursday). This was Robinson's portrait, and Sarah said that it was a good likeness. She stated that the person who was with Helen on Saturday was the same person who was with her on Thursday, and on Robinson's being pointed out to her at the coroner's inquest, she identified him, as she had seen him at both times.

By Mr. Phenix--When Rosina Townsend was examined at

the police office, she was under oath. Mr. Resolvent Stephens, late clerk in the Police office, wrote down her answers to the interrogatories I put to her. Sarah Dunscombe was also examined under oath, and I wrote down her examination. The answers written down were precisely those given by the person under examination, in reply to interrogatories proposed to them. (The written examination of these persons was handed to the witness, and he identified it as being that which had been taken at the police office.)

By Mr. Hoffman—I remember that in the cross-examination of Mrs. Townsend and Sarah Dunscombe, the clerk, at one time, suspended writing, and Mr. Price requested him to go on with his writing, as the examination might be material testimony, in the trial of the prisoner.

By Mr. Phenix—Some questions were put, and answers given on examining Mrs. Townsend and Sarah Dunscombe at the police office, but were not written down. They were not written down because they were considered to be irrelevant, immaterial. I discovered a number of letters in Helen Jewett's room when I was at Mrs. Townsend's house on the morning when the murder was discovered. I read one letter in the room which I could again identify. The carrier took a number of letters away from the room of the deceased, which he subsequently brought to me. After they were placed in my possession, I took them home and read the most of them. [Some bundles of letters were here handed to the witness, and he identified them as being the same that were found by himself and the coroner, in the room, trunks, and bureau of Helen Jewett.]

Examination continued:—A bureau and two trunks were brought from Robinson's room to the police office without the knowledge or authority of Mr. Hoxie, but Mr. Hoxie was present when the contents were examined.

[Before the witness left the stand he explained to the court and jury an important error which he had observed in the diagram of Mrs. Townsend's house and premises, which had been exhibited as testimony in the case.]

Rodman G. Moulton, examined by Mr. Maxwell, for the defence—At the time of the murder of Helen Jewett I lived at No. 42 Dey street, in the same house with the prisoner at the bar. On the Thursday evening preceding the murder, I came to the house by 7 o'clock, and there saw the prisoner. I remained in his company from that until between 12 and 1 o'clock, until he went to bed. He went to the theatre on that night; this was on the 7th of April. The "Maid of Judah," and the "Dumb Belle" were the pieces represented there that night.

Cross-examined by Mr. Phenix—I cannot swear positively whether he went with me to the theatre, or whether he met me in John street. We were both in the theatre when the curtain rose. We remained there from the commencement until the end of the performance; both of the opera and farce. I think that we remained together in the theatre all that evening. We went into the pit until the first performance was over, and then we went into the boxes. I do not think that we discovered any person in the pit on that night we spoke to. I do not recollect to what part of the boxes we went to see the after piece. The theatre was very much crowded on that night. We were part of the time in the second tier, and part in the third tier. The theatre was not so crowded but that we could get a seat in the second or third tier. I saw no person in the third tier that I was acquainted with. I knew Helen Jewett by sight. She was at the theatre on that night. I saw Robinson talk to her on that night; we had met on former occasions, to go to the theatre, at Mr. Parker's coffee room, in John street. I cannot say whether he had on a cloak, on the night we were at the theatre. I have seen him wear a cloak. I cannot say the precise number of times I have seen him wear one. I think not as many as a dozen times. The first time that I saw him with one was during the winter, when the snow was on the ground. I think that I have seen him wear a cloak in the day time once. The one that he wore was a blue cloth cloak. It had a collar and facings of black velvet. There were cords and tassels attached to it.

[The cloak found in the rear of Mrs. Townsend's house on the morning of the murder was here shown to the witness, and he stated that it was in every respect of similar appearance to that worn by Robinson, but he would not positively swear that it was the same.]

Examination continued—I have never seen the cloak that Robinson wore since the murder of Helen Jewett. I do not know what became of his cloak. I have been out sleigh-riding with

Robinson on two occasions. The first time we went to Jamaica, L. I., and the second time to Harlem. I do not know that he had a quarrel with any one either of these times. He wore his cloak on both occasions. I believe Robinson had a night key to get into his boarding-house. All the boarders had night keys. I think, but I am not certain that I opened the door when he came home from the theatre, on the night of the seventh of April. I have been at the house kept by Rosina Townsend. I was there on the evening the murder was committed. I went there in company with Mr. James Teer. I do not know by what name Mr. Teer was known there. I never, to the best of my recollection, heard him called Frank Rivers. A female let us in there, but I don't know her name. I did not then know Mrs. Townsend. I had been to her house twice before the murder of Helen Jewett. I know Elizabeth Salters by name. I saw her on that night. I saw her in the entry. I did not speak to her. Mr. Teer went in with me. He had some conversation with her in the entry.

Mr. Phenix asked the witness what the conversation was, and Mr. Price rose to object to it. He said that a conversation between Miss Salters and Mr. Teer would hardly be evidence. Mr. Phenix withdrew the interrogation, and the examination of the witness proceeded—

Mr. Teer had spoken to Miss Salters about ten minutes. We did not got go upstairs. During one of our sleighrides, Robinson informed me that he had lost one of the tassels of his cloak. On the night that the murder was committed we took tea at our boarding-house at about seven o'clock—that was the hour we generally took it. I did not wear an overcoat on the night I went to the theatre with Robinson. Robinson did not stop any where before we went into the theatre. We both went directly into the pit.

Thomas Garland, examined by Mr. Maxwell, for the defence—I am one of the city watchmen. I belong to Captain Hall's watch. I was stationed on the corner of Thomas and Chapel streets on the Saturday night preceding the discovery of the murder of Helen Jewett. I was on my post from two to four o'clock on the Sunday morning. About twenty minutes past eight o'clock, as near as I can tell, I heard an alarm proceeding from a house in Thomas street, between Chapel and Hudson streets. I proceeded to the house, and found it to be the house of Mrs.Townsend. Not over one minute elapsed from the time of my first hearing the alarm before I got to the house. To the best of my knowledge I was the first watchman who entered that house. Mrs. Townsend told me that nc other watchman had been there. When I first entered the house I saw two men in the room on the right of the entry in company with Mrs. Townsend. From their attitude and appearance, and from their being in their shirt sleeves, I took it that the men were going to fight, and I went to the front door and gve an alarm rap. When I first entered the front door Mrs. Townsend told me that there was a girl murdered in the house, and the room was set on fire. Before I went up stairs I got the assistance of two watchmen, and we all three went up stairs. I went up a-head. This was about ten minutes after my first entering the house. When I got upstairs, I caught a young man in my arms who was standing near the door of Helen Jewett's room. He was undressed. It was dark when I caught him in my arms. After I had been in the house, I saw a female come out of one of the up stairs rooms, having in her hand a hat and band-box; she went downstairs with them, and I did not see anything more of her. or of the young man that I got hold of. As soon as I and the other watchmen got into the house I told Mrs. Townsend to lock the door, and let no one come in or go out but watchmen. At this time there were four men in the house. Shortly afterwards I discovered that the first man whom I had seen had left the house. A number of watchmen at that time had come into the house. After leaving the room where the murdered girl was lying, I went into the yard and looked into the cistern. The lid of the cistern was open. There was a step-ladder standing by the cistern. The cistern is not in the rear of the yard, it is close by the back of the house. If the step-ladder was found in the rear of the yard in the morning, it must have been removed there after I saw it. It was very damp and cold this morning. I found the murdered girl lying upon her stomach, with her back up, with a large cut in the side of her head. From the time that I entered Mrs. Townsend's up to the time that I entered Helen Jewett's room, it must have been fifteen or twenty minutes. I was the first person that threw water upon the fire to extinguish the flames. I called for water when I got in. There was no appearance of any water having previously been thrown upon the fire, or any other attempt having been made to extinguish it.

Cross-examined by Mr. Phenix—I was on the first tour of watch on the night of the murder. It was a dark, wet and drizzly night, but not very cold. I am not positive whether it rained or merely sprinkled on that night. Mrs. Townsend was standing at the door of the room on the right side of the entry when I went in, and the two men were standing inside. I merely thought that they were going to fight because they had their coats off. I don't think that it was one of those very men that fetched water for me; I think it was a female who brought me the water; I don't know that it was Mrs. Townsend; water was first brought up in a pitcher, afterwards in different description of vessels. When I went up stairs, Mr. Hall followed me with a light, and Mrs. Townsend followed him. I only saw two men in the house when I first went in—then I saw the other in the entry. I took hold of the man in the entry and did not let go of him until both he and Mrs. Townsend told me that he did not belong to Helen Jewett's room. After that I found another man, making four in all, that I found there. I don't know where they all went to or what time they got away. I did not see the young man that I found in the entry after I let him go. I did not stop in the room where the fire was burning until I thought it was out. While I was in the room there was a handkerchief found by Mr. Collyer. It was between the pillow and bolster of the bed upon which the murdered girl was laid. It was handed to me; I kept it in my possession, except showing it to a person who was standing near me. At this time some girls had come into the room, and one of them remarked " this is Frank's handkerchief;" I ultimately gave it to Mr. Noble, the assistant captain of the watch. The step-ladder that I saw in the yard is one of a similar description to those generally used in houses.

Jared L. Moore, examined for the defence, by Mr. Maxwell—I am a jeweller and watchmaker; I received a watch this morning from Mr. Hoxie. That watch was bought of me by Mr. Hoxie in March, 1834. [The watch was here exhibited, and it was identified as being the same that Mr. Furlong swore he saw in possession of the prisoner, on the evening of the 9th of April last.]

[Mr. Hoxie was called upon the stand, and he swore that the watch referred to and exhibited by Mr. Morrill, was the same that he had bought for the prisoner at the bar.]

James Tew, examined by Mr. Maxwell, for the defence—I am a clerk. Have been a clerk for four years. Boarded at the same house with the prisoner, No. 42 Dey street. We boarded there at the time of the murder of Helen Jewett. Saw him at his boarding house on the Saturday night preceding the discovery of the murder. We had tea together about seven o'clock, and we went out about half an hour afterwards. I walked out in company with Mr. Moulton and Robinson was with Mr. Tyrrell. We walked a little ahead of them and we missed them on the corner opposite the American Museum. He wore a cloak on that night. He had had that cloak about two months before that. I always understood that he got the cloak from a young man named William Gray, as security for money that he had loaned to Gray. On Saturday night, the 9th of April, I returned to bed about a quarter past eleven o'clock. I occupied a front room on the first floor of the house, No. 42 Dey street; Robinson was my room mate, and he occupied the same bed with me. We occupied the same bed together on the Saturday night preceding the murder. I went to bed first; I awoke during the night. Cannot say what time it was when I awoke. Had no light, or means of judging except from mere guess. As well as I can tell, it must have been between one and two o'clock. I then found the prisoner at the bar in bed with me. It was not at all unusual for me to go to bed before him. A second time during the night, I awoke between the time that I first awoke, and the time that the officers came to our room in the morning. I think it must have been between three and four o'clock when I awoke the second time. I did not look at my watch and had no means of judging except from guess. Robinson was in bed when I awoke the second time. I was awake when the officer came to our room in the morning. Robinson had a particular place for putting his clothing. He generally hung them over the testor of the bed. I saw nothing unusual in their arrangement or the manner in which they were laid when the officers came into our room. On the Sunday morning I heard a knock at the street door. It was an unusually hard knock. The servant went to the door, and on its being opened I heard some inquire if Robinson was within. As Robinson, as I thought, was asleep, I got up and opened our room door, and told the servant that if any one wanted to see Robinson to tell them to come up to our room, as he was in bed. Two men then came in, and as I was getting into bed again, I shook Robinson and told him that two persons wished to see him. He awoke and they asked him if his name was Robinson, and he replied that his name was Robinson. They then told him that they had something to say to him, and he asked them if it was necessary for him to get up; if they could not say what they had to say to him while he was in bed. One of them replied that he wished to see him in private. He got up, partly dressed himself, and went into the hall from the room. He went into the hall with the persons who were there. Did not hear anything that was said on that occasion. Cannot say how the conversation was conducted. Robinson returned to the room and finished dressing himself. After dressing himself he told me that the men wanted him to go with them, and he asked me to go with him. I replied that I would go if he wished it, and he then asked the men if I might go, and they said that they had not any objection. Before I got out of my bed, I called him to the side of the bed and asked him in a whisper, what was the matter. He replied that he did not know. His reply was in a loud voice and he said nothing to me that any person could not hear. From the time that I first awoke him, to the time we went out, I did not notice any confusion or emotion in him different from anything that I have always noticed in his conduct. We proceeded with the men in a carriage which they had at the door to the house of Mrs. Townsend. As we went up Dey street into Broadway, there was a general conversation amongst us. When I got into the carriage it was raining very fast. I remarked that the rain would clear the ice out of the river. Robinson I think, but I am not certain, joined in this conversation. Up to the time of our arriving at Mrs. Townsend's, I witnessed nothing in his conduct indicative of guilt. I remained at Mrs. Townsend's house until about twelve o'clock. Believe he was taken up into the room where Helen Jewett was laid, but I am not certain of this. I did not see him immediately after he saw the body.

By the Judge—I think Robinson was asleep when the officers came to our room.

By Mr Maxwell—When we took tea on the night before the murder, Robinson and I and Mr. Moulton made arrangements to ride out on horseback before breakfast on the following morning. The reason we did not go was that the morning was wet. I got up shortly before the time proposed to go out, and finding it wet, I told Robinson that we could not go. He agreed with me and said that it would be of no use to awake Moulton. At the house of Mrs. Townsend, Mr. Noble asked Robinson if some white marks which he observed on his pantaloons were whitewash, and Robinson told him "no, that it was paint."

[At this stage of the examination, it being half past three o'clock the court took a recess.]

At about three quarters past four o'clock, the court again met in session, and the proceedings were resumed by the continuation of the examination of James Tew by Mr. Maxwell. The witness continued: Was at the house of Rosina Townsend on the Saturday night preceding the discovery of the murder of Helen Jewett. From the time that I lost sight of the prisoner, near the American Museum, on the evening, up to the time that I found him in bed, at one or two o'clock in the morning, I did not see or meet him.

By the Judge—Was not awake when the prisoner came in on the Saturday night, nor did he awake me. Have no positive means of knowing what hour it was, when I awoke. When I awoke, I spoke to the prisoner, and asked him what time he came in. He replied between eleven and twelve o'clock.

Cross-examined by Mr. Phenix—I was examined before the coroner's inquest, between ten and eleven o'clock in the morning; I was also examined before the Grand Jury. The prisoner had, I believe, a night key, to get into the house at any time in the night he pleased. I am not positive of this. I have known him to come home frequently after I went to bed, and I suppose, after other persons went to bed. I have known the prisoner to come home late at night, but I cannot say that he was in the habit of it.

[Mr. Phenix here inquired as to the general habits of the prisoner, but Mr. Maxwell objected to any such questions being put—no proof of good character having as yet, being offered for the defence.—The court sustained the objection, and the examination was resumed.]

Witness resumed—I cannot swear positively that the prisoner ever had a night key, but it is my impression that he had.

I think the prisoner wore a black frock coat on the Saturday night, but I am not quite certain. I do not know positively what sort of pantaloons he then had on. When the officer came to our room in the morning, he put on a pair of drab mixed pantaloons; I am not certain that they were the same pantaloons that he had on when I left him at the American Museum.

By the Judge—I did not observe, on Saturday night, that Robinson had any paint or whitewash upon his pantaloons; on Saturday night, I did not observe any such thing, because I did not notice his pantaloons. I did not observe anything of the kind before we got to Mrs. Townsend's on the Sunday morning, nor afterwards, until it was spoken of by Mr. Noble. Mr. Noble asked Robinson, what is that on your pantaloons; is it whitewash? My attention was then called to it. Think he then had a frock or surtout coat on. It is my impression that it was a double breasted coat, with two rows of buttons in front. When Mr. Noble called Robinson's attention to his pantaloons, I observed there was a white mark on the left side of the right leg, below the knee. That, at all events, is my impression. I was then but a few feet from the prisoner. Cannot say whether that was before or after I was examined by the coroner's jury. Did not discover any white appearance on the other part of his pantaloons. Did not examine any other part of his pantaloons except that which I have spoken of. Cannot say how long I remained with the prisoner at Mrs. Townsend's after I observed the white upon the pantaloons; perhaps half-an-hour. When I parted with the prisoner on that morning, I left him at the house, in Thomas street. I went and spoke of the prisoner after I had been before the coroner's jury. Was before the coroner's jury half-an-hour, perhaps it might be longer. I cannot say how long I was with the prisoner after I had been before the coroner's jury, perhaps three-quarters of an hour; it might be longer. Don't know whether I observed the whiteness upon the pantaloons of the prisoner, before or after the coroner's inquest. Did not call the attention of the prisoner to the white upon the pantaloons at any time that I was there. I never stated that the white upon the prisoner's pantaloons was paint. I have never said, at any time, that Robinson told me he came home at a different time from what I now state. I have not sworn before the Grand

Jury, that Robinson told me he came home at twelve or half-past twelve o'clock, on Saturday night. Cannot say how often, prior to this affair, I had been to Mrs. Townsend's house; I had been there several times. Was in Mrs. Townsend's about two months before the Saturday night preceding the murder. Was known at that house as Frank Rivers. I was frequently called by the persons in the house as the cousin of the other Frank Rivers, (the prisoner at the bar). When I was so called, I never denied it. When I was there on Saturday preceding the murder, I neither saw her, nor made any inquiry after Helen Jewett. I saw no cloak in our bed room on the morning that the prisoner was arrested of the description that he was accustomed to wear. When we started from our boarding house together, on the Saturday night, the prisoner did not tell me where he was going. When he left home on the Saturday evening, it is my impression that Robinson had a quantity of cigars in his room; I cannot tell how many he had. He and Moulton had a box between them. I cannot say whether or not, there were any left in the box on the Saturday afternoon. I think I have seen Mr. Robinson write; I cannot say how often. I am not acquainted with his handwriting; could not tell his handwriting from his cousin's—Mr. B. F. Robinson—the young man who has gone to England. Cannot exactly say whether Robinson kept a journal or not.

[Mr. Maxwell here rose and stated that he thought the District Attorney had disclaimed any intention to go into the subject matter of the letters, papers, books and memorandum found in the bureau and trunk of the prisoner after his arrest. Mr. Phenix said that if it displeased the gentleman—and rather than they should think that their client had not had a fair trial, and had not been liberally dealt with—he would forego any interrogations in reference to these matters.]

Cross-examination continued—The prisoner generally wore a hat in the day time, and a cap at night. I think I have seen him wear a hat in the night time. Think when I spoke to Robinson on the Sunday morning about its being a wet morning, and about our being consequently unable to ride out, as agreed on, that he was only about half awake. Did not hear any charge made against the prisoner while in the carriage, on our way from Dey street to Rosina Townsend's. Did not hear Robinson say to the police officer while in the carriage, that he was at home, at his own house, on Saturday night between nine and ten o'clock. I had no conversation with Robinson before the officers came in the morning. Did not go to sleep again after getting up and looking at the weather.

By Mr. Maxwell—On the Saturday night preceding the murder, I went to Mrs. Townsend's between nine and ten o'clock. I should think it wat near ten o'clock.

William B. Townsend, examined by Mr. Price—I was foreman of the Grand Jury that presented a bill of indictment against the prisoner, for the murder of Helen Jewett. I remember that Mr. Brink was examined as witness. I remember asking Mr. Brink, (and told him to be very particular in his answers)—if, when he first accosted the prisoner, he gave any indication of embarrassment or guilt, or if he did anything that made any impression upon his mind, in relation to whether he was guilty or innocent. He said that while in the coach, after turning up Broadway, he told him that a dreadful crime had been committed. I asked him what impression, in telling him this, had been made upon his, (Brink's) mind. He said in the first place, his impression was, that he was guilty—in the next place, he thought he was innocent; but, on the whole, after mature reflection, he thought he was guilty I think I cannot be mistaken that this was his answer I read a report of Mr. Brink's testimony in one of the papers. I cannot say which, and I thought there was some discrepancy between what he then gave, and what he gave before the Grand Jury.

Cross-examined by Mr Phenix—I don't remember that Brink swore before the Grand Jury, that Robinson did not betray any emotion of guilt until passing the police office. In reference to the time that Robinson went home, and went to bed, on the Saturday night. I perceive, on now referring to my notes, that Mr. Tew, the witness who has just left the stand, swore before the Grand Jury, that he went to bed between eleven and twelve o'clock, and that he (Tew,) and Robinson went asleep together, shortly afterwards.

John Blake, treasurer of Park Theatre, examined by Mr. Maxwell—The Maid of Judah, and the Dumb Belle were the pieces performed at the Park Theatre on the night of Thursday, the 7th of April. These pieces occupy about four hours in their performance. The Woods sung in the Opera of the Maid of Judah, and it occupied a little longer when they performed, than on ordinary occasions, as their songs were frequently encored.

William H. Lane examined—I am a city watchman; have not been examined before in this case, nor have I until to-day, heard any part of the proceeding. I was on my round in the neighborhood of Thomas street, on the night of the 9th of April. Heard the alarm rap given by a watchman, from the house of Mrs. Townsend, No. 41. Immediately went there, and found several persons there. Mrs. Townsend said, in the course of some conversation on the subject, that she believed Frank Rivers was the person who had been with Miss Jewett on the night before. Mr. Collyer asked her if she knew him, and she said that she did not, only by his voice, as he always came into the house with his face muffled up in his cloak. There was some other conversation between Collyer and Mrs. Townsend. She said that there was a bottle of champagne called for. I don't know the precise time that she said it was called for. She said she carried it to the room door, and delivered it to the girl (Helen Jewett). I think she said she saw somebody in bed when she went up with the champagne. She said that she thought Frank Rivers had murdered the girl, but that she did not know him, nor would she know him if she met him in the street, as he always came to the house closely muffled up. The first time that I received a subpœna as a witness in this case was since four o'clock to-day.

Cross examined by Mr. Phenix—Mr. Collyer served the subpœna upon me. He told me that he had been examined as a witness to-day. He did not tell me what he said. He asked me if I remembered what Rosina Townsend said when he interrogated her. Told him that I thought I did recollect in part. He did not tell me that she said she would not know Frank Rivers by daylight. Cannot say whether she did say so or not. Mr. Collyer did not say anything to me that Mrs. Townsend told him anything about a light in the entry. Heard her tell him that there was a lamp in the entry hanging up, by which she let the person in on Saturday night. She stated to him that she found a light standing in the room at the end of the passage, about three o'clock in the morning. It was a glass lamp. Was in the back parlor of Mrs. Townsend's house, and I discovered a pier table there. There was nothing said that I know of, about the pier table in connection with the lamp and light. I cannot say whether or not Mrs. Townsend told Myers that she saw a man in Helen Jewett's bed when she went up stairs with the champagne ; but it is my impression that she did tell him so. Cannot recollect that she said whether or not the person was leaning on his elbow in the bed, or that he had a book in his hand. Do not think that she said anything about the door of the room opening towards the wall when she went up with the champagne. Forget who was in the room besides myself when Mr. Collyer and Mrs. Townsend had this conversation.

By Mr. Maxwell—Mr. Burill saw me at Mrs. Townsend's, but I don't know that he is acquainted with me. I went with Mr. Collyer for Mr. Brink. Mr. Brink must then know that I was there. I was not not examined before the Grand Jury.

Mr. Collyer, recalled by Mr. Maxwell—I was not called before the coroner's inquest or the Grand Jury. Mr. Brink saw me at Mrs. Townsend's, but I don't know that he knew me.

Mr. Brink recalled, by Mr. Maxwell—I have a pair of vases in my house. I bought them two years ago. I bid for a pair of vases at Mrs. Townsend's, and bought them; but I bought them for another man. I bought them for Mr. Tompkins, the police officer. I cannot say why I forgot the vases when I gave my testimony on Saturday. I did not think of them, on Saturday, that's certain. I bought the clock in my own house, and got Welch to pay for it. I think I told the auctioneer that Welch and I and Rosina would settle for the things that we bought.

Alderman Benson—Now recollect, sir, you are under your oath. Did you, or did you not, pay for the vases that you bought?

Witness—Upon my honor, sir, I cannot recollect.

Alderman Benson—Is it not a fact, sir, that there was an understanding between you and Welch and Rosina, that you were not to pay for anything you bought at the sale?

Witness—There was no such understanding that I know of, sir.

Alderman Benson—Now, sir, you have sworn that you paid for the clock; did you do so?

Witness—It was settled for, sir, by Welch; you had better ask him about it.

Mr. Maxwell—No. sir. we want an answer from you.

Witness—All I can say, sir, is that all I got I expect was settled for.

By Mr. Phenix—I and Welch were employed to attend Mrs. Townsend's house at the sale, and one or two days after the murder.

Rosina Townsend, recalled by Mr. Maxwell—There was a clock sold at my sale for thirty dollars. Mr. Brink, I believe, bought it. There were two vases which he also bought. I think for eight dollars. Mr. Welch bought some small pictures. The auctioneer never received any money for them. They settled with me for them. I don't believe they ever paid me any money, but we squared accounts any way. I gave them five dollars a day for their attendance and services.

By Mr. Phenix—I had officers in attendance at my house because of some threatening letters that I received, I know not from whom, in reference to my giving testimony against Mr. Robinson for the murder of Helen Jewett. I gave them five dollars a day, and would have given them more, if I could have afforded it. Sometimes they were at the house both day and night, and sometimes all night.

By Alderman Banks—I do not consider that five dollars per day was too much for the services of the officers. I would have given more if I could have afforded it.

Dennis Brink, recalled by Mr. Maxwell—I did say that I paid the auctioneer, or settled with him, for the clock that I bought at Mrs. Townsend's. I now wish to correct myself.

Alderman Benson—You now wish to correct yourself. I will strike what you have said out of my notes.

William Schrueman, the coroner, recalled by a juror—When the cloak was found in the rear of Mrs. Townsend's yard, it was damp, as if it had been lying upon the ground some time.

By Mr. Maxwell--It had evidently been on the ground, from its dampness, more than half an hour. It must have been there an hour and a half.

By Mr. Phenix—I heard of a watch and gold chain having been found in Helen Jewett's room, and I got them from Mrs. Townsend. I have a clerk; his name is George Runyan. I don't know whether or not he is here to-day. He attended with me the coroner's inquest upon the body of Helen Jewett. There was a box of books and papers brought for safe keeping to me, by one of the police officers, from Rosina Townsend.

The counsel for the defence here rested the case for the prisoner.

Mr. Phenix resumed for the prosecution, and called Daniel Lyons, the keeper of Bellevue Prison, who testified as follows,— I remember Mr. Furlong's calling at Bellevue Prison to see the prisoner. He told me the object of his visit, and said that he suspected that he would be a witness for him if he was the same man that he supposed he was. He said that he had read a description of him in the newspapers, and he expected that he was the same young man who had been in his (Mr. Furlong's) store, on the Saturday night preceding the murder. He said that he (Robinson) had been in his store, and that they compared watches at ten o'clock. When he saw Robinson, he went up to him, and reminded him that he knew him; said that he had seen him in his store on the Saturday night before the murder, and remembered his buying a half a dollar's worth of cigars. Robinson said that he remembered it, and he thanked Mr. Furlong for the trouble that he had taken in his behalf, for the purpose of identifying him, and for his good wishes. Mr. Furlong, on leaving Robinson, told me that he was the man he had expected, and that he should volunteer his testimony to Mr. Hoxie. I remember on a second occasion, Mr. Furlong coming up; but I don't know who let him in to see Robinson. Think I heard something about an order from Mr Hoxie · but I never heard anything said about rejecting an order for admission to the prisoner, because it was from a Whig. Robinson had his head shaved while he was in prison. The first time that I noticed anything particular about Robinson's head was when a young lady was with him, and she said Richard, or Dick, how thin your hair is getting behind. I looked at his head then, and observed a bald spot on the back of his head.

By Mr Hoffman—Know that previous to Robinson having his head shaved, his hair came out continually, and I believe he was advised by Doctor Allen, a surgeon attached to the prison, to have his head shaved. I did not find out that a barber had been called in until he got half through with the operation, and I was then very angry about it, and made some inquiries in relation to it. Thought it was calculated to injure me very seriously. I did not see the bald place in Robinson's head until nearly a week after his arrest, and I know that when you (Mr. Hoffman) heard of it you were very angry, fearing that it would militate against the interests of the prisoner, and said that nothing should be done without consulting counsel.

By Mr. Phenix—I don't exactly know who the girl was that was with the prisoner, when she remarked upon the bald spot on his head. She observed, after noticing the place, "never mind Dick, I will put a patch upon it some of these days."

[At the conclusion of this witness's testimony, Mr. Hoxie got upon the witness stand, and addressed the court in a brief and energetic address, entirely exonerating Mr. Lyons, and his deputy keepers from any imputation as regarded an alleged want of courtesy to him, and the unhappy young man at the bar, during the incarceration of the latter; at the same time testifying to the uniform politeness, kindness and attention as far as their conduct had fallen within his observation. There was a disposition among the audience to applaud his remarks at the conclusion of his address, but the court immediately put a stop to the plaudit.]

Henry Burnham, examined by Mr. Phenix, for the prosecution—I am deputy keeper for Bellevue. I know Mr Furlong. He was admitted by me to the prison to see Mr. Robinson. Was there when he came; Robinson had been at Bellevue three or four weeks when Mr. Furlong first came to the prison:—He did not bring any order or request for admission when he came that I know of. He said he came to see if he could recognise Mr. Robinson as the person who was in his store buying cigars on the Saturday immediately prior to the murder. Went with him to Robinson's cell. Robinson was lying down, and as soon as we went in, he got up. Mr. Furlong said to him, how do you do, Mr. Robinson, and he answered, how do you do, sir, and shook hands with him Mr. Furlong then told him that he thought he had seen him in his store on the Saturday before the murder. Robinson replied that if he had anything to say he had better speak to his counsel. Nothing further of any importance was said by either of them I think I mentioned these circumstances to one or two of the police officers. I think I saw Mr. Furlong at the prison about a week after the time he first called.

Cross-examined by Mr. Hoffman—Knew Mr. Furlong at the time he came to the prison. He said he wanted to see if Mr. Robinson would recognise him. Did not notice any bald place on the prisoner's head. If there had been a bald place, I must have seen it. Almost four weeks after he came to the prison, his hair began to come out, especially on the left side of his head, and when Dr. Allen passed his hands through his hair it came out in clusters. I cannot be mistaken about their not being a bald place on the back of the prisoner's head. I have seen him standing up and lying down, and almost all positions, and have been close behind him, and I have never witnessed anything of the kind. It is about three weeks since Robinson's head was shaved.

By a Juror—I have the utmost confidence in Mr Furlong's integrity and oath I have known him for eight years, and I never knew anything of him but good.

At the close of this witness's examination, the juror who proposed the last material question, stated that the object of his asking it was merely to satisfy some of the jurors who did not know Mr Furlong as well as some of the others.

Mr. Phenix now proposed to read the four letters that had been proved, as having been found in Helen Jewett's room, written by the prisoner at the bar to the deceased. Two of the letters were dated in August, 1836, one without date, and one dated in November.

Mr. Hoffman objected to the letters being read on strictly legal and technical grounds, but the court overruled the objection, and Mr. Morris was about to read them, when

Mr. Maxwell rose and presented to the court an additional objection to their being read, stating that the obvious intent of submitting them as evidence against the prisoner was to show that he had at some distant period entertained malignant feelings towards the deceased, and had, on one or two occasions threatened her with injury. The learned counsel said that if such threats and such letters had not been written immediately antecedent to the murder they ought not to be made use of to prejudice the mind of the jury against the unfortunate accused, and he appealed to the well known magnanimous and benevolent feelings of the District Attorney, and to his mercy and sense of justice, to withdraw the proposition he had made.

Mr. Phenix replied that it was his sense of public justice, and in obedience to the oath he had taken as attorney for the people, that he was induced to urge the proposition he had made, and he did so with feelings towards the unhappy prisoner at the bar, far from being harsh, unfriendly or unkind. Inasmuch, however, said the learned gentleman, as there were some circumstances detailed in the letters referred to which related to other persons entirely unconnected with the prisoner. and an exposure of which pehaps be calculated to do some serious injury, he would, before insisting upon their being read, submit them to the court, for their erasure of any particular which should, by them, be deemed as irrelavent, and not pertinent to the issue on trial.

At the conclusion of the learned counsel's address, he handed the letters in question for the perusal of the court, and while the judges were deliberating upon the disposition they should make of them.

Messrs. Maxwell and Price, alternately rose and addressed the court in opposition to their admissibility as testimony against the accused, principally upon the ground that they were calculated to prejudice his general character in the estimation of the jury, whereas, no attempt had been made by the counsel in his behalf to sustain his good character and reputation.

The learned gentlemen were replied to in a forcible address, by the District Attorney, at the conclusion of which Judge Edwards delivered the opinion of the court, stating that the majority of his associates were of opinion that the letters were not admissible.

[It being now a quarter past nine o'clock, the court was adjourned until ten o'clock next morning.]

FIFTH DAY.

Soon after the judges took their seats next morning, Mr. Phenix rose, and stated to the court that since the adjournment on the previous evening, he had maturely reflected on the decision of their honors in reference to the admissibility or inadmissibility, as evidence against the prisoner, of the four letters which had been proved to be in the handwriting of the latter, and which were found in the room of Helen Jewett after her murder, and he was firmly and decidedly of the impression—with all due deference to the opinion of the court, that the decision which had been given was founded on misapprehension or error. One of the letters (dated November 14th, 1835), was, said the learned counsel, of the utmost importance as regarded its connection with some material evidence that had been already adduced for the prosecution, and he begged, therefore, that the court would reconsider the proposition that had been made, and deliberate upon it, and permit him, at all events, to introduce this document.

Mr. Maxwell (in the absence of his associate counsel, who had not yet arrived in court), said that to obviate any further difficulties in reference to this proffered testimony, and to avoid further discussion, he would, in behalf of the prisoner, consent to the reading of the letter which the gentleman deemed to be so important, if the gentleman would, on his part, stipulate not to offer or read any others, and would permit the counsel for the defence to make use of the other three letters if they should deem it necessary or proper. The District Attorney replied that he would willingly consent to the proposition of the learned gentleman, and the court gave its consent to this arrangement.

Mr. Phenix then read the letter to which he had reference. It was addressed to Miss Helen Jewett, at Mrs. Berry's, Duane street, and was evidently written in a disguised hand, notwithstanding that it was identified to be the prisoner's writing. At that time the deceased generally went by the name of Maria Benson, although she was known to some persons by the name of Helen Jewett. The following is the letter, precisely as it was written, with the exception of a few alterations in the style of punctuation:—

"Miss Maria—I think our intimacy is now old enough for both of us to speak plain. I am glad you used that expression in your note yesterday—"And as long as you pursue a gentlemanly course of conduct," &c., &c. I don't know on what footing I stood with you. Any deviation from the line of conduct which you think I ought to pursue, and I am' blown. All of your *professions, oaths, and assurances*, are set aside to accommodate your new feelings towards me. *Even this very letter* will be used as a witness against me to avenge a forced insult, received at my hands Poor Frank has a thousand insurmountable difficulties to encounter. Banded about like a dog, who as he becomes useless, is cast aside, no longer worthy of a single thought except to be cursed. No sooner extricated from one difficulty than he is plunged into ruin and disgrace by one who he had confidence in, one who professed attachment more sincere than any other, who swore to be true and faithful, and let all *others* be false, she would be my friend till death parted us. Oh, has it come to this, and she the first to forsake me, whom I so ardently endeavored to gain her lasting regard and love: *then* are all vows false, or Frank is indeed altered. He has but two wishes left, either of which he would embrace, and thank his Heavenly Father, *with all the ardor of his soul*, *death*, or a complete alteration and make me what I once was—'tis strange yet 'tis true.

"After reflecting on our situation all night, I arose this morning feverish and almost undecided, and so ill as to be able to attend to but a portion of my business of the day. I have now come to this conclusion, that it is best for us both to dissolve all connection. I hope you will coincide in this opinion, for you well know that our meetings are far from being as sweet and pleasant as they once were, and moreover I concluded from the terms of your last note, that you would not regret such a step. I am afraid it will be the only way for me to pursue a gentlemanly course of conduct. *In my opinion, my conduct*, the last time I was at your house, was far from being gentlemanly or respectful. I behaved myself as I should never do again, let the circumstances be what they might, even if I had to prevent it by never putting my feet into your house again. I was very sorry for it, and now I beg your pardon. I have done to you as I have never done to anybody else (in the case where other gentlemen are concerned). *This*, I hope, will be forgiven, as there's no harm done, and let the circumstances justify the act. H., as we are about to part, allow me to tell you my genuine sentiments.

"I have always made it a point to study your character and *disposition; I admired it more than any other female's I ever knew*, and so deep an impression has it made on my heart that never will the name and kindness of Maria G Benson be forgotten by me; *but for the present we must be as strangers*. I shall call on you to-night to return the miniature and then ask you to part with that which is no longer welcome. That you should think I would use subterfuge to obtain the cursed picture, wounded my feelings to the quick, for God knows *I am not*, nor ever was, as mean as that. *Your note of Wednesday I never received, that I am aware of.* I would not insult you by leaving you to infer that another will receive my visits, for "Pius" I shall remain. Now I have only to say, do not betray me, but forget me; I am no longer worthy of you.

"*Ne ex memoria amitte et ero tuus servus.*

"Respectfully,

"FRANK.

"November 14, 1835."

After the reading of this letter, Mr. Phenix called as a witness for the prosecution

Silas Bedell, the crier of the court, examined by Mr. Morris—

I know the house No. 41 Thomas street. Knew the premises before; two houses, which form the house as it now is, were joined together. Have been in the house since it was joined in its present way. I have been there several times. The partition between the up-stairs back rooms, is, I believe, of brick. I am not, however quite certain that it is so. The house has a brick front, but I am not certain that it is brick in the rear.

[The witness then explained the manner in which the two houses were joined into one—stating, however, in the course of the explanation, no material fact, either for or against the prosecution. He was not cross-examined by the counsel for the defence.]

David L. Rogers, M. D., recalled by Mr. Phenix—I was of opinion, when I first saw the axe which was found in the rear of Mrs. Townsend's yard, that there was blood on it.

Cross-examined by Mr. Price—It would be difficult for me to say whether the bruised appearance of the axe,—the discoloration which appears upon it,—is blood or rust. The places where I thought the blood was, was upon the back of the axe. When I was examined before respecting the axe, it was before the coroner's inquest.

The District-Attorney here called the coroner and his clerk, Mr. Relyea, both of whom he wanted as witnesses, but in consequence of their not being present, and having no other witnesses to examine, he rested the case for the prosecution.

The counsel for the defence, then called George D. Woole, who testified as follows:—I am assistant secretary of Jefferson Fire Insurance Company, of this city. Mrs. Townsend had a policy on the furniture on the 9th of April last, to the amount of thirty-five hundred dollars. In June, 1834, the policy was only fifteen hundred dollars, and twelve months afterwards it was renewed for the large amount I have stated.

Cross-examined by Mr. Morris—It was either in May or June 1835, when Mrs. Townsend renewed her policy for thirty-five hundred dollars.

Joseph Hoxie, Jr., recalled by Mr. Hoffman—We had part of our store in Maiden Lane, painted on the Saturday preceding the murder. I got some paint upon my clothes, and the prisoner also got some paint upon his clothes. The paint was white. The elbow of my coat was painted. The prisoner got some paint upon his trousers. He also got it upon the right leg, below the knee, and upon the left thigh near the hip.

Cross-examined by Mr. Morris—I don't know what time in the day we got paint on our clothes. I recollect the circumstance, because I got some spirits of turpentine to get the paint out. Tried to get it out of his clothes, but could not, nor could I get it entirely out of mine. Am not very positive whether the paint was inside or the outside of the prisoner's trousers. He then had on a sort of mixed dull kerseymere pantaloons.

Laban Jacobs, examined by Mr. Price, for the defence—I manufactured the hatchet now shown to me, (the hatchet with which the murder was committed). Know it, for we had a great number manufactured for us in 1834. My firm was then Latman and Jacobs, and our mark was L. & Jacobs. We had 2,500 manufactured for us in 1834, in Connecticut The handles were put in here. Know that by the handle.

Cross-examined by Mr. Morris—We sold a great many hatchets like that, and I presume that they are nearly all alike. They were sold in nearly all the hardware stores in the city. Know nothing about Mr. Hoxie having had such an axe as the one now presented.

Mr. Phenix now offered to prove that the prisoner on being brought for examination before the police magistrates, refused to give any answer at all to any interogatory put to him.

Judge Edwards stated that such testimony was altogether inadmissible.

Mr. Phenix—I was undert he impression, if it please your honor, that I had a strict legal right to introduce this fact to the Jury.

Mr. Hoffman—"*Me me adsum qui feci.*"—If it please your honor, if the refusal on the part of my client to answer any questions that were put to him at the police office be a crime, it may be justly chargeable to me, for he acted entirely under my direction and advice.

At this stage of the proceedings, Mr. Phenix stated that some witnesses who had been subpœned on the part of the prosecution at the early part of the trial, and whose testimony would be very material, could not now be found, and he therefore was under the necessity of resting the case for the people.

The counsel for the prisoner remarked that they had no

more witness to introduce in behalf of their client, and if the court pleased, they would immediately commence summing up the defence. The court replied that they were ready to hear the summing up.

A few minutes before twelve o'clock, Mr. Price, counsel on the part of the accused, commenced an able speech, elucidative of the testimony, explanatory of the abstruse and seemingly dark portions of the evidence, illustrative of the infamous character and conduct of Mrs. Townsend, and her household, to the former of whom he imputed the probable perpetration of the murder. He swept away by the force of his reasoning, the inauspicious circumstances attending the paint on the pantaloons, the baldness of the head, the finding of the coat and hatchet, and attempted to show their deposit in the yard by other hands, than those of the prisoner. He spoke in the strongest terms of detestation of the infamous and abandoned course of life of Rosina Townsend, reaping her polluted resources, and supporting her wretched life by the prostitution of yound and tender females, whom she had inveighled into her toils, to vegetate in vice of the most abominable kind, to wear out their lives in her odious service, and to die in misery and disgrace. One Maria Stevens, he said, who declared she knew the murderer, had since died in the brothel of Mrs. Galagher, under circumstances of suspicion; and he protested in the strongest terms against reposing any confidence in the testimony of such a woman as Rosina Townsend, corrupt, and rotten and abandoned as she was. He considered her incapable, from her deep depravity, of telling the truth in a case like this, where her own character and interest and safety were at stake. He spoke of her repeated contradictions of herself in her several statements made before the police, the grand jury, to other persons, and here; and also exposed the discrepant statements of the black girl, and the other girls of Mrs. Townsend's family. He spoke of the presence of the prisoner at Mr. Furlong's store, for an hour after the time he was sworn to have been at Thomas street; and went on at great length to attack and overturn by his arguments, the whole mass of testimony against the prisoner.

Mr. Price continued speaking until eleven minutes past one, when he closed his remarks in a burst of powerful eloquence, having spoken an hour and thirteen minutes. After the lapse of half-an-hour or more, spent in interlocutory conversation, in relation to the further order of the proceedings.

Mr. Morris for the prosecution, commenced his summing up argument at thirteen minutes before two o'clock, and after speaking until four minutes past three, gave way without finishing his speech, for the court to adjourn for dinner.

After an adjournment of more than an hour, the court met, at twenty-five minutes past four o'clock, to resume their business. At twenty minutes after five, Mr. Morris recommenced his address, during which he reviewed, and commented on the entire testimony, replied fully to the remarks of Mr. Price, and contended strenuously for the guilt of the prisoner, concluding his remarks at half past five o'clock.

Mr. Hoffman then commenced his summing up speech, and continued to address the court and jury with great energy and eloquence until after eight o'clock, having spoken fully three hours. After he concluded, the audience, who had listened with profound attention to his speech, during its delivery, broke forth in loud plaudits, which for a while interrupted the proceedings of the court.

Mr. Maxwell then rose and cited and read several authorities on the subject of evidence necessary to work a conviction, particularly evidence of a circumstantial character, which he interspersed with appropriate observations, and illustrated by pertinent comments and remarks.

The reading of these authorities and comments and remarks upon them, occupied until nine o'clock. Mr. Maxwell concluded by submitting to the consideration of the court the following propositions, viz:

1st. Every man is presumed to be innocent until his guilt be proved. The guilt charged must be proved to the exclusion of all reasonable doubt.

2d. No conviction can be had except upon proof of guilt. The mere preponderance of evidence will not warrant a conviction, unless that preponderance should convince the jury of guilt to the exclusion of all reasonable doubt.

3d. Circumstantial proof may be sufficient to convict, but to warrant a conviction, the circumstances proved, ought fully to exclude the belief that any other person could have committed the crime

4th. The proof in this case consists of coincident circumstances, but taken severally or united, they do not necessarily exclude the hypothesis, that some other person ought to be guilty of the murder, and if they do not, the prisoner ought not to be convicted.

5th. The coincident circumstances as proven, may create a probable ground for presuming guilt, but each and every circumstance, severally, or united, are no more than inconclusive probabilities, and do not warrant conviction.

Mr. Phenix, the District Attorney, then commenced the closing speech in favor of the prosecution, and after a patient and able argument of two hours and more, concluded at eleven o'clock.

His honor Judge Edwards then charged the Jury at length, recapitulating the prominent parts of the testimony, and laying down the law for the guidance of the jury. He said that the jury, however, were as well the judges of the law, as of the facts. That it was a principle of law as laid down by Blackstone, that it were better ten guilty persons escape punishment, than one innocent person suffer. He stated that if, after a careful and candid investigation of all the facts and circumstances of the case, they did not arrive at a full conviction, that the prisoner was guilty beyond all reasonable doubt, they ought not to convict him.

That this principle was to govern them throughout; and if all the facts and circumstances brought by evidence against the prisoner did not bring them to the conclusion that the guilt of the prisoner was established beyond all reasonable doubt, they were to be laid aside as insufficient for conviction. The jury were also to consider well the character of the persons brought forward as witnesses; the manner in which they testified; whether they were consistent throughout; and whether the facts they stated were in accordance with other facts indubitably established. In this case, the testimony principally is drawn, confessedly, from persons of very bad repute,—from one of the most infamous houses in this city. When persons are brought forward who led such profligate lives, their testimony is not to be credited unless corroborated by testimony drawn from more creditable sources. The law therefore says, if testimony is drawn from persons of this description, in the judgment of law you are not entitled to convict upon it, but if it be corroboroted and strengthened by other credible testimony, then give it all the credibility to which it is in justice entitled. That there was a murder there can be no doubt—the question for your consideration is, was the prisoner at the bar the murderer? Your attention is directed to the circumstances connecting the prisoner with the crime with which he is charged: 1st. There is a cloak found in the yard; 2nd. The hatchet found in another yard, and 3rd. The miniature which was proved to be in the possession of the deceased on Friday, and was found after the murder in the possession of the prisoner on Sunday. These are the three facts to be relied on for connecting the prisoner with this transaction. First, as to the cloak, Mr. Terril, testified that he saw it on the prisoner at half past seven or eight o'clock, and Mr. Furlong testifies that at half past nine o'clock he was at his shop without it. It must then have been left at some place in the intermediate time. If he had been at Mrs. Townsend's house after he parted with Terrill, he might have left it there early in the evening, and returned to Mr. Furlong's without it; or else he may have taken it home, and after he left Mr. Furlong's he may have gone and got it. The cloak, however, was found in the yard adjoining the house in Thomas street, spread out, where it was dropped by some person. Further, Mrs. Townsend testifies, as do also her girls to precisely the same facts viz., that the prisoner came to their house at nine or half past nine o'clock, while Mr. Furlong testifies that he did not leave his store till half past ten o'clock. His Honor considered the statement of Mr. Furlong as the proper one to be relied on to the exclusion of those of Mrs. Townsend. How the cloak came in the yard, he, however, could only hypothetically account for. As to the hatchet, he said, it was sworn to by Mr. Hoxie's porter; it had been taken from the store on the Wednesday previous to the murder, found in the yard of Mrs. Townsend on Sunday morning with the string round it, and not missed by the porter until Monday morning. His honor then attempted to furnish a satisfactory solution of this matter. As to the miniature, he stated the facts proved in relation to that; so with the fire, the discovery of the fire; the calling of the watch to extinguish it, the contradictory statements of Mrs. Townsend and her girls with that of the black girl, &c.; all of which circumstances he stated and commented upon with some severity, as regarded the females who testified; but he admitted that some of the circumstances were enveloped in a mystery difficult to be unravelled. The result of his Honor's convictions was generally adverse to the credibility of the female witnesses against the prisoner. He concluded by charging the jury that if they entertained any reasonable doubt of the guilt of the prisoner, those doubts were the property of the prisoner, they were bound to acquit him ; but if they were without a reasonable doubt of his guilt they should find him guilty.

His Honor closed his charge at half past twelve o'clock, when the jury retired to their chamber, and in about ten minutes returned into the court with a verdict of NOT GUILTY.

As soon as the verdict was announced, the court-house rang with loud and reiterated plaudits, which the officers were for some time unable to suppress. The prisoner was then formally discharged from custody.

THE END.

The result of Robinson's trial astonished many. There is no doubt but that the evidence was strongly against him, and how the jury arrived at a verdict of acquittal was a matter of much surmise Some asserted that the jury had been bribed ; while others laid bribery at the door of officials high in the confidence of the community. These assertions may or may not have had some foundation ; or it may have been that the jury had really arrived at their conclusion from a conscientious conviction of the prisoner's innocence.

As to what became of Robinson after the trial, it appears that he left New York and settled in Texas, where he married, and became the father of a large family. He is now dead, and gone before that tribunal where his guilt or innocence has been fully determined, and the measure of his reward or punishment justly awarded.

JOHN C. COLT.

HIS TRIAL AND CONVICTION FOR THE MURDER OF SAMUEL ADAMS IN THE YEAR 1841.—SKETCH OF THE MURDERER AND HIS VICTIM.—THE EVIDENCE FOR AND AGAINST THE PRISONER IN FULL.—EXCITING INCIDENTS OF THE TRIAL.—THE HEAD OF THE MURDERED MAN EXHIBITED IN OPEN COURT.—INTERESTING EXAMINATION OF CAROLINE HENSHAW, COLT'S MISTRESS.—THE VERDICT.—ATTEMPTS TO RELEASE COLT FROM JAIL—INCIDENTS OF HIS PRISON LIFE.—SUICIDE OF THE UNFORTUNATE MAN ON THE DAY SET DOWN FOR HIS EXECUTION.—THE TOMBS ON FIRE, &C. &C.

It was only four years after the murder of Helen Jewett, that the citizens of New-York were again startled by another assassination, equally appalling in its character, causing intense excitement among all classes of the community. The perpetrator of the deed was John C. Colt, a teacher of book-keeping, and brother of the well-known Colonel Samuel Colt, of patent revolver notoriety. His victim was Samuel Adams, a printer, both residents of New-York.

The atrocity of the deed or any of the palliating circumstances which may have surrounded it, is not a fit subject for us to dilate upon. We will leave the public to form their estimate in this connection on reading the report of the trial, which follows this preliminary sketch, together with the statement of the prisoner, which was read in court by his counsel, Mr. Robert Emmett.

John C. Colt was born in Hartford, Conn., and at the time of the murder was about thirty-two years of age. He lived with his mistress, Caroline Henshaw, at No. 42 Monroe street in this city, and occupied a room for his business in the granite building corner of Broadway and Chambers street, now the well-known Delmonico's. Few who to-day enter this celebrated establishment are aware of the fact that within its walls was enacted one of the most remarkable tragedies of the nineteenth century.

No human eye other than that of him who did the deed, witnessed the killing of Mr. Adams; but from the evidence brought forward on the trial, and the statements of Colt, there seemed to be no doubt as to the manner in which the unfortunate deceased was hurried into eternity.

It appears that Adams and Colt had business transactions, the former being engaged in printing a work on book-keeping for the latter. A small bill of some fifty or sixty dollars was due to Adams by the prisoner, and on the seventeenth of September, 1841, he called at the latter's place of business, corner of Broadway and Chambers street, in relation thereto. Colt's statement of the affair is that words came between himself and Adams as to the correctness of the bill. Adams called Colt a liar, when the latter resented the insult by slapping the former in the face. A scuffle then ensued. Adams seized Colt by the throat, and matters began to look serious. Colt, fearing for his life (according to his own statement) stretched out his hand for a hatchet, which lay near, and struck Adams a heavy blow on the forehead, which levelled the unfortunate man to the floor, and he died in a few minutes. Colt was now at a loss what to do. He left his room and locked the door, wending his steps to the City Hotel, where his brother, Samuel Colt, then stopped, to whom he intended to impart his secret, and consult as to his future movements. Samuel Colt was in the bar-room speaking to some friends, and he desired John to go up to his room, and he would rejoin him in a few minutes. The prisoner waited some time, but his brother not making his appearance, he hurried back to the corner of Broadway and Chambers street The body lay there covered with blood. He took a large box crammed the body into it, wrapped in a piece of canvas, tying up the legs close to the trunk, and then scattered salt and saw dust over all. There were marks of blood upon the wall and flooring which he washed off, and poured ink upon them, so that they could not be noticed. He remained in the room until late at night, when he returned to his home in Monroe street. Next morning at nine o'clock he hastened to his place of business, procured a carman, and sent the box, which he had previously nailed up, on board the steamer Kalamazoo, lying at the foot of Maiden Lane. The box was directed to a gentleman in St. Louis, by way of New Orleans.

Adams being missed by his family, inquiries were made, and it was ascertained that he was last seen going into the apartments of Colt. Those who occupied rooms in the building, had heard suspicious noises in Colt's room, the day of Mr. Adams' disappearance. These incidents, together with the fact of the body being found boxed up on board the Kalamazoo, led to the arrest of Colt.

A trial took place, which we append in full, as reported in a newspaper of that date. The jury, believing that Colt committed the murder wilfully, and not crediting the plea of self-defence which he set up, convicted him, and he was sentenced to be hung; but the law was robbed of its victim, as on the day set down for his execution, Colt committed suicide by stabbing himself to the heart with a dagger, furnished him for the purpose by some of his friends.

THE TRIAL.

At twelve o'clock, on Thursday, the 21st of January, 18 2, two days having been occupied in procuring a jury, the trial of Co t was commenced in the Court of Oyer and Terminer, before Judge Kent. The indictment set forth the facts that John C Colt on the 17th of September, 1841, being instigated by the devil, &c made an assault with a hatchet on the person of Samuel Adams and inflicted a wound on the right side of his head, of which wound the said Samuel Adams then and there died.

"It is for you gentlemen," said the clerk, addressing the jury, " by the evidence which will be presented, to say whether the prisoner was guilty or not guilty, as charged by this indictment.

Mr Smith, Assistant District Attorney, then rose and presented the particulars of the charge to the jury. It is the first time in my life, said he, I have been engaged on the part of the people in a case affecting life and death. It is a painful task for me, for you, and for all here present, to perform, but one that is necessary. You have been selected out of a large number because you have declared yourselves as having no bias You will give the evidence such weight as you think it entitled to. You are not to allow your sympathies to be improperly exercised. We may feel them, but the jury box is not the place for their display. The prisoner has been charged with the commission of murder, and such a murder, too, probably as is unparalleled in the annals of crime. You are bound faithfully to pass between the people and the prisoner. On the 17th of September Samuel Adams was seen for the last time by his friends. The prisoner and Adams had dealings by which the relation of debtor and creditor existed between them. Mr. Colt had made an arrangement with Adams for the printing of a work which he had written on book-keeping. It was in relation to a bill which Colt owed Adams that the latter called on the former on the day of the murder. [The circumstances attending the discovery of the body were then alluded to by Mr. Smith.] The counsel on the opposite side would, no doubt, endeavor to palliate the crime, but the violent character of the prisoner, which would be shown by the trial, and the contrary one of the deceased, left but little doubt that the murder was wilful and premeditated. It was for the jury, however, to pass upon the act, and afford that justice which the nature of the evidence demanded.

The District Attorney, Mr. Whiting, then proceeded to call his witnesses:

Asa H. Wheeler sworn—was a teacher of writing and book-keeping on the second floor of the granite building corner of Chambers street and Broadway. Was a married man and resided in 30th street; became acquainted with the prisoner in 1838, when he came to shew witness a system of book-keeping. On the 2d August last witness occupied two rooms, and the prisoner requested him to let one of them for six weeks; he did so; the rooms adjoing each other, and the entrance was on Chambers street; there was an entry way at the head of the stairs, running parallel with Chambers street towards Broadway, there were three or four rooms between the stairs and Broad way; Colt's room was the second door; the door swung in; witness' own room was at the corner, and there were folding doors between that and the one occupied by Colt; Mr. Riley had occupied the room previous to Colt having it; there was a lock on the door and it opened into Colt's room; the room had one window in it on Chambers street; had seen in the room a few chairs, a table, a box, and a trunk; the box was about three feet in length, and eighteen inches in width and height; it generally stood on the left hand side as you entered the room, the table stood on the west corner, right hand side as you went in. [A diagram was here shown witness, which he stated to be a correct one.] The window was op posite to the door; frequently met the prisoner in the hall and went into each other's rooms; in witness' room there was a writing desk, about seven feet by four, which, at the time Mr. Adams was missed stood against the folding door; there was another against the wall in Chambers street, extending from one window to the other: there was also one from the corner of Chambers street window to the second one in Broad way; chairs were used to the Chambers street table and long benches for the Broadway one; there was a secretary in the recess between the fire place and the door, which witness occupied; did not have any professional controversy, but some words had occurred between us, owing to my asking Mr. Colt for my rent; I told him it was not worth while to get wrathy about it;

he settled by giving me some books, and we became on familiar terms again: next evening, after my scholars went away, Mr. Colt came into my room; he was to pay me $10 at the end of four weeks, and $5 more at the end of the six—making fifteen dollars in all—so that I suppose it was about the 4th of September: no unpleasant words passed between us from the time; the time for his leaving had expired on the 13th: I was anxious to get the room in my possession; on asking him he requested to stay a week longer, which I agreed to; on Friday, the 17th of September I arrived at my room about half past 2; was seated at my desk writing in the Broadway corner of the room; was alone for some time; then entered a pupil of mine about 16 years of age. The young man's name was Seignette; about quarter past 3, I heard a noise like the clashing of foils; it was momentary, and I heard a violent fall on the floor. the young man exclaimed,—"what is that?" I said I did not know; I went into the hall and listened at Mr. Colt's door, but all was still: I looked into the keyhole but found that the drop was down inside. there was simply a ray of light through: I had my pen in my hand placed it in the keyhole and slid the drop on one side; I there saw, in about the centre of the room, close by the wall on the west side, a person in his shirt sleeves, in a position as if bending down over something. [The witness described the position, the left knee appeared to be resting on something, and the arms slightly moving up and down as a person would be in the act of sawing.] On a table I observed two black hats; the person remained in the recumbent position about ten minutes; he put something on the table, which I did not see, and returned to the same position: I then called the young man to stand in my door and watch Mr. Colt's door till I went up stairs to find Mr. Adams, the owner of the building, and procure advice or help; Mr Adams was not in; I then called at several of the doors, but the occupants were not there, it being the hour for dinner. I called the keeper of the house, Mr. Locklan, who with myself, endeavored to look through the keyhole, but found the slide down and the room darkened again; Mr Locklan appeared to be alarmed and agitated, but thought there could be nothing of the kind, and left me alone in the hall; another of my scholars then came in to whom I related the circumstance, and rapped at the door, but found no answer, all being perfectly still; I then went softly down stairs and returned with a heavy walk, supposing that Mr. Colt would think it a friend, and would open the door; I rapped again, but no answer; several more of my scholars came in soon afterwards, to whom I told what had occurred; we were in the room with the door open; I sent one of the scholars, Mr. Delnous, after an officer, who returned and said that the officers were then engaged, but that one of them would be there in half an hour or less; waited till candle light, when two of the scholars, Mr. Wood and Mr. Riley, went again after an officer. We continued to watch the door; the officers sent word back that they would not dare to open the door, but we must keep watch; I remained in my room till 9 o'clock, and left it in the care of Mr. Delnous, who was to remain. Heard no noise as of foils, loud words, or otherwise, after that time. The noise like foils clashing was momentary; previous to hearing the foils, there was a sound—a slight one—as of people stamping on a carpeted floor. At nine o'clock I left with Mr. Delnous. At half-past nine next morning I borrowed a key and went into Mr. Colt's room. He was absent; I only stepped one foot in and looked round; I discovered the box was missing that had stood there, and that the floor had been scrubbed. The part where I supposed I saw the person the day previous was more scrubbed than the rest; oil and ink had been spilt round the base of the floor, and thrown in spots on the wall. I closed the door and went into my room. The scrubbing had been more in the centre of the room, and was not quite dry. Locked the door again and returned the key to the owner. After being in my room about 30 minutes Colt rapped at my door. He inquired if my key would fit his door, as he had left his at his house, and wished to enter his room. I told him I did not know, but he might try; he did so, but it did not fit. He then commenced talking about book keeping and writing, in which we were both engaged. He was very talkative indeed. At last I got an opportunity to say a word, and observed, "Mr. Colt, what noise was that in your room yesterday afternoon?" He replied, "You must be mistaken, as I was out all the afternoon." I said there certainly was noise, as it had quite alarmed us. He said nothing more then, and went away. On Sunday I did not go to the office, and did not see him. On Monday, about half-past 10, I went to the office and was leaning against the folding door, when Mr. Colt entered his room. He commenced singing, which was very uncommon. I had a piece of writing which Mr. Colt had spoken of, and took it into his room as an excuse. He was smoking and had a bunch of matches in his chair. He asked me to smoke with him which I declined. He observed he had a very bad habit of smoking, doing so to a very great extent. He either said it caused him to spit blood, or he did it to prevent spitting blood, cannot say which; there were 30 or 40 specks on the wall. In the course of conversation I referred again to the noise. He said, "to tell you the truth, Mr. Wheeler, I upset my table, spilt my ink, and knocked down the books, making a deuced mess. I hope it didn't disturb you." On Saturday I called at the office of Mr. Adams, owner of the building, over my room, to ask his advice; he said it was a very delicate subject to meddle with, and we had better wait until we saw something in the papers. Colt and I met frequently in the hall during the week. On Tuesday I saw the notice of Mr Adams' absence in the papers, and went to the house of Mr. Lane, in Catherine street, but couldn't see him. Left word, and Mr. Lane called on me at my room in company with Mr. Loud. He brought with him Mr. Adams' books. We examined them. We then went to the Mayor, and informed him of what we knew. I continued to meet Mr. Colt in the hall up to the time of his arrest. On Thursday he urged me very politely to come into his room, as he wished to have some conversation on the subject of book-keeping, and obtain my advice as to the publishing of his work. Partly promised to go in, but did not. On Friday morning he invited me in again in a very friendly and urgent manner to come into his room. I was talking at the time with Mr. Barker, at the front door. Colt was arrested on Friday.

Arzac Seignette, sworn—I am sixteen years of age; reside at the corner of Fourth and Wooster streets; went to Mr. Wheeler's between half-past two and three, and took my seat at a desk facing Broadway, pretty nearly opposite the folding door Soon after going in I heard a kind of a rush, a sudden noise—it sounded as if you laid hold of a man and threw him down without much trouble; rose from my seat at about the same time with Mr. Wheeler, and I followed him; he looked through the keyhole and returned (objected to). He then went up stairs, while I kept watch at Colt's door. He returned with Oakland; they talked together, and Mr. O. went away. I tried to look through the keyhole, but it was stopped up. About five minutes had elapsed since Mr. Wheeler had looked through. He went out, returned again, and went to the door a second time. Two persons came in who were strangers to me—one of them was an Irishman—then Mr. Wood came in, and then Mr. Delnous; the latter came in about half-past four; no person had gone into Colt's door, nor did I hear any voice in the room. (The witness, in answer to other questions, confirmed Mr. Wheeler's testimony.) He left about half past three that evening; had not seen Mr. Colt that day, and did not know him.

By Mr. Selden—That was the first day of my becoming a scholar. Where I sat was about eight feet from the Broadway wall. Heard the sound like striking of foils on crossing each other. The fall followed immediately. Do not think it was foils, but cannot compare it to anything else. Heard the noise and fall almost simultaneously, with a difference of about a second. Listened at the folding doors, and thought I heard a noise as of struggling, or something like that. After trying to look through the keyhole, I returned into the room, and listened at the folding door; leaned on the desk, and got as near to the door as I could—within about three inches.

By Mr. Whiting—I listened near the center of the folding doors, and thought I heard a slight shuffling, but it was very faint. I think it was the sound of a foot.

John Delnous sworn—I am twenty-six years of age, and a bookkeeper by profession; reside at 129 Broadway. Was at Staten Island last summer, and told Mr. Wheeler that as I could not get the room I wanted from my landlady, I would take the one occupied by Mr. Colt when he vacated it, which he agreed to do. Went to Wheeler's that afternoon, who told me what had happened. I at first laughed at it, till I saw him go to the keyhole. I then listened at the folding door, but heard no noise whatever — everything being perfectly quiet. Mr. Wheeler asked me to go for an officer, which I did. Bowyer promised to come, but did not. I went to my tea about six o'clock, and returned. Mr. Wheeler left about nine, after which I remained still for about half an hour. I then heard some one unlock Mr. Colt's door from the inside, come out, lock it again, and go away. The person returned in about five minutes, and in about five minutes more I heard some one in Mr. Colt's room tearing something resembling cotton cloth; the next sound was the rattling of water—after that, some person scrubbing the floor very near the folding door, continually putting his cloth in the water and rinsing it. The next noise I heard was about six o'clock next morning, as of some person nailing a box, which sounded as if it was full. It was the first noise I heard after I awoke, or it might have been the noise which awakened me. I heard a sawing as of a person sawing a board, immediately after the hammering. It then went to breakfast. This was about seven o'clock, and no person had opened the door from the time that I awoke. Was gone to breakfast about an hour. On coming in, saw a box at the foot of the stairs, directed to some person in St. Louis, *via* New Orleans. It stood in the lower entry, about six feet from the door. The box was boarded up, the direction in writing, and seemed to be made with ink. The box was about three feet long, and two and a half feet wide and deep. There was no box in the entry when I went to breakfast. Had seen Mr. Colt two or three times—once in his room, when I went to ask him about the key in the folding door. He said it was in the door, and pointed it out Saw him the Friday after the murder, when he entered into conversation. He spoke of his own and other sytems of bookkeeping; also of different places he had been in—Boston, Philadelphia, and elsewhere. The box was removed the same afternoon that I saw it in the entry.

By Mr. Selden—Was not absent from Mr. Wheeler's after going there in the afternoon, except when I went to the police office, and when I went to tea. (Witness saw Messrs. Wood and Riley, and others that came in, as described by Mr. Wheeler.) Returned from tea about half-past seven. The weather was rainy. The keyhole of the folding door is above the desk. It was stopped up After my return from tea, Mr. Wheeler knocked again at Colt's door, but there was no answer. Thinks it very difficult when the omnibusses are rattling by, and windows are up to hear in Mr. Wheeler's room even loud talking going on in Mr. Colt's.

Law Octon, sworn—I am keeper of the granite building corner of Chambers street and Broadway. Reside in the third story. Am also sexton of a Baptist church. Know the prisoner, but had very little acquaintance with the tenants. On the afternoon already alluded to, Mr. Wheeler came up stairs, and requested I should go down with him to Colt's room. Went down, and Mr. Wheeler applied his eye to the keyhole, and endeavored to look in Everything was quiet. Returned up stairs, and came down in about an hour, when Mr. Wheeler went again to Colt's door. Between seven and eight o clock next morning saw a box in the hall at the head of the first flight of stairs. It was a pine box, and stood on one end. In a minute or two Colt came out of his room, laid hold of the box, and took it down stairs. He threw it over on its side, dragged it to the stairs, and slid it down, going before it, and placing his shoulder against the box to prevent it going too fast. It caught in going down, when he pressed his shoulder heavily against it, and raised up the lower end. I went up stairs; returned in about seven minutes, when the box was at the foot of the stairs, and Colt standing at the door. He had no coat or vest on, but was in his shirt sleeves. He seemed to look out for a carman. The box was directed to some person; saw the word "New Orleans" on it; the direction seemed to have been done with a kind of blue ink. Colt did not say any thing when he was getting the box down stairs. Never saw the box before, and have not seen it since, (The witness then underwent a long cross-examination by Mr. Selden, but nothing was elicited beyond a description of the building and the tenants occupying it.)

Richard Barstow sworn—I am a carman, 34 years of age, and reside at 392 17th street; saw Mr. Colt in Chambers street, near Church, the morning of the 18th of September, between a quarter to nine and nine o'clock; I came down Hudson street into Chambers and was coming through the latter; saw a man looking round as for some one; he beckoned to me and asked me if I was engaged; I told him not particularly; he stepped into the street to me; asked him what he wanted; he said he wanted a box to be taken to the foot of Maiden Lane; as that was on my way I agreed to take it; there was a spring cart opposite to the door, standing sideways, with the head towards Broadway; backed my horse up to it; the prisoner was dressed in black; he went in and I followed; he went a few steps up and pointed to the box; it lay alongside of the balusters; do not recollect his saying a word. The carman that was there with the spring cart took hold of the box with me, and we took it up and put it on my cart; Colt stood there while we were doing it; I went back and asked him to what vessel I was to carry it. He said he did not know the name of the vessel, but it was at the foot of Maiden Lane, and he would go with me. From time to time as I was going, I looked back to see if he followed me. He did so. I went down Broadway and Maiden Lane. I had noticed the direction, and supposed the box was going on board a vessel for New Orleans. Stopped opposite a ship bound for there, and pointed to the vessel to know if that was the one, and he nodded assent. I backed up my cart. The vessel was the Kalamazoo. The weather was rainy and the box very dirty, and had to be cleaned off before it was put down below. Dropped the box on the wharf the same as I would a box of sugar. Colt handed me two and sixpence, and I took it and cleared out. If he had asked me the price, I should have charged him three shillings, but supposed I would have more trouble to get the other sixpence out of him than it was worth. [Prisoner laughed.] In about a week afterwards saw the same box again in the hold of the Kalamazoo. Had to work very hard before we got it; it was opened, and contained a dead body. The box was then closed and I presume carried to the dead house. Did not see it again. The box was found down in the forward hatch. I was engaged from the first in removing the other boxes to find it. It was near the ground tier. The marks were still on it, very fresh. They were made with blue ink.

Thomas Russel sworn—I am a carman by profession; on the 18th of September last, when at the corner of Chambers street and Broadway, where I am employed, I saw the other carman come to the door of the granite building, and assisted him to put a box on his cart; Mr. Colt was there; did not take particular notice of the direction of the box; saw there was a large G to it; saw it again on Snnday the 29th; did not know the carman that took it; on the 25th was asked by the officers if I knew him; I replied that I did not, but thought I would know the horse; went in pursuit of him, and found him; we were then questioned as to size of the box and the description; went down to the ship Kalamazoo together, and saw the chief mate; the bills of lading for that day were examined, and we commenced a search; the box was hoisted to the middle deck; saw it opened; first saw the awning, but on account of the stench I left, and went on the upper deck; saw the box hoisted on deck and over the side; did not see the body; when the box was opened the stench was so great I was compelled to leave.

Mr. Godfrey sworn—I am superintendent of carts; the mayor asked me if I could find out the cart spoken of on this trial; spoke to Russel, who thought he could tell the horse; went with him to search and found the carman at Peck Slip; asked him if he recollected about it; he replied that he did; went on board the Kalamazoo and saw the chief mate; asked him to let me see the bills of lading; got an order to take out the cargo, and the officers were directed to assemble at the mayor's office. On Sunday morning about nine o'clock, with a lot of stevedores we commenced taking out the cargo; when near the box Mr. Barstow recognized it; we hoisted it up between decks, knocked off the lid and took out the awning, when we discovered a dead body; there was a rope round his neck, and passed down round his legs, and his knees drawn down towards his head—his face was up; examined it, and supposed there was salt on the breast and body; the body was not taken out on board the ship. The chief mate then threw some chloride of lime over it, and the box was nailed up again. Put it on the cart and carried it to the dead house, opened it there and saw the dead body again. Was there when they commenced lifting it out. The mayor sent for me, and I left. The box was directed to R. P. Gross, St Louis, to the care of Mr. Gray, New Orleans. The salt on the body was partly dissolved; saw the breast; the body had a shirt on, which Mr. Mulligan, I believe, the deputy coroner, tore open; the body had a greenish cast to it, as usual, when the flesh became mortified; was in and out of the dead house during the examination of the body, but did not pay much attention to it; the body was taken out of the box and put on a board, and a person washed it off; the stench was great, and the man was paid six dollars for washing it off. Oceans of people have offered to bet me that Colt would be cleared; one last week, and, two this week; Mr. Kelpin is one; probably a thousand persons offered to bet, but I told them I had nothing to do with it;

cannot say whether the people have been sent to me or otherwise.

The District-Attorney then read the examination of the mate of the ship, who confirmed the testimony already given. Colt was pointed out to him, and he had an indistinct recollection of his countenance. Gave the man that accompanied the box to the vessel a receipt. The box was put into the hold exactly as it came to the vessel, and was not touched again until taken out by order of the mayor. The box he saw in the dead house was the same. He threw the chloride of lime over the box before he left the vessel.

Abner Milligan sworn—I am deputy coroner. The witness saw about two quarts of common salt in the box, also a black dress coat which had been cut or torn, also a stock which had been cut, and was smeared with blood on both sides, part of an awning, two pieces of matting about eighteen inches square, and some oakum; the coat and stock were underneath the body, the others with the body, folded in; the body had nothing on it but a shirt; the neck was drawn down to the knees by a rope.

By Mr. Selden—The salt was mixed in with the clothes; discovered it before the chloride of lime was thrown in; the body was examined by Drs. Gilman and Kissam; there was a small ring on the left hand, which the coroner took off. The coat appeared to have been a new one, but it was much cut and torn. Everything inside of the box appeared to be damp. Decomposition had taken place, and there were white worms inside of it. Had the things found in the box washed. About a pound of chloride of lime was thrown into the box. The cleaning of the body took place in the presence of several individuals, from the beginning to the end of it. The whole of the box has been preserved. The stock was cut in two in front, the buckle remaining fast. Saw no wound except that on the head. The articles found in the box were cleaned by a young man named E. D. Warner, an apothecary. He cleansed them with a process to destroy the putrid matter. The articles were placed in a cell at the Halls of Justice, and a solution thrown upon them; also several pails of water. They smell offensive still, never having been removed since the first day.

Robert H. Morris, Mayor, sworn—I was applied to on Thursday, the twenty-third, in relation to the murder of Samuel

Adams. On the evening after, a statement had been made to me by three gentlemen, that something wrong had transpired at the granite building. I went over to the building and examined several persons, among them the keeper. I then associated Justice Taylor with me, who, on Friday morning, took depositions, and issued a warrant against Mr. Colt. I was induced, from something that had been told me, to go to the room in person; and Justice Taylor, A. M. C. Smith, another officer, and myself, went to the building in order to arrest Mr. Colt. Mr. C.'s door was locked, and a label left on it that he would be back soon. One of the officers was stationed at the head, and the other at the foot of the stairs, and Justice Taylor and myself went into Mr. Wheeler's room. Mr. Colt came to his door and was arrested. I told Mr. Colt who I was, and told him I wished to see him in his room. We all went in and closed the door; I told him that he was arrested on suspicion of having killed Mr. Adams; the officers proceeded to search him to see if he had any weapons; the prisoner assisted in the search, and seemed disposed to yield everything. I then showed him the affidavits on which the arrest was founded; he was taken to my office at the hall, when Mr. Selden was sent for, also the prisoner's brother; the former came, but the latter was out of town; Mr. Colt was then committed to prison; I sent an advertisement to the papers, asking any carman who had carried such a box from the building to the slip, to give notice at my office, and succeeded in finding him: I went to the coroner's office, and learned particulars as to the marks, and on Sunday morning we got the box out; I assisted as did all the officers, in getting out the cargo, and was there when the box was opened; was not sufficiently near to observe if there had been salt in it, but was close enough to see that there was a dead body in it.

By Mr. Selden—Did not hear anything about the salt till after the coroner's inquest; the box was bottom upwards in the hold, and the direction damp, as if blood and matter had oozed through. The two things were started simultaneously, to find the box, and to find Mr. Colt's residence; Justice Taylor took charge of one branch, and I the other; Colt's residence was ascertained on Saturday; we moved with as much secresy as possible, in order to prevent a knowledge of these proceedings coming to the parties.

Thomas Taylor, sworn—I am a police magistrate, attached to the upper police office; on Thursday received a note from the Mayor to meet him at his office; we took depositions, and went to Mr. Colt's room, who was absent; he soon came, and was arrested. I read to him the affidavits. In consequence of remarks made by Mr. Colt, got down the keeper and examined him on oath. Dr. Chilton came and endeavored to ascertain the character of the spots on the wall. Samuel Colt came to the Mayor's office on Saturday morning, and told me that the residence of his brother was forty-two some street, and he thought Thomas street, but was not sure, and thought if I went to the City Hotel with him, he could tell me certainly. Went to 42 Thomas street, and inquired for Mrs. Colt, and was introduced to a young woman who was called such. I asked her what apartments Mr. Colt occupied, and where his trunk was; she drew from a recess in a room in the third story the trunk that is now in court. It was opened in his presence in the police office; found some things in it, among them a book, with several names in it; also some stamps, with "Colt's Book-Keeping" on them; also cards for his lectures. There was also a watch. The Mayor and myself, in consequence of information, took the watch to a watch case manufacturer in John street, and also to Platt & Brothers, in Maiden Lane.

By Mr. Selden—The spots on the wall were larger near the centre, opposite the folding doors, than anywhere else. We took up a piece of the floor near the folding door, on account of a dark spot there. It was taken away by Dr. Chilton. Saw one place more scrubbed than the rest. From the Mayor's office, Mr. Colt was carried to the upper police prison. In a day or two afterwards he was taken to the Halls of Justice. Was present when the box was opened on board the ship, but did not observe anything like salt about it. Colt and the woman were both at the police office, but did not observe that they said much to each other. Found at Monroe street, besides the trunk, a carpet bag, which is here; everything is in it now, except a piece of newspaper, which I gave to Mr. Clinton (objected to). The shirt here shewn was also found at the house; it is marked "J. C. Colt, No. 5." Both of the wristbands were off. There is no name or mark upon anything but what I have mentioned.

By Mr. Selden—The shirt was neither in the carpet bag nor

the trunk. Got the key from the female and wished her to open the trunk, but she declined, when we took her to the police office, and opened it in presence of her and Mr. Colt. The room in Monroe street was a small one, and the trunk was in the entry. The carpet-bag did not appear to contain any clothing, but small pieces of rags and boots; it is a sort of "receivable" bag. The piece of paper was about in the middle of the bag. I think it was a portion of the *Sun*. The watch found in the trunk was not wrapped in paper.

The Mayor recalled—After Mr. Colt's room was locked up, the key was brought to me, and I took from the room such articles as I thought would be necessary on the trial. They are here in the same situation as when I first took them. There are some pieces of cloth, pieces of towel, and pieces of a shirt, which were taken from a trunk in Mr. Colt's room; also pieces of a handkerchief, and a pamphlet, which, by request of Mr. Emmett, I put my initials on at the time—also four stamps of Colt's bookkeeping, which are here present; a ball of twine, which Mr. Emmett also asked me to take charge of—some papers, some letters, a receipt, two pocket books, (nearly empty) which I merely took because they were pocket-books.

By Mr. Selden—Mr. Colt was in custody at the time. I put padlocks on both of the doors, (as evidence had been presented to me that one of them had been entered by a key that did not belong to it), and kept the keys for some time. In one of the pocket books was a paper, endorsed, "Hair of Sarah Colt, my mother; Margaret Colt, and Mary Colt, deceased." There was also a package containing documents endorsed, "My little old aunt," different numbers; also some two or three letters from some individuals, a discharge for John C. Colt from the marine service, dated Connecticut—(the prisoner appeared to be very much depressed during this examination, leaning his elbow on the back part of his counsel's chair, with his hands over his eyes).

By the District Attorney—There were a great many other articles found in the room, several papers and books; also a hatchet, which is here shewn, (it was a perfectly new shingle hatchet, apparently very sharp)—found no rope in the room.

David Kelso, sworn—I am thirty-eight years of age. Reside at 42 Monroe street. Am a pilot. Became acquainted with Colt in the middle of May last. He came to board with my sister-in-law, who lives there. He had a lady, whom he called Mrs. Colt. They messed with the family and occupied a front room in the third story. They had two black trunks and a leather bag, which I assisted him in taking up stairs. One of the trunks stood in a recess in the entry. Was not home when Justice Taylor came. The prisoner at the bar is the same man.

By Mr. Selden—My business requires me to be absent a great deal. Have often seen the trunk in the entry.

Dr. Chilton sworn—I am practicing physician. Was called to the room of Mr. Colt, corner of Broadway and Chambers streets. Saw spots on the wall, some of them an eighth of an inch in diameter. I preserved them for examination. Did not observe any on the base. There were an immense number of spots on the folding doors. Also took the hatchet, which was placed in my charge; also a piece of the floor, having a stain on it. That was all I took at the time. I applied the test, and the spots proved to have been blood. Blood was on the hammer side of the hatchet, which had been inked over, as also on the handle, near the eye of the hatchet, which had been inked. Examined the spot on the piece of floor, which proved to be blood; oil had been thrown round the base of the floor, under which was blood. There was also a piece of newspaper, which had much stains upon it. It was opened, and showed much blood on it, and was also much torn. It was part of the New York *Herald* of June 13, 1841. Applied the tests to this, too, and found the spots to be blood. A key and pen-knife was also subsequently handed me by an officer, but I did not perceive any blood on them.

Mercy Octon (a light colored woman), sworn—I am the wife of Law Octon. Knew the prisoner well. Was in the room he occupied after Mr. Wheeler received the key back, and cleaned out the room. Mr. Colt asked me on the sixteenth of September to lend him a saw. He did not say what he wanted of it. It was a little after four in the afternoon. I had not spoken to him more than to pass the day when I met him. I lent him the saw [a common hand saw]. I took it to his room.

Dr. Gilman, sworn—I am a practicing physician. Examined the body of Mr. Adams. It was on a Sunday. I was requested by the coroner to go to the dead-house and examine a dead body. I went in company with Dr. Kissam. I there found the body of a man very much decayed. The body was lying upon a table, and alongside of the table was a box, from which they told me the body had been taken. The body was tied with a rope around the knees and carried to the head. The thighs were strongly bent up, and the head a little bent forward. The body was excessively offensive, and covered with vermin. After observing the general appearance of it, had the rope cut, and the body extended. We then proceeded to make an examination of something that appeared about the head. The skull was fractured in several different places. The right side of the forehead, the socket of the eye, and a part of the cheek bone were broken in. On the left side the fracture was higher up. The brow had escaped, but above that the forehead was beaten in. The two fractures communicated on the center of the forehead, so that the whole of the forehead was beaten in, also the right eye, and a part of the right cheek. On the other side of the head, directly above the ear, there was a fracture, with depression of the bone—it was not detached, it was dented in. This fracture was quite small. There was also a fracture on the left side of the head, a little behind and above the ear, in which there was a round, clean hole, so that you might put your finger through it. There was no fracture on the back part of the head. Two pieces, about the size of the head of an ordinary nail, were chipped or scaled off; it was the part of the skull termed the occiput. The head was so much decayed that the scalp could be removed from the bone by a rub of the finger. Examined the cavity of the skull; found nothing but some pieces of bone, some of the size of half a dollar. Examined the body—one of the legs, I think the left one, showed a dark mark near the instep, but whether from an old sore or a blow I could not tell. There was a gold ring on one of the fingers, which we took off. Measured the body—it was five feet nine and a half inches in length. The body was that of rather a stout but not a fat man. The hair was long and black. There was a small place on the back of the head from which the scalp was detached; but such was also the case where the fractures occurred. Cannot say deceased was any way bald. The whiskers were very small. The sore was hard, dry, and almost perfectly black. The rope passed from one knee to the other, and then to the head. All the blows on the head could readily have been made by the hatchet here produced, except the round hole, which, I confess, I am at a loss to see how it could have been made by it, but it might have been so. Do not think the sound in giving such blows would resemble the clashing of foils. Have never been in an adjoining room when foils have been struck. There must at least have been five blows given—perhaps a good many. If a ball had been fired from an air gun, it might have made such a hole as that in the head, and a person receiving it would be instantaneously killed, and unable to make any noise. Did not find any ball in the skull. A single blow from a hatchet, sufficiently strong to drive in the skull, as we found it, would prevent a person from crying out. The person would not probably bleed much. There would be more blood from such a blow than from a pistol ball.

By Mr. Selden—The outer skin of the surface first changes color and decays, then the brain, which becomes a semi-fluid. The wounds on the right side of the face and the skull must have been made by more than one blow, unless struck by the head of a large axe. The wounds were probably done by a blunt instrument (the hatchet shown has a hammer on one side). The blow on the back part of the skull may have been done by a sharp instrument or by a blunt one. The upper part of the cheek bone was beaten back, as if from a front blow. Cannot reconcile the idea of a hole in the head being made by the hatchet; a large nail being driven into the skull would leave such an appearance. Examined the body before it had been cleaned. There were vermin about the body, and lime, but I saw nothing else. Heard observation there about salt, but saw nothing of it. The examination continued from one to two hours. Saw the body two or three times that day, but not afterwards. [A human skull was shown, also a bust, from which Dr. Gilman described the situation of the wounds.] Have seen a skull in which the back part has been an inch thick. The brain would not bleed very profusely on a fracture of the skull. I omitted to mention on the direct examination another wound that was observable. It was a fracture of the lower jaw on the right side, about an inch from the centre of the chin. If cut with a sharp knife, wounds at this point would bleed freely, but they did not appear to have been made with such. Blood would cease to flow after life was extinct, except from gravity power, and then very slightly. The hole was round, with slightly ragged edges, and similar to what would have been made by a ball.

Dr. Kissam, sworn—Heard the examination of Dr. Gilman. Saw and examined the body he described. The features were not recognizable. Do not know that the hole in the side of the head could have been made by a hatchet—would rather suppose, as Dr. Gilman observed, it resembled what would have been made by a nail. Never saw a wound in the head that had been made by a ball. Had this been a ball hole, would suppose it to have looked more regular. Examined the body before it was washed, and saw nothing that looked like salt. Chloride of lime had been thrown on the box. Saw no wounds except those on the head and the remains of what appeared to have been one on the left temple. Think the wounds, other than the hole, could have been made with the hatchet. Those on the right side of the head could have been made by a single blow from the side of the hatchet, and that on the left by one blow from the hammer-side. The skull of deceased was about of the ordinary thickness; that part where the hole appeared is generally thin. The forehead on the left side was not broken directly through.

By Mr. Whiting—The blow on the right side would have struck a man down, and instantly caused death. The wound on the left side might have been produced by a very heavy fall. Do not think a person oould receive such a blow on one side and then turn the other. Cannot say how the hole was made. It was a circular hole, with broken edges. It is barely possible the wound was made with the hatchet. Thinks there might have been considerable blood.

By Mr. Selden—My impression is that on such a blow being given there would be an immediate relaxation of power. Have heard of increased muscular action being caused on receipt of a gun shot wound, but have seen nothing of it. A wound of the kind would create at once an insensibility. The doctor underwent further examination, confirmatory of what had already been said.

Dr. Archer, coroner, sworn—Witness examined the body and described the wounds. Took a ring from the finger of the deceased. Showed it to Mrs. Adams at the time. Thinks it unlikely that a blow from the hatchet would have made the hole in the head.

By Mr. Selden—Was on board the vessel when the box was opened, and also at the dead house. Saw nothing that looked like salt. Thinks if there had been I would have seen it.

By Mr. Whiting—Assisted Mr. Milligan in removing the body. Thinks their labors were about equally divided. Examined the box after the body was removed—there was part of an awning, a coat, stock, pieces of mat, and oakum; saw no appearance of anything else. The stock was cut through, and there was a corresponding cut about the lower jaw.

Mrs. Adams, widow of the murdered man, attended by her father, was then placed upon the stand; she was dressed in deep mourning, and seemed calm and composed.

Emeline B. Adams sworn—My husband's name was Samuel Adams. At the time of his death, he was aged about thirty years, and a printer by profession; his place of business was at the corner of Ann and Gold streets. My husband was last at home on the 17th of September, at noon, to dinner. He went away a little after. Do not know where he intended to go when he left home. He did not return. An advertisement was put in the paper on Wednesday. He wore a black coat when he left home, vest, gambroon pantaloons, a cotton shirt and black stock, and had a ring on the small finger of one of his hands. Did not see the body at the dead house. The ring was shown to me by the coroner (ring handed to witness); this is the same. The coat shown to me was his. Think it doubtful if I should know the shirt again if I saw it. The stock shown was his. (The coat was here held up; it was sadly torn and mutilated.) I know the stock, for I made it myself. He had a watch, with a gold chain, key and seal. The watch and key shown are the same. The key I wore two years myself. Am positive he had the watch with him, when he left home. Do not know exactly how long he had it. Was in the country when he got it, and had been gone for four or five weeks. The watch had been a subject of conversation. He sat on the foot of the bed on Wednesday night; took the key of my chain and endeavored with my pincers to get the dents out. He was at 90 Chatham street Wednesday evening with me, and had it.

After the cross-examination of witness, she was handed from the stand by her father, and immediately left the court.

Mr. Adams' foreman, sworn—I am a printer, and have been foreman to Mr. Adams about thirteen months; knew Mr. Colt; we published a system of book-keeping for him; Mr. Adams made the charges in the book himself; Mr. Adams left the office on the 17th September, about 2 o'clock in the afternoon; he did not say anything at the time of leaving, and do not know what way he went; had on a black coat, black stock, and gambroon pantaloons; did not see the body, nor the stock and coat, at the Alms House; he did not return, and on Tuesday I wrote an advertisement; I saw Mr. Colt in Mr. Adams' office about a week before the time of the latter being missed; there was a book printing for him then; it had been finished; saw Colt also on the day after the advertisement was issued; he called at the office between ten and eleven o'clock and enquired for me; we occupied three floors of the building; he came suddenly upon me and asked if Mr. Adams was in; he said he had seen the advertisement in the newspaper; I told him he had been missing since the previous Tuesday, and that if I had known where to find his office I would have called to enquire of him; he replied that he had known Mr. Adams for about three years, and had always found him very kind and accommodating; a gentleman came into the office and Mr. Colt introduced himself to him; I told Mr. Colt that some of the sheets of his work remained in the office, and he asked me to take care of them; he spoke of some work that Mr. Adams had formerly done for him, and I referred him to Mr. Wells, a book-binder; I asked him if he did not owe Mr. Adams about two hundred dollars; he replied he owed him about fifty dollars; he then left me and went nearly opposite to see Mr. Wells; did not see him again previous to his arrest.

The box in which the body had been found was here brought into court. It was a middle sized packing box of the ordinary appearance, with cleats. The awning which had been stowed around the body was in it.

[The prisoner seemed to wince at the appearance of the box, but young Mr. Emmett got into conversation with him and seemed to draw him off from the examination.]

John Johnson sworn—I am a clerk at No. 8 City Hall Place. Do not know Colt. Knew Mr. Adams since January, 1841;

saw him in the month of September, particularly on the seventeenth, when I saw him three times, at his office, at the office of the Board of Foreign Missions, and in Chambers street near the Post Office, about 3 o'clock P. M. He was going from Centre street to Broadway, on the side next the Post Office; did not speak to him at the time; he was walking moderately. I was going from the Post Office newspaper room to Chambers street; he used to speak to me when we met, but did not on this occasion, and I suppose he did not take notice of me; I turned and looked after him; he kept on; I did not see him after that time Previous to that, between twelve and one, I had seen seen him at his office; went to get a proof of a job he had been in the habit of printing. He did not give it to me, but said he would bring it to the office.

Objected to.

Several witnesses were examined, who testified relative to the watch worn by Mr. Adams.

After this examination, the District-Attorney read an advertisement from the *Courier* relative to the ship Kalamazoo being about to sail for New Orleans. The advertisement was continued for two or three weeks.

An advertisement was also read from the *Sun* of September 22nd, stating that Mr. Adams was missing, and asking information relative to him to be left at the residence of his brother in-law, in Catharine street.

David Downs, sworn—I was acquainted with Samuel Adams, and had been intimate with him for five years; saw the body in the dead house, and believed it to have been his. Knew it by the foot, hair, and size of the person. Am a boot and shoemaker, and acquainted with the size of his foot. Considered him to be a man who was very reserved and of very good temper. I had a high respect for the man, and thought a great deal of him. I had made boots and shoes for himself and family, and got cards printed in pay.

Charles Wells, sworn—I am engaged in the book business at fifty-six Gold street. Was acquainted with Mr. Samuel Adams for five or six years. Had some business transactions with him. We were often at each other's places. His general temper I have supposed to be good, but never saw him under circumstances by which it would be tried. Saw him on the seventeenth of September at two o'clock. I had proposed that he should print a book for me, and take the pay in binding. He informed me soon afterwards that he was doing some printing for Mr. Colt, and asked me to bind that. The sheets were sent to the place where I have folding done. They came to the bindery, and a portion of them were finished on the morning of the seventeenth of September. Mr. Colt came in and said he had been in the bindery, and wished the books forwarded to Philadelphia. He had been there three times previous relative to them, and had made out invoices for the trade (or public) sale at that place. I went out and returned about one o'clock, when my people were bringing the books down below. Sent for Mr. Adams to get his directions. Told him that Mr. Colt had ordered the books to be sent to Philadelphia, and asked if it was all right. He answered "Yes, I believe it is all right. I am to get the proceeds." I remarked from what I heard Mr. Colt say in the morning, there must be some misunderstanding between them. He turned round and said he would go and see. The work had been delayed by Mr. Adams, which gave me some trouble. The trade sales had been held in New York on the thirtieth of August, and in Philadelphia on the sixth of September. Samples were sent by me to the New York sales. Said to Mr. Adams a misunderstanding was apparent, as Mr. Colt spoke of expecting to obtain the proceeds himself; he left my place after two o'clock, and I have not seen him since.

By Mr. Selden—The proceeds of the four hundred volumes would have been from one hundred and twenty-five to one hundred and fifty dollars; Mr. Colt informed me that the proceeds as sold by sample at Philadelphia, would be one hundred and seventeen dollars. Told Mr. Adams that Colt expected the proceeds; I thought it was my duty to tell him; he only said "I will go and see;" he did not show temper, but seemed surprised that there could have been a misunderstanding; he was a man of very few words; a great many persons have spoken to me on the subject; I do not recollect saying that Mr. Adams was vexed when he left my store; I hardly dared to say anything about it for the first five or six days, there was so much confusion; the work was not got out in season for the New York trade sale. Mr. Colt had said Mr. Adams was very kind to him; and had bought him paper for his works; but did not speak of the paper for this book. Mr. Colt appeared to be worried and anxious to get them off, so much so that I thought he intended to run away. The plates cost at least three hundred dollars,—perhaps more. I believe they are now in my vault. Do not know who put them there. Know it was a good work, and supposed I would endeavor to obtain the copy right. Conversed with Mr. Adams on the subject, and learned that Colt was not the owner of it. I thought from the tenor of Colt's remarks, that he supposed the delay was caused by me. He said if they could be got out any sooner by paying the cash at once, it should be done. I replied that the binding had been hurried as much as possible. There are two books—" The Teacher's edition," and a smaller one called the " Second edition."—Mr. Adams allowed me ten cents for binding the small one and fifteen cents for the large one—about half of each had been prepared in the four hundred copies. I believe the plates were put into my vault by Mr. Adams for safe keeping. I saw them there before knowing Mr. Colt. The work was a super royal octavo. The paper was bought of Mr. Field by Mr. Adams, and Mr. Colt's note given for the amount. At first felt grieved to think I had sent Mr. Adams to Colt's room, but on reflection supposed I was right, and under similar circumstances thought I should do so again.

By Mr. Whiting—He did appear to be vexed, the day subsequent. Mr. Colt came into my room and said, this is very strange, what could have become of him. I did not look up, but he came and put his hand on my desk. I said " I do not know; the last I saw of him he said he was going to see you." He did not appear to make much answer, but stepped back and appeared to make similar expressions as at first. We then began to talk about the books. It was between ten and twelve o'clock. He changed countenance a little and stepped back. I felt hurt a little to think I had told him, as I knew I should feel hurt myself to have such an expression made to me. He afterwards appeared to evade the question.

By the Court—The four hundred volumes were sent to Philadelphia on the next day. I understand that Mr. Colt has since received the proceeds. The invoice was under the name of B. W Foster & Co.

John L. Blake sworn—I am a clergyman residing in Brooklyn; knew Mr. Adams for five or six years; he occupied the upper part of the building in which I was (Blake & Co.'s, Gold street), for about three years; saw him frequently; he was in the habit of doing the printing for the establishment, and saw him over three times a day; he removed, and continued doing a portion of the printing to the day of his death; saw him probably a thousand times while he was engaged in his business; his temper was unusually passive and mild; his boys were frequently noisy, and he did not appear to have the necessary energy to keep them in proper discipline; I am not able to state what he would do under circumstances of irritation such as he experienced; but I never heard him saying as loud a word as could be heard across the room. The work at the latter part of the time was not done so well as it had been, as he employed a number of these irresponsible young men. Strong fault was found with him, but I never heard him answer in any petulant manner. I spoke harshly to him once myself unintentionally. He made no reply, but I saw that his feelings were much affected, and that he shed a tear.

Several other witnesses were examined, who testified to the mild character of Mr. Adams.

William M. Ironsides, sworn—Was employed in the granite building with Mr. Slocum. Slept in the third story; slept there in the month of September. Noticed something singular one night about twelve o'clock. Had shut up the store and was going up stairs. Heard a great hammering, and mentioned it next day. It was on Friday night, and in one of the rooms on the second floor, to the right hand side. It sounded as if some one was nailing up a box. I was frightened at first, and went back, but returned and proceeded to my room. Next morning I saw several boxes—they were coming and going all the time. I did not notice any in particular.

By Mr. Selden—Slept in the third story, with my uncle, Mr. Ironsides. He is not in the city now. I was asleep when he came home. Told the folks in the store next morning and my mother on the same evening, as I went home on Saturday night. Locked the hall door when I went up stairs.

Charles J. Walker, sworn—Am a picture-frame maker. Kept with Mr. Ritner in the granite buildings; asked Mrs. Octon for the loan of a saw on Thursday. She directed me to go to Mr. Colt for it. I went to his room, and knocked two or three times. Heard some one inside sawing. Finally Mr. Colt came to the door; I asked him for the saw, and he told me to go to hell. The door was fastened inside, and Mr. Colt opened it but a very little way.

John Golden, sworn—I am a milkman. Left milk at the basement saloon of the building corner of Broadway and Chambers street. Saw a man occupied in the vault of the saloon, opposite the area, the latter part of the week in September, working on boards. It was between seven and eight o'clock. The man was tall, and started when he saw me. He looked so wild I thought he was going to strike me. He had a saw and hatchet.

Mr. Monahan sworn—Was foreman with Mr. Adams for fourteen months. Saw him in a passion twice—once when a man threatened to sue him. He replied that the other would get his money no sooner. Did not make use of bad language. Have seen him vexed. His pay-day was every other Saturday, and would have been such the day after he was missed. His bills amounted to a hundred or a hundred and fifty dollars. Do not know that he had made any arrangements to raise the money.

By Mr. Selden—Understood that the Butcher's Bank had a mortgage upon the office. He might have been a little behindhand with his workmen, but not a great deal. [Witness was handed the books of Mr. Adams, with list of his workmen, as marked paid, and he declared them to be his.]

By the Court—Do not know whether he had any money with him on the seventeenth of September, or whether he carried a pocket-book.

Mr. Sparks sworn—I am administrator on the estate of Mr. Adams. He was a very good-tempered man.

By Mr. Selden—Have had the books in my possession since the thirteenth of October. They do not appear to have been regularly kept. Accounts were open which he should have credited.

By the Court—It is doubtful whether the estate is solvent or not.

Joseph L. Lane sworn—I am father-in-law to Mr. Adams. Had known him about five years. He was married to my daughter about three years ago. Recognized the body at the dead-house by the scar on his left leg. He usually carried his money and papers about him in a large pocket-book.

Nicholas Conklin, gunsmith, sworn—Reside at 90 Chatham street. Was acquainted with Mr. Adams, and know him to have been of an amiable disposition. Himself and Mrs. Adams were at my house the evening before he was missing. Know the watch, and talked of buying it from him. He had it with him then. Offered him eighty-five dollars for the watch, but he wanted ninety.

Officer A. M. C. Smith, sworn—Arrested Mr. Colt; found the hatchet under a lot of papers and a trunk placed over them, found a pail there, and also saw the other things already described.

John P. Brinkerhoff, sworn—Was called upon to have the contents of the sink at No. 42 Monroe street, cleared, and also that of the granite building raked, with a view to find clothing, but none was discovered.

Mr. Wheeler recalled—Told Mr. Colt that I had let his room to Mr. Delnoce, and he was anxious to get it. Also mentioned to him on the Saturday morning that he came into the room to see if my key would open the door, that I wanted his room, as Mr. Delnoce had been obliged to sleep in my room that night. Colt observed that he thought he saw a light in the room, but corrected himself as he had just before stated that he was absent the previous afternoon and evening. On the 13th September, on the evening of the day on which we had the controversy about the rent, Mr. Colt came into my room. We spoke of his brother, and I asked him if he (the brother), was the inventor of the patent pistol; he replied that he was, and asked me if I had seen any of his pistols. I replied that I had not. He said he had one in his room and would go and get it and let me see it. He went in and got it. It had a beautiful pearl handle, and four or six barrels—I think six; also explained to me a very ingenious mode of detonating with a cylinder; the barrels were about four inches in length. It had his brother's name on; I think at any rate he said it was his brother's. He did not explain its capacity for propelling.

By Mr. Selden—The person I saw stooping down after I heard the noise, had his side towards the hall door, and his head in a westerly direction. He was near the folding door. Cannot say as to the qualities of the pistol I saw; the handle and all was about eight and a half inches long. My attention was particularly attracted by the elegance with which it was wrought. I had it in my hand; I had often been in his room —oftener than he was in mine. Am certain he had the pistol three or four days before the 17th. Was not questioned by the Grand Jury in regard to the pistol. Told Mr. Whiting of it last Friday. Think I might have mentioned the circumstance to Justice Taylor soon after the affair, but am not certain. Thought of the pistol after the discovery of the murder.

Mr. DeForest, French consul, sworn—Had purchased a pair of Colt's pistols, of the pattern shown. We tried some of them on board the Belle Poule. When merely propelled by a cap the ball was sent one hundred and fifty or one hundred and sixty feet, struck and dented a board, and rebounded ten or twelve feet. When fired at twelve feet the ball went through two thick covers of a book. The sound is like the cracking of a whip; cannot say the sound is like the clashing of foils. The experiments were made with Colt's pocket pistol.

James Short sworn—Washed the body at the dead house; cut the rope from the neck and the right knee, and also picked the bones from the skull, washed them and gave them to the doctors. The rope was a very thick one. Washed the body after the doctors had examined it: I saw salt on the body, and washed it off. Deceased was salted, but I cannot say how much salt was on him; but am sure he was salted. Do not know how many pieces of skull there were. I took them out of the head, washed them in a pail, and the doctors took account of them The first piece was about the breadth of your finger, as if struck by a hammer. Took out at least three pieces of skull. Both eyes were in. Saw no cuts about the jaw; only saw the head as if beat in with a hammer. Put the body in a coffin. Forgot to put the bones in, but wrapped them in a piece of paper and ran to the burial grounds afterwards, and placed them in the grave with the coffin.

By Mr. Selden—The grave yard was down that way (pointing towards the Battery). I do not know the streets in this city. I am no scholar. The salt was all over the body. I got into the box and showed a gentleman how the body lay in it when found, with its limbs doubled up, and the head leaning on one side of the box and the feet on the other.

This closed the testimony for the prosecution, when District-Attorney Whiting here rose, and remarked that he would then rest.

THE DEFENCE.

John A. Morril, Esq., one of the counsel for the prisoner, then rose and remarked as follows: Gentlemen of the jury—it now becomes the duty of the counsel for the prisoner—their solemn duty—to enter more minutely into the examination of the evidence which has been produced against the unfortunate individual who stands before you—a young man just entering into life, who has no friend around him but a brother—who is deprived by misfortune of the presence of his father—you know where his mother is, and also where are his beloved sisters. While you have sympathy for him, I must admit that you must also feel the loss sustained by the widow of Mr. Adams, one who has been bereaved by the loss of a tender and affectionate husband. The people ask that the laws shall be fairly administered, but while they do so, are sometimes carried away, and without thought will condemn an individual unheard. But the jury must lay aside these feelings—must lay aside feelings not only for the unfortunate prisoner, but for Mrs. Adams and for public prejudice. You must take hold of this case with clear, dispassionate minds, remembering to blend with justice the attributes of mercy. The counsel on the other side is all powerful, and it was necessary to fight the cause, as we have, from one step to another, knowing that "trifles light as air" may have much effect on a case like this. A man will fight for his life, and the counsel will contend not only for that life but for justice to the prisoner. It is with this feeling, and not with the view to detain the jury, that we have been thus minute. Gentlemen, John C. Colt, poor and friendless, a fellow citizen, comes before you charged with crime. He comes before you in defence of that life which is dear to all. He asks you to mete out to him justice—it is all he asks, it is all we ask. We seek but one thing—it is that we may have mercy according to law—and if he has such, we have no doubt that he will find a safe deliverance at your hands.

Samuel Colt was the first witness called for the defence—I am the inventor of Colt's patent fire arms, and am acquainted with their construction. [Mr. Colt was then requested to show some experiments touching the power of the pistol with a cap. He placed balls in the cylinder of one about eight or ten inches long, and propelled them by percussion caps, which he stated to be of great strength. There was a loud report, and he caught the balls in his hand as they came from the barrel. He then fired at an open book at a few paces which he struck, the ball penetrating nine leaves and indenting twenty-four. He also tried a patent pocket pistol at a distance, which made very little impression.] Witness never made pistols with more than one barrel except at first, about ten years ago, and then only kept them as models.

Dr. Zabrisky, sworn—I am practising physician and chemist. Had at one period charge of the patent arms store in Broadway. Have fired off the pistols with a cap thousands of times, in order to exhibit them. Do not suppose, from my knowledge of the human skull, that it could be penetrated by a ball propelled only by a cap—it is impossible that the skull could have been more than bruised. I was never able but once even to indent a fire-board with a ball sufficiently deep to make it stick. The patent article, when fired with powder, makes more noise than common firearms.

By a Juror—The impression did not appear to be so great at five feet distance as at twenty feet. Think it would be impossible for a ball to make a hole such as represented, in the head of deceased, by a ball from Colt's pistol, propelled by a cap.

The District Attorney here stated it was necessary to have Mr. Adams' skull produced in Court, Dr. Mott being present, who wished to examine it.

The Coroner, Dr. Archer, stated that the body had probably been re-interred by this time; a minute examination of the wound had been made.

Dr. Gilman, sworn—Was present that forenoon at an examination of the body, which laid in a small building inside of the burial grounds. We first examined the cavity of the skull. There was no foreign substance there whatever. Our attention was then directed to the round hole over the left ear, a little back. My little finger passed in, and rested at the second joint. The wound is slightly oval—one part is a very trifle larger than the other. On the anterior portion of the hole was beaten in the twelfth part of an inch. It was made as if a round file had been applied to the inside of the hole. Some of the physicians thought the skull was not so thick as usual, but I did not see that such was the case. It is inconceivable to me how it is possible that such a hole could have been made by a hatchet; it is more easy to suppose it could have been done by the driving of a nail; a nail might have been driven in it, and the working of the body caused the circular hole. The appearance of the wounds in front are as if made by the hammer part of the hatchet. My opinion is changed from what it was. I think it improbable that the hole was made by a ball of any description.

Dr. Rogers recalled—It is impossible to say what particular degree of injury would be necessary to create insensibility. In some cases, it is created by a very small sized wound—in others, even where the whole front of the top of the head was broken in, as a wound caused by the falling of a block from a masthead, where the man preserved his senses throughout, and got well. The witness, James Short, got into the box, as he described, to show how the body lay. It was a kind of across the box; the left side of the head lay against the inside of the box. A nail projecting into the box about an inch, I should suppose, must have penetrated the head of the body in any way it moved.

By a Juror—A blow that struck in the right side of the skull might also have injured the cheek bone.

Witness resumed—Think, from the wounds shown, that the hemorrhage was great and instantaneous. The wounds on the forehead and right side might possibly have been made by a single blow from the side of the hatchet. The man got into the box yesterday to show me how the body lay. The nails in the box were about two inches long, and the one I alluded to projected about an inch.

By the Court—Think the action of the body in carrying it to Maiden lane, putting it on board the vessel, and afterwards carrying the body to the dead-house, might have been sufficient to drive the nail through the head. Do not think the force shown by the ball in the experiments this morning would even have fractured the skull.

Victor Becker, sworn—Lived at No. 3 Murray street from May, 1840, to May, 1841. After we moved away, Mr. Colt went in. We left an awning in the garret. Saw the one at the Tombs. It was the same.

By Mr. Whiting—My father's family now live down at 144 Fulton street. Know the awning by a piece of linen I had fastened to it. My father left the awning in the front of the house. Did not know Mr. Colt. Mr. Nelson occupied the house afterwards. The awning was still on the house on the first of July. My father said he was there on the second, and it was gone. Have been to the granite building, but not to see Mr. Colt. My father does not speak English very plain. My father left the awning because he supposed the person who moved in might want to buy it. No one bought it, though it was taken away. It was fastened to the house by iron rings. My father went to France last Saturday. I was requested by Mr. Colt and Mr Robinson to go up and look at the awning. Did so about three weeks ago. Have no doubt but it is the same.

John N. Lee, sworn—I am an engraver, and keep at No. 3 Murray street. Mr. Colt moved into the building in May. Saw a box in his room. He was preparing his work. He brought in a hatchet one morning, and said it was very handy. I bought one afterwards. Mine is not like the one here shown, but has an axe form. He had been in the habit of borrowing a hammer from me. He had moved away, and the awning was gone, but I did not suppose he took it. I never saw any irritability about him. He was gentlemanly in his appearance to me, and I the same to him.

By Mr. Whiting—Did not know his associates. Have seen men in his place.

By a Juror—He showed me the hatchet before leaving Murray street.

Cyrus W. Field, sworn—I am a paper dealer. Made paper to order and on account of Mr. Colt in July and August, 1841. The terms were to be one half cash and one half a good note. He gave the direction No. 3 Murray street. In August sent to inquire, and he was not there. Soon afterwards, Mr. Adams came in, having in his hand a letter from Mr. Colt, dated Boston, and requesting I should let Mr. A. have the paper. Told Mr. Adams the terms. The latter said Mr. Colt had always paid him, and the books should not go out of his hands till the money was paid. I let him have ten reams. The balance of the paper was delayed in coming from Hartford here, and Mr. Adams was very anxious about it. On the twenty-fifth of August Mr. Colt came in, and said it was too late for the trade sale, but, if I would give him time, he would take the balance of the paper, and have the work perfected for the Philadelphia trade sale, getting his returns in time to pay for the paper. Mr. Adams thought the note of Mr. Colt would be good for the amount. The two lots came to one hundred and twenty-one dollars and sixty-eight cents, for which I took Mr. Colt's note at three months, which note is unpaid. The paper was sent to Mr. Adams' office. Understood the plates cost over three hundred dollars.

By Mr. Whiting—I never saw Mr. Adams excited, but, on the contrary, supposed him to be extremely amiable; indeed, too easy.

[The head of Mr. Adams was here brought into court by the physicians and coroner, while the latter sat with it in his lap, wrapped up, beside the reporter's table. Colt sat on one side, within a few feet of it. The hand that struck the blow and the head that was still in death came nearly in contact.]

Doctor Mott had been subpœnaed by the counsel for the defence, and he requested through the District-Attorney that he might now be examined.

[Mr. Selden, the District-Attorney, Doctors Mott and Archer, and others, agreed that the head of Mr. Adams, which was in possession of the coroner, should be taken into an adjoining room and be examined, and Doctor Mott afterwards give his evidence. The District-Attorney announced the fact to the court, who acceded to it. The prisoner looked towards the head as the coroner took it out. What must have been his feelings!]

Dr. Rogers, recalled—Have examined the head of Mr. Adams. Am well satisfied from the examination and comparing the hatchet with the wound, that the hole was made with the sharp side of the hatchet. It fits the wound precisely.

The District-Attorney requested that the skull and axe should be shown to the jury.

Mr. Selden objected.

Judge Kent stated that, however painful it was, justice should be administered, and the head produced, if the jury thought it necessary.

The District-Attorney observed that they were only seeking truth ; desperate efforts were making to break down the testimony. If it could be avoided he would gladly agree not to have the skull exhibited, but it was necessary that the jury should see it.

The skull was then handed to Dr. Rogers by the coroner, and exhibited to the jury. Never was there a more thrilling sight. The court room was crowded to excess, and the head was held up in his fingers by Dr. Rogers. He placed the corner of the axe in the hole over the left ear, which precisely fitted it. He then put the hammer part in the fracture or indentation on the other side, which joined in it fairly as a mould. He then explained the wounds in front. It was, indeed, a dreadful sight.

Colt held his hands over his eyes while the examination was going on.

Dr. Archer, sworn—The body has been twice exhumed today, and the skull taken from the coffin which bears his name and age. The hole in the head seems to agree with the corner of the axe ; but the blow most likely to have caused insensibility was one struck behind, which the hammer part of the hatchet exactly fits.

The jaw bone was also produced, which was broken in halves. Dr. Archer went on to explain the nature of the wounds, and the head was minutely examined by the jurors.

Dr. Mott sworn—He examined the skull. Think the small hole was inflicted by the hatchet. If the hole was made from a ball, it was different from what I have ever seen. Believe it to have been given from the front. Also examined the wound behind. It is impossible to say how the party stood. Do not think the front part of the head could have been driven in, as this one shows, by a single blow. Do not know what blow created insensibility. There are no two cases alike. Either of the blows here shown would have knocked any man down. I have seen a man recover and walk with nearly a quarter of his skull knocked in. No man can tell how many blows have been given. Have no dobt that the hole was made with the hatchet.

Previous to this thrilling examination, all the ladies in court had retired.

Nathan G. Burgess, sworn—Am acquainted with John C. Colt. Have known him since 1837. Was engaged with him in

Cincinnati in that year publishing Delafield's Antiquities of America. He was engaged previously teaching book-keeping. The work was got out in New York by subscription in 1839, we having come here for that purpose. It was published in the name of Colt, Burgess & Co., and we lost a thousand dollars by it. I am still indebted to Mr. Colt. He always treated me like a gentleman. He kept in Cortlandt street after coming here.

Mr. Selden here called several witnesses who did not answer. He then asked if Miss Henshaw was in court.

The crier called Caroline M. Henshaw.—[The mistress of Colt.]

Miss Henshaw then advanced to the stand, and created quite a sensation among the audience. She wore a dark bonnet, black veil, and light cloth cloak. She was handed a chair, threw back her veil, and presented an interesting appearance.

On being sworn, she testified as follows—Am acquainted with John C. Colt. Have known him fifteen months. Knew him before I came from Philadelphia here. Came on soon after him from Philadelphia; about three months after. Had lived with him from the eleventh of May to the time I understood he had been arrested. I reside at No. 42 Monroe street. Have been in this city since January, and reside at Captain Hart's, corner of Catharine and Madison streets. Mr. Colt was generally in from half-past nine to ten o'clock in the evening. He was engaged in book-keeping. His office was at the corner of Chambers street and Broadway. On the evening of the seventeenth of September, I think he was not home at the ordinary hour, but can't state positively. He was frequently out with a gentleman named Moore, and I generally went to bed soon. Do not recollect of his being out one evening later than usual. Recollect one evening when he returned home after I had gone to bed, and supposed it was late. It was within the week before his arrest. Think he was out till eleven or twelve o'clock. He had not been in the habit of being out late at night. He was always home before ten o'clock.

By Mr. Selden—He had been absent some time in the latter part of the week before. His deportment was different after that night. He seemed strange in his conduct, and disinclined in conversation. I was asleep when Mr. Colt came home that evening. I woke up when he had got on his night-shirt, and asked him what time it was. He said it was a little after eleven. Next morning he went away early. I awoke as he was just about to leave the room, and asked him where he was going so early. He said he was going to the boat; he might be back soon, or might not be back to breakfast. He returned about ten or half-past ten o'clock. After his return he undressed, bathed himself with spirits, and went to bed. He bathed his shoulders and neck. After he had got into bed, I went to the bed side, it being unusual for him to go to bed in the day. He was not asleep. I observed on his neck a black mark. I commenced speaking, and he said [objected to by the District Attorney]. The marks were on one side of his neck, as I could only see one side. He generally slept with his night-shirt open, but for two or three nights afterwards he slept with his night-shirt pinned up. Cannot say which side of the neck it was. He continued to rub his neck afterwards with spirits.

By Mr. Emmett—Remember being called upon by Justice Taylor. Had heard that Mr. Adams had disappeared on a a Friday. Believe the night that Mr. Colt was absent was on a Friday night. As he lay in bed after his return, his night-shirt was pinned high up in the neck by the binding. He showed no unwillingness to state what had occurred. [Objected to by Mr. Whiting, who said he was unwilling to allow in evidence what Mr. Adams had said.] He appeared very stiff, as if he had caught a cold or something of that kind. The stiffness continued up to the time of his arrest.

[The witness was directly opposite the prisoner during the examination, within about ten feet, and seemed favorably disposed towards him. Colt kept his eye steadily meeting hers.]

By Mr. Whiting—First became acquainted with Colt at Philadelphia, at the house of Mrs. Stuart. He first made arrangements to come to New York in January, a year ago. Became acquainted with him in the month of August preceding. Mrs. Stuart was not a relation. I visited at her house. Mr. Colt did not board there, but came with a gentleman. Did not live with him before I came from Philadelphia. At Mr. Hart's I passed by the name of Mrs. Colt. We did not furnish our own room. Mr. H. furnished it for us. Nor did we at 42 Monroe street, though we had a few articles. Was also known there as Mrs. Colt. Occupied a room in the third story. Messed with the family we lived with. Occupied no other room in any part of the house. Mr. Colt's trunk stood in the entry. It was the same that Justice Taylor took, as was also the carpet-bag. We moved from Catharine to Monroe street. Was not in the habit of going to bed at a particular hour. Sometimes early and sometimes late. When Mr. Colt went out of an evening I generally went with him. He was very seldom out, but when he was out I did not sit up for him, but generally woke up when he came into the room. Did not keep a light burning in the room through the night. Sometimes I put out the light when I went to bed at times when he was absent. There were matches in the room. Do not remember whether I put out the lights that night or not. Do not well remember the night of the seventeenth. Only remember he was out late if that was the seventeenth of September, Remember his being out late on the night before the Saturday he went out early. It was the Saturday previous to his arrest. I went to bed early in the evening; cannot say the hour. The family took tea about seven o'clock. I cannot say whether he was home to tea or not. He was home to dinner. A lady (Mrs. Burke) who boarded in the house, came into the room and we talked some time before I went to bed. We had a very small clock over the dressing-table, but do not remember having looked at it. It was not a dressing-table, but we called it such; the glass stood in a frame. Mr. Colt wound up the clock every morning. Went to bed and soon to sleep. Do not remember whether I put out the light or not. I slept soundly, and generally did. The door was not fastened. I did not wake that evening before Mr. Colt came home. When I first saw him he was undressed, and had his night shirt on. There was a light in the room, and he stood directly opposite to the glass. I then saw his side face. I did not get up. The dressing-table stood by the window, at the foot of the bed, our feet to it. I remained lying in the bed after I saw him. There was no space between the table and the bed. In looking into the glass a person lying in bed could see the right side face of a person standing in front of the glass. Could not see the face of the clock as I lay in bed. Mr. Colt blew out the candle immediately on my awakening, and came directly to bed. I do not remember speaking to him, but think it very likely I did, as I generally spoke to him as he came into the room. He came into the bed about a minute or two minutes after I first saw him. Cannot say what he was doing those one or two minutes. He might have been fixing his clothes. He did not go out of the room. I turned over, and as I did so he came into bed. He generally threw his clothes over the back of a chair. The chair stood at the foot of the bed, but do not remember seeing his clothes on it. I went to sleep again, and woke in the morning when it was broad daylight, and Mr. Colt was leaving the room. The sun rises early at that season, but as the blinds were thick, could not see whether the sun rose or not. Mr. Colt was in the habit of getting up between the first and second ringing of the breakfast bell. He went out that morning before the ringing of the first bell, but I cannot say whether it was a very long or a very short time. He did not return to breakfast. I did not observe that he had anything in his hands. Was surprised at his going out so early and spoke to him. I think if he had had anything in his hand I would have seen it. The carpet-bag was kept under the head of the bed,—the room was so small we had no other place to keep it. It was never left outside, and I had access to it after I had washed his clothes and put them in it.

By Mr. Whiting—Was he dressed? He was; do you suppose a gentleman would go into the street without? Am not positive the clothes were the same as those he wore the day before, but they were like them. He had three or four pair of pantaloons, and two coats; one pair of the former were black cloth, and the others lighter, something of a pearl color. One of the coats was a black dress, and the other a frock. Do not remember which he had on that day. He had long blue socks which he wore on Friday. He was in the habit of putting the clothes away himself. Remember going to the carpet-bag that morning. The litter we made in the room we generally put into the bag. Did so after he went out that morning. Put some rags and things in it that lay about the room, but did not put a newspaper in. Went to a trunk that morning, but did not take anything out, or put anything in. Do not remember why I went to it. Do not know whether he changed his linen or not. The way I know he came in about eleven, the ladies had company that night, and they did not have company very late, and they said he came in about that time. I mean to say he was absent two nights of the week previous to his arrest—the first night I knew the time by the clock, the Friday night by what the young ladies told me. It was Miss Ann Kelso who told me. The two nights were before the preceding Sunday of the arrest. The first time might have been eight or ten days before the Saturday morning. Mr. Colt, after he went to bed, said he felt unwell, and didn't wish to converse, so I took my sewing and sat down. I do not remember what clothes he wore on Friday; think on Saturday I was going down as he came in. Met him at the front door. He went up, and I went down, where I staid a few minutes. When I went up he was undressing himself. When I first went in supposed he was going to change his dress. I took a seat. Did not aid him to undress. Did not see him put on his night-shirt. I was sitting on a chair looking out of the window, and did so for five minutes after he got into bed. The night-shirt had a button in front, as usual. I had made the shirt. His linen shirts were marked with his name and number, and I think his night-shirts were. He wore linen shirts in the daytime. When I came to the bedside, observed his clothing on the back of the chair. His shirt was the last garment placed there. Did not look at it. He generally threw it over so that the bosom was smooth, and not soiled. There were no spots or marks on it. If there had been, I think I would have observed it. Think I can say that there were no such. It was after he had gone to bed that I saw the black spots on the neck. He was lying on his side, and had gone to sleep. We slept in a small square front room. From the position he lay in bed, think it was on the right side, and the mark was on the left. His feet were towards the river. The spot was black and blue, round, near the front; it was about as large as a sixpence. I began conversing with him on the subject, and he put his hand and pushed me away from the bed. Did not see any other spot. He lay in bed, I think, to the hour of dinner, but am not certain. He put on the same clothes he had taken off. He returned to the room after dinner, but do not know whether he went out that afternoon or not. Do not remember having assisted to dress him for dinner. Might have done so without remembering it. Think he wore the same clothes that he took off on undressing at ten o'clock, as he wore them in the evening. Cannot say that they were the same which he wore the day previous. He generally changed his linen three or four times a week, and think he changed it on first getting up that Saturday morning, as it appeared to be clean. Do not know what became of the shirt he took off. I might have seen it and washed it, but did not observe. Have not seen any shirt in his basket that had been soiled. I generally washed on Monday, but did not that week until Wednesday. Observed a shirt that I thought the stiffness or starch had been washed out of the wristbands. He had a shirt which wanted mending. It was the Thursday before his arrest, as he lay in bed. I ripped the wristbands off, and threw them under the bed. I think he was home the whole Saturday evening; am not sure that he was so in the early part of the evening. On Sunday morning I took his breakfast up stairs to him; think he was up, and that he went out in the forenoon, but went to bed in the afternoon again. He was all the forenoon or all the afternoon in bed on Sunday—I cannot say which. He slept soundly in the day, but did not sleep much that night. I had been at his room in Chambers street before. Cannot say when—it might have been a month. He appeared to be restless on the Saturday as he lay in bed, but did not appear to sleep much; appeared to be coughing; do not recollect his turning over and I discovering the other side of his neck. Never saw any other spot. Do not recollect having ever seen any mark on his hands or face. When I was at the bedside I was going to ask him if the mark was a pinch or something of that kind. On Friday he was arrested, and I sat up for him the whole night. The clock did not strike the hours.

By Mr. Selden—The shirt I was washing on Wednesday I thought had had the stiffening washed out of the bosom as well as wristbands, but am not sure. His conduct during the week previous to his arrest did not appear such as usual. He did not talk nor go into the parlor in company, as before. I tried to persuade him to do so, but could not. He was always very kind, very mild; treated me kindly always, and I do not recollect that I ever saw him in a passion.

By Mr. Whiting—I am a mother by Mr. Colt. My own mother never called to see me at 42 Monroe street. Think I am acquainted with his disposition and temper. Never gave a reason to any person why I left him and returned to Philadelphia. Mr. Colt instructed me in writing while we were at Monroe street.

By a Juror—Do not know anything about the watch, and did not see it.

By Mr. Whiting—Did not know there was a watch in the trunk when Justice Taylor took it, nor did I know then that he had been arrested; I did not know Adams; he was never at our house.

The witness then left the court, attended by Samuel Colt.

Sarah Hart sworn—I know the prisoner, Mr. Colt, and Caroline Henshaw; they lived in my house from the last of February, or beginning of March, to the middle of May; Mr. Colt was of very mild temper, very pleasant, and every day alike, always pleasant and mild.

By Mr. Selden—How did Caroline Henshaw act? (objected to by Mr. Whiting.)

Mr. Selden stated to the court that he meant to show that the only ground why she and Mr. Colt did not form the relation of man and wife, was owing to the breaking up of his business, and his inability to provide an establishment, but they both looked forward to the day when they could be united. His relation with her was one of the acts for which he has been called upon by public sentiment to answer, but she was no prostitute except as regarded him. He did wrong and she did, but adverse circumstances alone caused them to live together in the illegitimate manner they did; still her character, every other way, was good. She came into court under circumstances which went to impair her reputation as a witness, and he wished to show by this witness that she was deserving of confidence.

Mr. Whiting said, he had no objection to allowing that the conduct of Caroline Henshaw had been good both at Catharine and at Monroe streets. They had not impeached her character; but should the parties be permitted privileges now, be allowed to testify for each other, when they would be denied if they stood in the relation of man and wife, and still further, produce evidence of correct conduct?

Judge Kent stated, that unless the character of a witness was impeached the testimony should be allowed. It was unnecessary to produce evidence as to the character of the last witness.

Mr. Selden requested the court to notice the counsel's exception to the decision.

Henry W. Root sworn—I reside in the city, and have so done for ten years. Am a native of Hartford. Was acquainted with John C. Colt in early life. We went to school together. Never saw him quarrelsome so far as to make remark. I may say one thing—John Colt was the leader of the boys in our neighborhood.

Richard B. Pullen sworn—Know Mr. Colt. Have been acquainted with him for three years. Think Mr. Colt would be the first man to resent an insult and the last man to give it—one that would insult no man unless they first insulted him. Have been at his rooms in Chambers street and felt pleasure in keeping his company. He was a man of extensive information, and I called upon him almost every evening. He generally wore a watch, but do not recollect any one in particular.

Isaac Hart sworn—John C. Colt and Caroline M. Henshaw boarded with me from February to May, 1841; his conduct was mild and good; I saw nothing whatever by which I could find fault with his behavior.

Samuel S. Osgood sworn—I am portrait painter, at the corner of Chambers street and Broadway; my room is No 11, directly opposite Mr. Wheeler's, and contains three windows; entered it in August; when the windows are open the inconvenience from noise in the street is so great that I have frequently to stop conversation; was never in the room after dark but once; am a native of Boston, and resided in Hartford twenty years since; Mr. Colt and myself went to school together; he was ardent in his feelings, but for what I know very amiable. I was absent from home when this circumstance happened.

George Andrews sworn—Have been acquainted with Mr. Colt since 1838; I am a merchant tailor, and have had business transactions with him; never discovered anything but that he was an amiable person; he always paid cash down like a man.

Fredrick Cary called—Am a clerk with R. Ashton & Co., in 8 Cedar street. Have known John C. Colt since August, 1840, when he was keeping a book store in Philadelphia, corner of Fifth and Minor streets. I came here in January 1840, and have seen him often since. Have been at his rooms in Murray street, and also at Chambers street. Saw a box and other things, as already described. Saw a piece of looking glass in his room, which was against the wall, and a piece of paper kept over it. Saw the hatchet in his room at Chambers street, about the 1st of August. Saw him have a new gold watch in September, some time after the 4th, cannot say which day.

By Mr. Whiting—I was in his room five or six times and staid about ten minutes each time. He was the only one I knew here from Philadelphia. I saw him with the watch the 11th or 13th of September. It was in his room, and I saw it as he held it up to tell what time it was. I said "you have got a new watch;" he replied (objected to); I saw it had a gold face and engraved back. The day he moved into Chambers street saw a piece of cloth in his room larger than a sheet, also a rope round his trunk. Never saw him out of temper. Did not see him have a watch either before or after the day I mention. Read an account about the watch and key in the *Sun*—remember fully as to the key, that it had dents on it; no one gave me a description of the watch that had been found in the trunk. [This witness seemed to have been extremely deficient in both sight and recollection as related to particular occasions.]

Mr. Selden then declared that the defence would rest.

The prosecution proceeded to introduce some testimony in rebuttal.

Robert Hoe, sworn—Was acquainted with Mr. Samuel Adams; have known him intimately since 1835; our intercourse had been principally of a business kind; he called upon us almost every day; I always had a great respect for the man, and considered his character and temper very good indeed; have seen him upon very many occasions when his temper was tried; do not think he carried a cane; he was a plain, unassuming man; never knew or heard of his giving or receiving a blow.

Other witnesses were called, who testified similarly as to the character of Mr. Adams.

Solon Humphreys, sworn—I am clerk to the Patent Arms Co. I charged the pistols on board the Belle Poule. The ball was thrown the length of the ship, about one hundred and fifty feet, and struck a board. The pistol was fired only by a cap. The ball must be rammed home to be effective. A very small quantity of powder introduced would have great force.

John Ehlers, sworn—I am treasurer of the Patent Arms Co.

When a pistol is charged in the proper manner a ball can be thrown by a mere cap a hundred and fifty to two hundred feet. At a hundred and thirty-five feet it leaves a mark. If the ball does not show power, it is because the ball is not driven home, or the cap properly put on. Think a ball thrown by a cap would not go through a skull at a distance of five or six feet. A very small quantity of powder, say half the charge of a cap, in addition, would drive a ball at a distance of nine or ten feet through a half-inch plank. Think the experiments made in Court have been fairly done, and that the caps were of the best kind, better than are usually sold, and can only be had at our establishment and one other.

Mr. Whiting here declared that the prosecution would rest.

The defence then recalled Mr. Brinckerhoff, superintendent of the Poudrette Co.—Had cleaned the sink at Monroe street, with a view to see if anything could be discovered. Put a man down the sink at the rear of the granite building some few days ago, with a light and a rake, and he discovered nothing. Within the last two days, however, the sink had been cleaned. Had a tub, in which was placed what was discovered. We found some cloth, some portions of a towel, and a bundle which contained shoes from its outside appearance, all of which were placed in the tub. Put the tub in the rear part of the wagon, and carried it into the Tombs. Remained there till morning, when we went to see Mr. Selden, Mr. Whiting, and others. I told Mr. Fowkes I should take the bundle into my own possession. Took it down to Nassau street, placed it in the cellar under lock and key, and from that took it to the factory, where the bundle was opened. There was found in it a hat, a pair of shoes, a pair of pantaloons, part of a shirt, a pair of suspenders, and a vest.

Mr. Selden—Was it there, sir, when you made the first examination?

Mr. Whiting objected, as it would only be a matter of judgment.

Witness continued—From the condition of the bundle and the state of the garments, supposed the bundle must have been overlooked on the first examination. I stated so to Mr. Conklin. Have no doubt, from the garments being rotted, that they have laid there. The soil has not been thoroughly examined yet. Some things were found this morning—a pencil case, some keys, a half-dollar piece, and other things. They were not found in the bundle. I came here early, by request of Mr. Selden, and did not have time to examine the whole of the soil. Had cleaned the sink at Monroe street in the early part of October, but merely raked that at the granite buildings. Have a piece of the pantaloons and vest in my pocket. [Showed the pieces, and they were examined by the jury.] The pantaloons were gambroon, and the vest may have been yellow. There was also a pockethandkerchief and a pair of stockings. The bundle was tied in a hard knot, the diagonal corners of the handkerchief tied. The contents under the third apartment had been raked. The hat had been cut from the rim to the crown, directly opposite, and pressed together. It was so cut, apparently, by a sharp instrument. The vest was folded up; there was nothing in the pockets. The shirt had been saturated with blood. Cannot say about the hat and vest, they are so much soiled. The suspenders were thrown in. There was only part of a shirt. The pantaloons were doubled up. The shoes were at the bottom of the bundle. There were six or seven pieces of cloth, the largest about the size of an ordinary towel.

Robert Emmett sworn—Called upon the Mayor a week or ten days after the arrest of the prisoner. I am not sure I stated to the Mayor I wished to have the privy examined, but I said I wished to have his aid. [Objected to.] I asked him if he did not feel bound to aid in efforts at discoveries tending to convict or clear the prisoner, without communicating the result to the District Attorney. At first he thought he could, but his final answer was in the negative.

Justice Taylor and Mr. Brinckerhoff were recalled—They gave more additional unimportant testimony as to the examination of the sinks.

Tennis Fowks corroborrated the testimony as to the finding of articles in the sink at Chambers street.

Mr. Blake recalled—Thought the pencil case found in the sink might have belonged to Mr. Adams; he had one that made a similar noise when it was drawn out. Do not recognize any of the keys.

Mr. Monahan recalled—Thought the key here shown was

the one that Mr. Adams carried in his pocket; it belonged to his office door.

The District-Attorney and the counsel for the prisoner, both stated that they had ended.

Mr. Whiting then read the points on which he should rely as to circumstantial evidence.

Mr. Robert Emmet then rose and addressed the jury, opening in an impressive manner, for the defence. He spoke substantially as follows:—We will admit that Colt took the life of Adams, and we now propose to tell you, as far as possible, how it was done. As the counsel for Mr. Colt, I state what he would if he were to stand up before you. It is not for you to receive it other than as a statement of facts, which you are authorized to reject or receive. I will read what would be the statement of Mr. Colt, were he called upon to give the facts in reference to it. We have a right, as none but the God above us saw the transaction, to show the manner in which the act was done. I shall speak in the first person.

Samuel Adams called on Friday at my office, as near as I can recollect, between the hours of three and four o'clock. Whether he had any special object in view in coming at that time or not, I cannot say. When he entered my office, I was sitting at my table, as usual, and was at that time engaged in looking over a manuscript account book, as I had been engaged in this work for one or two days previous, that is, I was reading over the entries and reconsidering the arithmetical calculations belonging to the entries, &c. Mr. Adams seated himself in a chair near the table, and within an arm's length of myself, so near that if we both leaned our heads forward towards each other, I have no doubt but that they would have touched. I spoke of my account, which he had at my request handed to me ten or twelve days before. I stated to him that his account was wrong, and read to him at the same time the account, as I had made it out on another piece of paper, and requested him to alter his account as I had it. He objected to it at first, saying that I did not understand printing. He however altered his figures as I read them from my account. I made the remark that I would give ten dollars or some such sum if I was not right. After he had altered his figures, and on looking it over, he said that he was right at first, and made the remark that I meant to cheat him. (In the meantime we had both been figuring, on separate papers, part of the account.) Word followed word till it came to blows. The words "you lie" were passed, and several slight blows, and until I received a blow across my mouth, and nose which caused my nose slightly to bleed. I do not know that I felt like exerting myself to strong defence. I believe I then struck him next violently with my fist. We grappled with each other at the time, and I found myself shoved to the wall, with my side and hip to the table. At this time he had his hand in my neck handkerchief, twisting it so that I could scarcely breathe, and at the same time pressing me hard upon the wall and table. There was a hammer upon the table which I then immediately seized hold of, and instantly struck him over the head. At this time, I think, his hat was nearly in my face, and his face, I should think, was downwards. I do not think he saw me seize the hammer. The seizing of the hammer and the blow was instantaneous. I think this blow knocked his hat off, but will not be positive. At the time I only remember of his twisting my neck handkerchief so tight that it seemed to me as though I lost all power of reason. Still I thought I was striking away with the hammer. Whether he attempted to get the hammer from me or not I cannot say ; I do not think he did. The first sense of thought was, it seemed, that his hand or something brushed from my neck downwards. I cannot say that I had any sense or reflection till I heard a knock at the door. Yet there is a faint idea still remains that I shoved him off from me, so that he fell over; but of this I cannot say. When I heard the knock at the door, I was instantly started, and am fully conscious of going and turning the key so as to lock it. I then sat down, for I felt very weak and sick. After sitting a few minutes, and seeing so much blood, I think I went and looked at poor Adams, who breathed quite loud for several minutes, threw his arms out and was silent. I recollect at this time taking him by the hand, which seemed lifeless, and a horrid thrill came over me, that I had killed him.

About this time some noise startled me. I felt agitated or frightened, and think I went to the door to see if I had fastened it, and took the key out and turned down the slide. I think I stood for a minute or two, listening to hear if the affray had caused any alarm. I believe I then took a seat near the window. It was a cold, damp day, and the window had been closed all day, except six or eight inches at the top, which I let down when I first went to the office, and which remained down all the time I occupied it. I remained in the same seat, I should think, for at least half an hour, without moving, unless it was to draw the curtains of the window close, while they were within reach. My custom had been to leave the curtains about one third drawn from the side of the window towards Broadway. The blood, at the time, was spreading over the floor. There was a great quantity, and I felt alarmed lest it should leak through into the apothecary's store. I tried to stop it, by tying my handkerchief round his neck tight. This appeared to do no good. I then looked about the room for a piece of twine, and found in a box which stood in the room, after partially pulling out some awning that was in it, a piece of cord, which I tied tightly round his neck, after taking the handkerchief off, and his stock, too, I think. It was then I discovered so much blood, and the fear of its leaking through the floor caused me to take a towel, and gather with it all I could, and rinse it into the pail I had in the room. The pail was, I should think, at that time about one third full of water, and the blood filled it at least another third full. Previous to doing this, I moved the body towards the box, and pulled out part of the awning to rest it on, and covered it with the remainder. I never saw his face afterwards. After soaking up all the blood I could, which I did as still and hastily as possible, I took my seat again near the window, and began to think what was best to do. About this time some one knocked at the door, to which, of course, I paid no attention. My horrid situation remained from this time till dark, a silent space of time of still more horrid reflection. At dusk of the evening, and at the same time some omnibusses were passing, I carefully opened the door, and went out as still as possible, and I thought unheard. I crossed into the Park, and went down from thence to the City Hotel, my purpose being to relate the circumstance to a brother who was stopping at that house. I saw him in the front reading-room, engaged in conversation with two gentlemen. I spoke to him, a few words passed between us, and, seeing that he was engaged, I altered my purpose, and returned as far as the Park. I walked up and down the Park, thinking what was best to do. Many things I thought of—among others, was going to some magistrate, and relating the facts to him. Then the horrors of the excitement, a trial, public censure, and false and foul reports that would be raised by the many who would stand ready to make the best appear worse than the worst, for the sake of a paltry pittance gained to them in the publication of perverted truths, and original, false, foul, calumniating lies. All this, added to my then feelings, was more than could be borne. Besides, at the time, in addition to the blows given, there would be left the mark or evidence of a rope drawn tightly round the neck, which looked too deliberate for anything like death caused in an affray. Firing the building seemed at first a happy thought, and all would be enveloped in flame, and wafted into air and ashes. Then the danger of causing the death of others (as there were quite a number who slept in the building), the destruction of property, &c., caused me at once to abandon the idea. I next thought of having a suitable box made, and having it leaded inside, so that the blood would not run out, and moving it off somewhere and burying it. Then the delay of all this, and great liability of being detected.

After wandering in the Park for an hour or more, I returned to my room, and entered it as I had left it, as I supposed, unobserved. Wheeler's door was open, and he was talking to some one quite audibly. I went into my room, entering undetermined, and not knowing what to do. After I was seated in my room, I waited silently till Wheeler's school was out, and his lights extinguished. During this suspense, it occurred to me that I might put the body in a cask or box, and ship it off somewhere. I little thought at this time that the box which was in the room would answer; I supposed it too short and small, and entirely unsafe, as it was quite open. Wheeler's school being out, I still heard some one in his room, and, as I then thought, laid down on some benches. The noise did not appear exactly like a person going to bed. I could hear the rustling of no bed-clothes. I felt somewhat alarmed, but then the idea occurred to me that it might be the person who Wheeler stated was going to occupy the room that I then occupied as a sleeping room as soon as I gave it up, which was to be in about ten days' time, was temporarily occupying his room for that purpose. Relieving myself by this thought, I soon lit a candle, knowing that no time was to be lost; something must be done. This was about nine o'clock, I should think. Having closed the shutters, I went and examined the box to see if I could not crowd the body into it. I soon saw that there was a possibility of doing so, if I could bend the legs up, so that it would answer if I could keep some of the canvas around the body to absorb the blood, and keep it from running out. This I was fearful of. It occurred to me, if I bury or send this body off, the clothes which he had on would from description discover who it might be. It became necessary to strip and dispose of the clothes, which I speedily accomplished, by ripping up the coat-sleeve, vest, &c., which removing the clothes, the keys, money, &c., in his pockets caused a rattling, and I took them out and laid them on one side. I then pulled a part of the awning over the body to hide it. I then cut and tore a piece from the awning, and laid it in the bottom of the box. I then cut several pieces from the awning for the purpose of lessening its bulk, supposing it was too much to crowd into the box with the body, *i. e.*, it would not go in. I then tied as tight as I could a portion of awning about the head, having placed something like flax, which I found in the box, with the awning. (This flax or swindling tow came from a room I had previously occupied, No. 3 Murray street, also the awning.) I then drew a piece of this rope around the legs at the joint of the knees, and tied them together. I then connected a rope to the one about the shoulder or neck, and bent the knees toward the head of the body as much as I could. This brought it into a compact form. After several efforts I succeeded in raising the body to a chair seat, then to the top of the box, and turning it round a little, let it into the box as easy as I could back downwards, with head raised. The head, knees, and feet, were still a little out, but, by reaching down to the bottom of the box, and pulling the body a little towards me, I readily pushed the head in and feet. The knees still projected, and I had to stand upon them with all my weight before I could get them down. The awning was then all crowded in the box, excepting a piece or two which I reserved to wash the floor. There being still a portion of the box, next to the feet, not quite full, I took his coat, and, after pulling up a portion of the awning, crowded it partially under them, and replaced the awning. The cover was at once put on the box, and nailed down with four or five nails, which were broken and of but little account. I then wrapped the remainder of his clothing up, and carried it down stairs to the privy, and threw it in it, together with his keys, wallet, money, pencil cases, &c. These latter things I took down in my hat and pockets, a part wrapped in a paper, and a part otherwise. In throwing them down I think they must have rattled out of the paper.

I then returned to my room, carried down the pail which contained the blood, and threw it into the gutter of the street; pumped several pails of water and threw it in the same direction. The pump is nearly opposite the outer door of the building; then carried a pail of water up stairs, and repeated said washing to a third pail; then rinsed the pail, returned it clean and two thirds full of water to the room; opened the shutters as usual, drew a chair to the door, and leaned it against it on the inside as I closed it. Locked the door and went at once to the Washington bath house in Pearl street, near Broadway. On my way to the bath house, went by a hardware store, for the purpose of getting some nails to further secure the box. The store was closed. When I got to the bath house, I think by the clock there it was eight minutes past ten. I washed out my shirt thoroughly in parts of the sleeves and bosom, that were somewhat stained with blood from washing the floor. My pantaloons in the knees I also washed a little, and my neck handkerchief in spots. I then went home; it wanted, when I got home, about five ninutes of eleven o'clock. I lit a light, as usual. Caroline wished to know why I came in so late. I made no excuse, saying that I was with a friend from Philadelphia, I think, and that I should get up in the morning early to go and see him off. I went to the stand and pretended to write till she became quiet or went to sleep. I then put out the light and undressed myself, spread my shirt, &c., out to dry, and went to bed. In the morning, at about half past five o'clock, I got up, put on my shirt and handkerchief, which were not yet quite dry, into the bottom of the clothes-basket under the bed. Always changed my shirt on going to bed. In the morning put on a clean shirt and handkerchief and was nearly dressed when Caroline woke up. I said to her that it was doubtful whether I should return to breakfast. Did not return; went to the office, found all apparently as I had left it. Went after some nails; got them at Wood's store; the store was just opening; returned to the room; nailed the box on all sides; went down to the East river, to ascertain the first packet for New Orleans. Returned to my room—marked the box—moved it myself, but with great difficulty, to the head of the stairs—did not dare to let it down myself—went to look for a cartman—saw a man passing the door as I was going out—requested him to help me down with a box—he got it down without any assistance—preferred doing so—paid him ten or twelve cents—went down Chambers street for a cartman whom I saw coming towards Broadway—hired him to take the box to the ship, foot of Maiden lane—went with him. While he was loading the box I went to my office for a piece of paper to write a receipt on—wrote a receipt to be signed by the captain, on my way down the street—did not offer the receipt to be signed, but requested one, which the receiver of the box gave me. A clerk was by at the time and objected to the form of the receipt, and took it and altered it—wished to know if I wanted a bill of lading. I first remarked that as there was but one box, it was not very important; however that I would call at the office for one. Did not go for a bill of lading. Tore up the receipt before I was two squares from the ship. Returned to my office, by way of Lovejoy's Hotel in the park. Went to the eating room, called for a hot roll and coffee; could not eat. Drank two cups of coffee. Went to my office, locked the door, and sat down for some time. Examined everything about the room. Wiped the wall in one hundred spots. Went home and to bed.

We had intended, said Mr. Emmett, to state the facts to the public, but circumstances induced us to await the trial. When I first saw Mr. Colt he was a perfect stranger to me. After hearing the particulars, it was our intention to make the matter public, but decided otherwise. Mr. Colt consented to it only with the understanding that he should yet make the statement.

[The District Attorney asked if such a course of remark were proper. The judge answered that the communications made by Mr. Colt were not admissible.]

Mr. Emmett then explained the law upon the subject, and went fully into it—read the various laws and precedents governing the case, reviewed the evidence, and concluded by a most eloquent appeal to the jury.

Mr. Smith, for the prosecution, spoke for two hours in a most impressive and masterly manner.

Mr. Selden for the prisoner commenced by stating that his remarks should not extend to a length unnecessarily to trespass upon the time of the jury. He alluded to the comments which had been made upon the law, and stated that the statute gave to the jury the decision as to the law as well as the facts. The act in relation to concealing the body must not be connected with the idea itself. Even if he adopted the suggestion that breaking in the frontal bone was to conceal the body, it can have no bearing upon the decision as to the guilt or innocence of the defendant. Did they suppose it was a feeling of cruelty, for the purpose of mangling the body at his feet, as alluded to by the prosecution. He believed the wounds were given before the body of Mr. Adams was struck down. Mr. Colt would not have resorted to disfiguring the head to insure concealment; it was the last course that a man of mind would resort to. Adams lay prostrate at the foot of the prisoner—he fell, and the attention of those in the adjoining room was attracted by the noise—they listened—not a sound was heard, not a groan uttered. Where was the prisoner then? He was hanging over the body of his victim, contemplating the ruin that had been created. The transaction took place at half past three, and it is said his room was watched till nine. Do you not believe that he knew the movements of those outside? What sensations would likely be produced in his mind? No one put their hand upon the door for the purpose of entrance. He was in terror of his situation. He knew that no person had witnessed the act—that his situation, living in a state of profligacy, was against him—he had nothing on which he could fall back as to connection or character—and was not in a condition by which he could hope for credence in making his situation known. There is no man but under such circumstances would have resorted to concealment rather than disclose what occurred. He determined upon the plan, and set out to put it in execution. "Poor Adams is dead," said he, "and I shall have to meet the consequences or conceal what has been done by means within my power." Yet the means had nothing to do with the offence unless collected for that purpose, and that they were not so has been proved. He resorted to the plan of placing the body in a box—it could not stay in his room—to attempt bringing it or throwing it into the sea, would be certain to cause detection, and it was disposed of in the best manner he thought possible. The body was discovered. In relation to the catastrophe itself, Adams was standing on his feet, and fell dead upon the floor, and face to face. The testimony of Mr. Wheeler, on looking through the key-hole, shows the body to have been near the table. Suppose Colt had Adams by the throat, there could have been no outcry. Adams could not, and Colt would have had no reason to; but in that case Colt would have been the victor, and had no need of resorting to other means of defence. But, on the contrary, Adams had Colt by the throat, and there was necessity of resorting to other means of defending himself. The axe lay on the table, where it would necessarily in that small room be placed. Colt seized it, and in self defence struck the blows. It was all done in an instant's time. The first blow may have deprived Adams of speech, but had the muscular power continued, it would cause him to hold with stronger grasp on the neck-cloth of Mr. Colt. General Hamilton, on being shot, sprung from the ground before he fell; and young Austin, after he had been shot in the head, advanced upon Selfridge, and struck him some violent blows before he fell dead. The effect of the blows on Adams' head, while he held Colt by the neck-cloth, would cause him to hold with still greater pertinacity. His head would necessarily be thrown back to avoid the hatchet, and placed in a position which would be likely to receive the blows that have been shown. As to the idea of the pistol, is it probable the prisoner would have used the hatchet when he had the other, whereby he would have avoided detection,—for, although the ball might not penetrate through the skull, a very slight addition of gunpowder would have caused death. With what caution circumstantial evidence should be received, is shown by the testimony of Mr. De Forest, for had it not been for subsequent proof to the contrary, it would have been believed that the deceased could have been shot by the mere action of the cap, and had been so. As to the motives of the prisoner, let us glance at them. The prosecution had been commenced with an idea that the box was prepared, and the hatchet newly purchased for the purpose, and a sort of mortification appeared observable when it turned out that the prisoner had owned them so long. Is it likely, if he had contemplated killing Adams, he would have brought them into his own room, from which he would have been compelled to remove the body, and where he would be so likely of discovery? He did not take his life from motives of revenge—he had none to gratify. Was it for gain? Had he been disposed to seek money in this way, he would have marked out a more wealthy victim than poor Adams. On the contrary, the supposition of a sudden quarrel between them is borne out by the fact that Adams left Mr. Wells' store between two and three o'clock, in an angry state of mind, for the purpose of going to Colt's room. It had been stated that the idea was conceived by Colt after his arrival, for the purpose of plunder. The evidence of the articles found in the sink, and which had been there since, shows this not to have been the case. Had he premeditated to kill Adams for the sake of the watch, he must have known also that the body would have to be disposed of. Broadway was extremely noisy at that time of day, and sounds were not heard; but would not Colt have known that there was but a thin door between him and Mr. Wheeler, and the cry of a victim would probably be discovered? It was shown that Colt had a pistol. How easily, had he premeditated taking life, could he have decoyed Adams to some other place, where he would have no trouble with the body. Had he taken the life of Samuel Adams for the sake of the watch, would he have not told his friends at Monroe street that the plunder was in his trunk, would be discovered by the officers of police, and bid them to remove it, twenty-four hours having elapsed from the time of his arrest, during which he had continued intercourse with his friends; and the house being searched, the watch fell into his possession as the other things did, and he thought no more of it than of the others. Osgood, who occupied the room next to Wheeler's, went to Boston, carrying his carpet-bag, and the District-Attorney seemed desirous to fasten on the idea that Colt had chosen the time when Osgood was away, to effect a premeditated purpose. Is it inconsistent to suppose that Adams gave Colt possession of the watch previous to the quarrel in order to perfect a sale, in which case it would not be thrown away as the other things were? The idea might have occurred to him that Samuel Adams left but little, and here was some valuable property that at some day might be restored to his family. The learned counsel said this morning that Caroline Henshaw's testimony was not entitled to confidence,—that she was living in a state of adultery with Mr. Colt. If he means to apply that to her general course, he is much mistaken. I have seen those who pretended virtue guilty of vice—have seen the wife whose word was no better than that of the mistress. She may have been guilty on one point, but is entitled to credit as regards every other. Her testimony showed that she loved the prisoner, yet was determined to tell the truth. Caroline Henshaw had access to the trunk, and Colt knew it. He was aware that the watch was an elegant one, of peculiar workmanship, and must be discovered in case he afterwards attempted to wear it. Is it likely he would have plundered another of such an article as that, and have committed murder in order to do it? Except what was shown yesterday, in respect to the articles found in the trunk, there is no evidence that Samuel Adams had anything about his person. He was not a man likely to have had money about him—he was pressed on all sides, and his books disclose it. There is nothing on the books that gives evidence of his having received a dollar of money. Had any money been in possession of Adams, Lane, Mrs. Adams or his foreman would have known it, and the Dist.-Att'y. been ready to prove the fact. The subject shall be dismissed, then, assured that nothing has been shown to prove anything legally wrong in that point. Now for the quarrel—God forbid we should say anything against Mr. Adams, his character or his conduct. The name of John C. Colt is stamped upon the record of criminal jurisprudence—he has been represented as if he had been born for blood,—has been persecuted and maligned; but it is not for us to visit the idea upon the unfortunate deceased. Adams went to Colt's room in a "vexed mood," having expressed surprise to Mr. Wells that Mr. Colt expected the proceeds of the sale. Mr. Colt owed Samuel Adams only seventy-one dollars, but he contended that he owed him more. Out of that account words came up, which produced blows, and terminated in death. Mr. Adams had hold of Mr. Colt in a manner to prevent him crying out, and caused him to use the hatchet in self-defence. The plates and residue of the books were in possession of Mr. Adams. The temper he repeatedly exhibited may have grown out of misfortune. On three occasions he has shown it, by saying "You intend to cheat," or, "you intend to swindle me," and he called the surrogate of Kings County a liar. The present quarrel is involved in darkness, and who commenced it is not proved, but enough is shown to convey an idea of the fact. As to the wounds on the back of the head of decased, they could have been produced by the fall, and probably were so—or may have been caused by the prisoner, in efforts to get the body into the box, or in other ways subsequent to the quarrel. The pieces chopped off were found in the box when opened at the dead house. Everything bears the evidence of wounds being given in self-defence. The counsel said we should have shown where we purchased the nails. It would be as easy for a storekeeper to prove the transfer of a cent, as to prove who bought a penny's worth of nails. It was also said that the mark on the neck of Colt was caused by getting down the box. The mark seen by Caroline Henshaw was on the jugular vein—a man receives a weight on his shoulder, not on his neck. The pinning up of his shirt shows a feeling of innocence rather than guilt. The counsel also said that the new engagement to occupy the room a week longer, showed a premeditated design. Mr. Colt could have easily got the watch without planning it for a week, or resorting to an act of violence. The counsel, when he spoke of the little mementos of hair, said they were found among the rubbish. He has subverted the testimony—they were found in the pocket-book. In regard to the saw, the witnesses were alarmed—the cry of blood had gone forth—and the circumstances were represented as occurring at times different from when they took place. Mrs. Octon said Colt got and returned it on Thursday, and yet Delnoce said that he heard it going on Saturday morning. Mr. Colt was publishing a book, and is it too much to suppose he had been engaged in sending some of them off? The witnesses no doubt intended to represent things truly, but they have confused the dates. The man who wanted to borrow the saw said Mr. Colt uttered an oath, but that was not uncommon. The prisoner had not been treated by the prosecuting officers with ordinary courtesy or ordinary kindness. When examinations were made in the sinks at Monroe and Chambers street, nothing had been stated by the police to the prisoner, so that some person in his behalf could have been present to witness that it was done fairly. Mr. Brinckerhoff gave evidence as to the clearing of the sink, showing that the articles had been placed there from the first; but an effort was made by the prosecuting officers to show that the property had been placed there after the indictment was found; but it had failed. The government has as good a right to protect as to prosecute the prisoner, and testimony should not have been presented that was not well founded. It was sworn that deceased had been salted down, but it was sworn by persons not entitled to credit, and it is satisfactory to find that the indignation which had been created in the public mind is changed to simple curiosity. The witnesses all testified differently, and poor Jemmy Short, on leaving the stand, said that Adams was salted. But did any of them feel the chrystalized matter with their hands? Jemmy Short first said he washed the body before the doctors examined it, and afterwards stated the reverse. Justice Taylor, (who, with the head of the city government, is the only man who has shown any mercy to the prisoner), together with the Mayor and highly respectable physicians, say there was no salt on the body. The officers of police, many of whom are not men of confidence, were allowed to testify, and Dr. Chilton sent to examine the spots, but no one could analyze the articles found with the body.

[The District Attorney said that the salt had been analyzed, and they might bring additional testimony to the stand.]

So much the worse, then, said Mr. Selden ; the prosecution should have shown it, and not left us in the dark. When the wife was here, one of the salt men was directed to bring up the bloody garments and shake them under her very nose. Although the death of Adams had not been denied, the testimony must be brought up to make an effect on the audience. Even the grave was opened, and the head severed from the trunk. The physicians said they could examine it in another room, but it was necessary to place upon the table of a court the head, in order that you, gentlemen of the jury, might be influenced by the feelings observable among the multitude. A charge was made that a pistol had been used, and the brain searched to find a ball. Could the prisoner have obtained the exhuming of the body to prove his innocence. The activity of the police has been brought into exertion, in a manner such as I have never known, in order to convict the prisoner, and his case has withstood them all. He is entitled to the sympathy of a jury of his country. I ask only for the exercise of that principle of law, which says that where there is a doubt, it must be placed in favor of the prisoner. When there are two degrees in the statute—one that will cause a limited degree of punishment, and the other show excusable homicide, if there is a doubt as to which the case belongs, the jury is bound to present a verdict of acquittal. The jury has been kept aloof from external events, and can now see that what a first seemed murder, is but an accident. A prisoner is not bound to show justification—it is for the jury to decide. Gentlemen, after nearly a fortnight's trial, the cause of the prisoner is now committed to your hands,—a young man just entering into life, his prospects probably have been permanently blasted —but still it is for you to pass upon the fact,—we leave his cause with you, requesting you to bear in mind justice as well as mercy, is a portion of the attributes of the criminal law.

Mr. Whiting, District Attorney, then rose and remarked:—We are about to close. Blood has been spilt—shall we flinch in the performance of our duties, or fulfil our oaths—not only do justice to the unfortunate person, but to ourselves and the country. The counsel has not attempted to show that the prisoner is not guilty, but I have been placed on trial, and charged with doing everything malignant. If I am such as they describe, the sooner you get another to fill the office of District-Attorney the better. If doing everything to facilitate counsel for the prisoner—if ever having read the accounts in the papers, makes me guilty, then I am so—then have I persecuted their client to the death—if furnishing copies of all the affidavits, and showing favor to the prisoner, such as none ever was shown—then am I guilty. But I appeal to twelve honest hearts whom I see before me, that I have done nothing since this trial has commenced but what was strictly enjoined upon me by my duty. What do the counsel mean by their aspersions? As to the last gentleman who has spoken, if, peradventure, a little jealousy has entered into his feelings I will only say, that if I ever go to the legislative halls, I will return to the people having performed all the pledges that have been enjoined upon me, and when I go from this trial to the bosom of the community I shall feel that I have performed the oath that I have taken. As to the threats of the other gentleman, that I deserved impeachment, I can only say that his threats have no terrors. Perhaps I deserved blame—let not a hair of the prisoner's head be hurt—think not of me—they said I had a feeling of triumph—triumph of what—if it were in my power, I would unclose this man's chains and say "go." I would, after performing my duty, take that man's hand and hear from his lips that I had done no more than my duty. Has John C. Colt been unfairly dealt with? After making every effort to procure evidence, the counsel were offended because we proved the contents of the box; they observed that they intended to make a confession. That confession we do not hear of before, not even when the counsel first opened the case. Suppose we had been contented to do as the counsel spoke of. They had the confession in their pocket, and yet cross questioned every witness that came up, and even stated, in opening, that we had not proved our case—yet they charged us that we had kept the jury day after day. I advise the counsel to beware how they sport with the lives of their clients; how they come to defend a case and still claim to have a confession in their pocket. Had the gentleman said, we do not dispute that he killed Adams, put him in a box, and put him on board a vessel, how long would it have taken to try the case? and how much more would it have redounded to the credit and ingenuousness of the counsel? But this is a circumstantial case, and the counsel had time to write a confession, but it is at variance in all its main points with the evidence and the probabilities of the case. Our duty is to ascertain the truth. The gentlemen say we are seeking triumph, but gentlemen that know not themselves know not us. We ask you faithfully to perform your duty—no man need to have his frontal marked with any better character. "Well done, thou good and faithful servant." If we maintain the laws against the lawless and against the bandit it is all the success we ask. —Would to God I could look into the testimony this day and aid you to relieve this prisoner rather than convict him But are we never to convict?—what have you or I to do with the consequences?—you are to remove all doubts from your minds and pronounce upon the guilt or innocence of the prisoner—you owe that to your oaths, your country and your God. You come from the body of the community; I could have rejected every man from that box who had ever seen his face, but I did not press it. I would take twelve of his friends to try him, provided they were men of truth and integrity; you are simply to enquire into the circumstances of the case; if he killed Samuel Adams to get rid of a debt or without apparent cause it is murder; but if Samuel Adams went there armed—

made an attack upon him and he found it necessary to use the hatchet in self defence, it was justifiable homicide; you are to pass upon the facts without reference to the excitement without these walls, and the excitement within. One of the counsel for the defence has told you that you must give a verdict of acquittal, even if you did so at the risk of your lives in passing through the crowd—they have told you that the mind of the community is made up—they have complained of the public prints, (which have been sedulously kept from you), and said everything to operate on your prejudices. We claim this case to have come under the first class of murders. Killing a human being is not murder—it is the killing with an evil mind—with a bloodthirsty heart. The law was beautifully laid down three thousand years ago. "He that smiteth a man will surely die," &c. He that comes upon his neighbor with guile to slay him shall be destroyed, said the Almighty. We now appeal to the laws of man as well as of God—show me the land where the laws are not administered, and I will show you the innocent in despair; but let me see that where the laws are observed, and I will exhibit the smile of the Almighty God upon it, I will present the facts without reference to the confession, which the gentlemen had no right to offer unless they put in a plea of guilty; but I shall examine it; if you can bring in a verdict less than the charge, do so; but you must do so without reference to the confession, for that will not bear you out. What are the facts? Samuel Adams went to this man's room. He possessed the reputation of being more mild than men in general—but even suppose that he was a little irritable, is that any excuse for his being killed? These books were to go to the trade sale; not to bring four hundred dollars, but one hundred and twenty-five dollars; Mr. Adams probably wanted all the money he could get; he was told that Mr. Colt meant to appropriate the proceeds; it was said he "was vexed," "surprised," but even say that he was "angry." His answer was I will go and see. Mr. Wells said he was not violent "by any means," Mr. Adams did not take the direct line to Colt's. His passion, even if he had any, had had time to cool, as the heat of the iron from the forge of the blacksmith, when exposed to the atmospheric air. His gait, when seen, was of the ordinary description, not faster. We cannot say that there was an agreement between them to meet, because the evidence does not fully go to show it.—We saw him at three o'clock at the door of Mr. Colt—how did he get in—did he knock or did he go in unasked—the confession does not tell it—where had he been the previous day?—Neither are we informed on that point. Mr. Colt occupied a little room in Murray street, his furniture was an empty box, a table and some chairs; he moved to Chambers street, and all the witnesses, with one exception, agree that the furniture in that room, up to the 17th of Sepember was the same. There was no awning; even the clerk in the dry-goods store, that saw something, could not tell whether it was a piece of cotten or woolen cloth. The boy tells you that the awning was in the garret in July, but the father of the boy was permitted to go to sea on Saturday, without being brought on the stand. (Mr. Morrill said it was Saturday week, as he was with him himself.) I care very little about it; I care very little what was said; I wish he could have sworn his father went away six months ago. But the mind of the boy was still uncontaminated. Things have been so ordered, unfortunately for the prisoner, that what the testimony for the prosecution failed in proving, that brought by the defence confirmed. The little boy proved that he took the awning. What for? for what purpose was the awning taken? He knew that a great noise had been made about the awning being gone, yet said nothing about it. The prisoner would not steal it; he was a man of too high honor; the woman clamored about it, and had it been long anterior to this deed, the woman would have been placed on the stand to testify to it; but she did not come, and was a stranger to us. It was said that the box and the hatchet had been some time in his possession. Had I pursued this prosecution as the counsel stated I did, I should have hunted up the woman that owned the awning; I should have found men that knew Colt; I should have seen every cent that was paid to Adams; but I gave such evidence as was presented to me. [The court stated that the woman missed the awning in July.] Mr. Whiting, in reply, observed that he knew that was the case, but no evidence was shown that Colt for the first time got it then. The woman could have been brought here as well as the boy. But be careful how you believe even that. We infer he took it on that night, but suppose he had taken it before; for some object, for some purpose, for men do not take an awning unless they have some use for it, or intend to raise money. It will be recollected that his Honor, the Mayor, and Justice Taylor were placed upon the stand, to state what Mr. Colt said at the time of his arrest,—how he came into the possession of the awning and box; but the counsel for the prosecution would not permit it, and the confession says nothing about it. He had not shown from whence the box came or where it was made, nor if the cleets were on. As to the hatchet,—where is the testimony that the hatchet was there? One called it a shingle hammer, and the other did not know. But this hatchet is a new one—the handle is new—the blade is new. As to the place where he would be likely to keep it, even if it had been in his room,—would it likely have been kept on his table, when the windows were open? When he is in his shirt-sleeves, in summer time, is it likely he would have it on his table, or would it be kept in his empty box, or some corner? The hatchet still had the string on it, and that is not usual for an old hatchet. But still it was on the table, as stated by the counsel, when Mr. Adams came into the room. Mrs. Octon said the day before he borrowed a saw. Mr. Selden could only account for it by the witness being mistaken, or that another box had been previously sent away; but had that been the case, proof could have been shown when it went away, and where it went to; but the evidence of Mrs. Octon and the man both declared it to be that day—the door of Mr. Colt's room was locked—he was secretly occupied in his little room, and the answer was "go to hell." The District-Attorney contended that a murder was intended, but whether on Samuel Adams or some other could not be stated. This gentleman is represented to be everything mild, kind and affectionate—and yet when interrupted shows a diabolical temper. What did he want the saw for? If we assume the box was already there, he might have been sawing the cleets, or he might have been making the cover—at any rate we have reason to believe he was doing wrong, because he was acting in secret. Had there been no improper intention, he would not have locked the door. [Mr. Emmett stated that the confession was made two months ago. The court said that it was not evidence, and hoped it would be excluded in summing up. The District-Attorney replied that the confession had been given, and he hoped he would be allowed to refer to it. The court assented.]

Colt had the saw for half an hour, during which there had been time probably to make the cleets, and not the cover. I am willing to shut out the testimony of the milkman, but as it has been referred to, we will mention that he saw a tall man at the foot of the stairs of the vault, with a box, a hatchet and a saw. At the time of Samuel Adams' going into Colt's room, did he knock, or did he go in without? did Colt immediately strike him from behind as he entered the room? As the gentlemen say, none but the Almighty God and themselves knew what happened. I will show that by the evidence of those who examined the skull, that when they came to express opinion, it clashes; it does not matter when Adams came into the room, whether he was struck by the hatchet, or was shot—it is still murder. When Dr. Gillman referred to the hole, the idea flashed upon my mind that a pistol had been used, and such appears still to have been the case. Why should every blow leave a fissure but this? All the rest exhibit such, but here is a clean round hole. I would ask the professional gentlemen how they account for the difference? Did Dr. Mott, or any other gentleman, ever see an oblong round hole that had been made by a hatchet? I do not mean to say it was made by a pistol ball; I do not know how it was made; perhaps Adams did not; perhaps none but he (pointing to prisoner) knew. How is it possible for such a blow to have been made from in front by a hatchet; the man who has nothing but the defence God has given him when attacked by another with a hatchet, will seize the arm; but will Dr. Mott, or any other physician, place his professional reputation on the idea that blows from a hatchet represented the sound of foils. Adams must have received his death-blow about fifteen minutes past three. No sound was heard, no voices, nothing but the momentary clash and the fall. If Adams had been a man sufficiently strong to hold the prisoner off at arm's length, would the blows from the hatchet have been struck on the rear of the head or directly in front? How, then, did the blow come, and could the deceased have kept his hold when his head had been stove in? Dr. Rogers gives some little idea of the kind, but he must speak of some other order of men. If men can strike so hard as Austin and others are said to have done—can hold their grasp so fully after being struck as has been represented, soldiers, before going to the field, should have their brains knocked out, as they would fight much harder. Dr. Rogers said the whole of the front part might have been knocked in by a single blow; but had that been the case, pieces of the hat as well as the brain would have been knocked in. But Dr. Mott sets the matter at rest by saying that several blows were given. We have to judge of the fact, and the skull exhibited deep cruelty in the murder. [Mr. Emmet stated that the skull was shown as it h d been taken from the coffin. Mr. Whitney said that he spoke of Dr. Gillman's testimony, shown by the bust, before the body had been exhumed.]

I have done everything that has been asked of me, and the remarks of the gentleman in allusion to me were made because he does not know me. I should have said to him had he called upon me, that I felt the life of this prisoner was in my hands, and I will do everything in justice that is possible to save him from the strongest penalty of the law. If, gentlemen of the jury, I have pushed this case too far, blame me; but, as a prosecuting officer, have I done so? If the hat had been knocked in by the hatchet, why cut it in the center?—was it to chip out the marks of a pistol ball? The testimony has not been allowed to show us whether the hat was cut at the sides or in rear and front, nor whether a piece was cut out or not. But why destroy the hat? Even allowing the bundle to have been put into the sink that night, it was placed there by him, and why did he cut it? Would a man who had unintentionally taken the life of his neighbor have proceeded in the formal manner he did to fold up the pantaloons, the suspenders, cut the hat, and then place them where he did, or would he, in his trepidation, have thrown in the things as he found them? It has been said by counsel that Adams had Colt by the neck, but would that have produced the clash [Mr. Whiting struck his hands together] as of foils? There would have been a scuffle, —a noise with the feet,—but nothing of this kind was heard, but a slight clash. What made the noise? The flashing of a percussion cap would do it, and the introduction of a few grains of powder, even by the most favorable testimony for the prisoner, would have driven a pistol ball through the hat and skull. Had a quarrel taken place, as pretended, noise would not only have been made, but Colt would have been more likely, unless bent upon murder, to strike with a chair than a hatchet; and, even if he had done the latter, a high-minded man would have at once exclaimed to those around him, "I have struck a blow which I shall regret all my life,"—and have shown contrition for the act. Had the quarrel taken place as said, would the words "you lie" have been made in a low voice? Would it not have been heard? That man, there is no doubt, was struck down by the first blow. Where was the neckcloth? Had it been a common stock it would have been twisted. Caroline Henshaw had given evidence that he had neckscarfs and stocks, but why was not the one worn presented? Had Adams been pressing Colt by the neck, the marks would have been left, and what man refuses to show such to his bosom friend? We hear of a trifling mark, but nothing such as would have appeared there. We hear of Caroline Henshaw going to his bedside; she asked him, as Portia did Brutus, when he came from the Senate House and committed a murder, what ailed him? He pushed her away, and she dared not, after that, ask this kind friend to see the marks on his neck—she dared not speak. Tell me if a man takes to his arms one who gives herself up to his embraces, one who yields herself to him to her destruction here and forever, is entitled to more feeling than if honorably engaged to her. God forbid I should say anything against that witness—she was about to become a mother—and if there was any one who would pray for that man, that he might be blessed forever, and would come here to testify for him it would be her. She approached his bed, he threw her from him. She knew she was not his wife, and dared not press it. Had she been his wife, she would have persisted. But do not blame her, do not blame that slight girl—blame the one whose heart was such that he could seduce her, and keep her in abjection. Had she been his wife, he could have poured his sorrows into her ear; she would have clung by him; she would have gone with him to his prison; she would have accompanied him even to the gallows. Let this be a warning to women—let them learn not to put their earthly and eternal happiness in the keeping of such a man as that. That poor unfortunate girl must go down to the grave with the stain that is upon her. Caroline Henshaw, according to her testimony, had gone to bed, not dreaming that he would come home steeped in guilt. He had on his night-shirt when she first saw him, and it was said it was then eleven o'clock. By that time he must have gone systematically to work, prepared his victim, boxed him up, had the box ready to ship, the blood washed up, and everything done so coolly as to show it had been previously planned. We contend that this murder had been premeditated. Does the law require it shall have been a long time before? No, not even a single minute, if the intention is to produce death, and the blow is unnecessarily produced. [The District Attorney then gave precedents in point. He gave the case of a farmer who had killed an officer in his barn, buried him in his field, and ploughed it next morning; but the very precautions he taken led to his arrest. The officer was missing, as Adams was, and suspicion became excited to the ploughed field.] If the Kalamazoo had sailed, would there have been any evidence of Colt's guilt, or would suspicion even dare to be attached to him? The night after, the boy, in shutting up his store, heard the noise as if of nailing. How did Colt know the Kalamazoo was up? The box was directed to New Orleans that very night;—was this accident? He might have shown where he got the nails, but the counsel said there was but a pennyworth; but even then "straws show which way the wind blows," and even this small quantity might have shown the fact. As to the mark on the neck, it could easily have been made in moving the box down stairs. Counsel for the defence said if Colt had been guilty he would have sent to Caroline, when he had been arrested, to put away the watch; but the body had not been discovered then. He told Mr. Wheeler, at first, that he was not in the room, but afterwards contradicted himself. The vessel seemed to have been most providentially detained. Colt knew that, unless the body was found, there would be no need of sending to Caroline Henshaw. He was aware, on putting the box on board a ship, that poison would be created by the putrid atmosphere, and used salt to preserve it. There is one error I have made which I endeavored to correct last night. Who, except the guilty, is afraid of a human skull — as it was — battered in. The counsel wished to have it examined but only that physicians should do so, and in an adjoining room—but doctors are but men as others —and the court, jury and others, had a right to examine for themselves. Complaint has been made that the bloody garments and the ring should be shown to Mrs. Adams, but could anybody else identify them; as to the body of poor Adams even the impress of his maker had been obliterated by the hand of violence; and without Mrs. Adams' testimony, gentlemen, would you believe that the body found in the box was that of Samuel Adams. Now, gentlemen, as to the pocket book. Mr. Adams had been in the habit of carrying one, and whether he had money or not we cannot say.—Mr. Colt may have known it. It is also said of the watch that Colt had it before or that he would not be likely to plunder such an article. Had the vessel sailed, the watch might have been carried into the country, and would probably never again been heard of. I have alluded to the principal points, and could speak two hours more on the subject, but shall be brief. I ask you to review the evidence, and mete out fair and ample justice to the prisoner. If favorable, it is for you to say so. A chain of circumstances have been presented in the case astonishing to think of. It is for you to weigh them and bring in your verdict of guilty or not guilty. As to the temper of the deceased, what Dr. Barber has asserted showed him to be of good temper rather than otherwise. I asked the doctor if no other had ever treated him equally bad, and he appealed to the court for protection. Mr. Wheeler was a lawyer, and was engaged in a case where Adams felt aggrieved. The case of Mr. Cornell shows that Adams would not tread upon a worm. Cornell opened the door, and said. "Presto, be gone," and Adams was off. Adams appears to have been a man that would run rather than fight. The District Attorney then made a powerful appeal to the jury. If courts and juries, said he, refuse to do their duty, who will protect our houses from burning. If it is to be understood that prosecuting officers are to have the stiletto, who will protect the community, our streets will be washed in blood, our altars be desecrated. Gentlemen, I have endeavored to do my duty. If I have been too warm, appreciate it. But, as regards the excuse of the prisoner, if the memorials of the mother and sisters had been pressed closer to his heart, it would have been better for him. I believe that life was taken by John C. Colt. I believe if, by laying down his own life he could restore that man to his family he would gladly do it.

[Colt had his hands over his eyes, leaning on the back of his counsel's chair, and freely wept, the tears falling from his face.]

I believe he would gladly give his life, but is that an excuse for taking the life of Adams? It is for us to do our duty—there is on that bench a judge whose heart is alive to every kind feeling. If mercy is deserved it will be shown; but you have a simple duty to perform. I have endeavored faithfully to do mine. If erroneous, correct it—deal leniently and mercifully with the prisoner; do justly to yourselves. There are in this city three hundred thousand souls committed to our care, and much rests upon us. Act in a manner that you can answer to your consciences hereafter; deal justly, but deal firmly and honestly between the people and the prisoner.

CHARGE OF JUDGE KENT.

Judge Kent then proceeded to charge the jury as follows:—Gentlemen, it becomes us to close the last scene. My remarks shall afford you some time for deliberation, and do away with the excitement thrown around the case by the speeches of counsel. My duty will soon be done and yours begin. Some allusion has been made to the excitement out of doors. I am inclined to believe it is over rated. Had I not so, I would have postponed the trial. It would have been strange if, in the city of New York, the public mind would not have been shocked by the murder, but I have no doubt that every justice has been done to the prisoner. The court has kept everything uninfluenced by contamination from without, and I have no doubt but reliance can be had upon the sound heads before us. I was sorry to find some acerbity of feeling shown among the counsel, but I see no occasion for it. Never have I known more talent or industry displayed than in this cause. No blame is deserved on either side, and as to the District-Attorney he has discharged his duty ably and eloquently, and without any feeling but that of his duty. It is now my place to address to you a few remarks. The degrees of homicides are four—justifiable and excusable homicide, murder and manslaughter. There is very little difference between the grades of the two former—the one is where an officer kills another in the performance of his duty—the other to prevent an attempt to kill where a man is allowed to defend himself even in taking life. If you think Colt killed Adams to protect himself from an attempt at murder or felony he is justified. It is also justifiable when a design is evident to inflict some great felony, such as to main or murder, as where a man raises a large bar of iron to strike another. If you think this to have been the case, no ame is attached to the prisoner. We now come to the grade where the law says blame is deserved, but where there are mitigating circumstances—such as correcting a servant and death ensues, or a person in building lets fall a brick, and some person is killed—or where there has been some unexpected combat without dangerous weapons, and where it was not intended to take life. Words do not authorize one man to kill another, but where in resisting an assault death ensues, and it is not intended to kill, nor done in a cruel manner, it is excusable homicide. Cruel and unusual manner may have been by such a weapon as this—it cannot be considered excusable. If not justifiable or excusable, it is a murder or manslaughter. In the former there are no shades; in the latter four degrees. The first is premeditation, and where it is done with an instrument regardless of life. Where a person discharges a loaded pistol into a crowd, it shows a depraved mind, and where he takes life, it is murder. As to premeditation, I differ from the District-Attorney as to a point of law. It was said that if a homicide was committed the law implies malice, such as the case where a black man cut a woman's throat in Broadway, but I cannot agree with that doctrine. You may say that Colt designed to take Adam's life, if so it was murder. But you must show premeditation. This is not necessary to have been previous to Adams going into his room. If you think he did, not in hot blood, or in a fracas, it is murder. But if you do not think such, it is manslaughter, and you must bring it within one of the grades. The first is, if a boy throws a stone at another, and kills him, or if a man kills another in a fight previously intended. If Colt intended to beat Adams and killed him, it is manslaughter in the first degree, but in the heat of passion he did so, it is in the second degree. Third degree is, where it is done without the use of a dangerous weapon.

The first question is, was the offence committed? This has been admitted. What degree of crime does it come under? The counsel has placed out of view much that was the object of several days' inquiry. The pistol idea is settled, and not necessary to touch upon. It was well to produce the skull. It became necessary on account of the physicians not being clear in their testimony. I was averse to producing it and harrowing up the feelings of the prisoner himself, and the relatives of the deceased, but it was necessary. In regard to Colt's confession, it is difficult to exclude such. The counsel introduced it in his argument, and it was irregular. It is in, however, but it is not testimony, and you (the jury) are bound to throw it out entirely so far as it goes to exculpate the prisoner. After all the testimony that has been presented, the case lies in a nut shell. Except so far as illustrating the character of John C. Colt, the mass of evidence goes but little way beyond the admitted murder. The pistol idea has not been given up by the District-Attorney, but you have the opinion of Dr. Gillman that he did not believe in it, although it had been his first impression; and Drs. Mott and Rogers declare it not to have been. You must discard the idea that the wound was given by the pistol. In regard to the watch, it has also been admitted to have been taken. The question then is as to murder or manslaughter. I shall now look at the homicide and the subsequent proceedings. In regard to the latter, they are of importance in judging of the character of John C. Colt, and throwing a reflective light upon his character. Dismissing his own statement, and what do we find?—I am not going to detain you. The chain of facts are remarkable, and show him to be an uncommon man. The homicide occurred at half-past three o'clock. Mr. Wheeler went to the door—then up-stairs—told all he met—and yet Colt gave no signs of life or emotion. After nine o'clock Delnoce heard him go down-stairs, return, wash up the floor, and next morning heard the sawing. Next day, we have the testimony of Mrs. Octon, to show that he came in, passed his door, and sat down by Mr. Wheeler's. It is a trait of character in his favor. He did not care to see his victim. Like Macbeth, he appears to have said, "I'm afraid to flee from what I've done; look on it I dare not." Then again we see the body placed in a box, and packed up in a manner unparalleled in crime. He goes out to get a carman, assumes a careless air, and told the carman to convey the box to a New Orleans vessel. Almost any other man would have gone on that box and kept by it till it was safe; but he entrusted the carman to knock it around and throw it down as an ordinary package. He then gets a receipt, tears it up, returns to his office, and obliterates the marks. On Monday he assumes a gay air; he went to Adams' office, and also to Wells'. It shows him a man of intrepidity and coolness, such as rarely can be met with. Such is the impression on my mind, but you can judge of it. In regard to the idea of salt, I do not look upon it in any other light than that of additional foresight. Using salt in order to preserve the body, was to guard against discovery, but it showed no greater atrocity. Whether the salt was there or not, it made no difference. It is not fully proved—the witnesses say they are not certain. The warmth shown by counsel was unnecessary. The thought might have an effect in inflaming the public mind, but as regards the fact, it only shows, if true, the foresight and providence of John C Colt. We now come to the point of Samuel Adams being in the room. The witnesses we have are Wheeler and Seignette. Is there proof of design, anterior to his entering the room, that Colt intended to kill him? Colt was, perhaps, in want of money. At any rate Mr. Wheeler had asked him for his rent, and he could not pay. He was also desirous of sending off the books, so as to raise money. The District-Attorney thinks the fact of the saw important. The evidence is conclusive that he borrowed one, but the circumstance is too light to say much, unless coupled with something else. The stuffing of the box with paper seems to have some weight about it, but you will judge of the fact. Then, again, his having the window shut may look like preparation. These two points are all I see that look like preparatory design. Had Mr. Wheeler tried the door and found it locked, it might have been an important circumstance; but Mr. Wheeler did not try the door, and you must not look at it. Was the mere fact of Adams being in the room sufficient to fasten crime? The hatchet appears to have been in Colt's possession two months, and the box so for a long time anterior. The awning is said to have been taken from Murray street some time before, and this seems to have been the case. The inference is in favor of the prisoner. The box, the hatchet and the awning, were in his possession. The place in which parties were, seems to be inconsistent with the idea of premeditation. In that small room, and at that time of day it is difficult to suppose that there had been a premeditated design to take life. Now as to the occurrence itself. We must look again at the conduct evinced by Colt in packing up the body. Does this show an evidence of guilt? The law gives concealment as evidence of guilt. A boy killed another and hid the body, and it was evidence against him. Is any deduction necessarily drawn from the fact, but his desire to avoid punishment? Does this show that John C. Colt wished to avoid the State's Prison, which the law provides as the punishment of manslaughter? It may have been accompanied by guilt, but is any other idea apparent? The public mind was shocked, and every one felt it, and you may have imbibed the idea. The concealment was as likely to have been caused by a wish to avoid the punishment of manslaughter as well as of murder. We have the evidence of Mr. Wheeler and others. Mr. Wheeler acted precisely as a prudent man should have acted—it was so improbable that at noon day a murder had been effected that Mr. Wheeler may have been pardoned for not pushing his inquiries further than he did. The philosophy of evidence is, that persons agree on subjects, if their attention is drawn to the same object, but two persons in looking at a landscape, one may observe something that will escape the notice of the other. [The judge then read a case in point.] There is some little discrepancy as to whom first went to the police, and other small points, but it is certain that they heard a noise and the fall of a heavy body—on that they speak positively. He heard the clashing of foils, something like a movement of feet, and a fall, but nothing beyond. It does not follow that they could hear the beginning of this controversy; ordinary conversation could not probably have been heard; their attention was first called to the falling of a heavy body. Now as to the wounds themselves. We hear of a clash and the fall. After the most deep inquiry I am at a loss to account for the manner in which the wounds were inflicted; it is a matter for you to solve, not me. The wounds must have been given before the fall on the floor, as no noise was heard afterwards; but whether while deceased was standing, or from before or from behind, the jury must weigh. Dr. Mott and the others do not appear to agree, and the chain seems broken. Dr. Gilman speaks of two pieces being hacked off the back of his head, but it may have been done, he said, while putting it in the box, but this is not satisfactory to my mind. Whether the blow was struck from behind, may or may not have been the case. There is mystery; how these wounds were given is a subject of strong inquiry. The first wound appears to have created insensibility—if it had not been so the piercing cry in the accent of fear would probably have arose over everything else. That there was a fracas appears evident from the nature of the case, and also from the testimony of Caroline Henshaw. That testimony appears to be worthy of confidence. That interesting young woman comes here under adverse circumstances. Her manner was childlike—she did not appear desirous of pushing her remarks, and the impression on my mind was decidedly in her favor. She stated that the mark was no larger than a sixpence, and she spoke with much caution. I believe her story, but the jury can weigh the fact? Does it then imply a fracas? Octon said he saw Colt take the box down stairs, and press his neck against it as it went down stairs. I believe Octon, and particularly as he said he was afraid of that box. His suspicion was awakened, and if you look at the statement of Colt, still Octon's testimony is deserving, even if Colt's was admissible, of the greatest weight. The weight of the box accounts for the stiffening in his limbs, but the mark on the neck seemed like a pinch or grasp by the hand. Was the case murder? You have heard the evidence. The desire of revenge is a prominent trait. A savage has been known to kill another to see how he would fall from his horse. It is hard to know the feelings that enter into the heart of a guilty man. But it is for the jury to think if there was any adequate motive. There appears to be no desire to preserve reputation, as Adams knew nothing against Colt, nor was there any old grudge—avarice may have entered his mind; his books were going to Philadelphia, and he might have got possession of the money though not be free from the debt, by Adams being put out of the way. It is possible he may have done it for the sake of his money, but we have no evidence that Adams had any about him. It had been stated that he carried a pocket book, but there was no evidence. He had a watch in his possession, that is certain and fully proved. Cary's testimony, that he saw a watch on a former day in Colt's hands appears to be insufficient. The watch was in Colt's possession. Suppose he killed him in an affray, what was he to do with the watch? Persons have been known to kill another for feeling; Colt may have been governed by such, but was it probable? Adams lay dead at his feet, and the possession of the watch is not inconsistent with the idea that he kept it some day to give it to his family. There appears to have been no grudge—very little motive for lucre, for the probability is that he would have selected a richer man.

The firm manner in which he walked on a precipice, one false step on which would have been fatal—the coolness of character he displayed—if you think these sufficient to believe him capable of premeditation, bring him in guilty of murder; if you do not think they show premeditation, he is not guilty of murder, but of manslaughter. As to the latter, we have the character of the slayer and the slain; the evidence is favorable to both. Adams was shown to have been amiable; nevertheless, he was capable, as appeared by three witnesses, of using language of an insulting character, but nothing seems like his having ever been engaged in an affray in his life. As to Colt, also, he has been shown to be kind, pleasing and elegant in his address, yet we have evidence that he was disposed to show temper—the testimony of the man with the saw, Mr. Wheeler, and the case where he had become responsible for a debt. Mildness is sometimes shown by the sternest character, but Colt has exhibited nothing improper. Now as to his taking life, and his liability in the charge of manslaughter, the certainty that Adams was capable of showing temper, was sufficient to convey an idea that he might have come upon Colt when in a feverish state of mind, and a fracas occurred between them. But I leave it with you—give the doubts for the prisoner—give the lowest degree of punishment to which you feel the case belongs. Let it be a doubt fully formed. But I leave it with you, feeling the utmost confidence in you. Do justice whatever may ensue. You are bound to spurn all excitements—must not cherish a mawkish sympathy—examine the subject coolly, bring in a verdict according to what you really believe, and do your duty to the prisoner, your country, and your God.

Mr. Emmett said he begged to offer slight exceptions, alluded to the statute and declared that this case would be excusable homicide unless the prisoner was armed with a hatchet at the commencement of the affray, or had prepared it before hand. It was so allowed.

The jury then retired in the charge of officers to deliberate.

THE VERDICT.

Next morning (Sunday), at a quarter before three o'clock, the jury having come to an agreement, Judge Kent was sent for. At four o'clock the judge, in company with Aldermen Purdy and Lee, took his seat upon the Bench.

The jury was then brought into Court, and the clerk after calling over the names, asked if they had agreed upon a verdict,

Foreman—We have.

Clerk—Gentlemen, what is your verdict?

Foreman—We find the prisoner, John C. Colt, guilty of wilful murder.

Mr. Morrill, the only counsel for the prisoner present, then applied to the Court for time to prepare a bill of exceptions, &c. The application was granted, the prisoner remanded to the custody of the Sheriff, when the Court adjourned.

EFFORTS FOR A NEW TRIAL.

On the 31st of January the case of Colt was again brought before the Court of Oyer and Terminer on application for additional time of two weeks to file a bill of exceptions. The application was granted. Further delay was experienced afterwards, however, and the bill of exceptions was not formally entered until the 28th of February.

On the 1st of March the bill of exceptions was allowed, and the case sent before the Supreme Court for adjudication.

May 5. A motion was made before the Court of Oyer and Terminer to grant the prisoner a new trial, upon the additional ground that one of the jurors who had tried the case had expressed an opinion, previous to being sworn in. Colt was in Court. Affidavits were read both on the part of the defence and prosecution. Mr. Emmet argued the case for the prisoner, and District Attorney Whiting opposed. The Judge took the papers and reserved his decision.

May 12. The prisoner was again brought into Court. The motion for a new trial was denied.

May 27. The bill of exceptions was called up in the Supreme Court, the District-Attorney being present. Counsel for the prisoner did not appear, and the Court ordered a nonsuit, and directed the District Attorney to proceed by default.

May 31. Counsel for the prisoner appeared in the Supreme Court, and the default taken by the District Attorney was opened, and argument ordered, to be presented at the next term of the Supreme Court to be held at Utica in July.

Supreme Court, Utica, July 16. After hearing arguments, on application for new trial, made by Messrs. Morrill and

Selden in behalf of the prisoner, and District Attorney Whiting opposed, the Court denied the motion, and sent back the prisoner for judgment to the Oyer and Terminer.

THE SENTENCE OF DEATH.

On the 27th of September Colt was brought up in the Court of Oyer and Terminer (Judge Kent presiding), to have the awful sentence of the law passed upon him. The court-room was crammed by a crowd of spectators of all classes, anxious to get a glance at the prisoner. Aldermen Purdy and Lee were upon the bench with Judge Kent. Colt was accompanied by his brother Charles, and his counsel, Messrs. Morrill and Selden.

The Clerk asked the prisoner if he had anything to say why sentence of death should not be pronounced against him.

Colt said that he had some written remarks which he would hand the Court to read. This paper alluded to the unjust manner in which the trial had been conducted, and asserted that the evidence had been trampled upon by the jury.

Judge Kent then proceeded to pass sentence. He was sorry that any unjust allusions had been made as to the conduct of the jury. It was due to justice, and it was due to one of the most intelligent juries that ever sat in a court of justice, that he (the Judge) should not allow them, in this, their proud tribunal, to be insulted, without entering his solemn protest against it. The jury were selected out of three hundred of our most respectable citizens—taken indiscriminately from the city, selected under the most vigorous exercise of the peremptory challenge by the prisoner—and in every instance where objections were raised and allowed, it was in favor of the prisoner. Their demeanor in Court was such as to entitle them to the highest consideration of the tribunal in which they took part. They had been separated from their families and from their business, confined in a sort of prison for eleven days, and he (the learned Judge) never saw one of them exhibit the slightest impatience. On the contrary, they bore, with most exemplary patience, the tedious, even unnecessary, delays in the progress of the trial. Calmly, honestly, unfalteringly earnest in their efforts to discover the truth from the mass of evidence spread before them. Had these men been followed to their rooms, we would have seen the same calm, unimpassioned inquiry characterizing their deliberations. As far, therefore, as the paper expressed dissatisfaction with the conduct of the Court and Jury, it was his (the Judge's) conscientious opinion that the asseverations were untrue and unjust. He would now allude to the offence for which the prisoner had been convicted. No man ever doubted that it was a crime of the greatest magnitude and enormity. It was a crime, too, which had sunk deep in the community. Leaving out of view all the appalling circumstances, with which he would not distress the prisoner or himself in recalling, no doubt could exist but that the deed was executed under the influence of ferocious passions and sanguinary cruelty.

Colt said that if the Judge had read the document he would find that he (Colt) did not charge the jury with wilful wrong, but that they were mistaken. As to any allusions made by the Judge, he could assure him that he would rather leave his case with God than with man. He never did a deed in his life but he would repeat, had it to be gone over again. The prisoner then went on to say, "I am not the man to be trampled down in my own office, and look tamely on. It was not my intention to kill the man; but he made the assault, and must take the consequences. I am sorry the Court thought proper to make the remarks it has. For myself, I had intended to say something more; but, not expecting to be sentenced to-day, I was not prepared. I am ready to receive sentence, knowing that it cannot be avoided."

Judge Kent—Sentence will now be pronounced, with expressions of deep regret entertained by the Court at the callous and morbid insensibility exhibited in your last speech, and which shows that any further remarks would be lost. John C. Colt, the sentence of the Court is, that on the 18th of November next you be hanged till you are dead, and may God have mercy on your soul.

The prisoner was then removed. During the sentence he assumed a bold and careless air.

COLT'S PRISON LIFE—EFFORTS MADE FOR HIS RELEASE.

From the date of Colt's sentence up to the day set down for his execution the most energetic efforts were made upon the part of his friends to have the death penalty commuted to imprisonment for life. But all such exertions failed. The Governor could not be moved. Application was also made to the Chancellor to have the case removed up to the Court of Errors, but the application was denied, and nothing now remained to be accomplished but the last final act of the law.

Several attempts were now made to release the prisoner from jail. One evening one of his friends went to the Tombs attired in woman's clothes, the plot being matured to let the prisoner walk out of the Tombs in the female costume, while the latter should remain in his place. Rooms were prepared in Brooklyn for the reception of Colt, and every arrangement made so that he should be hidden when he again emerged into freedom. But the plot was discovered. On the party arriving at the Tombs and applying for admission they were informed that their conspiracy was well known, and they were advised to withdraw, and nothing would be said about the movement.

When all attempts failed, a certain doctor of the city undertook to resuscitate Colt after he was hanged, in case the body was not too long suspended. This doctor asserted that Colt's neck was of such thickness that it would require a longer period than is usual in such cases before the unfortunate man would be strangled. A room was taken at the Shakespeare Hotel, where the body was to be brought direct from the Tombs, and there all efforts made for its resuscitation.

Every attention was paid to the physical wants of Colt during his term of imprisonment. Each day he was visited by his friends. Caroline Henshaw was faithful to the last. For hours she remained in his cell, and offered him all the consolation her presence and conversation could afford. Colt really was attached to this woman, as on the 18th of November—the date set down for his execution—he married her in the Tombs.

THE DAY OF EXECUTION—SUICIDE OF THE PRISONER.

At last the eventful day came—the 18th of November—when Colt was to expiate his crime upon the gallows. There was the greatest excitement throughout the city. Crowds hastened to the Tombs, which was thronged inside by those who held passes, and in the outside neighborhood by those whose morbid curiosity had to be satisfied with a view of the prison walls within which the awful judgment of the law was about to be carried out.

Four o'clock was the hour announced for the execution to take place. During the day Colt was visited by his friends and others. Rev. Dr. Anthon administered to his spiritual wants. At twelve o'clock Caroline Henshaw arrived, and was immediately shown to the condemned cell. Colt was much affected on seeing the girl, to whom he was undoubtedly very much attached, and by whom he had one child—a son. The pair were then united in wedlock. It was a singular and a solemn ceremony. In three hours the bride was to become a widow.

At one o'clock Caroline Henshaw—now Mrs. Colt—took leave of the unfortunate man. Deputy-Sheriff Hillyer shortly after entered the cell, and bade Colt farewell. He was the last man that saw him alive. A few minutes before four o'clock Sheriff Hart, Deputy-Sheriff Westervelt, and Rev. Dr. Anthon proceeded to the cell in order to inform Colt that his hour had come. The preparations were all complete. The noose dangled in the breeze from the scaffold ready to receive its victim. Outside, the crowd awaited in breathless silence the appearance of the mournful procession.

On opening the cell door the visitors started back in horror. Lying at full length upon his couch was John C. Colt, a corpse. A small clasp-knife, with the handle slightly broken, was stuck in his heart. The body was still warm, but the spirit had departed before the throne of its Creator, where eternal sentence had already been pronounced. The law had been robbed of its victim, but Samuel Adams was avenged.

Just then a cry of fire was heard. The cupola of the Tombs was found to be in flames. The news of Colt's suicide spread among the crowd, and a rush was immediately made among the large concourse of people assembled. The fire, however, was speedily extinguished; and after considerable exertion on the part of the police, the assemblage dispersed, when order was restored.

THE END—RUMORS.

An inquest was immediately held upon the body, when all the above facts were sworn to. A verdict was rendered setting forth that John C. Colt came to his death at his own hands. The body was then removed by the friends of the deceased, and placed in the vaults of St. Mark's Church.

Rumors of the most extravagant nature were circulated throughout the city for several days after the consummation of this fearful tragedy. Some asserted that Colt had not committed suicide at all, and that the setting fire to the Tombs was simply a *ruse* in order to facilitate the escape of the prisoner. These rumors, however, appear to have had no foundation, as the most incontrovertible facts were brought forward to prove that Colt had really taken his life with his own hands.

AN ACCOUNT OF COLT'S SUICIDE BY MR. L. GAYLORD CLARKE.

A very interesting account of the circumstances anterior to and succeeding the suicide of Colt, has been written by Mr. L. Gaylord Clarke, which we append:—

I have no doubt that hundreds and hundreds of people, in this State, and in border States, are at this moment in the full and undoubting belief that John C. Colt, who took the life of Adams in 1842, is still in existence!—that he never entirely "killed himself," but that he was "spirited away" from the triple-barred and triple-guarded "strong immures" of the Tombs, and is now in a foreign land, safe from further peril!

Why, not two months since, I heard a magistrate from one of the lower counties of New Jersey say—a man accustomed to deliberate, and carefully weigh evidence, that "he has no more doubt that John C. Colt was among the living, than he was that he himself was alive!"—and I have heard at least fifty persons affirm the same thing.

Few persons took a deeper interest in the case of Colt, from the very beginning, than myself. Firmly believing that the killing was never premeditated, but was the result of a quarrel and a blow suddenly given, when the parties stood face to face, with each other (and this was shown by the cast of the head, showing the mark made by the hatchet, which Dr. Rogers and a committee, of which I was one, took up to Albany, and laid before Governor Seward) say, firmly believing all this, I never could consider Colt a deliberate murderer.

Nor was he. He was convicted for concealing the body of his unfortunate victim. Does any one suppose that if Colt had rushed out into the hall, after having struck the fatal blow, and said, "I have killed a man!—we have had a little difficulty—I have struck him with a hatchet, and have killed him!" does any one now believe he would ever have been convicted? Never! But this apart.

I believe I am the only survivor of those who left John C. Colt in his cell at the Tombs, in company alone with his brother Samuel, some three quarters of an hour before the time appointed for the execution.

The late Rev. Mr. Anthon, John Howard Payne, Samuel Colt, the unhappy condemned, and myself were the only persons in the cell at this time. It was a scene never to be forgotten.

The condemned had on a sad colored morning-gown, and a scarf tied loosely around his neck. He had a cup of coffee in his hand, and was helping himself to some sugar from a wooden bowl, which stood on an iron water-pipe near the head of his bed. His hand was perfectly steady, as he held the cup and put in the sugar; and the only sign of intense internal agitation and excitement was visible in his eyes, which were literally blood red, and oscillated, so to speak, exactly like the red and incessantly-moving eyes of the Albinoes.

Our interview was prolonged for half an hour, which was passed in conversation with Dr. Anthon, Mr. Paine, and his brother. And when we were about to depart, and some one, looking at his watch, said that he thought he must be some ten minutes fast, poor John replied, "May you never see the time that when those ten minutes will be as precious to you as they are to me! But, after all, we have all got to go sooner or later—and no man knows when!"

As we closed the cell door, leaving him alone with his sorrowing, faithful brother, the unhappy man kissed us all on each cheek, and bade us "Farewell!" with emotion, too deep for tears—for not a drop moistened his throbbing, burning eyes.

We made our way with difficulty from the Tombs, by the

aid of the surrounding police, who opened a space for our carriage through the crowd, which, in every direction, for two or three blocks, filled the adjacent streets, and reached, on Franklin street, nearly if not quite to Broadway.

I resided at that time in Seventh street, between Eighth and Ninth avenues, and Rev. Dr. Anthon lived in St. Mark's Place, in Eighth street. We deposited the good doctor at his door, and after calling at the same time to acquaint the family with the last sad scene we had witnessed, Mr. Payne and I were driven quickly over to the New York University, in the southern tower of which, in the upper story, Mr. Samuel Colt had his incipient pistol-manufactory, or rather his Invention and Improvement Office.

As we entered, he was sitting at a table, with a broad-brimmed hat drawn over his brow, his hands spread before his eyes, and the hot tears trickling through his fingers.

After a few moments silence, at his request, I took a sheet of paper, and commenced, at his dictation, a letter to his brother, Hon. Judge Colt, then of St. Louis.

I had not written more than five lines, when rapid footsteps were heard on the stairs, and a hackman rushed into the room, exclaiming in the wildest excitement:

"Mr. Colt! Mr. Colt! your brother has killed himself—stabbed himself to the heart! And the Tombs are a-fire! You can see it a-burning now!"

"Thank God! thank God!" exclaimed Mr. Colt, with an expression almost of joy.

We raised an eastern window of the tower, stepped out upon the battlement, and by a short ladder, stepped out on to the roof of the chapel, or main edifice, and saw the flames licking up and curling around the great fire-tower of the Tombs.

There was something peculiar about the air—the atmosphere—on that day. One felt as one feels on a cold autumnal night, while watching, uncovered in the open air, the flickering of the aurora borealis in the northern sky. As early as half past three o'clock that afternoon, two stars were distinctly visible through the cold thin atmosphere. This was regarded at the time as a remarkable phenomenon.

Now everybody knows, or should know, that the body of John C. Colt was found as exactly as described by the hackman; that life was totally extinct; that the corpse was encoffined, removed, buried, and "so remains unto this day."

The Tombs tower caught fire from an over-heated stove; and yet, all the doubters of Colt's suicide, whom we have ever met, contend that the burning was part of the plan; that it was hired to be set on fire, and that in the confusion the condemned man escaped.

L. Gaylord Clarke.

THE MURDER OF LORD WILLIAM RUSSELL.

TRIAL OF FRANÇOIS BENJAMIN COURVOISIER.—HIS CONVICTION, CONFESSION AND EXECUTION IN LONDON.—GREAT SPEECH OF MR. CHARLES PHILLIPS IN DEFENCE OF THE PRISONER, &C. &C.

Courvoisier was a native of Switzerland, having been born in a small village called Monte-la-Ville, in the month of August, 1816. His father, Abraham Courvoisier, was a small farmer. François was at an early age placed in one of the common public schools in the village, and after leaving this, he was engaged in assisting his father up to his twentieth year. In 1835, he left Switzerland, and came to England, of the language of which he was, however, wholly ignorant. He had an uncle in England, a butler in the establishment of a baronet, through whose influence he is said to have obtained a situation as footman in the establishment of Lady Julia Lockwood, where he remained for about seven months. He left this service in March, 1837, and entered that of Mr. J. M. Fector, M.P., at Dover, where he remained as footman for three years. He quitted Mr. Fector's service on the 31st of March, 1840, and entered the establishment of Lord William Russell, where he was, when, on the morning of May 6, 1840, his Lordship was found murdered in his bed, under circumstances that led to the committal of Courvoisier on trial for the crime.

The deceased nobleman was a posthumous child of the Marquis of Tavistock, eldest son of the fourth duke (who was killed during his father's lifetime, by a fall from his horse, March, 1767), by

Lady Elizabeth Keppel, daughter of the second Earl of Albermarle. The present Lord John Russell is a member of the same family. Lord William was the third and youngest brother of the two last Dukes of Bedford, Francis and John. He was born five months after his father's death,—namely, 1767, and was consequently in his seventy-third year. He married in July,, 1789, Lady Charlotte Anne Villiers, eldest daughter of the fourth Earl of Jersey, who died in August, 1806. By his wife he had seven children:—1. Gertrude Frances, born in November, 1791, and who married, in 1816, the Hon. Henry Grey Bennett, brother of the Earl of Tankerville, who died in May, 1836. 2. Lieutenant-Colonel Francis Russell, born in March, 1793, and who died unmarried in November, 1837. 3. George, born April 7, 1795. 4. John, Commander R.N., born in July, 1796, and who died in April, 1836, having married Sophia, Baroness de Clifford, by whom he has left five surviving children. 5. Charlotte Frances, born in 1798, and who died the first year of her age. 6. William, born in July, 1800, who married Emma, daughter of the late Colonel John and Lady Charlotte Campbell, of the family of Argyll; and 7. Eliza Laura Henrietta, born in January, 1803, who married her first cousin, the Rev. Lord Wriothesly Russell.

Lord William Russell was educated at Westminster School, and entered Parliament at an early age. He subsequently filled more diplomatic offices, but never distinguished himself in any particular manner.

Strange circumstances attended the commencement as well as termination of his career. His father, as we have already stated, was killed by a fall from his horse, and his mother died of grief soon afterward, a martyr to her affection for her deceased lord.

THE TRIAL.

The trial of the prisoner commenced at the Central Criminal Court, Old Bailey, on the morning of Thursday, the seventeenth of June, 1840, and terminated on Saturday evening.

By nine o'clock in the morning many of the best seats in the court were occupied by ladies, and on the bench were the Earl of Cavan, Lord Arthur Lennox, the Hon. Mr. Villiers, Sir Montagu Chapman, the Lord Mayor, Sheriffs, Under-Sheriffs, Alderman Sir Mathew Wood, Alderman Harmer, and Alderman Humphery. Shortly afterwards, Mr. D W. Harvey, Lady Granville Somerset, the Earl of Mansfield, the Earl of

Sheffield, and other noblemen, gentlemen, and ladies, entered the court.

The counsel for the prosecution were Mr. Adolphus, Mr. Bodkin, and Mr. Chambers; and for the prisoner Mr. Charles Phillips and Mr. Clarkson.

The attorney for the prosecution was Mr. Hobler, and for the prisoner, Mr. Flower.

At half-past nine o'clock, a model of the house in which the unfortunate nobleman was murdered, was brought in and placed upon the table in the centre of the court.

At a quarter before ten o'clock the Duke of Sussex entered the court, attended by the Sheriffs and the Swordbearer.

At ten o'clock the prisoner, Courvoisier, was brought into the dock.

The clerk of the Arraigns then proceeded to read over the indictment to the prisoner, and told him, as he was an alien, he had the privilege of being tried by a jury composed half of foreigners and half of Englishmen, and asked him whether he wished to have six of the jurors foreigners, or whether he was content with a jury consisting entirely of Englishmen?

The prisoner replied that he was content to be tried by Englishmen.

The jury were then sworn.

Lord Chief-Justice Tindal and Mr. Baron Parke entered the court as the jury were being sworn, and took their seats by the side of the Common Sergeant.

Lord Chief-justice Tindal then directed the foreign jury to be discharged.

The prisoner having pleaded *not guil y*,—

Mr. Adolphus rose to address the jury for the prosecution.—He commenced by calling upon them to dismiss from their minds whatever they might previously have heard of the murder of the most illustrious, learned, and amiable nobleman who had fallen a victim to the hand of the assassin. He dwelt upon the awful manner in which the late lord had been hastened to another state of existence; alluded to the history of several members of the noble house of Russell, who had come to a sudden and untimely death, but the late Lord William Russell had been cruelly and basely murdered in his own house, under circumstances of the most melancholy description. The learned counsel then proceeded to state that the deceased nobleman was seventy-three years of age, and although in sufficient good health to enjoy life, he was feeble and weak upon his feet, and lived in such a manner, in tranquility and retirement, as to allow the flame of life to be gradually extinguished. He lived in a house of small dimensions, at 14 Norfolk street, the model of which was now upon the table of the court; and his household consisted of two female servants and a valet within the house; and a coachman and a groom who lived out of the house. Such was the state of his lordship's household up to the time of his death. The learned counsel then proceeded to point out to the jury the different apartments of the house, and next called their particular attention to the back part of the premises, showing how difficult it was to gain access to it, from the manner in which it was blocked up by stables and other buildings. both at the sides and in the rear The female servants were persons of unexceptionable character. The prisoner had lived in his lordship's service for five weeks, and previously to being in his lordship's service had borne an excellent character —in fact, up to the moment of this crime being imputed to him there seemed not to be a blemish on his character. On the morning of the fifth of May, his lordship rose at his usual hour of nine, then went out, and spent his morning as noblemen do spend their mornings, leaving several messages with the prisoner, some of which the prisoner had expressed fears he should forget. His lordship afterwards returned to his dinner at the usual hour, subsequently took his coffee, and retired to bed about his usual time. He laid himself down on his bed that night never to rise any more. The next morning he was found mangled and a corpse. The learned counsel then detailed the circumstances of the prisoner having forgotten to send his lordship's carriage to Brooke's club house, as he had been told to do, as well as the conversation which ensued between the servants on the subject, and the fact of the prisoner's having procured beer for the servants, after taking which they had felt sleepy and gone to bed. On the next morning, about six o'clock, the housemaid, Sarah Mancell, rose, and in coming down-stairs the first thing which she remarked was the warming-pan, with which the prisoner had warmed his lordship's bed, standing in the passage, appearing as if he had, instead of taking it downstairs as usual, immediately after warming the bed, gone up to his own bed-room. Mancell went down into the passage, and there saw things scattered about, and the door unlocked and unbolted, as if the house had been burglariously entered. She alarmed the cook, who told her to go to the valet, Courvoisier, which was very natural. She did so, and the prisoner came down in an unusually short time. There might or there might not be anything in this circumstance, but it was his duty to state it to them. The first of the prisoner's acts was to remove the warming-pan, and carry it down to its proper place. After reading the list of the articles found in the passage, he called the attention of the jury to the fact of these articles being left behind, and to the inference which it led to, that no real burglary had been committed, but that every attempt had been made to give the appearance of one. He next called the attention of the jury to the suspicious manner of the prisoner when he first went into his lordship's bed-room; his silence and his inactivity, while every one else was in a state of bustle and confusion. It had at first been supposed that his lordship had committed suicide, but, independent of the improbability of this from his lordship's character, it had been satisfactorily proved that his lordship could not have inflicted the wound which was the cause of his death, for no instrument of death was to be found, and it was impossible that the dead man could have put it out of the way. Besides, the body, and even the face, of the deceased, was covered up in such a manner as no person could have himself done after committing suicide. The next suspicious circumstance against the prisoner was the broken state of the back door, to which he had pointed as the place where the thieves had entered. Neither the tiles, nor the walls, nor the white-wash of the walls, had been displaced or discolored in any way whatever; and it would have been impossible for any one to come over the leads, or tiles at the back, without leaving marks in the dust upon the leads. Even a cat's foot would have left a mark upon the dust. But the dust was not disturbed, and there was no mark of importance, even of a cat's foot. Scientific men, and persons acquainted with such matters, had given their opinion that the marks made upon the door had not been made from the outside, but from the inside of the door. And if this was the case, it was a damning circumstance against the prisoner. After alluding to the screw-driver and other things found, he called the attention of the iury to the state of the rushlight found in his lordship's bed-room. It was usual for his lordship to burn a rushlight, but on the morning of the discovery of the murder, the rushlight was found to have been very little burnt, while a wax-candle was found in a candlestick burnt down in the socket. The presumption was, that the rushlight had been put out immediately before or immediately after the murder, and the wax-candle had been used by the murderer to see his way about the house. He now came to the discoveries made upon a more minute examination. In his lordship's bed-room there was a watch-stand, but no watch in it; and on the prisoner being asked whether his lordship's watch was in it the night before, he replied that it was; but it was not found for several days afterwards, and then under most suspicious cirumstances. The prisoner, on being asked if his lordship had any money, said that the had a ten pound and a five pound note previously to his murder, and the ten pound note had been found subsequently under circumstances, and in a place, to lead to the suspicion that no one but the prisoner could have placed it where it was found. This ten pound note would become a very material point of the evidence. It would be proved that it had been entrusted to his lordship for a charitable purpose—for his lordship was a charitable man, as every one knew who was acquainted with his character. He dwelt upon the suspicious fact of his lordship's keys being found on the hearth-rug. After the premises had been generally searched, the prisoner's box was searched, but nothing was found, and it was hardly necessary to say that no one would be such a fool, if he had taken the property under such circumstances, as to put them into his box, which he must know would be searched. He stated once for all, that he did not rely on anything which was found in the prisoner's box, from first to last; but on subsequent examinations, behind the skirting-board in the pantry, five gold rings, undoubtedly his lordship's property, had been found; and behind another part of the skirting-board was found a Waterloo medal; and the ten pound note was also found at the same time. This note the prisoner had admitted was in the note-case in the bed-room the day before the murder, and if a burglar had taken this note, was it likely that he would have concealed it in such a place as this, or would he not have taken it away with him? Subsequently a locket was found in the prisoner's pocket, and on its discovery, the prisoner said, 'That's my locket.' On the ninth of May, another locket was found, which would be a very important link in the evidence. A few days before the unhappy catastrophe, his lordship had gone to Richmond, accompanied by the prisoner only. While at Richmond, he went over to Hampton Court to see his relative, Lady Sarah Bailey. During his stay there, and in the midst of a conversation with her, he dropped the locket out of his pocket. He went to the chapel at Hampton Court, and on his return from the chapel the locket was returned to him by Lady Sarah Bailey. He put it into his pocket, and never saw it afterwards. He made frequent inquiries after it of Lady Sarah Bailey, and also wrote a letter to the innkeeper of Richmond, which did honor to his feelings. But the locket was never more seen, until found under the hearthstone in the butler's pantry, after the murder, and it was impossible that any person could have placed it there but the prisoner. The watch, which the prisoner had said was in his lordship's bed-room the night before the murder, was also subsequently found under the lead of the sink, having never been in any other human possession but the prisoner's. He was obliged to anticipate the defence, for he knew not what it would be. It was difficult to conceive what motive the prisoner could have had for the perpetration of the murder, but such was the constitution of the human mind, that there were motives which no one could conceive. The prisoner had complained that he was dissatisfied with his place; he had said, "I am sorry I came here; I have given away a sovereign for seventeen shillings in silver." It was probable that the prisoner had supposed his lordship had a good deal of money in his possession, and that his motive in committing the murder was plunder. He left it to them to say whether this was not a just view of the case. If the prisoner had no motive, who could have had a motive? If the prisoner could not have done it, who could have done it? It would be said, he knew, that the evidence was circumstantial. It was so; but if all the parts, if each atom of the evidence were complete, he thought it was as good evidence as could be had. It would not do to consider the parts of evidence separately. They must be taken together, and if the chain of proof were complete, the objection to such evidence fell to the ground. He quoted the opinion of Lord Chief Baron Macdonald upon circumstantial evidence—namely, that when the witnesses neither contradicted each other nor themselves, it might be even more satisfactory than direct evidence. An attempt had been made to throw discredit on the evidence of Sarah Mancell, but he could not help saying that she remained altogether unimpeached.

He combated the insinuation thrown out against the police, —namely, that they had tried to 'get up' this case for the sake of the reward; and after saying how unworthy was the supposition, that the noble family for whom he appeared were capable of hunting down a foreigner in a strange land, he proceeded to tell the jury their duty in the case before them. It was a case which required firm and upright hearts, and clear and intelligent heads. Should their verdict be an acquittal, no one could blame them for that; but if, on the other hand, they found the prisoner guilty, they would do so according to the evidence laid before them, and would know that they had done their duty. The evidence was then gone into.

Sarah Mancell examined by Mr. Bodkin—After stating of whom the establishment of the deceased nobleman consisted, and the fact of his lordship giving the prisoner certain orders on the morning preceding the murder, before he went out, witness said—After dinner the prisoner went out to deliver his messages, and returned a little before five, and he then said he should put out his lordship's things to dress. Soon after this the upholsterer's man came to the house. This was about five o'clock. He stayed a short time and then left the house, after doing some little job that was required. The prisoner went up stairs with the upholsterer's man, and while they were gone, an acquaintance of the prisoner's, named Carr, rang the area bell. He came down the area steps into the kitchen, and stayed and took tea with them after the upholsterer's man was gone. While they were at tea, the coachman came in by the area steps, when something was said about the carriage not being sent for Lord Russell, and the prisoner said he had forgotten to order it, and he should tell his lordship that he had ordered it at half-past five; adding that his lordship was very forgetful, and he must pay for his forgetfulness. The coachman upon this left the house, and the prisoner then went into his own pantry with Carr.

A model of the house was here shown the witness, and she described the situation of the kitchen and the pantry.

Examination continued—His lordship came home in a hackney cab, about twenty minutes to six, and the prisoner went up and let him in. His lordship immediately went to the dining-room, which was directly over the kitchen. She soon afterwards saw the prisoner come down with a letter in his hand, and he said he was going to take it to the stables, and he went out, accompanied by Carr, and they were absent about sufficient time to enable them to get to the stable and back. The prisoner told her that his lordship appeared angry when he first came home, but that he afterwards got quite good-tempered. When the prisoner came from the stables, he brought a dog with him, and his lordship went out and took a walk with the dog, as was his custom before dinner every day, and the prisoner was then engaged in making arrangements for the dinner. The dinner-hour was seven, and a few minutes before that hour, a bell-hanger came to fasten the handle of his lordship's door. His lordship dined alone on that day, and was waited upon by the prisoner; after his lordship had dined, he went into the back drawing-room. She went to bed, and to her knowledge he did not go again into the dining-room. About nine o'clock the coachman came to fetch the dog. The cook went out, and witness and the prisoner supped alone about nine o'clock; and while they were at supper, they had some conversation about changing servants. The cook was going away, and a new cook was expected. The prisoner said that his lordship would take any servant that he recommended. He also said that he did not like his lordship's service. On the 22d of April, which was the day his lordship returned from Richmond, the prisoner said his lordship had been very cross and peevish, as they had changed his rooms three times while he was stopping at the Castle Hotel there. The prisoner also said that his lordship had lost a locket while he was staying there; and he did not know how it was lost, but he could not find it. He also said he could not tell how the late valet had stopped so long, as his temper would not allow him (prisoner) to stop with his lordship. All this took place on the 22d of April. Between that time and the 5th of May, she heard the prisoner say he must write about the locket to the porter. He did not say what porter he meant; and she did not hear him say anything in reference to the locket after this time. On the evening of the 5th May, the cook went out and returned a little after ten, and the prisoner let her in by the front door. After the cook came in, the prisoner went out by the area steps to fetch a pint of porter, and returned by the same entrance. He was only gone a very few minutes. She did not know whether he locked the area gate or not; it was the duty either of the cook or the prisoner to have fastened it. She left the kitchen to go to bed about a quarter or twenty minutes past ten o'clock. Her bed-room is directly over that in which his lordship slept, and the cook slept in the same room, but in a separate bed. It was her duty, every other night, to light a fire in his lordship's bed-room, and she did so that night, and after lighting it went to her own bed-room. The prisoner slept in an adjoining room. At this time every thing appeared to be in its usual state. The room behind Lord Russell's bed-room was not at this time used for any purpose. His lordship's door was covered with green-baize, but the others were not. The door at the foot of the attic stairs was sometimes left open at night and sometimes closed. The cook came to bed in about a quarter of an hour or twenty minutes after witness got to bed. Neither herself, nor the cook, to her knowledge, left the bed-room any more; on that night she heard no noise, and was not disturbed at any time during the night. It was the duty of the prisoner to remain up until his lordship went to bed, and to leave a supply of coals, or any thing that might be necessary. Witness awoke on the following morning about a quarter past six o'clock, and at this time the cook was in bed and asleep, apparently. She then proceeded to state what she saw upon going down stairs, as mentioned in the opening speech of the learned counsel. After the police had been called into the house, her attention was directed to his lordship's gold pencil-case, gold tooth-pick, and a napkin, in which both those articles were folded, a silver sugar-grater, a silver caddy-spoon, a silver top of a salt-dredger, a pair of silver spectacles, and a silver cayenne-spoon. She recognized the napkin as the same she had given out on Monday at his lordship's dinner, and she saw it again on the Tuesday. The things mentioned were kept in different parts of the house. The cloak was generally kept in the dining-room; the opera-glass in his lordship's bed-room; the trinket-box in his dressing-case. His spectacles, she believed, he generally carried about with him. The other articles were generally kept in the cupboard in the butler's pantry. Some of the articles were also kept in the cupboard of the side-board. After this she went to the cook and said something to her, and afterwards went to the prisoner's room and called out, 'Courvoisier, do you know of any thing being the matter last night?' He opened the door immediately: about ten minutes had elapsed from the time when she first knocked at his door; he was dressed all but his coat when she went the second time. It was his usual custom to go down and wash himself in the pantry. There was nothing peculiar in his dress on this morning. He had his shoes on. The moment she saw Courvoisier, she said, 'Do you know that all the silver is about?' He looked very pale and agitated, but gave no answer. He put his coat down, and went down instantly. He went first, and she followed after him. He took the warming-pan down with him into the dining-room. It was her custom to call the prisoner in the morning. He was never down so soon as on that morning after her calling him. Sometimes he was half an hour, sometimes a quarter of an hour, and sometimes an hour. The first room he went into was the dining-room, and there he left the warming pan. She did not hear him say anything on going into the dining-room. He next went down to his pantry. There is a door near the pantry which opens into the back area; but she did not notice the state of that door. She followed him into the pantry; there were a cupboard and drawers in the pantry, which were all open. The prisoner went up to the drawers, and said, 'My God! somebody has been robbing us.' Witness then said, 'Let us go up stairs,' and on getting as far as the passage, she said, 'Let us go and see where his lordship is.' They went up stairs, prisoner first, and she following. He entered by the green door. The door closed on him, and she went in immediately afterwards. One of the windows of the room is directly opposite the door. As she entered the room she saw the prisoner in the act of opening the shutters of the middle window. To do that a person would have to pass the foot of the bed. She went about half way round the foot of the bed, and noticed blood on the pillow, but before she saw that she exclaimed, 'My lord! my lord!' on which the prisoner said, 'Here he is,' or 'There he is,' she did not know which. On seeing the blood she screamed, and ran out of the room, and out at the street door, and then over to No. 23, in the street, and rang the bell. Finding there was no answer at No. 23, she rang at No. 22. She was not gone ten minutes. On her return to the house, she went into the dining-room, and found the prisoner sitting on a chair, in the act of writing; he had a pen in his hand, and a small piece of paper on a large book. She said, "What the deuce are you sitting there for? Why do you not go and see for some one, or a doctor?" He said, "I must write to Mr. Russell," and continued writing. Witness said, "Some one must go for him." Mr. Russell was a son of Lord William Russell, and lived at 9 Chesnut-place, Belgrave-square. There was a sort of laboring man going past, and prisoner beckoned to him, but she told him not to call such a man as that, and the man went on about his business. The coachman and Young, Mr. Latham's servant, came in a few minutes afterwards, and went up stairs. She then ran down, to send some for Mr. Elsgood, a surgeon in Park-street, who arrived soon afterwards, as did also the police. Witness went up with them, and then saw his lordship's face, and noticed a quantity of blood. There were two pillows, and they were generally placed side by side, as if for two persons. They were in that state w en she saw them that morning. His lordship lay on the right side of his person, his face towards the window. He was lying with his head on the pillow next the window, and the other pillow was lying behind him. There was a dressing-table in the room, with the white cloth, on which his lordship used to put his pencil case, and also his rings. On the morning after the murder there were no rings, nor was there a gold pencil case upon the table. She saw a purse there; it was empty. The police have remained in possession of the house from that time to the present. She had conversations with the prisoner on the subject of money. The last time was on the Tuesday morning, the 5th of May. He said that he had no money at home, and that he never took any out with him, nor had he any at the bank. He afterwards said he had eight pounds some odd shillings in the bank. In the course of the same conversation he said all the money he had was five pounds, and when that was gone he must ask his lordship for more; he had eight pounds on his books against his lordship. She asked him if he had got rid of all the money she had seen him take out. He had taken out some sovereigns with him on the Monday before; he had put them in his waistcoat pocket; he had fetched the sovereigns out of his bed-room. It was to that she alluded. He said, in answer, he had, for he had paid a tailor's bill. He said before that he was not so well off now as when he first came to England, and he said it again at tea-time, when Carr was there. On the Tuesday morning he said he had only five pounds left. He spoke of the five pounds before he said he had the eight pounds in the bank. She had heard him speak of Lord W. Russell's property on two occasions. The first was before his lordship went to Richmond. He said old Billy was a rum old chap, and if he had his money he would not remain long in England. She said his lordship was not a very rich man, and he repeated what he had said. The second time was after his return from Richmond. In the course of the day, May 6, she asked the prisoner if he heard her knock at his door; he said he thought he would begin to dress, but did not say whether he heard her or not. She had frequently seen the prisoner in his lordship's bed-room, and noticed that he always was looking into all his lordship's property. She asked him what he was going to do, and he always said he was looking after something, but did not say what. This occurred before he went to Richmond. She could not say what particular articles he was looking at in the bed room. He was, on one occasion, looking at the dressing-case; he had it down in the pantry. He was looking at his lordship's property not only in one room, but in every room. When he went to Richmond, the little box covered with Russia leather, which his lordship called his cash-box, was unlocked; he was looking into that. It was usually kept by the side of his lordship's bed. The prisoner brought it down, and said it was unlocked. His lordship was then out for a walk. The prisoner brought it down into the dining-room.

The witness was searchingly cross-examined by Mr. Charles Phillips, but nothing of any special importance elicited.

Mary Hammell, cook in Lord W. Russell's service, and who had lived with him two years and nine months, was then examined, and confirmed, in almost all respects, the evidence of the preceding witness. In her cross-examination, she said that, when the murder was discovered, the prisoner appeared to be much alarmed at the time. He said he should never get a place again. He was alarmed and agitated like the rest.

She also stated that there was some quantity of plate that has never yet been found.

[The next day's proceedings show the extraordinary discovery of this missing plate, during the progress of the trial.]

William York, who was coachman to the late Lord William Russell, and Emanuel Young, coachman to Mr. Lather, 3 Norfolk-street, were then examined, but they only deposed to some of the facts already spoken to by Sarah Mancell.

Mr. Henry Elsgood, examined by Mr. Chambers—I am a surgeon, residing in Brook-street. I was called to the house of the late Lord William Russell on the morning of the 6th of May, at half-past seven. I went into his bed-room, and saw his body in bed covered up. The bed-clothes were over the body, and the towel over his face. I turned the clothes down, and removed the towel. The body was lying on the back, inclining to the right side. There was some blood on the sheet, on the pillow, and on the towel over his face. His shirt collar was wide open, and there was a sort of worsted comforter over the chest. I divided it, and saw a wound extending from the top of the left shoulder across the throat and neck, dividing the throat. It was decidedly sufficient to destroy life immediately. It was about four or five inches deep at the commencement, and about three at the termination; it was made with one incision. Great force must have been used in making it. It might have been made with a knife, or some such instrument. I have not been shown any knives that were found down stairs. It is impossible his lordship could have inflicted it himself. I found no instrument near his lordship with which it might have been done. I again examined the body on the following Friday. The ball of the thumb of the right hand was nearly cut off. When I first uncovered the body, the left hand gripped the sheet. There was blood upon the corner of the pillow lying by his side, down by his head, as if it had been used to prevent the gush of blood by holding it over the wound.

Mr. John Nussy—I am an apothecary, residing in Cleveland-row, and was the medical attendant of the late Lord Wm. Russell. He was 73 years of age, of spare and feeble habit, and subject to asthma. I was sent for to his house on the 6th of May, and found Mr. Elsgood there. I examined the wound, and have heard the evidence of Mr. Elsgood, and agree with him in what he has said. I could feel the neck-bone in the wound. I requested those present to place the things exactly as they hadbeen at the time of the discovery. They did so. Courvoisier assisted in doing so. Thomas Selwyn, servant to Mr. Cutler, residing nex door to the late Lord William Russell's, in Norfolk street, corroborated part of the evidence of the housemaid.

John Baldwin examined by Mr. Chambers—I am a policeman. I was on duty in Norfolk-street on the morning of the 6th of May. I went to Lord William Russell's a few minutes past seven. A female let me in. Rolls was with me. I asked if there was any man-servant. I saw a person sitting behind the door who was pointed out to me as the man-servant. He was sitting with his hands over his face. I asked him why he did not get up. He made no answer, and did not move his hands from his face. I addressed him three times, and said to Rolls, "Rolls, he must know something about this." He never made any answer. I remained there, putting up the things together. I then went down into the kitchen with Rolls, and examined the back kitchen door. I found it standing open. I observed some marks of violence on the door. I went into the butler's pantry, and found a person sitting behind the door, with his elbows on his knees, and his hands to his face, apparently the same I had seen in the dining-room. I had told him he had made a devil of a pretty mess of it, that he must know all about it—(Laughter, in which the prisoner joined heartily)—but I had no answer. I went into the yard, and got up out of the area into the top yard, and examined the party wall, between 14 and 15. It is a whitewashed wall. Near the top there is a ledge of slate projecting about two inches. There were no marks on the wall. The steps were standing in the yard, against the wall, but not in such a position as any person could get up them. They were not open. Rolls pulled them out. I got up and saw the lead flat: it was covered with dust, and there were neither foot-marks nor finger marks. No person could have passed over it without marking it. I tried it with my hand, and my hand made a mark on it.

Cross-examined by Mr. C. Phillips—What were you doing when you were angry with the prisoner for not giving assistance? Witness—I was inquiring what was lost. The females never told me anything. When I examined the kitchen door

I thought at first some one had broken in, when I saw the door was open, but on further examination I saw there was no break-in. I never saw the placard offering a reward, and I do not know what it is to this day. I have heard of no reward in this case. I have been in Lord William Russell's house three or four times. I have not talked to my brother policemen about it; it may have been mentioned. I have spoken to policemen about it. I will not swear I have not spoken to twenty about it. I never heard talk of any reward. I can write and read a little, but not much. I belong to the Vine-street station. I am there every day.

Mr. C. Phillips—Did you never hear of any reward of five hundred pounds being offered for any of the missing spoons and forks?—There was something about it read out in general orders, but I do not know what it was about, nor what the amount of the reward was. I cannot tell when it was read. I cannot tell if it was a week ago, or four days ago, or if it was yesterday.

At the conclusion of the examination of this witness, the Court adjourned to ten o'clock on the following dav

SECOND DAY.—FRIDAY.

The Court resumed this morning, and was crowded in every part.

At ten o'clock, Mr. Sergeant Arabin opened the Court, and the prisoner was placed at the bar. He appeared firm, but rather fatigued, and not in quite such good spirits as on the preceding day.

Mr. Adolphus stated that he had to say, that in the course of yesterday a most important piece of evidence had been discovered, which he intended to offer to the Court, and that, therefore, if the Court wished it, he should open it.

Mr. C. Phillips said, that, in justice to the prisoner, the information ought to have been communicated to his legal advisers; he must deprecate any statement being made at present.

Mr. Adolphus—The communication was made immediately to you.

Mr. C. Phillips—Neither Mr. Clarkson nor myself heard anything about it until the last quarter of an hour, and there is our solicitor willing to make oath to the same, as regards himself. Let us know, therefore, to whom the communication was made.

Lord Chief-Justice Tindal—The evidence, I suppose, will be produced in the regular course. Let us have no more inquiry about it, but call the next witness.

John Tedman, inspector of the police, was next examined, and after stating similar facts to those related by Baldwin, he was cross-examined, and said—I asked the prisoner if anything was missing from the sideboard. He said some spoons and forks, but I cannot tell how many. I asked the prisoner if the cloak and other articles found in the passage were his lordship's property, and he said "Yes." I said no thief would ever leave this property behind. He said, "It is certainly very odd." I asked if he had locked the street-door at night when he went to bed. He said he had, and showed me, by putting up the chain, shooting the lock, and putting to the bolt. He bolted both top and bottom bolt. I asked him how he found it in the morning. He undid the chain, unlocked and unbolted it, and put the spring of the lock by the hook, and I said, As you see it now. There is a door at the end of the passage going into the garden. It is partly a glass door. The chain was on that door. It was bolted, and it had never been disturbed at all. There was an inside shutter to it. It was down. It could be pushed down without unfastening the door. The glass was whole and unbroken, and there was not a mark on the door; the area gate was uninjured; it was locked. There is no gate to the back area. I went to the pantry, and saw a press there with some drawers; they were open; the top of one was forced, as if by a chisel or a screw-driver, or some such blunt instrument. The lock was sprung, as if locked. The articles in the drawer were disturbed. There is a window in the pantry. I asked him if it was fastened last night; he said, "I do not think it was, but I cannot say exactly." I then went to the back door on the basement story; it was very much bruised, as I have before stated. The prisoner assisted in examining the door, and pointed out some marks which I had not seen. I said to the prisoner, on examining the door, "Some of you in the house have done this deed." He said, "If they have, I hope they will be found out." I said, "There is not much fear but what they will." I looked about to see how any body could have got into the house. I examined the wall. There were some slates which must have been disturbed, I should think, by any person descending that wall. There was a quantity of dust on the slates, which was undisturbed. I went with the prisoner into his bed-room. I found there a purse; there was a five-pound Bank of England note, and six sovereigns in it. I asked the prisoner how he came by the note. He said he had given his lordship change for it some days ago, and that the rest of the money he had had some time. He showed me his box. I examined everything in it, but found nothing to throw any light upon this case. The box was left in the room, and the key in the prisoner's possession. He left the box open. He appeared to have on quite a clean shirt that morning. The prisoner, although not in custody, was under the watch of the police, and the female servants were watched also. Care was taken to prevent their having conference with one another; but the prisoner was not hindered from having access to his own room. He was taken into custody on the afternoon of Friday, May 8, but was not taken out of the house until Sunday. On Sunday he was taken to the station-house, and on Monday, the 11th of May, he was taken before the justices at Bow-street. On the evening of the 13th of May, a person, representing himself as the uncle of the prisoner, came to the house and asked for some clean linen for the prisoner. I, having had directions to let him have what he required, went up next morning to his box to get it, and in doing so unfolded a shirt, from which the gloves produced dropped out. They are white cotton gloves. I had on the previous examination unfolded the shirts in the box, but had not shaken them. The gloves dropped down when I shook the shirt. On the former occasion I had unfolded the shirt without finding anything, and on this occasion I had unfolded the shirt without finding anything, but when I shook it, the gloves dropped out.

William Rose, a police constable, and Henry Beresford, an inspector of police, corroborated the evidence of their colleagues, in almost all particulars.

Nicholas Pearce, a division inspector of police, in the course of his examination by Mr. Bodkin, said—In searching the premises I found the poker produced in the fire-place in the butler's pantry. It was bent, as it now appears. Such an instrument would make a similar mark to that on the wood inside the socket of the bolt. In the same pantry I found the screw-driver produced on a shelf. I applied it to some of the marks on the door, and it corresponded. I found the pair of tongs produced. I found the hammer produced in the cupboard in the pantry. I fitted it to the marks in the door and door-post, and it fitted them when the door was shut from the outside. It would be impossible to force the door open by such an instrument, if bolted on the inside. The marks on the socket of the upper bolt could not have been made by a person from the outside, if the door had been fastened. The socket of the lower bolt had been started from its place, but not off. The bolt was rusted, and did not appear to have been used lately. There were considerable marks of violence about the lower bolt, which would have been unnecessary if the bolt had not been shot. I found marks which could not have been made if the bolt had been shot. One of a screw-driver on the rabbeting, which could not have been made from the outside. In my judgment, no breaking into the house could have taken place from the outside. I was present when some experiments were made on the half-glass door. Until they were made, the door was uninjured. I made the first mark on it myself. I saw an experiment made while the door was on the latch, by placing the claws of the hammer between the door and door-post and pressing the handle down. It did not force the latch, which resisted the pressure. The mark produced was equally deep with that on the door below, and quite similar. I applied the tongs to the door of the safe in the pantry, which had been forced open. The mark corresponded with the tongs. [The door was produced, for inspection.] I also found a screw-driver, which I compared with the marks in the safe, and found it to correspond. On the Monday I made some inquiry of the prisoner respecting the missing property. I asked him if he knew what money or property had been taken. He said he had seen a 10*l.* note and a 5*l.* note in a purse a few days ago. I asked him where the plate was kept that was found in the passage. He pointed out a cupboard in the sideboard in the dining-room. On the Friday I searched the prisoner's boxes with Shaw. I never searched them with Tedman. I searched a portmanteau, a deal box, and the drawers. I saw two clean shirts in the portmanteau, but cannot say that I examined them minutely. On the same day I made a search in the prisoner's pantry. At that time workmen were in the house, to take up the drains. I was searching in the pantry, by the side of the fire-place, near the sink under the window. I took away a piece of the skirting-board which runs from the fire-place to the corner under the sink. When I pulled it down, I saw the purse produced, about two inches in behind the skirting. I perceived that the mortar had been disturbed before I took the skirting away. I found in the purse five gold coins and five gold rings—one a wedding-ring—and a small piece of silver. I then took away another piece of skirting-board, and found a Waterloo medal, and, further on, a 10*l.* Bank of England note; all of which I now produce. This note was folded up; it was not wrapped up in anything. The skirting was quite dry; it was on the side of the fire-place. The prisoner was in the dining-room when I found these things. I went up to him directly afterwards; Constable Collier was with him. I laid the things I had found on the table before him, and said, I have found these things concealed in your pantry, behind the skirting-board. He said, 'I know nothing about them; I am innocent, and my conscience is clear; I never saw the medal before.' I then took him down into the pantry, and pointed out to him the place from whence I had taken them. He again said,—'I am innocent; I know nothing about them.' He remained in the pantry for some time. I then proceeded with my search in the presence of the prisoner. There is a water-pipe going round the room, and is continued into an adjoining scullery. In removing that pipe between the pantry and the door, I saw Collier put his hand to the pipe, and take a ring behind it down. Some one had previously said 'Hollo! there is a ring.' The ring produced is the one; it is a split ring. I continued the search, but found nothing more concealed that day. I afterwards went up into the prisoner's bed-room, and searched his person. I found about 5*s.* in silver, a small locket, and a bunch of keys upon him. He said the locket was his, and I have no reason to believe the contrary.

Mr. Clarkson—Was it not to get a confession from the prisoner, that you told him those things were found in his pantry? Witness—I suspected he was the person who put them there, and thought it my duty, at that stage of the proceedings, to acquaint him with it.

Mr. Clarkson—Did you intend to obtain from him anything like a confession? Witness—I expected the prisoner might make some remark, which might be either for him or against him. I had naturally a great anxiety to obtain every information on the subject. Mr. Mayne, the Commissioner, was in the room. Mr. Hobler was there at the time.

Mr. Clarkson—Did you not say to the prisoner, 'I found this property concealed in your pantry—can you now look me in the face?' Witness—I said so among other things.

Mr. Clarkson—Did you think that language calculated to intimidate the prisoner? Witness—It was likely to do so, if he were a guilty man; but if I had thought it so, then I should not have used it. There is a reward offered. I expect to get a portion of it, if the prisoner is convicted. I have nothing yet; I have never had a farthing from any one. The property was found behind the skirting-board before I was aware that any reward was offered.

George Collier, a police constable of the C division, corroborated Pearce's testimony, as to the articles found concealed behind the skirting board, and as to the finding of the split-ring behind the leaden pipe. The prisoner continued in the pantry two or three hours. While there, I asked him if those were his lordship's rings which Mr. Pearce had found. He said they were, and that his lordship had worn them yesterday. I asked him where his lordship had placed them when he went to bed, and he said on the table in his bed-room. I asked him if his lordship had a gold split-ring. He said he had, and he used to keep his seals upon it. I said, 'It is a most shocking thing.' He said, 'It is; I am innocent of it; but it would not look so bad against me, had not the property been found in my pantry.' I said it looked very suspicious. The prisoner said 'I shall say nothing till the last until I hear if the whole truth is told.' He was then taken up stairs and searched, and from that time kept in strict custody. On the next morning, the 9th, I searched the scullery with Sergeant Shaw. I assisted to take down the plate-rack, and behind the pipe which runs along the wall close to it I found the seal produced, with a coat of arms engraved on it. I marked it and showed it to Shaw. I searched another pipe in the scullery leading from the pantry. I found the ring produced. It was bent as it is now as if by being pressed behind the pipe. It is a seal ring. It could not be seen behind the pipe. I took the plumber and the carpenter on Wednesday, May 13, and had the floor of the pantry taken up. Under the second board which was removed, the plumber took up a handful of rubbish close by the scullery door, and in it was found the sovereign produced. On the following morning myself and Cronin went into the dining-room and saw Tedman. In consequence of what Tedman said, I went up stairs with Cronin, and in a portmanteau in the prisoner's bed-room I found the two handkerchiefs produced, one cotton and one silk, near the top, they were marked S. C. the silk, and B. C. the cotton, and likewise the shirt front. The handkerchiefs are marked with blood-spots; there are several spots. I was in the room when that portmanteau was examined previously. I attended to the examination, but I cannot swear I noticed either of those things. I did not find anywhere a shirt to which the front found will match.

Mr. Phillips—Why did not you, or the rest of the police, lock up and seal that box and room, to prevent any one having access to them?

Witness—I had nothing to do with that. I had not charge of the house. No one could miss finding the handkerchiefs, nor could any, I should imagine, miss finding the shirt-front, on searching the box, if they had been there. I do not think the prisoner was in the house when I made the search.

F. Shaw, police sergeant, corroborated Collins' testimony.

Cross-examined by Mr. Phillips—I had assisted in searching the prisoner's room on Friday afternoon, May 8. The search was not a careless one; we missed no article; we saw there was nothing more in the box. No one else was in the room; I did not search the box after the eighth

[The portmanteau was produced, and appeared to be an ordinary travelling portmanteau.]

Paul Cronin, a police constable 168 C, corroborated Pearce's testimony as to the finding of the property concealed in the pantry, and added, I went to the house again on Tuesday, May 12; the search was continued. I searched the floor of the scullery on that occasion, with a brick vault adjoining. I passed my fingers along the bricks to discover if any of them were loose, as it was very dark. My fingers struck against something, which I pulled out with great difficulty, and which proved to be part of a watch-key, with the pipe broke off. On the following day, in the upper yard, I raised two or three stones with an iron chisel. I went round the yard, and saw a leaden sink, cased in wood. It had been a fixture in the butler's pantry, just over where Mr. Pearce found the property. I examined round the edge of the sink, and in one place it appeared to me that the lead had been taken up, and put down again very carefully. I turned the front up with the iron chisel, and looked inside, and saw a watch, which I now produce. There was no glass on it when I found it.

James Ellis, examined by Mr. Bodkin—I am at present in the service of the Earl of Mansfield. I was in the service of the late Lord W. Russell two years and eight months. I left him in April, of this year. The prisoner entered his lordship's service two days before I left. The witness identified most of the articles produced as the property of Lord W. Russell, and then said,—I have seen a small locket in Lord Russell's possession, but I am not positive it is the one produced, as I have never had an opportunity of examining it. His lordship always had a lighted rushlight in his room. I never knew his lordship to be in the habit of reading in bed. He was always very careful on the subject of fire. I saw the prisoner two or three times after Lord William Russell's return from Richmond. On one occasion prisoner asked me if I had any recollection of a locket. I told him I had. He then said his lordship had lost the locket while out of town at Richmond. I then said I wondered how it could be lost, as his lordship always carried it in his note-case, The prisoner also said he could not account for its being lost, unless it had fallen from his lordship's clothes while he was brushing them. He said his lordship had written, or was about to write, to Mr. Ellis, at the Hotel, Richmond, about it. I rather think this conversation took place a day or two after the return from Richmond, as I saw the prisoner then, and did not see him afterwards, until the Monday before the murder. I delivered over the plate to the prisoner, and gave him a list of it. The plate box is produced; the list of the plate is inside it. I examined the contents of the box by my list before it was removed from the house, and before I deposited the list in it, there were missing four table spoons, four large forks, four dessert spoons, and two tea-spoons.

Mr. Comyn, a pawnbroker, here produced certain silver articles, which were shown to the witness, who said—They have the crest of Lord Russell upon them, and I believe them to have been his.

Mr. Richard Harrison—I am clerk to Messrs. Hoare, the bankers, in Fleet street. The Baroness de Clifford has an account there, and Mr. Wing, a solicitor, draws in her name. On the twenty fifth of April I paid a check for two hundred pounds, and one of the notes I gave in exchange for that check was the ten pound note now produced.

Mr Thomas Wing corroborated the witness as far as his share in the transaction was concerned, and the Baroness de Clifford proved that she had passed the note to the hands of Lord Russell, to be dispensed in charity.

Lady Sarah Bayley—I am related by marriage to the late Lord W. Russell, and reside at Hampton Court Palace. The deceased used to come to see me when he visited Richmond, and on one occasion I recollect something occurring about a locket. His lordship had a very great regard for the locket. The locket produced is the one I refer to.

William Winter—I am a plumber. I was employed in Lord William's house, and I saw a sovereign found under the boarding.

Mr. Charles Ellis—I keep the Castle Hotel, Richmond. I remember Lord William coming to the hotel on the fifteenth of April. On the twenty-fifth an application was made to me by his lordship respecting a locket he had lost, but no locket was found.

Charles Albert Klafhenberger, a watch-maker, identified the watch as belonging to his lordship.

Charlotte Piolane—My husband's name is Louis. He is a Frenchman, and resides in Leicester square. I am an Englishwoman. I know the prisoner, and have known him for four years. He came to take a place in our hotel as waiter. We used to call him "Jean" in the hotel. He stayed with us as a a servant for a month or five weeks, and I did not see him again until about six weeks ago, when he came to see us on a Sunday evening. He only stayed a short time, and then went away. I did not know him at first, and he said,—"You recollect me—I am Jean, who used to live with you some time ago." He then told me that he was in a situation, but did not say with whom. He came again the same evening with a paper parcel in his hand, and asked me if I would take care of it till the Tuesday following, and he would come for it. I consented, and received charge of the parcel, and he went away. I locked up the parcel in a closet, not at the time having the least idea what it contained. It was tied and sealed. I have never seen the prisoner since until to-day. I heard a public report of the murder of Lord William Russell. The parcel had been left long before that. I took out the parcel yesterday morning in consequence of an account I read in a French newspaper; and I sent for a gentleman named Carbonier, and Mr. Cumming, a friend of ours, and who is also an attorney. The parcel was never touched or opened until yesterday morning.

Mr. Cumming here produced the parcel.

It contained fourteen spoons, two pair of blue stockings, a pair of golden ear-trumpets, and a jacket. The jacket appeared to be wrapped round the other articles so as to prevent them from being discovered by the feel. So tow was also placed to prevent the plate from rattling.

The witness was cross-examined, with a view to show that her house was a common gaming-house, but there appeared no ground for the insinuation. On re-examination, she said, there is no pretence whatever for saying that our house is a gaming-house. I may, like other women, have conversed with my husband about the news of the day, and forgot it directly. I had no idea that Jean was the same person as François Courvoisier.

Louis Gardie—I was present when the parcel was brought to the hotel, and confirmed Madame Piolaine's account of the occurrence.

Mr. Richard Cumming, examined by Mr. Chambers—I am a solicitor, and carrying on business in the Old Jewry. In consequence of a communication I received, I yesterday went to M. Piolaine's, in Leicester place, and a brown paper parcel was produced, and I was consulted as to the propriety of opening it, and it was ultimately opened, and I observed the crest, and proceeded to Ridgeway's, the book-sellers, where I ascertained that the crest was that of the Bedford family, and I immediately proceeded to Marlborough police-office, and had an interview with the clerk and the magistrates, and in consequence of what transpired, I immediately proceeded to the Old Bailey in a cab and sent in a note to the solicitors for the prosecution, with whom I had an interview; and I subsequently, having placed my initials upon the parcel, handed it over to an officer. The paper produced is the covering of the articles.

Mr. W. Molteno—I am a bookseller. Lord William Russell was one of my customers. On the twenty-seventh of April I sent a glazed print to his lordship, the subject of which was the vision of Ezekiel. The parcel, to the best of my belief, had a ticket on it similar to that on the paper now produced, in which the plate was wrapped up.

Joseph Vincent, a Frenchman, proved that he was also present when the parcel was opened in the hotel in Leicester place.

[The witness was examined through the medium of an interpreter.]

Henry Carr, examined by Mr. Bodkin—I am an acquaintance of the prisoner, and served with him in the family of Mr. Fector. I have seen the prisoner wear a jacket something similar to this, while in the service of Mr. Fector.

Eleanor Banks—I have washed some things for the prisoner. The socks produced bear the prisoner's mark, but I cannot say that I ever washed them. These socks are marked on the heel. The prisoner's stockings are generally marked at top. Some of the prisoner's socks and stockings were marked "C. B."

Thomas Davis—I was formerly in the service of Mr. Webster, an optician. He served Lord William Russell with such a pair of ear instruments as those produced in June, 1836.

James Ellis, his lordship's late butler, re-called—Lord William Russell had such a pair while I was living with him.

Sarah Mancell, re called—I saw them in the house about a fortnight before the murder. I have seen such a jacket in the prisoner's possession.

This was the case for the prosecution.

The court then, at twenty minutes to eight, adjourned until the next day, Saturday.

THIRD DAY—SATURDAY.

The court resumed at ten o'clock in the morning. It was not so crowded as it had been on the preceding days, but there were several noblemen, and a large number of ladies, on the bench and on the seats that had been placed in front of it.

The jury having been re-sworn, Mr. Charles Phillips commenced his address on behalf of the prisoner.

[The speech delivered by him was at the time the subject of severe criticism at the hands of several of the newspapers, and a large portion of the British community. All are aware of the great responsibility which rests upon the shoulders of an advocate, in defending an individual who is put before a jury of twelve men to be tried for his life. The case of Courvoisier created intense excitement throughout England. Mr. Phillips, assisted by Mr. Clarkson, was retained for the defence a short time before the trial. The ground for the criticisms on the speech arose from the fact of the powerful argument which Mr. Phillips used to shield his client from the consequences of his terrible act, while at the time the learned gentleman was well aware, from a previous confession, of the guilt of Courvoisier. This confession was made to both counsel by the prisoner, after eight witnesses had been examined for the prosecution. Up to that time everything appeared to bear towards the acquittal of Courvoisier. But a new and important piece of testimony had been hunted up—that of Mrs. Piolaine, the wife of a Frenchman, who kept a place of entertainment, called *L' Hotél de Dieppe*, in Leicester place, Leicester square, London. This lady testified that a few days previous to the murder, Courvoisier brought to her house for safe keeping a quantity of plate, which was proved to be the property of Lord William Russell. Hearing of this testimony, and before Mrs. Piolaine was called, the prisoner confessed his guilt to Messrs. Phillips and Clarkson. As the scene is described, both gentlemen were astounded. Mr. Phillips remarked to the prisoner, "Of course, then, you are going to plead 'guilty?'" "No, sir," said Courvoisier, "I expect you to defend me to the utmost." This conversation took place in court. The prisoner's counsel held a consultation, and Mr. Phillips afterwards remarked, in speaking of his feelings at the time, that "my position at this moment was, I believe, without a parallel in the annals of the profession. I at once came to the resolution of abandoning the case, and so I told my colleague." Through the influence of Mr. Clarkson, Mr. Phillips was induced to remain in the case, and he subsequently condemned himself for this hastily formed resolution, saying—"I am satisfied that my original impression was erroneous. I had no right to throw up my brief and turn traitor to the wretch—wretch though he was—who had confided in me." Both gentlemen then concluded to ask the opinion of Mr. Baron Parke, who sat during the trial beside Chief-Justice Tindall, but who did not take any part in the legal proceedings. Mr. Phillips said that Baron Parke "requested to know distinctly whether the prisoner insisted on my defending him, and on hearing that he did, said I was bound to do so, and to *use all fair arguments arising on the evidence!*" This was the opinion of a great lawyer and sound philosopher, and Mr. Phillips went on with his defence. The newspapers of the day were divided as to the exact words used in several sentences of Mr. Phillips' speech in defence of the prisoner. Some asserted that he made use of the asseveration —"On my soul, I believe Courvisier innocent of the crime!"—while others gave a different version, but conveying the same inference. It was also asserted that Mr. Phillips made an effort in his speech to shift the responsibility of the murder on the shoulders of the female servants of the family.

We give the speech in full, however, obtained from an authoritative source, which may be relied upon as correct. It is one of Mr. Phillips' most brilliant efforts, and added new laurels, in a forensic sense, to that gentleman's high reputation.

The exact truth of Mr. Phillips' position was that the bigoted English press were bitterly opposed to his advancement among them as a member of the bar. Mr. Phillips was an Irishman, and at the Irish bar obtained a prominence second to none in the profession. He was a brilliant orator, an elegant writer, and an accomplished gentleman. When he came to England the press of that country let loose its foul attacks upon him, simply because he was an Irishman. Even if he was a little over zealous in defending Courvoisier, the responsibility of the advocate should have been a sufficient cloak to defend him from all blame. Lord Brougham, in his celebrated speech in the case of Queen Caroline, thus lays down the duty of the advocate:—"An advocate, by the sacred duty which he owes his client, knows, in the discharge of that office, but one person in the world,—THAT CLIENT AND NONE OTHER. To save that client by all expedient means—to protect that client at all hazards and costs—to all others, and among others to himself—is the highest and most unquestioned of his duties; and he must not regard the alarm—the suffering—the torment—the destruction—which he may bring upon any other. Nay, separating even the duties of a patriot from those of an advocate, and cast them, if need be, to the world, he must go on, reckless of the consequences, if his fate it should unhappily be to involve his country in confusion for his client's protection!"

Although the foregoing broad propositions as to the duties of the advocate, were advanced by Lord Brougham, yet the English press took no notice whatever of it. But when Mr. Phillips took the ground which he did in defending Courvisier, this press was the very first to condemn and malign him. In the discussion which some years after took place in the newspapers regarding Mr. Phillips' line of defence, we are, however, happy to be able to state that the gentleman was entirely exonerated in all blame in the matter.

However, Mr. James T. Brady, of the New York bar, has disagreed with Lord Brougham in the propositions which that learned gentleman laid down as to the duties of the advocate. Mr. Brady, in defending John Y. Beall (who was hung on Governor's Island for being a guerilla and spy), makes use of the following language—"I wish to say to this court, on the honor of a gentleman, that I never have supposed that Lord Brougham's definition of the duties or right of an advocate was correct. I have never entertained the idea that it proceeds, in the view of refined society, or in the view of any instructed conscience, further than this—that an advocate may fairly present honorably, whatever any man who is accused would have a right in truth to say for himself, and no more."]

THE SPEECH.

Mr. Phillips spoke as follows:—

May it please you, my lord and gentlemen of the jury—I suppose I need scarcely say that, after twenty years of no inconsiderable experience in the criminal courts of this country, I have seldom risen to address a jury under more painful feelings, or with greater anxiety than upon the present occasion. There are circumstances in this case, even as they were developed before the magistrates, to cause me much anxiety, and, if such be the fact, how much more must that anxiety be increased by the production of additional evidence before you, and that, too, without notice, by which the life of the unhappy man at the bar may be placed in the greatest peril, and the most fearful jeopardy. Not that I, for one moment, admit that such can fairly be the result of the production of such evidence on the part of the prosecution. Considering, however, all the circumstances, I cannot but feel the situation in which I am placed, but I am consoled by the recollection that I shall have your sympathy, and that I shall also have the sympathy of my associates. Of this I am fully assured, for we are all embarked in a common cause—we incur a common responsibility. You are to recollect that the life of a fellow-creature is intrusted to our keeping, and so surely as that life is unjustly taken away, so surely will we have to answer for it to the God of all. Gentlemen, I have not merely to deal with the facts of this case, as they appear in evidence, but I have to contend against the odious prejudices which have been engendered by the peculiar circumstances by which this case is surrounded. These things, therefore, fill me with apprehension. The crime of which the prisoner stands accused—the rank of the deceased—the fact that this case has not been dealt with in the ordinary way in which justice is usually administered in this country; but that inquiries on the subject have been stimulated by a government reward—as if the grave knew any aristocracy!—these things fill me with the greatest apprehension. And when I look around me, and see the numbers that fill this court, I think I feel the throb of indignation which all feel at the horrible crime that has been committed; and then, when I turn to the prisoner who stands charged with this heinous offence, I see a stranger —who is far from his native land—distant from all those who were his associates in early life—without a friend to assist him in his distress—a poor, isolated, helpless foreigner. These things are surely calculated to oppress me. But still I have one anchor of hope to cling to; I can rely on the independence of a British jury—I can rely on your strict integrity—I can rely on your sense of justice—I can rely on your generous feelings, upon those feelings which, no doubt, induced the prisoner at the bar to decline all foreign interference in the jury-box, and to trust his life to the watchful care of an English jury. I have, therefore, no fear in such a tribunal—I know that the whole case will be fully, fairly, and impartially considered.

Having made these observations, I shall now proceed to consider the most unparalleled circumstances of this painful case. Gentlemen, I have much to claim from your kindness and attention; I have much to claim from you, not for myself—for in a case like this I should be unworthy of the gown I wear, if I did not throw aside all personal considerations. But, gentlemen, I have much to claim from you on the part of the accused. I confess that there has nothing been urged by the learned counsel for the prosecution that I did not expect—nothing that I did not long ago anticipate. It is no new notion of mine, as the learned judges who preside here to day are well aware, that the consequence of an act of parliament which is now in operation, is to make a court of criminal jurisdiction an arena of angry passions, and to place the life of a fellow-creature in peril or safety, just in proportion to the skill and talent of the advocate. I should be glad to know from those learned judges, if it is not startling to them to find that such a thought should enter into the head of any advocate, as that of anticipating the defence of a prisoner, to comment upon that defence, and then to answer it; and also to find appeals made to the passions, where everything should be stated with calmness and with reason? Gentlemen, think in what a situation is the accused! 'The man is a foreigner,' says Mr. Adolphus, 'and foreigners always murder and rob.' In the name of the human race, I protest against such assertions, and such language. All who don't belong to this country, are foreigners to it; and I say, therefore, that it is a libel against mankind to utter such language in reference to the people of all other nations. When I heard the expressions, my countenance sunk; I was afraid to look up, because I might see some of those foreigners who crowd the Court; for fear I should see any of those individuals, and the disgust which must have necessarily manifested itself when they heard such slander on the part of an English advocate. Let us maintain the character of England, high and noble as it stands; but do not let us seek to uphold it at the expense and the sacrifice of other nations. Mr. Adolphus is a historian, and history ought to have taught him that such an assertion was not grounded in truth—history ought to have taught him that the people of

Courvoisier's country could not be denominated murderers and robbers. If there be a country in the world free from crime, it is that country, Switzerland, of which he is a native. Cast your eyes back, and I ask if you can see or point out a single instance of a murder in Switzerland? 'They murder,' he says, 'and they rob when they murder.' A man arguing in this case should not have endeavored to instil into your minds such poison, as that because a man is a foreigner he is also a murderer. But, gentlemen, I have had the experience of some days of the way in which you attend to the case, and the various circumstances connected with it; and I do believe, from my heart and soul, that the attempt to excite prejudice in your mind, on any such grounds, will be entirely frustrated. Let me beseech of you to suppose such a case as this—that you were in a criminal court of justice in Paris, or in Madrid, and that you saw an unhappy fellow countryman on trial for his life, and let me imagine that you saw an advocate rise, whose bounden duty it was to state facts calmly and dispassionately—let me suppose that in so doing, he had said, 'Gentlemen, this man comes from the country of Patch, and of Greenacre, and of Thurtell, and Englishmen murder and rob, without even a motive.' Gentlemen, let me suppose that all this had occurred; with what indignation would your hearts have been filled, to hear such a foul calumny upon your native country? And such, gentlemen, is what the Swiss have to endure here, when Mr. Adolphus tells a sworn jury, that they always murder and rob, without a motive.

But, gentlemen, let us pass from this monstrous assertion to another, which is equally unfair in the present case, and infinitely more absurd. He told us, forsooth, that it was not necessary for a man to have a motive for the commission of crime. He knows that if he were to ransack his ingenuity of thirty or forty years' experience, he could not point out a single case where a man had committed either murder or robbery without a motive, and if he ransacked it to the quick, he could impute no motive to Courvoisier for committing the murder, for which he is now arraigned. But Mr. Adolphus was addressing men of reasoning minds, and who well knew that the most trifling action of human life had its origin in some motive or other. He did not attribute any motive to Courvoisier; but said that the crime of murder might be committed without one. What motive had the man who the other day fired at the Queen? I trust it will appear that he is a maniac; I believe he is so; for would any man in his senses, for mere notoriety, have committed such an act? I believe that he would not. Would any man in his senses raise his hand, containing a destructive instrument, against the life of the Queen of England—against youth, innocence, and beauty, and talent—against the life of her who not only sits on the throne of state, but in the hearts of all her people? Could it have been done by any man who was not mad, or on the very verge of madness? Gentlemen, in this circumstance Mr. Adolphus has found a very bad illustration. I know that there are motives for the commission of crime. I could not be so long a member of the profession to which I have the honor to belong, without being convinced of it. There are motives of jealousy which instigate men to the commission of murder—there are motives of hatred and revenge which induce men to perpetrate that dreadful crime—and there are motives of avarice and plunder which may instigate men to other deeds of wickedness; but as to Courvoisier, what motive had he of hatred? None whatever. He was living with a master who loved him, and whom he loved—was confidentially in his service, and accompanied him in his journeys—saw him to his repose at night, and was entrusted with his keys. Was there in such a case any cause for hatred? Was there any motive of jealousy? None. There could not exist the motive of revenge, where he had been treated with so much kindness: and as to the motive of plunder—good God! why should he commit the murder from motives of avarice? I can fancy the midnight depredator getting into the house, and being alarmed in his progress at the fear of discovery. I can fancy that a man for his own individual safety may have committed the terrible act, to screen himself from detection. Was it necessary for Courvoisier to break into the house of which he was an inmate, and when he had hourly an opportunity of committing plunder? Was it necessary for him to have murdered his master in order to conceal his plunder? He had daily an opportunity of escaping with that plunder, six or eight hours before it could have been missed, and to have carried it, perhaps, a hundred miles, with every certainty of effecting an escape. Nay, more, if he was the man who committed the offence, do you think that he was in his senses? Do you think he could be in his senses, and remain in that house after the commission of the deed, with the certainty of being detected? When a man commits the most trifling crime in the street—setting aside the crime of murder—what does instinct prompt, nay, compel him to do? Why, to fly—to fly while there is a chance for him. He may not be detected—he may outstrip his pursuers—and, possibly, he may not be pursued at all; but here is a man committing, according to them, a crime of the most serious nature, affecting his life, and yet he remains in the house after having committed it; and having done so without a motive, he did not seek to avail himself of the opportunity to escape.

Gentlemen, this is a case in which you have no clear proof before you—it is, as you have been truly told, a case of circumstances alone; and it will be my painful duty, perhaps, to trouble you with some remarks upon the evidence which has been adduced against the prisoner. But, gentlemen, it is not my case which is before you; in it is involved a question of the gravest nature known to our law; and thank God, that not upon my fleeting breath depends the irrevocable doom of a fellow-creature! But, gentlemen, it will be your duty not to let any circumstance, however trifling, escape—not to think any hour tediously employed when investigating the circumstances connected with the case, in such a manner as to lead you to a just conclusion. Gentlemen, I have now demonstrated to you that which the counsel for the prosecution has been obliged to admit—namely, that he could assign no motive for the commission of the act. Therefore, the first thing you will have to consider is, whether or not the prisoner had any motive for perpetrating such a deed. A motive has been sought after, but not found, and consequently counsel have been driven to the declaration that there is no occasion for a motive for the commission of crime. Now, gentlemen, I believe that I have no occasion to entreat that which has throughout these proceedings been voluntarily vouchsafed, namely, the kind attention of the learned judges; and I say that it will be laid down as a doctrine, not to be controverted by those learned judges, that it will be the duty of the prosecution to bring home, without a single doubt, the commission of the crime to the prisoner at the bar. It is not for me to do so. Such is the task they have undertaken—they must prove that the murder has been committed by that man, and unless they do so, he must be acquitted I am not called upon to rend asunder the dark mantle of the night, and throw light upon this deed of darkness. They are bound to show to you, not by argument such as has been used, but to prove to you, to downright palpable demonstration, that Courvoisier has been guilty of its perpetration. Let us see how they seek to do so.

In the first place, Mr. Adolphus called a woman named Sarah Mancell. But let me do myself justice, and others justice, by now stating, that in the whole course of the narrative with which I must trouble you, I must beg that you will not suppose that I am in the least degree seeking to impute crime to any of the witnesses. God forbid that any breath of mine should send persons depending on the public for their subsistence into the world with a tainted character; such is not necessary for the support of my case—the God above alone knows who is guilty of the terrible act of which the prisoner stands accused. Now, the first imputation cast upon this man was the agitation he displayed. Let us try this by the test of our own hearts and consciences. Here he is, having seen his master, perhaps in a state of repose, and in the morning he is alarmed by the housemaid, who was up before him, with an outcry of "robbery," and some dark, mysterious suggestions of murder having been committed. "Let us go," said she, "and see where my lord is." Gentlemen, I must confess that that expression struck me as very extraordinary. If she had said, "Let us go and tell my lord that the house is plundered," it would have appeared different. But why should she suspect that anything had happened to his lordship? She saw no stains of blood about the house, and, why, therefore should she suspect that his lordship was not safe? Courvoisier and all the other inmates of the house were safe, and why should she have suspected that her master had been injured? Courvoisier did as he was desired. He was the first person to enter the bed-room, and he very naturally proceeded to open the shutters; the housemaid sees the spot of blood on the pillow, and runs out screaming. Was not agitation displayed by the woman, rather than the prisoner? Mr. Adolphus has said that he will allow me to use every deposition, and that he will not insist on the right of reply. I trust the learned judges will look carefully into the depositions that were taken before the coroner—that they will consider it their duty to ascertain if what the different witnesses swore when they were examined before the coroner is the same as what they swore when they were examined before this court. I think it necessary and proper, in the discharge of my duty to the prisoner, to throw out this suggestion. I asked, it will be remembered, the witness Mancell whether she saw a spot of blood on the pillow, and if that was the first thing she saw. She replied she did. Before the coroner, she said that the first thing she saw was his lordship lying murdered in his bed. I will, however, pass that by, and come now to what took place afterwards.

The windows were thrown open, and daylight was let in upon the dreadful spectacle. Was it to be expected that any man would remain unmoved at the dreadful exhibition that then presented itself? An aged nobleman, one who was universally respected and beloved, was found lying on his bed with his throat cut, weltering in his blood; and because the prisoner was agitated at the awful sight, Mr. Adolphus wished that to be taken as a proof of his guilt. What, I should like to know, would Mr. Adolphus have inferred from it, if the prisoner's nerves had remained unshaken? what would have been thought of the prisoner, if, on seeing the state of his master, he had remained firm, cool, collected, undisturbed? Why, that a man who could so act was capable of contemplating or even committing the dreadful deed that had just been perpetrated. It, however, would be a gross libel on human nature to suppose that any man could look on such a scene unmoved. But Mr. Adolphus talks of the prisoner's agitation being a proof of his guilt; let me remind him that the female servants, his own witnesses, were in the same state of agitation, and I think the better of them for it, for I hold that in such a case, agitation, so far from being a proof of guilt, is a proof of innocence. I happened accidentally to be passing through the park at the time when the late outrageous attack was made upon our gracious Queen. I wish Mr. Adolphus—who affects to consider agitation as a proof of guilt—had been there at that moment, and had watched the countenances of the bystanders; he would have seen that men of the stoutest hearts were completely appalled by the event—that their limbs trembled—that they were agitated and dismayed; and if agitation is to be taken as a proof of guilt, I should say that there was not a man in the park at that moment who might not have been convicted of an attempt to murder the Queen. I say that no man could look upon such an appalling scene as that which presented itself when the shutters of his lordship's bed-room were thrown open, without being agitated. But then it is said the prisoner did not render any assistance. Gentlemen, the fact is not so; that assertion has been disproved by the witnesses for the prosecution. It was proved that the prisoner, as soon as his agitation had in some degree subsided, offered all the assistance in his power. But could he be expected to assist at a moment when his nerves were unstrung by the dreadful sight before him?—Could he properly be called upon to assist on the instant? But as soon as he recovered himself from the shock which he had sustained, what did he do? Why, that which was most natural for him or any other man to do under such circumstances: he sat down for the purpose of writing a letter to the son of his deceased master, in order to apprise the representative of the family of the dreadful deed that had been perpetrated, and while he was so engaged the housemaid came up to him, and made use of this extraordinary expression,—'Why, what the devil are you doing there?' Well, what did the prisoner do the moment after he had written the letter? Why, he ran out of the house and gave it to a man he met in the street, with a request that he would convey it to Mr. Russell's house immediately. The housemaid, on witnessing what he did, said, why do you send such a man as that with the letter: as if it was of any consequence by whom the letter was conveyed; but whatever the unfortunate prisoner did, he was thwarted in by somebody.' The housemaid suggested that he should have mounted a horse and rode off to Mr. Russell, with the melancholy intelligence.

And here let me ask you whether, if the prisoner had been guilty of the crime alleged against him, he would not have gladly availed himself of the means of escape which was suggested to him by the housemaid? Would he not have mounted a horse, and, under the pretence of going to the house of Mr. Russell, soon got beyond the reach of all pursuit? Is not that the course, which, in all human probability, a guilty man would have adopted? But to return to the statement that the prisoner did not render assistance. It was clear that he could render none to the unfortunate deceased, and those who com plained that he did nothing would perhaps point out what he could have done, under the circumstances. Instead, however, of escaping from the house, as he might have done, he remained in it; he answered every question that was put to him by the numerous policemen, and others by whom he was surrounded. Of the conduct of the police on the occasion, I shall have to say a word or two presently. A multiplicity of questions were put to the prisoner, every one of which he answered truly, and without hesitation or delay; his replies to each question were prompt, and, what is of more importance, they were also true. I implore the jury not to forget that. In asserting that the prisoner's replies were true, I do not state that which cannot, and, in fact, has not been proved. From the moment when he was first confronted with the police, he was subjected to the strictest scrutiny. Attempts were made to intimidate him. The most torturing interrogatories were put to him, and one of the police went so far as to say to him, 'Dare you look me in the face.' Under the circumstances in which the unfortunate prisoner was placed, every answer he gave to the numerous questions that were put to him increased and aggravated the suspicion against him, in the minds of those by whom those questions were put; and because he told the truth, he was the more suspected. At this time he was no more in custody than any of the other servants in the house; but at length a locket was found, and the prisoner was questioned respecting it, and what was his reply? Why, that the locket was his own. His assertion was disbelieved by the police, and Ellis was called in, who very fairly said he could not swear to the locket as having been the property of his lordship. Well, after all the suspicion that had been so unjustly excited against the prisoner, what was the fact? Why, his lordship's locket was found, and the account given by the prisoner was proved to be true. But I implore you, gentlemen of the jury, to consider what would have been the consequence had his lordship's locket not been found. Would it not have been said that the one found on the prisoner was his lordship's property? And the fact was, that he was not taken into custody until the finding of a locket in his possession, which afterwards turned out to be his own. Gentlemen, there is another circumstance to which I wish to call your attention, by way of proving that the replies given to the questions put to him were true.

You will recollect that there was an impression of a seal found upon him, and that was alleged as a proof of his guilt. He was questioned respecting it, and what did he say? Why this—it was given to me by Mr. Russell. Send for him, and he will prove that what I have stated is true. But no, Mr. Russell was not sent for. The solicitor for the prosecution did not think proper to make this inquiry, even in a case where the life of a fellow-creature was at stake. Mr. Wing, however, the solicitor to the Russell family, much to his honor, did make the inquiry suggested by the prisoner, and found that his statement was true. That was the second instance in which what the prisoner said was alleged to be false, yet afterwards proved to be true. When asked to identify the property, he did so; not tardily, but promptly; and I contend that that circumstance is another proof of his innocence. It was insinuated that though a book was found on a table by his lordship's bedside, the candle was not near enough to enable him to read it. That has been disproved. The prisoner's trunk was searched, and because nothing suspicious was found in it, Mr. Adolphus said that was not surprising, as the prisoner would have been a fool to have placed there any evidence of his guilt. The trunk was searched on the 6th, and nothing found. It was searched again on the 8th, and why? It was searched again on the 13th, when he sent his uncle for a change of linen from that very trunk. Would he have done so, if there had been anything suspicious in that trunk? When the trunk had been once searched, it ought to have been locked and placed in safe custody, but instead of that it was left open, in a room to which every one in the house had access, where any villain, tempted by the offer of 450*l.* reward, might put anything he pleased in it, to be afterwards produced as evidence of the prisoner's guilt. The whole gang of police had access to that trunk. Did he not know that in that very trunk some evidence of murder would be found? That evidence of guilt which was found on the 13th of May, was not there on the 6th. 'I unfolded the shirts,' says Inspector Tedman, 'on the 6th, and could see nothing;' but when Mr. Policeman Collier subsequently examined the shirts, 'I unfolded them,' says he, 'and out dropped the pair of bloody gloves' Who put them there? My learned friend (Mr. Adolphus) asks, who murdered his lordship? I ask who put the bloody gloves and the bloody handkerchiefs in the box of the prisoner? I say openly and fearlessly, that those articles were placed there by some of the police, for reasons best known to themselves. Now, I beg you to call to mind what Inspector Tedman said. He told us that he minutely examined the trunk on the 6th of May, and notwithstanding all his vigilance, neither gloves nor handkerchiefs were found. The contents of the trunk were actually ransacked over and over to find evidence against the prisoner, and yet Mr. Collier, the constable, tells us that he found the two bloody handkerchiefs on the very top of the trunk; and, adds Mr. Collier, in order to make the assurance doubly sure, and to add to the weight of guilt which attached to the unhappy man at the bar—Mr. Collier says, that the handkerchiefs must belong to the unfortunate prisoner, because his initials were on them. But the trunk had been examined, not only once, but three times before Mr. Collier says he found the gloves and handkerchiefs in it. But why, I would ask, was it necessary to repeat the searches so often? Why should those policemen go to the prisoner's trunk days after the unfortunate man was sent to a gloomy dungeon, at least three miles distant, for the purpose of doing what?—of producing evidence against him which was not existing before. I will suppose for a moment that the gloves might have been overlooked on the 6th and 12th of May, but what can be said about the handkerchiefs, and how did it happen that they should be placed on the very top of the very articles which had been previously turned over and ransacked again and again? Now I ask this question—who put these things in the trunk, and for what purpose were they placed there? The prisoner Courvoisier conld not have placed them there, even if we could for a moment suppose that he would have risked his neck by so doing. But why, after the first search of the trunk—why, when Inspector Tedman had searched it so minutely, was it not corded and sealed up to prevent the possibility of any villain tampering with it in order to fasten guilt upon the wretched man at the bar? I ask, is this fair play towards a man placed in this awful position? I say that the finding of these things in the trunk of the prisoner is a circumstance of deep suspicion, not against him, but against others who have sought to make him the victim of their foul machinations. It is clear, beyond a doubt, that the handkerchiefs were placed in the trunk after Courvoisier was sent to his dreary dungeon, and I suppose that no man will charge me with going too far when I say that a strong suspicion exists against some one respecting it.

But I leave this part of the subject, and shall turn now to the conduct of Mr. Inspector Pearce—that merciful and exemplar officer who would not, of course, attempt to intimidate a prisoner once within his fangs, or extort a confession from him by threats. Now let us see what was the conduct of this man. After finding the things in the pantry, he takes them up to the parlor, and places them before the prisoner's face. Now, if the prisoner had been guilty of this crime—had he one particle of guilt upon his conscience—would he not have shrunk back in fear and horror on beholding these silent proofs, dug from the earth as it were on purpose to confront him, and call to his mind the dreadful crime he had committed? But what was the conduct of the prisoner? Did he shrink back in conscious guilt and betray his agitation? No: his manner exhibited proofs that he was an innocent man. But what was the conduct of Mr. Pearce when he produced the things? 'Look here, sir,' said he to the prisoner, 'dare you now look me in the face?' Merciful God, gentlemen, was this an expression to be used by an officer of justice to an unfortunate man like the prisoner? But he did look Mr. Pearce in the face, and told him, 'I am innocent, my conscience is clear. I know nothing of these things.' My learned friend (Mr. Clarkson) asked Pearce, 'Upon your oath, sir, did you not use that expression to the prisoner for the purpose of extorting a confession from him?' 'Oh no,' replies Mr. Pearce, 'I merely asked the question in pursuance of my duty as an officer;' and after fencing with my learned friend for some time, then he at length declares positively that he did not use the words for the purpose of intimidating the prisoner and inducing him to confess. Now I will ask,—Is there any person in this court who believed him when he said so? And let it not be forgotten, gentlemen of the jury, that Mr. Mayne, the commissioner, was present at the time, and knew that Mr. Pearce was about to show the articles to the prisoner. I will not say that Mr. Mayne, the commissioner, directed Pearce to act as he has done, but it is very strange that Mr. Mayne, who, we are told, is a magistrate, should have permitted such conduct in one of his officers. Mr. Hobler was also in the house at the time, but notwithstanding the presence both of that gentleman and Mr. Mayne, this fellow Pearce was suffered by them to go upstairs to the prisoner and exhibit the things before him; and I would ask you now, as men of sense and men of the world—do you not believe that the object of Pearce was to get a confession from the prisoner? Would it not have been more prudent and more just to the prisoner to have merely placed these things before him, and then said, 'These things were found in your pantry, have you anything to say about them?' But no, that course would not suit Mr. Pearce, who was anxious, of course in pursuance of his duty merely, to get a confession from the prisoner. Was it right of Mr. Mayne, the Commissioner of Police, and a magistrate to boot, to send this inquisitorial ruffian Pearce to a private-room with the prisoner, in order to browbeat and frighten him into an admission of his guilt? Of course, Mr. Pearce was not at all influenced by the reward of 450*l.* But I forgot—he had the candour to admit that he expected to receive some portion of the reward. Yes, gentlemen of the jury, the money is to be divided upon the coffin of my unfortunate client, should you pronounce him guilty, and Mr. Inspector Pearce and the rest of the police myrmidons will, when they receive their respective shares, write the receipt in the blood of the prisoner. I had hoped, gentlemen of the jury, that the days of blood-money had passed away. I thought the atrocious system had been put an end to by the praiseworthy interference of an alderman of the city of London; but I am afraid that I am mistaken, and that the system is about to be revived again. You will bear in mind that the reward of 450*l.* is not to be paid unless the prisoner is convicted, when the money will be shared upon his coffin. It is certainly very strange that we should not have heard a word of reward being offered for the discovery of the murder of Mr. Templeman until a nobleman lost his life by the hand of an assassin.

Now, gentlemen, allow me to ask you, do you remember Mr. Baldwin, the constable, and how he gave his evidence? When I asked him about the reward, do you not recollect the manner in which he attempted to baffle my question? Poor man! he did not know how to read, and he never heard anything about a reward, and yet that miscreant bloodhound was obliged afterwards to admit to me, that he had heard the placard offering the reward read at the station-house over and over again. Now, I will tell the Commissioners of Police, and I tell the Government from this place—I tell them with the freedom and independence of a man who has nothing either to fear or expect from them—that they are acting upon a bad and vicious system in offering rewards to their men for hunting out the blood of their fellow-creatures. I shall not mention what the consequences were of offering a reward for the discovery of the murderer of the deceased Mr. Templeman, because I do not wish by any observations of mine to prejudice a case which is likely to be tried here shortly. There is another expression of the prisoner which is supposed to operate to his prejudice. But, to my mind, there is not anything more natural than the expression to which I am going to refer; and I would remind the jury that they are not to canvass too strictly the expressions of a foreigner. The expression to which I allude is this—'It would not go so hard against me if those things were not found in my pantry.' Then came the question, who hid them there? But is not the fact of these things being found in the pantry a proof that they were not put there by the prisoner? What! he who, if the statement made be correct, was up all night roaming about the house—who had bed-rooms and passages, and other places, to conceal those things in—could he be supposed to be the person to go and place these things in his own pantry? Could he have selected this place in particular in order that he might the more securely place a rope about his own neck? Who hid the handkerchiefs? Who hid the gloves? The pantry, you will recollect, was open to every one, and was it not the very place where every one wishing to place the crime at the prisoner's door would hide the things which were found there? These matters may be trifling in their nature, and they may appear to my mind of greater importance than they do to yours; but of this I am sure, that they ought to be considered with the greatest care by you, and that they will be I have not the smallest doubt.

Another expression of the prisoner's has been caught at with a view to his prejudice—they can find no trace of actions, and so they are obliged to fly to words. The prisoner is reported to have said—'If I had as much money as my master, I would not remain any longer in this country.' This expression he used in the presence of the two female servants; so they want to say that the prisoner premeditated robbery and murder, and that he did so in the presence of two witnesses, and those witnesses his fellow-servants. I will do the witnesses the justice to admit that the prisoner did make use of these words. But unless you can believe him to be insane, you cannot suppose that in using them he was influenced by any improper or base motive. But these were perfectly consistent with the views and feelings of an innocent man. You, gentlemen, are fond of the land that gave you birth. But supposing you were far from that land, toiling with industry and zeal for your existence, but away from all those whom you loved most dear, and anxiously desiring to return home to the land that you loved, the friends of your youth, and the companions of your childhood—what more natural for you than to exclaim, if you saw a rich man passing, 'I wish I had that man's money, and I would not remain longer in this country!' And recollect who the prisoner is! He is not only a foreigner but a Switzer, who love their native land with an intensity amounting to enthusiasm! Although the land is barren, and its mountains rugged and bare, still, not all the enchantments of creation, not all the splendour of scenery which may adorn and decorate the face of nature in other countries, can wean a Swiss from the love and affection which he bears his native land, or destroy that desire which burns within him, again to behold it upon the first opportunity that presents itself.

> "Dear is that shed to which his soul conforms,
> And dear that hill that lifts him to the storms,
> And as a child by scaring sounds oppress'd,
> Clings close and closer to its mother's breast,
> So the rude whirlwind and the torrent's roar
> But bind him to his native mountains more."

So it was with the prisoner; and it was this feeling that no doubt prompted the expression which the prosecutors in this case caught at with so much avidity. And this circumstance has been alluded to as confirmatory of the prisoner's guilt—namely, the possession of a five-pound note, which originally belonged to the late Lord Russell. Why, surely the prisoner must have known that, if he came improperly by that note, it could be traced to be his master's, and that in such an event it would be highly prejudicial to him. But he kept this 5*l.* in his pocket, and he fairly accounts for its possession. The prisoner was also asked if the late Lord W. Russell was in the habit of keeping money about him, and he answered that he knew he had a 10*l*. and a 5*l*. note in his possession. Now surely, if the prisoner was guilty of the crime imputed to him, he was, by making this statement, fixing the guilt upon himself in the most marked manner. But was it at all likely that, if the prisoner were really guilty, he would have made this statement? But is there no evidence of contrivance on the part of other persons, with the view of affecting the character of the prisoner? What! were valuable things left behind, and a woman's thimble, worth eighteenpence, stolen! The gold watch was left behind —the plate and spoons were neglected, but the servant's eighteenpenny thimble was amongst the articles which were to be carefully carried away. They were asked to find the prisoner guilty of the crime imputed to him upon circumstantial evidence. Are there, then, no circumstances against other parties in connection with this case? You are to recollect that, if you find this man guilty, you doom him to death upon mere circumstantial evidence.

I shall be able to show you by-and-bye, that you can, without putting your own souls to any hazard, find him guilty of the offence by which he will be liable to punishment little short of that to which he would be consigned if he were found guilty of the dreadful crime of murder, and this you may do without hazarding your own salvation. Look at the way in which the prosecution is supported. It suits those who have come forward against the prisoner to impute criminality to every circumstance connected with him; and thus it was that the housemaid talked of the ale which the prisoner gave her to drink on the night the murder was committed. She said, "After drinking the ale I became drowsy, and a sleepy sensation came over me." Now, what was the inference that was evidently intended to be drawn from this statement? Why, that the prisoner had drugged the ale. Do you not believe that this was the object which she had in view in giving this testimony; and yet she says upon her oath that she had no intention of suggesting that the ale was drugged. Now, could they believe this assertion? This was what was said before the police-magistrate, but the point was afterwards given up. I think I can point to the individual who advised that this evidence should not be relied upon. I think I can put my finger upon him. Yes, this gentleman pointed out the absurdity of relying on evidence of this kind, for, no doubt, he said, "Don't you see that, if you make this a part of the case, the counsel on the opposite side will start up and ask you, if the prisoner did not himself partake of this very ale?" Yes, the prisoner, who had such a mighty work before him as was imputed to him, did drink of the same ale which had caused drowsiness in the housemaid; and this fact having been made known to the gentleman to whom he had adverted, he at once, no doubt, observed upon the absurdity of resting any part of the prosecution upon the assertion that her drowsiness was intended to be caused by the ale, which was equally partaken of by all parties. So much, then, for the statement that the housemaid became sleepy or drowsy from that cause. Then again, it was assumed, because of the stain of blood upon the white gloves, that therefore the prisoner had been guilty of murder? What! was it usual for a man to commit the crime of murder in white gloves? Then, again, a part of a shirt was discovered in the prisoner's trunk, and this circumstance is fixed upon as operating to his prejudice. What! a man commit murder, and because spots of blood might appear upon a part of his shirt, he was so to economise his linen that he would throw one portion of it away, and keep another, and then, in order that he might give every chance against himself, he was to place the reserved part in his own trunk, where it was sure to be found by any person looking over it? Why, the thing was absurd. And then let it be recollected, that the part preserved was the breast of the shirt—that part most likely to have a stain upon it, if it were stained at all.

It was said that no person could get into the premises in Norfolk street without the police seeing them. But are you satisfied of this? Is their vigilance so remarkable? Are the late circumstances which have transpired in this town proof of the vigilance of the police? And are you, upon the facts stated in reference to the gloves and to this shirt front, to impute to the prisoner the crime of murder? Was any blood observed upon his person? Where were the stains under the finger nails, which, like the spot on Lady Macbeth, no water could wash out? And then, gentlemen, you are to recollect that all these discoveries are made on the fourteenth of May, eight or nine days after the commission of the murder, and when the prisoner was away from the premises where his trunks were deposited, and while he was confined within the walls of a prison. There is a matter which I wish here to draw your attention to, and that is the relative situation of the female servant's room to that in which Courvoisier slept. I wish, gentlemen, that you had seen the house, but I must admit the witnesses have pretty fairly described it to you. Now what I am going to say is this—Why have not the prosecutors placed before you, in the model on the table, that part of the house in which the servants slept? What was the reason that the exact situation of these rooms was not presented to you? There was only a thin lath-and-plaster wall between the room of the female servants and that in which Courvoisier slept. It appeared by the evidence that the female servants heard the prisoner going to bed—at least they heard him chain the door. I beg also to draw your attention to the circumstance that the housemaid swears, when she got up the cook was asleep, whereas the cook swears she was awake. Was it not extraordinary that during the whole of the night not a breath was heard by either of these witnesses from Courvoisier's room, which surely must have been the case, if he had been up and engaged in the commission of the crime with which he is charged?

I have now gone through all that part of the case which was brought against the prisoner before the magistrates, and which my learned friend and myself were prepared to meet on the first day. I now come to that part of the case of which I think we have a right to complain. I allude to the evidence which was adduced against the prisoner for the first time yesterday. Is it not most extraordinary that, after this case has been before the public for such a length of time—after it has been frequently brought under the consideration of the police magistrates, that, for the first time on Thursday last, we heard of the additional evidence which was adduced yesterday? I complain that we were not made acquainted with the name of the party who was to give this evidence, in time to enable us to make inquiries relative to her character. But let us examine the evidence given by this Mrs. Piolaine, and if it should be found that she is not worthy of credit, then all the corroboration which she may have received will go for nothing. Well—where does this witness live? In a hotel in Leicester place—a foreign hotel in Leicester place—where a billiard-table is kept. The jury were probably aware of what sort sort of places these foreign hotels in Leicester place are. Then here was this Mrs. Piolaine—who heard of Lord William Russell's murder—who had her husband always near her—but who never once thinks of looking into the parcel left her, as she says, by the prisoner, until the day previous to that on which she is made a witness. Gentlemen, on this part of the case let us examine a little more. Both my learned friend and myself have been taken quite aback, and well we may. It was not sprung on us until the end of the first night of this investigation, and was it not an odd time for such a discovery to have been made? They kept it to themselves all night, and then sprung upon us in the morning, when every moment of ours was engaged with the other part of the proceedings. A French paper, forsooth, was translated to the lady, and I beg the particular attention of your lordships and the jury to this circumstance:—Courvoisier was never known in that house by the name of Courvoisier—he was known by the name of "John," and how therefore could a French paper have directed Mrs. Piolaine to him? There is no proof that she had heard he was in the service of Lord William Russell; and it is mighty odd, therefore, that at the eleventh hour this should have been found out behind our backs, and that still the proof has been left thus imperfect. This most important part of the case depends on the testimony of one woman. Except through her they don't trace it to Courvoisier. She says it was Courvoisier who brought the parcel a week or a fortnight before the murder; she remembered so little about the man that she did not know him; and she says that in a day or two after the trial began, she opened the parcel in the presence of some half-dozen of persons, who signed a sort of round-robin, as an inventory of what it contained. This is all very well, but how has it been proved that is was Courvoisier who brought it her? They told you that they could identify the clothes which the parcel contained, and they produced the housemaid, and the man Ellis, neither of whom could swear that the jacket belonged to Courvoisier. But they also produced his washerwoman, whose testimony was to this effect —"Upon my oath, no sock of Courvoisier's that I ever washed —and I have washed many—was ever marked in the heel as this is; his are marked on the top, and the letter upon them is not in the way—even if the place was the same—in which he marked them. He did not mark them with a C, as this is marked, but with the letters B C." Why, this is disproof, if anything, of the fact which they wished to establish. Now, if even the stolen property had been traced to Courvoisier, is it conclusive that he had committed the murder? Gentlemen, that is a question upon which the learned judge on the bench will give you his most valuable opinion. It may be conclusive of the robbery, and of the theft the prisoner may hereafter be convicted, and transported for the term of his natural life to one of our penal colonies. But gentlemen, the fact of the murder has not been proved against the prisoner, and it is not upon suspicion or upon any moral doubt, that a man is to be found guilty of such a crime. He is liable to a terrible penalty if he should be found guilty of having committed the robbery; but better, far better, will it be if of that crime only he is guilty, than that he should be guilty of the foul crime of murder, which, for the sake of his eternal soul, I hope he is not. In such a case it would be better, far better, for him to be allowed to atone for the deed in the solitude which he must necessarily undergo, under such circumstances, than you should send him, on the dawn of his manhood, to an ignominious death. I say that the proof adduced is not conclusive of the murder, though it may be of dishonesty on the part of the prisoner, with which latter crime he does not at present stand charged.

And now, gentlemen, having travelled through this case of mystery and darkness, my anxious and painful task is ended. But, gentlemen, yours is about to commence, and I can only say, may Almighty God guide you to a just conclusion! The issues of life and death are in your hands. To you it gives to consign that man once more to the enjoyments of existence and the dignity of freedom, or to send him to an ignominious death, and to brand upon his grave the awful epithet of a murderer. Gentlemen, mine has been a painful and an awful task; but still more awful is the responsibility attached to the decision upon the general facts or circumstances of the case. To violate the living temple which the Lord hath made —to quench the fire within a man's breast, is an awful and a terrible responsibility, and the decision of "Guilty," once pronounced, let me remind you, is irrevocable. Speak not that word lightly—speak it not on suspicion, however strong—upon moral conviction, however apparently well-grounded—upon inference—upon doubt—or upon anything but the broad, clear, irresistible noonday conviction of the truth of what is alleged.

I speak to you thus in no hostile feeling: I speak to you as a brother and a fellow Christian. I thus remind you of your awful responsibility. I tell you that, if you condemn that man lightly, or upon mere suspicion consign him to an ignominous death, the recollection of the deed will never die within you. If you should pronounce your verdict without a deep and irresistible conviction of his guilt, your crime will be present to you during the rest of your lives—it will pursue you with remorse, like a shadow, in your crowded walks—it will render your deathbed one of horror—and, taking the form of that man's spirit, it will condemn and sink you before the judgment-seat of your God! So, beware, I say, beware what you do!

The effect this speech had on the jury was to make them hesitate on their verdict for a full hour and a half; and considering that the confession of the culprit had set at rest all question of his guilt, it is painful to reflect how the permission to prisoners to address juries by counsel may be made the means of violating the stern demands of justice.

The influence of the learned gentleman's address was very visible on almost every person in the court; it was less visible upon the prisoner, perhaps, than upon others. He stood at the bar with great firmness, and his cheek did not appear to be in the least degree blanched.

Several witnesses were then called for the defence, who testified to the prisoner's good character.

This having closed the evidence, the court adjourned for a quarter of an hour, and on the learned judges resuming their seats, Lord Chief-Justice Tindal proceeded to sum up the evidence, which he did at great length. The jury retired at twenty minutes after 4, and at half past 6 returned a verdict of GUILTY.

After the lapse of a minute, the Lord Chief-Justice Tyndal, having put on the black cap, said: "Francois Benjamin Courvoisier, you have been found guilty, by an intelligent, patient, and impartial jury, of the crime of wilful murder. That crime has been established against you, not, indeed, by the testimony of eye-witnesses as to the fact, but by a chain of circumstances no less unerring, which have left no doubt of your guilt in the minds of the jury and all those who heard the trial. It is ordained by Divine authority that the murderer shall not escape justice; and this ordination has been exemplified in your case, in the course of this trial, by the disclosure of evidence which has brought the facts to bear against you in a conclusive manner. The murder, although committed in the dark and silent hour of night, has nevertheless been brought clearly to light by Divine interposition. You felt no compassion for your helpless victim, whose infirmities ought to have found a protector in you, who was his servant; but you felt no regard for the tie that should bind a servant to his master, you felt no regard for that sacred duty; but, in the dead hour of night, you cruelly murdered an aged, amiable, and unoffending nobleman, and destroyed for a period the domestic happiness and comfort of the noble family with which he was allied, by a shock almost unparralled in the history of crime. The precise motive which induced you to commit this guilty act can only be known to your own conscience; and it only remains for me to recommend you most earnestly to employ the short time you have to live, in prayer and repentance, and endeavoring to make your peace with that Almighty Being whose law you have broken, and before whom you must shortly appear."

The learned judge, in delivering the sentence, was so affected that his voice at times was scarcely audible. The prisoner heard his fate pronounced without evincing the slightest emotion.

PREVIOUS TO THE EXECUTION—THE CONDEMNED SERMON, ETC.

On Sunday, July 5th, 1840, Rev. Mr. Carver, the ordinary of Newgate, preached what is called the condemned sermon in the chapel of Newgate. The sheriffs, in consequence of the innumerable applications made to them for admission to the chapel, determined to open once more the gallery which had been closed since the execution of Fauntleroy, and to issue cards. Although the service was not to commence till half past 10 o'clock, the avenues to the common door of entrance to the prison, as well as to the door of the governor's house, were completely blocked up before 9 o'clock by those to whom the governor had given the privilege. The arrangements were, however, so judiciously made by the authorities, that not the slightest inconvience was sustained by the numerous congregation.

Immediately before the service commenced, Courvoisier entered the chapel attended by two of the turnkeys, and sat on a bench before the pulpit. He appeared to be quite aware of the situation in which he was placed, and never once raised his eyes during the service. In fact, his looks denoted extreme sorrow and contrition, and he seemed to suffer great inward agitation when the ordinary particularly alluded to the crime for the perpetration of which he stood condemned. He was as attentive as possible to the service, and held the Book of Common Prayer with a steady hand.

The ordinary took his text from Job, chap. 34, ver. 21, 22: "For his eyes are upon the ways of man, and he seeth all his goings. There is no darkness nor shadow of death where the workers of iniquity may hide themselves."

The following are the passages which referred to the wretched criminal more especially. The preceding portions of the sermon illustrated, from the Old and New Testaments, the omniscience of God:

"How awfully true must the lesson and illustrations of our text appear to one amongst us this morning, and how fearfully and dreadfully appropriate the adaptation of its language to his special and almost unparalleled case! "The eyes of the Omniscient were indeed upon his ways, and he saw all his goings." There was no darkness nor shadow of death where he could hide himself.

"Yes, and that special deed of darkness which has subjected you, the midnight assassin of an aged, amiable, and unoffending master, to prison and to death, has yet, and in a few hours too, to be judged th by Him 'whose eye is upon your heart (as well as upon your ways), and who sees all your thoughts as He saw all your goings.

"In the solitude of your confinement, far more appropriate for serious reflection on your part, and profitable ministration on mine, than on this exciting occasion, before a large and public assembly—in that retired cell I have daily endeavored, in simplicity and fidelity, as the minister of God, to prepare you to meet Him, urging the duty and necessity of penitence, abiding, abject, abundant sorrow, godly sorrow, for your dreadful sin, which ignominiously closes your earthly career, and ushers you to your eternal destiny. With other matters, in which I have sought to be faithful and serviceable, for my own and public satisfaction, I have pressed upon you the necessity, as well as propriety of evincing the sincerity of your repentance, and making some small compensation, and small indeed it is, to outraged society, by a voluntary, ample, and explicit confession of all the circumstances connected with this unprecedented deed of darkness. The enormous crime itself has been by you tardily, though I trust penitentially acknowledged; but the evasions, subterfuges, and inconsistencies, which have appeared in your recorded verbal statements on minor details, have very naturally induced the fear that your 'heart is not right in the sight of God.' You had almost reached the very verge of a triumph that would have included the deepest sorrow to the guiltless, at almost the eleventh hour. So strong was the impression of your innocence, from your long-established character for mildness and probity, that a mortal stab was about to be inflicted upon the reputation of your fellow domestics and other innocent persons. You reposed in quiescent security of acquittal. At the critical juncture, God, in the wonderful workings of his providence, by a marvellous chain of circumstantial evidence, with unerring certainty fixed upon you the guilt of murdering one whom every tie of religion and morality bound you to love, reverence, and respect—yea, to peril your own life, if necessary, to save that of your master from the assassin's blow. All who reflect upon this wondrous event cannot but exclaim, 'Verily this is the finger of God; verily there is a God that judgeth the earth.' God has vindicated his attributes of omniscience, justice, and mercy, and with an eloquent tongue speaks to you, and to all who indulge in secret sin—'Be sure your sin will find you out.' The Book before me, from which alone I derive authority to preach glad tidings of a free and full salvation to lost and perishing sinners, through faith in the all-cleansing blood and righteousness of the Lamb of God, says indeed, 'Blessed is he whose transgression is forgiven, whose sin is covered;' and again, 'Blessed is the man unto whom the Lord imputeth not iniquity.' But it adds, and I cannot but press the important context on your mind—'and in whose spirit there is no guile.'

"In that charity which believeth all things, hopeth all things, I trust that your confessions (though I would they had been more explicit and faithful from the first, and less marred with at least apparent incongruities and inconsistencies) are sincere and honest, that your professed repentance is heartfelt, and that with the eye of faith you are looking on that blessed Saviour whom you have pierced. If not, your blood, and the blood of your aged, helpless, injured, and unoffending master, whom you hurried into the eternal world without a moment's warning, be upon your own head! I have faithfully and affectionately warned you not to deceive yourself. But if, as I would yet believe and hope, you do feel the burden of your sin, humbly confessing it, and keeping yourself humble, concealing no circumstance, however minute, in the horrid and loathsome detail of it, it becomes me, as a minister of truth as it is in Jesus, as the ambassador of God, to announce even to you that there is a fountain opened for sin (all sin)—for uncleanness (all uncleanness)—and that though your sins be as scarlet, they may be made white as snow; though red like crimson, they may be as wool."

The prisoner soon after entered into conversation with the gentlemen who manifested interest in his eternal welfare. Being of a taciturn habit and contemplative turn of thought, he appeared more at his ease when left with no other person than the turnkeys, one of whom was his constant companion by day and by night, and with whom he sometimes conversed, always rationally, and sometimes cheerfully. From first to last he devoted a good deal of his time to reading, for which he appears to have had a natural predilection, and he was amply supplied, beyond the Bible and Common Prayer Book, with publications calculated both to beguile his tedious hours, and instruct his mind. During the days of his trial our reporter conversed with several persons who had known him ever since his arrival in England, and they all concurred in expressing their surprise that a person with a mind so constituted as his appeared to be, could on a sudden swerve from the path of moral rectitude and become a murderer.

On the Saturday before the condemned sermon Courvoisier passed a very restless night, and frequently gave way to paroxysms of grief and despair. His appetite had left him, and he scarcely partook of any food. He dwelt with much anguish on the disgrace and dishonor he had brought on his family and country.

Soon after he left the chapel he was visited in his cell by the Swiss Consul, who handed to him a letter from his mother, conveying her forgiveness, her blessing, and her farewell. He wrote with a steady hand a few lines in answer to the letter, and received a promise from the Consul that it should be delivered. The answer was an attempt to console the unhappy parent for the misery and disgrace which his crime had brought upon his family.

He was subsequently visited by a Swiss clergyman who had been frequently to see him since his conviction.

The Sheriffs and others remained in prison with him until after eight o'clock in the evening, when they retired to their homes, and left the unhappy object of their solicitude to his meditations. The prisoner was spared one pang which native culprits have to undergo, namely, a separation or last farewell from those who are endeared by the ties of kin or consanguinity. We have heard many convicts similarly situated declare that when that was over, 'the bitterness of death was past.' Courvoisier was far from being deficient of filial affection, for he always alluded to his far distant relatives in terms of ardent affection.

THE EXECUTION.

The following account of the execution is taken from a leading newspaper of that date:

At an early hour on Monday, July 6, the Rev. Mr. Carver and other divines arrived at the gaol, and proceeded to the room which was occupied by the prisoner during his confinement. He entered without reserve into conversation, and expressed his reliance on pardon and mercy. Notwithstanding that he appeared resigned to his fate, yet there was a quivering of the flesh—and no wonder, as natural instinct [reason apart] has implanted in man a clinging to life. The Reverend Ordinary prayed with him some time, and put several questions to him, as to whether he was fully penitent, and whether he believed in the atonement of Jesus Christ. He replied in the affirmative in whispers barely audible, accompanied by an expression of countenance plainly indicating the deep anguish of his soul. He wrung his hands, and, as far as the ropes with which they were bound would admit of, raised them upwards.

The Sheriffs, Under-Sheriffs, and other of the municipal authorities, &c., entered the prison by way of the Justice Hall between seven and eight o'clock, and on visiting the convict he made his grateful acknowledgments to them for the kind attentions they had paid him during his confinement; indeed, he seemed grateful to every one, and his steady conduct almost banished from the minds of those who kept watch and ward over him, that he was a convicted murderer.

At a quarter to eight o'clock a great number of reporters were admitted to the Chapel-yard, contiguous to the room in which the convict was with his spiritual advisers, and with whom he had partaken of the Sacrament. The Sheriffs entered about the same time, attended by many of the Aldermen, Lord Powerscourt and several other noblemen, and numerous gentlemen. Mr. Kean, the actor, was also present. His father, the celebrated Edmund Kean, witnessed the execution of Thistlewood, with a view, as he himself said, to his professional studies. The executioner having pinioned his arms and wrists, and divested his neck of his satin stock, to which dreadful preliminaries the culprit submitted with his wonted amenity of manner, repaired to the platform in readiness to receive the prisoner. As the clock struck eight, the Sheriffs proceeded to the condemned room, attended by their Under Sheriffs and several persons of distinction. Then followed the Reverend Ordinary, and on his appearance in the yard the prison bell commenced tolling, which was a signal to the dense crowd outside the prison, and caused loud vociferations of 'hats off,' which could be distinctly heard in the prison yard. The prisoner then made his appearance, walking with a firm step; he looked downcast, but not despondingly. Immediately that he passed the wicket to the avenue of the prison, leading to the winding passage, there was a general rush made by those present, whereby some of the Aldermen were prevented from gaining admission: confusion ensued, and cries of 'Shame! shame!' were loudly uttered. The Reverend Ordinary at length commenced reading that portion of the burial service beginning with 'Man that is born of a woman hath but a short time to live, and is full of misery: he cometh up like a flower, and never continueth in one stay.'

The malefactor mounted the steps leading to the scaffold with a firm step, and took a circuitous gaze of the vast crowd who had assembled to witness his exit. At this moment there were considerable hootings, hissings, yells, and whistling from the crowd, and some very coarse expressions were uttered. The executioner having placed the cap on the prisoner's head, and the rope round his neck, the Ordinary proceeded to read a further portion of the liturgy, and he speedily gave the signal, when the sustaining bolt of the platform was withdrawn, and after a few severe struggles, the wretched murderer ceased to live, move, or have being. His hands were slightly convulsed and his legs considerably bent and drawn upwards, until pulled down by the executioner from below in order to shorten his sufferings.

The crowd outside the prison was greater than was ever known on any former occasion, and there were present a vast number of livery servants of noblemen, &c. As early as six o'clock there were as many present as generally assemble on ordinary occasions, and before seven the spacious area was completely filled, so that it was impossible to pass one way or the other. Every window, as far as the eye could reach, had its numerous occupants, and the roofs of some of the houses were crowded. Soon after the platform fell, the assembled multitude sought egress by the two principal entrances, but they were met by a rushing counter-crowd, which caused a good deal of struggling, and the loss of divers hats, shoes, &c. One of the principal barriers gave way, but nothing serious occurred in consequence; nor was there any accident, excepting that of a well dressed woman falling from a first-floor window upon the shoulders of the persons below, but without any great damage or bodily harmbeing done to any party.

During the hour the culprit was suspended there was a continual influx of new comers, so that the crowd lost but little of its density. Some of the spectators who had hired apartments had occupied them from eleven o'clock on the previous evening, and appeared to have been well supplied with cigars and potations. There were several persons in a state of great exhaustion from having stood for five hours pressed against the barriers, but retreat was impossible.

When the clock struck nine, the body was cut down and

taken to tne dead-room, where some artists were in attendance to take a cast preparatory to its interment, which took place in the evening, in the usual burying-ground, within the walls of the prison.

An immense crowd being anticipated, the Sheriffs and civic authorities caused additional ranges of barriers to be placed in the area in front of the prison, so that extreme pressure might be avoided, and a recurrence of the catastrophe which occurred at the execution of Holloway and Haggerty prevented—an event the most tragical that ever occurred within the purlieus of Newgate.

Even at an early period of the previous week, housekeepers who reside in front of the prison were applied to with the view of obtaining an eligible and cheap seat at one of the windows of their respective houses. Many asked extravagant prices—and, to use a Smithfield term, 'overstood their market;' nevertheless, every window had its occupant, as had also the parapets and roofs of the dwellings. In some houses the windows and frames were altogether removed, in order to give a view to a greater number. We were informed that five pounds were bidden for the attic story of the Lamb coffee-shop, and we know to a certainty that a member of the press paid two pounds for one window on the first floor, for the accommodation of his literary and anxious friends. At the George public-house, to the south of the drop, Sir W. W. Wynn, Bart., had hired a room, which, with a party of friends, he occupied previously to and during the execution; and Lord Alfred Paget, with several friends occupied a window in the adjoining house, an undertaker's. It is with extreme regret that we noticed one circumstance which derogates from the alleged sensitiveness of the fair daughters of Eve. It is lamentable to behold the matrons and maidens, snbjects of an amiable British Queen, mingling with the crowd on such an occasion, because, to say the least, it is 'unfeminine' for such to gratify a morbid curiosity by witnessing the last writhing struggles of a dying man!

THE CONFESSION OF COURVOISIER.

After the verdict had been returned, it was generally reported that the prisoner had made a full confession of his guilt; which, on inquiry, was found to be strictly correct.

The confession was taken down in writing, and on the following day, Tuesday, June 22d, transmitted to the Home Office. It is as follows:—

"NEWGATE, June 22, 1840.

"On the Friday before the murder was committed, I began two or three times not to like my place. I did not know what to do; I thought, if I gave warning, none of my friends would take notice of me again, and I thought by making it appear a kind of robbery, he would discharge me; and on the Saturday before I took this plate to Leicester-place. I had a mind to rob the house on Monday, and after I had forced the door down stairs I thought it was not right, and went to bed—nothing further happened on the Monday. On Tuesday night, when his lordship went to bed (he had been rather cross with me about the carriage), he gave me two letters, one for the post, and told me rather angrily, that he was obliged to write those letters in consequence of my forgetting the carriage; this was in the drawing-room, about 11 o'clock at night. I then went down stairs into the kitchen, and stood reading a book for some time. About 12 o'clock he rang the bell; I went up to him and took the lamp out. After that I thought he had gone upstairs to his bed-room; and when he rang his bed-room bell I thought it was to warm his bed, and I took the warming-pan up with coals in it just as usual, and he began to grumble because I did not go up to see what he wanted instead of taking up the warming-pan. I told him he always used to ring the bell for the warming-pan, and that it was for that purpose he had rung; and he said that I ought always to go to answer the bell first, to see what he wanted. He took off his clothes, and I came down stairs again with the warming-pan, and I waited there until about twenty minutes past 12. He rang again for me to warm his bed. He told me rather crossly that I should take more notice of what I was doing, and what he was telling me, and pay him more attention.

"I did not answer at all, as I was very cross. I went down stairs, and put everything in the state it was found in the morning. As I was in the dining-room with a light, he came down stairs to the water-closet; he had his wax-light; I was in the dining-room, but as he had his slippers on I did not hear him come down. He opened the dining-room door, and saw me. I could not escape his sight. He was quite struck, and said, 'What are you doing here?—you have no good intentions in doing this; you must quit my service to-morrow morning, and I shall acquaint your friends with it.' I made him no answer. He went to the water-closet, and I went out of the dining-room down stairs He was about ten minutes in the water-closet, and I waited to see what he would do after he came out. While he was in the water-closet, I put some of the things to rights again in the dining-room. When he left the water closet, he went into the dining-room where he stayed about a minute or two. I was on the corner of the stairs that goes from the dining room to the kitchen. I watched him up-stairs. I stopped perhaps an hour in the kitchen, not knowing what I should do As I was coming up stairs from the kitchen, I thought it was all up with me, my character was gone, and I thought it was the only way I could cover my faults by murdering him. This was the first moment of any idea of the sort entering into my head. I went into the dining-room, and took a knife from the side-board. I don't remember whether it was a carving-knife or not. I then went up stairs. I opened his bed-room door and heard him snoring in his sleep; there was a rushlight in his room burning at this time. I went near the bed by the side of the window, and then I murdered him; he just moved his arm a little, he never spoke a word. I took a towel which was on the back of the chair, and wiped my hands and the knife; after that I took his key and opened the Russia leather box, and put it in the state it was found in the morning, and I took all the things that were found down stairs—the towel I put over his face; I took a purse; I also took a 10*l.* note from a note-case, which I put in the purse, and put them in a basket in the back scullery; the day after I thought it would be better to put it behind the skirting-board. I had before I went to Richmond lost a shilling behind the skirting-board, so I thought that would be a good place to put it.

"While at Richmond Lord William's locket dropped from his coat while I was brushing it. I picked it up, and put it in my trousers pocket, but had not the least idea of taking it. I intended to have returned it to his Lordship while I dressed him in the morning. I put my hand in my pocket at that time, but found I had changed my trousers; this was on the morning we left Richmond for Camden-hill. I did not put the trousers on again while we were at Camden-hill. I did not recollect the trousers being different, and thought I had lost the locket. I then thought it best to say nothing about it. On the Friday morning I was looking at some of my old clothes; the policeman who had cut his chin was watching me, and in taking the trousers out of the drawer in the pantry the locket fell out of the pocket: it was wrapped up in a piece of brown paper; the policeman opened the paper, and looked at it and said, 'What's that?' I said to him it was a locket; but in the position in which I was, I did not like to say that it was Lord William's locket, as if I told the truth I should not be believed; the policeman then returned it to me, and I put it in my trousers pocket.

The watch and seal were in my jacket pocket which I had on until the Friday morning, and then I undid the ribbon, and took the seal off; it was the day the sweeps were in the house, which was either the Thursday or Friday; having the watch in my pocket, the glass came out, I did not know what to do with it, as the police were watching me, so I took the watch from my pocket and put it in between the lining of my jacket, and twisted the pocket until I smashed the glass; after that I dropped some of the pieces about the dining-room, and at different times put the large pieces in my mouth, and afterwards, having broken them with my teeth, spat them in the fire-place. The watch I had by me until Friday morning. I then burned the ribbon, and put the watch under the lead in the sink. I kept the seal in my pocket until they came into the dining-room to show me the ring they had found behind the skirting-board. When I was called to go down to the pantry I let the seal fall and put my foot upon it, and afterwards put it behind the water pipe in the scullery. Beresford and Cronin, the two masons, were there at the time taking the drain up, but did not see me do it. The watch, the seal, and the locket, together with two sovereigns, I had about me until the Friday, and if they had searched me they must have found them; but they did not do so until Friday, after I was taken into custody in my bed-room. The two sovereigns I afterwards (on the Friday, when I slipped the locket under the hearth-stone) also slipped down near the wall under the flooring. There is no truth in saying I put anything in the ale or beer, for all that time I had no idea of committing the deed. I had scarcely had any beer all the week, and the ale that I had drunk that night, together with the wine, and some more I took after the cook went to bed, affected me. The gloves were never placed in the shirt by me or to my knowledge. When I left Mr. Fector's, I gave all my white gloves to the coachman. The handkerchiefs that were found in my portmanteau were never put there by me, They were in my drawer where I used to keep my dirty linen, or in my bag with my dirty linen in the pantry. If there is blood upon them, it must have been from my nose, as it sometimes bled. I know nothing whatever of the shirt-front. I turned up the coat and shirt-sleeves of my right hand when I committed the murder. I did not use the pillow at all.

After I had committed the murder, I undressed and went to bed as usual. I made the marks on the door on the outside, none of them from the inside, for the purpose of having it believed that thieves had broken in. I never made use of the chisel or the fire-irons. I placed the things about the house to give the appearance of robbery. It is not true that the bottom bolt was never used to secure the door, it was bolted that night. I took the jewellery after I had committed the deed.—All the marks on the door were made from the outside on the Monday night, for I got out of the pantry-window and broke in at the door, and while getting out of the pantry-window made a little mark on the wall outside, near the water-pipe, which the witness Young saw, and mentioned in his evidence. I did not wash my hands or the knife in the bedit in his lordship's bedroom. Sarah Mancell knew nothing about it. Neither did the cook, or any of the other servants. I am the only person who is at all guilty.

"FRANCOIS BENJAMIN COURVOISIER.
"22nd June, 1840.

"Witnesses,
"Thomas Flower,
"William Wadham Cope."

The following is a verbatim copy of the confession made to Sheriff Evans on the following day, as it was taken down on paper by the sheriff:—

"After I had warmed his lordship's bed, I went down-stairs, and waited about an hour, during which time I placed the different articles as they were found by the police. I afterwards went to the dining-room and took one of the knives from the sideboard. I then entered his bed-room, and found him asleep. I went to the side of the bed, and drew the knife across his throat. He appeared to die instantly.

"FRANCOIS BENJAMIN COURVOISIER."

"PRISON OF NEWGATE, June 23, 1840.

"This declaration was made before me this twenty-third day of June, 1840.

"WILLIAM EVANS,
"Sheriff."

On the Saturday before his execution the prisoner wrote another long confession, and delivered it to Mr Carver, the Ordinary, and Mr. Baud, Minister of the French Protestant chapel in Threadneedle street, who afterwards read it over to him, and asked him if there was anything that he wished to add to it, and he replied nothing whatever. The confession is written in the French language, with a slight mixture of Swiss. The man's discrepancy is in his denying his former statement, that Lord Russell came down-stairs, and caught him in the act of plundering the house. He said he first made this assertion, thinking that the less the crime appeared premeditated, the less obloquy would attach to him; but, on the solicitation of his uncle, he had determined to tell the whole truth.

THE MURDER OF THE DUCHESS OF PRASLIN BY HER HUSBAND.

FULL PARTICULARS OF THE TRAGEDY.—DOMESTIC DIFFICULTIES IN THE FAMILY.—THE MURDER.—EXAMINATION OF THE ACCUSED AND OF MADEMOISELLE DE LUZY DESPORTES, THE GOVERNESS.—ELOQUENT LETTERS, IMPRESSIONS AND DIARY OF THE DUCHESS.—CAUSES ASSIGNED FOR THE DEED.—SUICIDE OF THE DUKE.—EFFECTS OF THE CRIME ON THE PEOPLE OF FRANCE, &C.

No bloodier, or more inexcusable murder is recorded in the pages of history than that of the Duchess of Praslin by her husband—the Duke de Choiseul-Praslin. No event of its terrible character had ever, perhaps, such sad results, or exercised such powerful influences. History has traced it as being one of the principal causes of the French Revolution of 1848, even the upsetting of the monarchy itself, in consequence of the fact that the Praslin and Bourbon family were related. Every vice of the time was traced to the aristocracy. The people, but a few years before merging from a revolution of blood and terror, looked upon the nobility as the cause of all their troubles. They believed that the immoralities and tyrannies of an idle nobility had hurled destruction upon their country, and they now watched with suspicion every act of this class which tended to recklessness or immorality. The nation was in this state when the Duke of Praslin murdered his loving wife. That this lady loved him with an ardent attachment, there seems to be no question. That she was a woman of the most excellent accomplishments, warm disposition, and possessed of all the virtues which should adorn the wife and the mother, her eloquent letters must incontestibly establish. It is then no wonder that the assassination of such a woman sent a thrill of horror, not alone throughout France, but throughout the whole civilized community, where the details were published.

To the American reader the recital at this time must prove of great interest. The governess in the Praslin family—Mademoiselle Deluzy Desportes, at the time of the tragedy — left Paris some time after the murder, and is at present residing in the City of New York. We annex her examination before the French court, together with that of the Duke of Praslin. We also print a number of the eloquent letters of the Duchess. From the most authentic sources we have obtained the history of this tragedy, and we will now proceed to relate the facts, as detailed shortly after the occurrence.

THE family of Choiseul-Praslin is of origin almost coeval with the sovereign line of Bourbon itself. The old blood-royal of France flows in its veins. Raynard Sieur de Choiseul, Count de Langres, married, in 1182, Alix de Dreux, grand-daughter of King Louis VI. Their descendants have been great for ages. Charles de Choiseul, Marshal of France, died in 1626, after having, in his country's service, commanded nine different armies, assisted at forty-seven engagements, and received thirty-six wounds. Stephen Francis de Choiseul, Duke of Choiseul and of Amboise, who died in 1785, was successively ambassador at Rome, at Vienna, Minister of Foreign Affairs, Minister of War, and Minister of Marine. His influence for good or evil had much to do with the destinies of France: for he it was who first subjected Corsica, the land of Napoleon, to French dominion, and who counseled the assistance given by King Louis to the colonies of America, when achieving their independence under Washington. To this Duke de Choiseul the French navy owes its rise into importance. The duke, who died in 1817, wrote a celebrated, and, in its results, very effective, work on the emancipation of Greece. This then was the house, upon which its representative, Charles Laure Hugo Theobald, Duke of Choiseul-Praslin, was to cast a stain of the blackest dye for ever. Despite of all antecedent glories, the name of Praslin cannot be mentioned in future without bringing remembrance of one of the most wicked and cruel, the most heartless and cowardly murders that bring additional disgrace to the annals of crime.

But the story needs no comment. The simple facts, as gathered from the various pieces of evidence adduced, are terrible and startling enough in themselves. To begin the narrative with the conjugal position of the duke. He was born in 1805, and, in 1825, he married Fanny, daughter of the late Count Frances Horace Sebastiani, a distinguished French general, since a peer and Marshal of France, by his wife Frances Jane de Coigny, sister of that Mdlle. de Coigny who inspired the unfortunate poet, Andrew Chénier, (already of record in this volume), her fellow prisoner in St. Lazarus, with his touching elegy of "La Jeune Captive."

The Duke and Duchess of Praslin had by this union three sons (of whom Gaston Louis Phillipe, born the 7th August, 1834, is the present duke), and six daughters. At the period when the dreadful tragedy happened, the two eldest of these children, who were daughters, were married. The one next in seniority, also a daughter, was in her eighteenth year. The youngest child, a boy, was eight years old. Fanny, Duchess of Praslin, was at this time in her forty-first year, some two years younger than her husband. She was born in 1807, at Constantinople, during the embassy of General Horace Sebastiani, her father, to the Ottoman Porte.

A short time after her birth, Mdlle. Fanny Sebastiani lost her mother, whose in-urned heart, according to custom, was transported to Olmetta, in Corsica, the home of the Sebastiani family: the motherless child was brought up by her aunt. When her marriage was arranged, Baron Pasquier, since a Duke and Chancellor of France, was the Duke of Praslin's first witness at the signing of the matrimonial contract; he afterwards sat as judge upon the murder. The husband inherited the honors of his house in 1841, on the death of the Duke of Praslin, his father, formerly Chamberlain to the Empress Josephine, and colonel of the National Guard, in 1814. By this succession he became chief of the third branch of the ducal house of Choiseul; and he was a made a member of the Chamber of Peers on the 6th of April, 1847.

From the time of the death of the old duke his father, he and his duchess and family lived at their Château of Vaux-Praslin, near Melun, in the department of the Seine and Marne. This Château of Vaux had once been one of the most sumptuous of the residences of Fouquet, the princely but unfortunate minister of Louis XIV. The duke and duchess were latterly not happy in their union. Grave discord had arisen between them. Their dissensions had become matter of public notoriety both in town and country. One serious cause of quarrel was said to be the influence which the governess of his daughters, a Mdlle. Henrietta Deluzy-Desportes, had gained over the duke. But differences had crept in as far back as 1837, long prior to the entrance of the governess into the family. The duchess objected to the continuance of this lady in the family, and particularly complained of her estranging from her the affections of her daughters, This subject of discord increased with years, and eventually grew to such a height, that at last Mdlle. Deluzy had to quit. She did not, however, leave France, as the duchess expected, but went to reside in a boarding-school near Paris. Here the duke visited her, and here she was about to get an appointment as instructress; but the principal of the establishment required a prior letter of recommendation from the Duchess of Praslin. Such a letter, therefore, became vital to Mdlle. Deluzy, and the duke undertook to procure it. He was to have obtained it the very morning the duchess was found murdered. The departure of Mdlle. Deluzy from the Praslin family took place at Paris, the 18th July, 1847, just about a month before the occurrence of the fatal catastrophe. The duke and duchess were then apparently reconciled, and they went from Paris to their country château together with their children. The people, assembled at Melun for the celebration of the patron festival of St. Ambrose, saw them there together arm in arm, and were glad in consequence, for the family of Praslin was popular with them; it was believed that they had become perfect friends for the future.

The duchess herself was much and generally beloved for her active charity and benevolence; the peasantry about her surnamed her "the good lady of Praslin." This semblance of concord between the duke and duchess was, however, a mere shadow; she still had her sorrows; she would often feel and express a kind of presentiment of her approaching end. One day the duke requested her to descend into the funeral vault at Vaux, which had recently been repaired; she refused, saying, "Shall I not soon go into it for ever?" It was under this state of circumstances that on the 17th of August, 1847, all the Praslin family left their château, and came to their superb residence in Paris, in the Rue du Faubourg St. Honoré, No. 55, at 8 o'clock in the evening, by the Corbeil Railway. After their arrival the duke, with three of his daughters, and the youngest of his sons, went to Mad. Lemaire's, the mistress of a boarding-house mentioned, to visit Mdlle. de Luzy Desportes; he saw her about the letter, and left her at ten o'clock; he arrived at his house a little before eleven, then conducted the young ladies to their apartment, and immediately retired to his own.

While the duke was out, the duchess with her two eldest sons took a hackney-coach, drove to a bookseller's in the Rue Coq-Saint-Honoré, and after staying a short time there, returned home at half-past nine; the duchess then retired to her sleeping apartment, where she put on her night-apparel, ordered and took some orgeat, laid herself down tranquilly, and beginning to read in bed, dismissed her maid with a desire that she would call her at six o'clock the next morning. The maid never saw her alive again: at five o'clock on that morning the duchess had ceased to exist. Her body, thrown down near the chimney, with the head and back against a sofa, there she lay deluged in her blood, and pierced with more than forty wounds. The news spread like wildfire, and all Paris was excited. An investigation instantly began. According to the opinion of the experts called in, three kinds of weapons must have been used in the perpetration of this crime; one a cutting, one a pointed, and one a bruising weapon; or at least they said, the assassin made use of an arm which had at the same time a point, a blade, and a stout handle, like a yatigan.

The blood had spurted on all sides. It formed itself into pools, gutters, drops, and various stains. It was seen upon the bed, upon the curtains, on the bell-rope, and indeed upon almost all the furniture in the room.

Everything proved that the duchess had attempted to escape from her assassin, either by rushing towards the doors to get out of the bed-room, or by endeavoring to pull the bell-ropes that her domestics might come to her aid,—also by running from one piece of furniture to another, that she might make a rampart of them. It was thought the first blows were given her while in bed, and that she made her most desperate efforts at the chimney.

The murderer, necessarily covered with blood, must have left traces of it on his way; and that stained way was found to be towards the apartment of her husband, the Duke of Praslin. Drops and marks of blood were visible from the door of the duchess's cabinet to the door of the duke's bed-room.

These indications at once put justice on the scent. Its further enlightenment is detailed in the following portions and summaries of the interrogatories and other evidence. The first declaration was that of the Duke of Praslin, which was made on 18th of August, the day of the murder, to the magistrates charged with the earliest investigations. It was as follows:—

"This morning at break of day," said the duke, "I was awakened by cries, when I caught up a pistol and descended into the chamber of Madame de Praslin. I found the duchess seated on the floor, her head against a couch. Her face was covered with blood. I had scarcely attempted to afford her aid, when I heard a knocking at the door communicating with the saloon. I went and unbolted it, and found there my valet, my porter, and other people of the house, coming also to the assistance of the duchess. In attending to my wife, I had stained myself with blood. My head was quite gone; I returned to my chamber and washed my hands. I endeavored to clear off with water the blood-stains upon my breast and my dressing-gown; I did so that I might not alarm my children, to whom I wished to communicate what had befallen their mother, but I had not the courage to tell them. Very soon after the General Viscount Sebastiani, the uncle of the duchess, came, and he was still with me when M. Bruzelin, the commissary of police, also arrived. My first care had been to order that the commissary and a physician should be sent for."

In consequence of this declaration, and other information already collected, the magistrates put various questions to the Duke of Praslin, which they set down, (as follows), in the minutes, together with the answers received.

"We asked the duke what use he made of the pistol with which he had armed himself. He replied that at the moment of his attempting to help the duchess, he let it fall near the body; but that afterwards in his agitation, he had picked it up again, struck it against the ground, and left it, he no longer recollected where.

"We asked the duke how it happened that the fragments of a silk handkerchief were found in his chimney? He replied, 'I took this handkerchief to bind about my head; but finding it in a very bad state, I flung it into the chimney, where there was a great quantity of papers. This morning I threw a match into the chimney, which I used, I know not for what purpose, and the things took fire.'

"We asked the duke whence came a piece of green cord, such as for a bell-pull, found under his braces? He replied that the cord belonged to a pounce-box, but he could not explain why he had it on him, and under his braces. (The bell-pull over the duchess's pillow, it should be observed, was cut off beyond her reach.)

"We asked the duke whence came five ends of rope, and one end of white cord, stained with blood, found in his dressing-gown? He replied, that he knew not how the cords could have fallen into his pocket; as to the stain upon the white cord, he might have caused it by touching the cord with his blood-marked hands.

"We made the duke observe that the pistol left by him in the duchess's chamber had blood upon the barrel and the ram-rod; that hair, and a small piece of skin, were sticking to the butt-end, glued to it by blood; that these were circumstances which raised against him the gravest suspicions. The duke hung down his head, and held it between his hands, while the Procureur du Roi earnestly exhorted him to reply with frankness. He ended by saying, 'I formally deny having struck Madame de Praslin with that or any other weapon. As to the sticking of hair and flesh upon the butt-end of the pistol, it is impossible for me to explain it.'"

The next deposition was that of Augustus Charpentier, the duke's valet-de chambre. It ran thus:—

"On the 18th of August, 1847, towards five o'clock in the morning, I was awakened by an extraordinary sound of bell-ringing from the chamber of the duchess. She rang at the same time for the valet-de-chambre, Maxime, who was not in the hotel, and for her lady's maid, Madame Leclerc. I descended hastily, and with the key that hung upon a nail, unlocked the door of the duchess's ante-room, but could not get in; the door, contrary to custom, being bolted inside. At the same time piercing shrieks issued from the duchess, and I heard a confused noise, as if there was a running about the room. I kicked the door violently with my foot, but could not burst it open. The lady's maid now came, and we both rushed round, to enter by the grand saloon; but here also the door was held fast by a bolt on the inside. This door I pushed against with violence, in hopes of breaking it in, but without success. At intervals, my ear caught the death-rattles of my unfortunate mistress. I flew to the garden. I knocked in vain at the window of the bed-room, and at that of the boudoir. On arriving, however, at the south-west end of the house, I found open the door of the wooden staircase which leads to the ante-room between the duke's chamber and that of the duchess. The door of the dressing-room, and the two doors communicating from this cabinet to the duchess's sleeping apartments, were quite open. By this way I got as far as the entrance of the latter. All the shutters were closed; the darkness was complete; I did not hear the least sound. I thought I experienced a smell of powder and blood. I was alarmed, and retracéd my steps. I rejoined the lady's maid, and flew to Merville, with whom I came back again, with a lamp and sword. At the moment of turning round the south-west corner of the house, we perceived that the Venetian blinds of the ante-room were open. I did not stop, however; Merville followed; we percived no one. The second time I reached the entrance of the duchess's bed-room; and there, by the help of my lamp, I saw her stretched upon the floor, and weltering in her blood. We instantly alarmed the whole house. While repassing the yard, I remarked a considerable quantity of smoke issuing from the chimney of the duke's chamber, and I mentioned the circumstance to Merville.

"Our call brought the porter, also Madame Merville, and many other persons. We were about to pass through the great saloon, to make the circuit I had before made, when the duke opened the door communicating from this room to the duchess's bedroom. We were not at the moment knocking there, as we knew it was bolted within. The duke said, 'Does she live still? Run, and fetch a medical man.' I hastened to fetch Dr. Simon.

"This morning when General Viscount Sebastiani arrived, he expressed himself as feeling suddenly unwell. I went to the duke's room to beg a glass of water for him, but the duke replied he had none. In fact there was no water in the duke's ewer, but the pitcher was in the middle of the room, and I wanted to take some water from it, when he told me not to touch it, for it was stale. This pitcher he took and emptied into the garden. A minute afterwards I was arrested and confined in my room; when I saw them act so with me, I said they would do much better to go and examine the duke's chamber." This witness also testified as to the reported intimacy which existed between Mlle. Deluzy and the duke.

The depositions of Margaret Leclerc, lady's maid to the duchess, of the porter, and also of Merville, the Duchess of Orlean's valet-de-chambre, alluded to the reported adulterous intercourse of Mlle. Deluzy with the duke, and agreed with those of Charpentier, but were less long in detail.

Euphemia Merville, wife of the valet of the Duchess of Orleans, was more minute in her evidence. When they rushed into the room, crying out that the duchess had been assassinated, that her dying groans could be heard, she replied, "We cannot let her die without help;" and she instantly flew to the fatal room. The porter was with her. To the best of her belief the murdered lady breathed her remaining life away in her arms, while she was laving her face with water. At this moment the witness saw the duke, and exclaimed, "Ah! my God! what a misfortune!" when he replied, striking her on the shoulder, "Good God! Euphenia, what will become of us?" He beat his hands against the wall, but she did not see him make any attempt to aid his wife.

The evidence of the porter's wife somewhat deviated from this. According to her, the duke, on seeing the dead body of his wife, exclaimed, "My wife! my poor wife!—the poor marshal! the poor children!—who will tell them of this?"

Charpentier was a second time examined, and gave these further answers.

Q. Do you recollect what the duke said on learning that you had seen the body of the duchess?

A. He asked me, pressing his head between his hands, "Who first entered the room?" Upon my replying that it was I, he demanded what I had seen; and when I said only the duchess, he asked what she had said. I told him she was dead, and could say nothing when I entered. It was then he exclaimed, "Who could have done such a deed? What will become of us—and the poor children?"

The next important evidence was the examination of Mlle. Deluzy Desportes, thirty-five years old, the governess of the duke's children, formerly acting in the same capacity to Lady Hislop, in England. According to Mlle. Deluzy's declaration, she had always paid due respect to the duchess, and done nothing to alienate from her the affection of her children. When she entered the family, "matters were," she said, "already on a very bad footing." The duchess wished to superintend the education of her children; but after three months, the duke, not approving of this, expressed his dissatisfaction, whereupon, for the future, she abstained from all interference. The following is a portion of the interrogation of Mdlle. Deluzy:—

Q. What were the causes of the dissensions between the duke and duchess?

A. On the part of the duchess it was a desire to rule the children, and, above all, her husband; on that of the duke, it was a fixed spirit of resistance, accompanied, however, with much gentleness.

Q. Is it not certain that the duchess, and more particulary during the last three months, believed that wrong relations existed between yourself and her husband?

A. The duchess never hinted at anything of the kind to me; she may have done so to others. Two years ago, in consequence of a libellous article in the newspapers, I wished to quit my situation, but Marshal Sebastiani, in whose house we were then living, in Corsica, was the first to oppose it at the time. The duchess treated me with much coldness upon my consent to stay, but since then she has been exceedingly kind to me. I was overwhelmed, therefore, when, about two months since, I was informed, through the Abbe Gallard, that my presence was the cause of trouble in the house, and that I must not stay.

Q. We have here a letter, without a date or signature, which appears to have been addressed to you, at no remote date, by the duchess, wherein she says, "If it is forbidden to go to rest without being reconciled to one's neighbor, it seems to me that a new year is a still more cogent reason for putting an end to all dissensions, and forgetting all complaints." She adds that it is with true good will she offers you her hand, and calls upon you to forget the past as she has done, in order that for the future you may live in good understanding with her. At that epoch, then, there still existed grounds of complaint against you?

A. This letter was written to me in 1846, and with it the duchess sent a bracelet for a new year's gift. Before this time she had treated me with much coldness, though without any reason. During last winter, on the contrary, she was far kinder. Every time she went to the play, she offered me a place in her box; and whenever she went out on a party of pleasure with the young ladies, I was invited to take a part.

From further questions it appeared that Mademoiselle Deluzy had been visited three times by the duke after she had quitted his service. Upon one of these occasions Madame Lemaire, with whom she was then staying, informed the duke of her wish to give Mademoiselle Deluzy a situation in her house, but that on account of the evil reports in circulation she could not do so without a letter from the duchess contradicting them. It was in consequence agreed that Mademoiselle Deluzy should call upon the duchess the next day to solicit such a letter.

The judge next demanded where she had slept on the night of the 17th of August, to which she replied, at Madame Lemaire's; and to further inquiries she answered that no one had slept in her chamber, but that she was so surrounded by persons near, that the least stir she made would have been heard by them.

Q. How did you learn the dreadful event that occurred yesterday?

A. I learnt it from M. Remy, professor of literature to the young ladies. He took me with him to his house, where I remained till eight o'clock, when an agent of the police came for me.

Q. Why did you leave Mme. Lemaire at such a time, without saying where you were going?

A. M. and Mme. Remy seeing me so distressed would have me go with them. I gave M. Remy's address to Mme. Lemaire, who told it to the police agents. I cannot say why the police remained at Mme. Lemaire's door without coming where they were to find me.

When the examination touched upon the duke's guilt, Mademoiselle Deluzy evinced the greatest emotion, falling upon her knees with clasped hands, declaring that it was impossible, and exclaiming:—"Tell me not that there are presumptions against him—say not that they are strong. My conscience assures me that he has not done it. But if he have—great God! it is I, it is I who am the guilty party, I who so loved the children, I who adored them—I was a coward, I could not resign myself to my fate ; I wrote letters to them—letters which you can see. I told them that I could no longer live, that I was a poor deserted creature, without other support than an old grandfather who threatened to suspend the little he was doing for me. I was terrified at my future prospects. O how wrong I was! I ought to have told them that I submitted to my fate, that I could be happy in my little chamber—I should have told them to forget me, and love their mother. But I did nothing of the kind. When I quitted the house, I was driven to such despair that I wished to die. *I had a vial of laudanum. I drank it. Unfortunately they recalled me to life, and life was to me so very sad!* For six years I had been so happy in that house in the midst of those children, who loved me, and whom I loved more than life, for without them it is insupportable. He must have demanded this fatal letter of recommendation, she must have refused, and then—'tis I, 'tis I that am the guilty one."

Q. It seems impossible that this excitement should merely belong to such feelings as might exist between you and the children. Was it to the children only that you addressed the despairing letters of which you spoke?

A. You are wrong, sir; excitement can belong to every feeling; do you not know that it can? But I will not say that, as I constantly saw the duke so kind, so generous to me, there may not have mingled with my affection for the children a tenderness—a vivid tenderness—for the father; but never did I bring into that house sin and disorder; I would not from regard to the children. I should have thought I had sullied those whom I called my own daughters if I had embraced them after I had become guilty. Can it not be understood that one may love with honor? I feel that I am wrong to use the words, my daughters—words that I have used only since I wrote to them. I have sometimes said, "my children," when speaking to the whole of this youthful family.

Q. Did the duke participate in this state of sentiment and excitement that you exhibit?

A. No; but the children were unhappy; they suffered in their health; their mother used them harshly.

Q. But supposing the duke to have committed this crime, one could never believe he did it to protect his children against the ill-treatment of their mother?

A. No; such could not have been the cause. That which excited and set him beside himself was the dread of a divorce, with which the duchess incessantly threatened him.

Q. This leads us far away from the conclusions that seem to follow from your first answers as to the causes which alienated the duchess from you. It is no longer a question of jealous suspicions, dissipated as soon as they arose, leaving no feelings behind. It is now, according to you, a case of serious dissension—the inevitable result to be a divorce. Your quitting was not caused by a first manifestation of jealousy; you were upheld by the husband against the wife; Marshal Sebastiani's interference became requisite.

A. These resentments were not manifested till the last moment; I am ignorant to what degree they were carried. The duke never showed any feelings for me but friendship and esteem, and I protest—to speak out plainly—he never was my lover.

Q. Nevertheless, it is one month since you left the house. In that interval are penned the letters, which you admit you did wrong in writing. In that interval occur many visits paid to you by the duke, three at least. To-day you were told to present yourself at the house, to request a letter of the duchess, and it was yesterday that she fell by the hand of the assassin.

A. I can only persist in the answers already given. Nothing wrong passed between me and the duke, nor was any future wrong meditated. Had the duchess died naturally, I would not for the sake of the children have consented to a *mesalliance*, the consequences of which might have fallen upon them. I had just as little idea of any other wrong. If the duke had loved me, I might have been capable of sacrificing my reputation and my life for him; but I never could have wished that it should cost his wife a lock of her hair. I speak the truth; you ought to believe me, gentlemen. Has not nature a tone which carries a conviction with it? You ought to feel that.

Q. The four beginnings of letters which we now show you, are they not yours?

A. Yes, sir.

Q. One of these has an unfinished sentence. "You say nothing of your father. I hope that he is well, and continues to keep up his spirits. It seems to me I should be less unhappy, if I were sure to suffer."—Will you complete the sentence?

A. It is probable I meant to terminate the phrase with the word *alone*, or perhaps with the words *for you all.* I know not why I broke off; it may be that I thought it better not to speak to the young ladies of their father.

Q. You did right; and precisely so, because the letter contained the expression of a community of feeling to which it was not fit the young ladies should be made a party.

The examination of the duke before the Chancellor Pasquier, President of the Chamber of Peers, was opened by an earnest adjuration on the judge's part that the duke should relieve his mind by a frank confession of his crime, and when he pleaded weakness as a reason for not entering into details, the judge replied that nothing was more requisite than *yes* or *no.* Still he urged his state of feebleness, but to various questions of detail he replied with sufficient readiness. From these it appeared that he had been wakened, as he thought, by shrieks in the house, and that he hurried into the chamber of the duchess, a recollection that seemed so much to overpower him that he begged of them to spare his life, to desist from questions. The judge, however, proceeded.

Q. When you were in the duchess's chamber, you could not be ignorant that every mode of egress was closed, and that you alone could enter?

A. I was not aware of it.

Q. You went several times in the course of the morning into the bedroom; was she in bed the first time that you went there?

A. No; unfortunately she was stretched upon the floor.

Q. Was she not lying in the place where you struck her for last time?

A. How can you ask me such a question?

Q. Because you did not answer me at once. Whence come the scratches that I see on your hands?

A. I got them while occupied packing up with the duchess the evening I left Praslin.

Q. I see a bite on your thumb; how did that happen?

A. It is not a bite.

Q. The surgeons have declared that it is.

A. Spare me; my weakness is excessive.

Q. You must have experienced a painful moment when, upon returning to your room, you found yourself covered with the blood you had spilt, which you tried to wash out?

A. This has been wrongly interpreted; I did not like appearing before my children with the blood of their mother.

Q. You are very unfortunate in having committed this crime.

The accused made no reply, but seemed lost in thought.

Q. Were you not urged to this crime by evil counsel?

A. I have had no counsel; people do not counsel to such things.

Q. Are you not devoured by remorse? and would it not be a sort of consolation to you if you told the truth?

A. My strength completely fails me to-day.

Q. You are always speaking of your weakness. I asked you just now to say *yes* or *no.*

A. If any one would feel my pulse, he must be sensible of my weakness.

Q. You have had sufficient strength to answer a tolerable number of questions in detail; you were not too feeble for that.

The accused made no reply.

Q. Your silence gives the answer for you, that you are guilty.

A. You have come here with a conviction of my guilt; I cannot change your opinions.

Q. You can do so if you give us reasons for a contrary belief—if you can explain otherwise that which seems explicable only by the supposition of your guilt.

A. I do not think myself able to change this conviction of your minds.

Q. And why do you think so?

After a pause, the accused declared it was beyond his strength to go on.

Q. When you committed this awful crime, did you think of your children?

A. Crime! I have committed no crime; as to the children, they are always in my thoughts.

Q. Do you dare to affirm that you have not committed this crime?

The accused sank his head within his hands, and for a few minutes remained without speaking. He then said, "I cannot reply to such a question."

Q. Monsieur de Praslin, you are in a state of torture, and, as I said to you just now, you may lessen this agony by giving me an answer.

The accused makes no reply, but begs, in mercy, that his further examination may be postponed till another day. This was assented to, and the investigation terminated.

A second examination of Mdlle. Deluzy now took place, and this time before the Chancellor Pasquier. Her statements would make it appear that the duchess had little intercourse with her children; for while the family remained at Paris she went out a great deal, and lived much at her father's; in the country she spent much of her time in her own room. Mdlle. Deluzy, according to her own showing, frequently wished to come to some understanding with her as to the education of the children, but her constant reply was that she did not approve of the duke's system, but that she had given him her word not to interfere with their education.

The judge then asked Mdlle. Deluzy if she did not think this isolation very painful to the duchess, and a cause of dissension between her and the duke? To this she replied, "Quite the reverse. I believe, upon my soul and conscience, Madame de Praslin was more occupied at that time with her feelings about her husband than about her children, whom she scarcely ever saw, and whom she sent away, when their father was present, in order to be alone with him. When he was no longer there, she voluntarily kept herself at a distance from the children, in order that she might use it as a weapon against him in her reproaches touching his way of managing their household. In the early part of my residence Madame de Praslin would never walk out in company with her children while we were in the country; since then she has changed. When the Duke de Praslin, while playing with the children, would happen to answer abruptly the questions the duchess incessantly addressed to him to divert his attention from them to herself, she would invariably quit the room with the liveliest expressions of jealous irritation. This was soon perceived by the children, who, with the innocent malice of their age, affected to brave this feeling by showing yet more attachment for their father, and by being perpetually about him. I perceived the evil arising from this sort of struggle, but I had not always the power to prevent the results. At a later period, the yet greater affection I felt for my pupils prevented me from being quite impartial in these daily-renewed disputes."

At this answer the judge rebuked the woman for endeavoring to turn all the blame upon the duchess, and for not having used the influence she had over the children in restoring their affections to their mother. To this Mlle. Deluzy replied that they had asked for the truth, and she therefore felt obliged to tell it without reserve; and added that the irritable, unbending character of the duchess made her totally unfit for bringing up the children. The examination then took another turn. She was asked if she had never felt that she was a cause of dissension—a stumbling-block in the way of the duke and the duchess? To this she replied that she thought but little at first of the estrangement of Madame de Praslin from herself, as the duchess evinced the same feelings towards every one who approached her husband. At a later period, when evil reports began to circulate, she had expostulated with the duchess, who, however, treated it as nothing more than vanity and self-love on the part of one who held a situation so beneath her own and her husband's rank.

Q. You have said that the Duke de Praslin ended by living chiefly with you and the children?

A. The Duke de Praslin did not live chiefly with me and the children; but, in country and in town, the habits of the duchess, who never left her father's saloon, except to mix in gay society, were the cause that in the hours of recreation during summer, as well as in long winter evenings, the duke walked with us, or passed some time in the school-room. The children were admitted for a few moments only into the house of their grandfather. Madame de Praslin never did desire us to pass the evenings in her drawing-room.

The judge again commented severely upon the evident desire of the witness to throw all the blame upon Madame de Praslin.

To this she replied, almost as she had done before, that, being interrogated, she felt bound to make her explanations as clear as possible; adding, "the conduct of Madame de Praslin was the same towards those whom she loved best; it was very unequal, and often quite incomprehensible. At one time she would grievously wound my feelings and self-esteem; at other times she would treat me with sympathy and kindness. Often in the space of an hour, after having charged me with my influence over the family, she would request me to use it for the accomplishment of some fancy she might have; often, after having inflicted some cruel anguish on me, she would make me a handsome present; even during the last days of my remaining with her, when she had refused to sit at the same table with me, when in the eyes of the whole house I was rather expelled than honorably dismissed, Madame de Praslin, meeting me by chance, showed herself all at once as kind as in our best days, and, more than that, actually sent me some books to amuse me."

The judge could see in this another proof of the duchess' goodness, while Mlle. Deluzy inferred from it that the duchess, displeasure must have proceeded from an irritability, which she could not control, rather than from any sense of wrongs done to her. The judge again objected to her evident desire to lay all the blame upon the deceased, to which she replied as before, but with considerable emotion, that she only endeavored to give the desired explanations, and that she would gladly die to bring the duchess back to life.

Q. In the last visit that the Duke de Praslin paid you with his three daughters, and his youngest son, what passed between him, you and them?

A. When the duke arrived with the children, the latter were much affected; at first there was nothing but tears and embraces. At length, embarrassed by the presence of the children, I said to the duke, in general terms only, that Mme. Lemaire, the directress of the establishment where I had been for a month, was willing to employ me; but that reports, unfavorable to my reputation, having reached her, she wished that Madame de Praslin would write her a letter, that might serve as a testimony of my character. The duke then saw Madame Lemaire. When he returned from the interview, I told him that it was not requisite for him to trouble himself much about this request, Madame Lemaire perhaps attaching more importance to it only to make me accept conditions that I did not feel disposed to comply with. A few moments afterwards the duke left me in haste, to save the children from the reproaches of their mother, on account of the visit they had paid me, and our last words were, "Farewell till to-morrow;" for we were all to meet again at noon, and it was agreed that at two o'clock I should respectfully seek a reconciliation with the duchess.

Q. Did the Duke de Praslin give you any assurance or hope of obtaining from the duchess the letter you required in your favor?

A. He told Madame Lemaire that he did not apprehend any difficulty, the duchess was anxious that I should pass into the employ of another.

Q. When the duke quitted you, did you observe any extraordinary excitement in him?

A. No, sir; he only said, "I am sorry for you. I play a vexatious part in this business." But he appeared calm.

Q. At what hour did he leave you?

A. A little before ten.

Q. Did he go away in a hackney-coach?

A. In a hackney-coach with his children.

Q. Did you hear anything fall from the lips of the Duke de Praslin that might lead you to think he was in a temper to proceed to extremities with the duchess?

A. By all that I hold in life most sacred, never! never! I know not whether it is allowable for me to mention here some facts that I alone know, and which prove that the violence was not on the Duke de Praslin's side. Often did I hear the duchess threaten to attempt her own life. Once at Vaudreuil, she wanted to stab herself, and the duke, in disarming her, wounded his hand; another time, at Dieppe, at the end of an explanation between herself and her husband, of which I was not actually a witness, but which the children and myself heard from the room where we were—she rushed into the street, threatening to fling herself into the sea; yet with that strong inconsistency of character already mentioned as belonging to her, the duke found her in a shop, making purchases, and quite calm.

Such was the sum and substance of this Mdlle. Deluzy's explanations. It is for the reader to form his own judgment of them. Not much more light was thrown on the horrible event. Its conclusion came abruptly.

The Court of Peers had been convoked by royal ordinance, issued on the 18th of August. The Procureur-General, M. Delangle, had immediately prepared the affair for the chamber; the Chancellor of France had forthwith associated to himself Messieurs Decazes, de Pontécoulant, de St. Aulaire, cousin, Laplague-Barris, and Vincens St. Laurent, to take the preliminary proceedings. He had, as already shown, gone through the examination of Mdlle. Deluzy Desportes, and of the duke. The court was now prepared to sit on the trial of the accused, and society awaited a great judicial example.

Suddenly a report spread that the duke was poisoned—that he was dying—that he was dead. The effect of this news upon the public is beyond description. The Duke de Praslin expired in the Luxemburg, whither he had been transferred in the darkness of night, to avoid the fury of the populace. In consequence of his death, the chancellor made the following report to the peers:—

"An account is due to you of how we used the powers committed to us, for investigating the murder of the Duchess of Praslin. The inquiry was conducted upon the presumption, which proved too well founded, that her husband, the Duke of Praslin, was the actual criminal. The time the duke was under your jurisdiction was of no long duration. At five o'clock on the morning of Saturday, he was committed to the prison of the Luxemburg, in virtue of an order that I had given on Friday, but which could not sooner be put into execution. He lived four days only from the date of his entering the prison, having, a few hours after the murder, taken a powerful dose of arsenic. On Tuesday, the 24th, at half-past four in the evening, he died, just seven days and a half after the perpetration of the atrocious deed. This short period, however, sufficed for bringing to light the truth in all its details. It is probable that the duke took the poison when he saw his plans defeated of hiding the murder, expecting its effects would be much more rapid than it actually was. At all events, he poisoned himself in the course of Wednesday, a little sooner, or a little later, and vomitings commenced at ten o'clock at night. These ceased with the end of Thursday, and were succeeded with great weakness, but the surgeon could detect no symptoms of poisoning, and imagined it was an attack of the cholera. After a few struggles the duke grew better, and at ten o'clock on Friday night it was decided by the medical attandant that he might be removed to the prison of the Luxemburg without inconvenience. Although the accused could not be brought to an actual confession of his crime, yet the absence of of all denial, even when the choice was formally given him between *yes* and *no*, may well be received as such. The conclusions drawn from the *procès verbal*, and the after minutes, bear that the poisoning of the duke, effected by himself, must have occurred in the middle of Wednesday, a few hours only after the commission of the murder. It appears also from the minutes, that all the results which followed, the intervals elapsing between them, and the duration of his state terminated by death, were the natural and habitual consequences of this kind of poisoning. As regards the duke all then is made plain, all is accomplished, the justice of man has no longer any power over him. But at the commencement of the preliminary inquiries, the ordinary judges did not hesitate to arrest Mdlle. Deluzy under suspicion of having been a party to the crime. For six years she had been a governess to the duke's children, and only left the house and her situation on the 18th of July last. I have continued this arrest, by issuing against her an order of imprisonment, in virtue of which she is still detained in the Conciergerie."

Mdlle. Deluzy was soon after set at liberty.

The duke's remains were buried at night, and in secresy. The people were so enraged against him, and were so incensed at the impunity he had obtained in the eyes of the world by dying, that many refused to believe he was really dead. Some there were who maintained that the noble families, interested in stifling the details of the scandal, had procured the government's connivance at the evasion of the miscreant. Those who had too much sense to credit so absurd a supposition, declaimed not less loudly against the system of tolerance, consideration and insufficient restraint allowed him, which enabled him to escape from the merited disgrace of a public execution.

The letters which the duchess wrote to the duke during the period of discord caused by the presence of Mlle. Deluzy, have obtained quite a literary fame from the purity and goodness of mind, and the energy of feeling they display. The correspondence minutely details and painfully lays bare the long agony the unfortunate wife must have endured. We give a number of these letters, impressions and diary addressed to her husband, and three letters to Mademoiselle Deluzy, together with other correspondence of the parties connected with this melancholy affair.

Some of those letters were found in the desk of the Duke of Praslin; others in the Duchess' chamber. Shortly after the assassination they were published in pamphlet form, and were the subject of considerable comment and eulogy. Had they been written by a person in humble circumstances they would not probably have obtained a general notoriety. But the writer was one of the first ladies of France, a Duchess, and daughter of a Marshal. Meeting with so tragical an end, her impressions and writings must necessarily be read with a good deal of interest. Their intrinsic merit as literary productions must also highly recommend them to the community.

LETTERS, IMPRESSIONS, AND DIARY OF THE DUCHESS DE PRASLIN.

Letter of the Duchess de Praslin, found in the Desk of the Duke, at Paris.

"May 21, 1840.

"Do not be astonished, my dear Theobald, at my fear of being alone with you. We are separated forever—you said so; a sad recollection will ever be attached to yesterday. You must have perceived yesterday that I felt its full weight, when in the presence of persons who have caused this separation, nothing betrayed that it had taken place. You will never have occasion to complain of me before the world—my conduct yesterday is proof sufficient. As long as I nourished hopes of a reconciliation—and latterly I had many—I was hovering between joy and fear, and gave way to fits of temper; but now that sacrifice is done, you need not fear. Before the children and the world, nothing will lead to the supposition that you have destroyed my peace. When I say 'you,' it is not you that my heart accuses, but to be alone with you would be too much for me. I must weep in solitude, and endeavor to gain sufficient strength to hide my misfortune from the world; my illusions are still too fresh, my love of too late a date, to assume at once toward you that cold reserve which my future position imposes upon me. My heart would overflow; it will need time to calm its movements. Then, *mon ami*, instead of avoiding you, I shall seek your presence; but at the present moment I love you too well. My future life will be one of mourning; my feelings will be always the same, but time will have softened down their form. Do not be angry with me, then, *mon ami*, if I avoid your society; I do so not to embitter your life. In the presence of a third I shall feel more at my ease, for then I can appear affectionate towards you, and those will be my only happy moments—and I hope that the occasion will often present itself. Surely after what passed between us in the morning, yesterday evening could only be a source of grief to me; and yet I appeared gay, and almost was so, for I thought that if we were reconciled I should have to act in such and such a manner, and I acted accordingly; but it was only an illusion. Alone with you, I must always be on my guard in presence of the sad reality. We are separated, and although it is now nearly three years that we have lived as if we were so, there still was hope; but that vanished yesterday.

"To act towards you for the future as I ought, I must endeavor to forget my past hopes. Time and habit can alone teach me to draw a line between Theobald and M. de Praslin. If I could but think that you would be happy at the price of all my sufferings, present and to come, it would be a consolation to me. Farewell! What pain is in that word: pain that I never dreamt of before. Farewell! and yet you loved me! We shall meet in heaven: refuse not this last prayer, the only meeting place I may now designate. May the thought sometimes cross your mind that I still love you."

Letter from the Duchess to her husband, written in June, 1841.

"Wherefore, my beloved, do you refuse to let me share your afflictions? You deprive our life of all the charms of affection. Do you then believe, or rather, do you wish to persuade yourself that independence consists in solitude? You say that I am *exigeante*, because I desire to share your sorrows. You do not like me to remark that you have any. Do you then wish to become quite a stranger to me, and for that would it not be requisite for me to become entirely indifferent to you? And how could I become indifferent to the person I love best on earth? Do you think it possible?—would not my heart break long before? You yourself are sorrowful to see me sad, and you know the reason of my sadness; you know how it is in your power to console me, and yet you withhold those consolations. I, on the contrary, see that you are sad: I feel within my heart a source of the deepest love, sufficient to calm and sooth all your sorrows, and you discard me. Am I not your wife, the partner of your life, she whose duty it is to share equally your pleasures and your sorrows? If you were ill, it is not my hand that should smooth thy pillow? And are not sorrows diseases of the mind—of the spirit? Wherefore, then, reject me? . . . You have a heart to appreciate the joys, the wants of a loving heart, in which to place full confidence and find relief for your sorrows. It is the violence of my manners that prevents you placing that confidence in me. Believe me, Theobald, four months of sorrow and repentance have chastened me: it is to love and console you, and not to torment you, that I seek your confidence. I give you my word never to try to gain an ascendancy over you; I am fully aware of your superior character and mind; I only wish to share your life, to embellish it, and pour balm upon your wounds. You left my room because you thought that I wished to gain an ascendancy over you. My friend, I swear unto you in the name of my love, in the name of yours, by all that I hold most sacred and most dear, I only seek your love and your confidence as you have mine. I will blindly obey you—I will no longer torment you by jealousy—I shall never give you a word of reproach or of counsel. My repentance is too sincere: I have suffered too much to return to my past faults.

We are both very young, Theobald. Do not condemn us both to solitude. How we love each other—we are both of us pure —and shall we live apart from each other both in body and mind ? Do not let your heart be a sufferer from a little feeling of *amour propre ;* I swear unto you that I only seek your affection and your confidence ; I shall be the loving and obedient partner of your life. My friend, confidence is the marriage of souls—their mutual confessions are their caresses, and union, happiness and virtue are their fruits. Believe me, I shall never abuse your confidence : your confessions will be received in my bosom with the same mystery and affection as thy caresses. Take again your own Fanny. Try her but for a short time with love and affection, and you will find that you will be much happier than living in solitude. You seek a change, but are you really happy ? Oh no, you are not, with a heart like yours, and the life we are leading. The only happiness of your wife consists in your love and support. Turn not, then, a deaf ear unto her entreaties—unto her vows—to her repentance ; for she loves you, and her whole life will be passed in love and gratitude towards you. You have driven her from your bed and from your heart ; could you do more if she was false ? She spends her days and nights in tears ; she waits outside your door, but dares not enter for fear you should reproach her for it on the morrow. *Mon ami*, in the name of the many dear remembrances which you bid me invoke, should I ever have offended you, hearken to me ; give me again your confidence and your love, and open your heart to the woman whose life is devoted to you. Oh, I will never abuse it. Oh, how have I offended you, my beloved, except by my suspicions and by my temper, and when did a kind word fail to sooth me ? Give not vent to your anger—be not inexorable. My heart is breaking. Theobald, pity ! pity on her who loves you. Trust your happiness to my keeping, as I trust mine to yours. . . . Do not break the heart that is beating only for you. You who once loved me so much, forgive me. When you confess to me your sorrows—your head upon my breast, your hands in mine, my lip upon your forehead—do you not think that they will be less than if pent up in your own breast ? Do not sacrifice our mutual happiness to an empty fear that I will abuse your goodness ; no, no, I will only share and console you in all your sorrows. But will you be the less a man to have a loving woman to share your pleasures and your sorrows? Let this union of our hearts be a sweet mystery of love between us. Oh, we could be so happy if you would but try it. You would always be met with a happy and smiling countenance, ready to follow you wherever you liked. Perhaps, after all, you are the more jealous of the two. God knows what suspicion you may nourish in your breast, for I am at a loss now to interpret your secret sorrows. If you knew what I suffered, my beloved! It is still in our power to be so happy. I cannot think that you wish to abandon me thus for ever, to deprive us of mutual happiness—life is so short, my beloved, and we have been separated already so long. Soon I shall not dare to make proposals—always refused, like my caresses. It is not in your character to make the first advances, and from custom your wife will fear you too much to make further attempts, and life will then pass by, and you will be unhappy, and your wife will die of grief. Oh, return, return unto her!"

The following are extracts from a diary, with a lock to it, found in the chamber of the duchess at the Chateau de Praslin. On the first leaf the following words are written—

For my Husband, the Duke of Praslin; for him alone.

"Jan. 13, 1842.—Twice have the pages of this book been covered with the outpourings of a broken spirit. I burned them in a moment of despair, to efface all marks of my sufferings, and only show you my happy thoughts at your return. Two years have passed, and my hopes are destroyed for ever; but I feel the want of expressing to you all the tenderness and love I have felt for you.

"You have taken my children from me. My children! do you think me capable of corrupting them? I loved you too well not to love my children, and you have now taken them from me, to place them under the care of a giddy young person, without any religion, and whom you only know from an eight months' acquaintance. Theobald, Theobald, was it not sufficient to abandon me, without depriving me of the affec tion and the esteem of my children? For five years, nearly, my pillow has been wet with my tears, and my health has suffered from it."

Jan. 24, 1842.—The duchess again complains bitterly of being deprived of her children:

"Each day adds additional sorrow to my existence. I have been calumniated, and perhaps you think me guilty; otherwise you would never have deprived me of my children, to place them under the care of a stranger who has usurped my place in your house, and yet, before God, I swear I never loved any one but you. Oh, if I was not certain that your heart is for ever closed to me, I would make a last attempt. I would throw myself at your feet, and entreat you, in the name of your father, of your old days, of our children, of our first love, to have pity on her who has never ceased to love you. What an existence—what a future! With a husband and children, to be condemned to live and die alone!"

"April 23.

"It is long since I have written, and my position has since become more and more painful. You seem to have changed, and put aside all external appearances. Mademoiselle D—— reigns absolute. Never was a governess seen to assume so scandalous a position. Believe me that it is a great misfortune, a great evil; for all this intimate and familiar conduct with you, this authority over the whole household, shows that she is a person who believes that she has a right to put herself above all propriety. With her all this is vanity, love of rule, domination and pleasure. Reflect that a fraternal intimacy between you and her, looking at your age and her position, is out of all consistency. What an example to give to young persons, to give to them, as a thing of course, a woman, aged only twenty-eight, going and coming at all hours, and in any state of costume, to and from the chamber of a man no more than thirty-seven, receiving him in her own chamber, being tete-a-tete with him for whole evenings, ordering furniture, directing journeys, parties of pleasure, etc. She has broken with her female friends in order to bring herself into greater relief, and thus engrosses you entirely to herself, always finding means to get rid of the children. Has she not had the effrontery to say to me, 'I regret, madame, that it is not possible to act as mediator between you and M. de Praslin; but, for your own interest, I recommend you to pay attention to your manner of conducting yourself towards me. I conceive that it would be painful for you to be separated from your children; but, after the positive resolution come to by M. de Praslin in this respect, I am sensible that he has reasons too well founded for coming to such a decision, for me not to feel it to be an important duty to conform to it.' Is it possible that your wife, who has ever been so pure, who has never loved but your children and yourself above all things, shall be constrained to hear herself insulted by her whom you entrust to bring up our children, whom you have known only a few months, and of whom you spoke ill to me in the first part of that time? You are afraid that I should corrupt your children—and yet you abandon them to a person who makes a mockery of all the decencies of life, trampling them under her feet, who regards as superstitious all the exercises of religion! You despise me so much that I dare not repeat the expressions you made use of in telling me so, because I blamed her manners and her arrogance.

It would be better for me to approve of that which is blameable, in order to obtain her permission for you to treat me better. Then, indeed, should I render myself despicable, when I submitted to purchase pleasure, even happiness, by baseness so vile. You are in such a state of irritation that you will not listen to me, and cannot comprehend me. I do not mean, as you always seem to conceive, that Mademoiselle D—— is your mistress in the full force of the expression. This supposition, on account of your children, is revolting to you, and you do not perceive that, in the eyes of all, her familiar relations with you, her absolute empire over the house, my isolation, are as fully established as if she were so openly. You have often concluded from appearances much less decisive, that there were criminal relations between others. Cannot you, therefore, conceive my grief at seeing my children torn from their mother, to be abandoned completely to a person who has no conception that good conduct and virtue have their own eternal forms, and ought never to adopt those of vice? How can I help being afflicted when I see them in the hands of a person who has avowed her contempt for me by what I have repeated to you above, and who establishes her empire by making you hate and despise me? You have always said to me, 'When there are suspicions they should always be cleared up.' But do you not find that she daily engrosses your time, and abuses her power over you by using it to aggravate our differences, and alienate us more and more from each other? The best weapon, if I take it into my hand, is sure to turn upon and wound me. To-day, feeling disgust at seeing you come from a *tête-à-tête* with Mademoiselle D——, I thought I was making a master-stroke by flying without saying a word; thinking by this to avoid a scene, and mark my disapprobation mildly and without risk. Good God! I was far from expecting the frightful rage into which my unfortunate mildness threw you! Certainly, no violence I could have used could have excited you further than to pursue me on the staircase with abusive language, uttered with loud voice and insulting gestures; and then, after retiring for a few minutes into your own room, coming into mine and breaking my Saxon vase, my silver-gilt ewer (*aiguière*), or rather that of Horace, and taking away two presents to which I was much attached, for you gave them me when I thought you loved so much—my little rose plateau and my small gilt vases. I trust you have not given them to her or to another. The other day, to punish me for having forced myself into your room, which she can enter whenever she pleases, you came and broke all my *ombrelles*. To-day, because I fled in silence to avoid a scene, you destroyed things most precious to me, and rob me of the memorials of a love which has been my entire happiness. You have already burned those letters which were the sole remaining testimonies of that tenderness; you have torn from me my children, you have condemned me to all the miseries of life for the present, without leaving any hope of happiness for the future, and now you deprive me of the memorials of the past.

"Oh, my God! I have loved him too much—you have struck true. I could have lost all with courage, with resignation, with joy, so long as his affection and that of his children had been left to me. Now I have no longer his esteem. In the bitterness of my grief I feel a proof of thy love for me by the magnitude of the trial. I feel in the bottom of my heart that each new grief is a new promise, oh! my God, of being again one day reunited to them in thy bosom. Strike! strike! oh! God, and deign to grant my prayer; give me strength in this world to support all that Thou art pleased to inflict. Often do I ask myself whether he loves me still; whether he is attracted by her, or whether simply by the children; and whether, under false ideas, he has placed himself upon such an improper footing with her. I cannot help believing that, at the bottom, there is much of the spirit of teazing and tormenting in all this that he does. What were his habits and connexions? Of what nature have they been for years past? Is it for her that he has renounced them? Frequently, and at this very moment (half-past one o'clock in the morning), I cannot help figuring to myself that she is perhaps with him in his chamber, gossiping with him, in defiance of propriety, without being what is called his mistress. How is it that he does not comprehend that there are many things wounding to the affections? All is not concentrated in one animal action, as regards the pains of the heart. I am convinced that, if we were separated, he would soon feel the necessity of observing strictly the proprieties of society with the governess of his daughters. Can it be true, my God, that he despises me; that he loves me no longer! Sometimes I entertain doubts, and fancy that it is only a plan to correct me. But, on reflection, I cannot but remember that for five years he has daily broken more and more with me; that I am no longer anything to him; that he has deprived me of my rights as a mother, as mistress of his house; that, on all occasions, my place is assigned to her by him. It is a lure he has held out to me, intimating that if I support all the severe privations he imposes upon me without uttering a complaint, he will restore to me all my desires! Does he imagine that he can, if he wishes to do so? Does he desire it? I often think he does. Could he then? This I very much doubt. Mademoiselle D— would bring forward the bargain between them, and he would not dare decide in my favor. And I well conceive that she has real advantages as a governess, but he thinks her superior to what she really is. He would see me submissive, and believe me content; he would think that the change would not be worth while, and in truth it is too certain that he has a very bad opinion of me. I have great faults, and I suffer too much from them to be ignorant of them ; but I am convinced he believes I have vices that I am not guilty of. This morning, in conversing, Madame de Dolonieu, before this frightful scene, said to me, 'Your husband has an entire and tender devotion to you, has he not?' I avoided the question, for I could not take it upon myself to say a thing I did not think, which I knew too well I could no longer boast of. He loves me no more! But, my God, to whom I have said, 'Deprive me, if so it must be, of his love, that only joy of my life—that life of my heart—but let him be saved, that we may one day be reunited with our children in Thy bosom, as the reward of this sacrifice.' O! tell me, my God, that he will love me again when he knows this—that he will not curse my memory, and my prayer will be granted. It is so new to me to see him give himself up to these violent fits of passion, and to which mine have never approached, that I frequently cannot help thinking that this violence is feigned, inasmuch as in general he does not break things to pieces until after he has reflected. God grant that this may be so! for if he be so anxious to correct me as to purchase my cure at the price of extravagances, with an air almost of *sangfroid*, then he still loves me: and yet, what horrible expressions of disgust! They cannot come from a feigned anger! But he did not say to me the other day, in the presence of Berthe, and throwing to me all he had broken in my absence, that he would do the same every time that I broke something in his apartment? This is a singular idea, since I never intentionally broke anything belonging to him. I only wished to force open the door of his chamber at the moment he was bolting it. He afterwards told me coolly that he would do the same whenever I happened to repeat the breaking. This, then, is a plan, a calculated resolution come to in advance. Why, then, should I take it for a real act of passion? To-day, however, I have neither said nor broken anything. Truly, this is paying dear for a silent mark of dissatisfaction. I cannot help thinking that it must cost Theobald dear to commit such follies as to break, like an untoward boy, things which belong to me. It is so little his character. He thinks he punishes me severely, and I confess that I do not suffer much at seeing him give way to a conduct so ridiculous, if it be not admirable from a design to correct me. He knows not, however, to what point material objects are in themselves indifferent to me since I have lost his affection, and the hope of bringing him back to my apartment, for I have never regarded my most precious objects other than as ornaments of the place to receive him. He has no conception of the love I bear him. At the bottom of my heart I feel that, were he but to return to me, I should love him as much, perhaps more, than ever. I suffer so much from my isolation. I should be so happy to see it brought to an end. But the will of God be done. I cannot conceive how matters will be arranged. I know not how to help thinking that a separation would be best. Things are becoming more and more envenomed. I wish to promote his happiness; but, as his life is now arranged, instead of contributing to it, I destroy it. I am suffering a thousand martyrdoms. If I were to go quite alone to Pretot, under the pretence of sea-bathing, he would have time to learn whether he is really more happy with the life he has arranged with Maidemoiselle D—— and the children, without having me as his wife, or whether it would be more agreeable to him to commence a new life together with me. Three months may be sufficient for his experiment, and I could resign myself with the greater facility to live alone down there, than to remain here in the position in which I find myself. I know that, as things are now, my absence would be rather a relief than a privation. 'Remember, most holy Virgin Mary, that it has never been heard that any of those who have had recourse to thy protection, who have implored thy succour, and demanded thy intercession, have been abandoned. Animated with this confidence, O Virgin of Virgins! I fly to thee; and, groaning under the weight of my sins, I prostrate myself at thy feet! O Mother of the Word, despise not my prayers, hearken unto my petition, and deign to grant it.' —*St. Bernard.*"

Undated Letter found in the Duke's Bureau.

"You have proved in so many ways that you have no esteem nor friendship for me, that you desire my children to partake your sentiments, I wish only to leave you to enjoy in peace the life you have selected, without my being perforce a spectatress. I suffer too much here, deprived of all in the place I love, and in the midst of those I cherish, and whom an *intrigante* tears from me. I do not understand why my sorrowful life should serve as a seasoning to your pleasure. Do what you will, but for pity do not force me to be a witness. If the baths are ordered for Aline, trust me to take her there. Ah! if you will allow me to consecrate my life to those of my children who give you the least delight, to whom nature has been least kind, it would be enough for me."

Also undated.

"You will not be surprised, sir, that after such an insult I can never consent that the person to whose ill conduct I owe it should remain under the same roof with me. You are completely blinded towards me, and towards yourself. You are, doubtless, free to do what suits you; but you are not free to have my daughters brought up by a person whom I despise as her shameful conduct deserves. For a long time I have sought an explanation with you; I have done what I could to obtain it, but you refuse it. I demand, then, that you authorize me to travel, to avoid greater scandals. During that time you will reflect on the course it will be suitable for you to adopt. The day will come, Theobald, when you will return to yourself, and will perceive how unjust and cruel you have been to the mother of your children, in order to please a crackbrain who respects nothing."

"May 1, 1842.

"It is evident that Theobald makes towards me what is for him great advances; he has ever shown me real tenderness, and a sincere desire to change our manner of life. But does he truly wish, as he tells me, to adopt, if I land myself to it (these are his expressions) a life of intimacy, and to restore me to my natural position as a wife and a mother; do we comprehend each other in this respect? Does he clearly understand that I cannot be happy unless I possess his unlimited confidence, nor content myself unless I am restored to the possession of my position as mistress of the house, and particularly to the surveillance and direction of my children? Will he ever admit that? Will he ever dare to signify such a thing to Mademoiselle D——? I doubt it, for she will put the case to him, 'Choose between her and me,' and she will carry her point. My defects and the qualities of Mademoiselle D—— he regards at the same time through the same magnifying glass; I fear that he will cause himself a complete illusion; that he will imagine that, whilst I shall be mild, his affection and his reconciliation will suffice for me, and that I relinquish with a good grace all my rights as a wife and a mother: but he deceives himself, for it is for me a serious and a positive duty, as it is desirable, to return to the enjoyment of my rights towards my children. Under these circumstances, my rights are duties, and of the most sacred kind. He has, unfortunately, ideas the most false and the most dangerous in the relations which he ought to have with governesses, and on their position in a house. He forgets that nothing in the relations, the position, and the conduct of a governess, should be capable of giving rise to unpleasant interpretation; he trusts too much to the purity of his intentions. Faults consist in bad actions, but scandal arises from appearances; for one can only judge from what one sees, and scandal is a great evil, particularly on a question so delicate for a man of his age, with so young a governess, and whose natural character is frivolous, inconsistent, familiar, impertinent, coquettish, without tact, without a solid religious foundation, and overruling. He treats governesses as certain persons treat nurses—they spoil them until they become odious. With all that, he has not returned the china he took from me. What has he done with it? has he them still? At the bottom I believe it; will he return them to me? there is a world of *ifs* on that subject. He has not expressed regret as to what he has broken for me—he smiles when I speak to him of it. I am inclined to believe that he felt a slightest degree of anger on that point. It is very evident that he had a mind to our being reconciled. Never have I so strongly believed in his inclination in this respect. Will they let him do it? I much fear that he may yet be impelled to do many things, against which I shall not know how to confine myself to a quiet regret. I strongly feel that, in spite of my affection for him I cannot be happy if I do not occupy, in a complete and irrevocable manner, the same apartment with him, so as to return to that intimacy which naturally and alone brings about that pouring of the soul, that unlimited confidence, that double existence, which is the happiness of marriage; neither can I be so unless I participate in all his cares for my children and their society. But, my God! snatch from me, if it be necessary, every happiness, the affection of all those that I love, and reunite us one day in your bosom. Save us, my God! Give us eternal happiness, and do with us what seemeth fit to you in this life. My God, thou knowest that this is from the bottom of my heart. I wish for what seemeth fit for you; but give me strength and resignation to support it."

Paper found in the Duchess de Praslin's Secretary.

"PRASLIN, Sept. 14. 1842.

"You are, Theobald, I am convinced, far from suspecting your harshness towards me, and how much it makes me suffer. It is a very slow but a very painful death, I assure you, to die of grief. Oh, Theobald, how much I loved you! how much I loved your children! I have no longer anything in this world. Of our union nothing remains for me but your name. I live alone, forsaken, despised, and I have a husband and nine children; another, before my eyes, enjoys all these blessings! and you would have me think that natural! Well, I do say, and truly, that of all tortures, the most cruel that could be imposed on me is the life I lead. My God! what crime would not be expiated by such anguish! you no longer love me! you abandon me! though of all pains this is the most acute for me, who have never ceased to love you with so much ardor. I understand it; but, to deprive me of my children, Oh! no, you have no right to do that, Theobald. Can you be so weak and so blind as to abandon my children to a brainless woman—a woman without shame, without principles, without tact?"

Extract from a Letter without Date, found in the Duchess de Praslin's Secretary at Paris.

"I go, my dear Theobald, for I confess I no longer know what conduct to adopt; I thought I yesterday acted very well in quitting in silence, in order to avoid the bitterness with which you reproach me whenever I open my mouth. This new plan so badly succeeded with me, that I require time to collect my ideas as to what course I shall pursue. You have frequently repeated that you despise me; you have for so long a time proved it to me, that I unfortunately can no longer doubt it; but I admit that I do not well understand it. Besides, you sadly misunderstand me; you always suppose that I fix all my ideas on one guilty act, and I comprehend that that idea revolts you, particularly under these circumstances. It is not only this which is blameable and painful to affection; certainly to see you prefer the society of another, to give her all my rights to your friendship, to your confidence, to your intimacy, all those which I had over my children; these are real and profound subjects of grief. Add to this the pain of seeing my children in the hands of a person, who, because she commits no fault, takes upon herself to be inconsistent and familiar; to employ her influence to direct you, and take possession of all the house: who looks upon the usage of society as absurdities —candidly there is enough in this to cause unhappiness, sorrow, and anger. To continue life in that way is impossible. Call to mind that before all things I wish for happiness; but I cannot secure it to the price of my conscience. If I remain . . . I will propose an arrangement to you—reflect. If you are willing I will get my physician to order me sea-bathing, and will go alone to Carteret. I will stay three months; if the life you lead with Mademoiselle D— and our children suits you for a permanency, without having the trouble of a woman who wants to be the companion of her husband, and the mother of her children—if, in short, you prefer being a widower, tell me frankly, and I will stay there; if, on the contrary, after three months, you remember that you have a loving wife, and if you feel the want of a friend who will devote her life to you, then you will tell me so, and I should arrive very happy, very grateful. Do not accuse me of thoughtlessness in offering you this alternative. I wish you to be happy; I know that my presence is a burden, that my absence will be no privation, as I am of no use to anybody for anything, as things have gone on for some time past."

This letter is addressed, "M. le Duc."

Letter, without Date, found at Praslin.

"When I arrived here I hoped to have some moments of amusement and truce: but the illusion has not lasted long: the steps of the carriage had not been put down, before I saw in your icy, disdainful, and discontented air, in the constrained expression of the looks of my children, in the little green eyes which appeared behind your shoulder, that I was about to be subjected to the most humiliating treatment, to the most pain ful life, to support the spectacle of the most improper things, not to make use of a more appropriate phrase. Believe it, Theobald, if I still struggle, it is because I am firmly conscientious—because it is my duty not to renounce the struggle to obtain a factitious peace and tranquility, not to give by my silence an appearance of tacit consent to a state of things which concerns my children, and which I strongly disapprove, and because I firmly believe it to be detestable, grievous for the present: pernicious, dangerous in the future! You may do all that you will, I am still the mother of those children whom you give to the first comer. I know very well that you are the master, that you can do all you will with me: but there is one thing in which the rights of a wife are almost equal to those of a husband—you entirely forget that. Do you know, then, that the laws, if I were to invoke them, would decide in my favor? You know that I shall never do that; but is that a reason for making a bad use of it? You believe yourself obliged to cede in all things in order to preserve Mademoiselle D—, at every cost. You believe that it would be possible to replace her near you, near my children.

"But why do you, who believe it so simple, so easy to replace a mother, think it so prodigiously impossible to replace a governess? If you had desired it, she might have been a good governess, but you have changed her functions, her position—

and those who shine in the second rank are cast into the shade in the first. How is it possible that her head should not be turned when your conduct says to her every day, still more clearly than your words, 'I have a wife, but I prefer your society, your attentions. My children have a mother, but, though I scarcely know you, and you are younger, I have more confidence in your principles, your experience, your attentions, your devotedness, your manners, your judgment, your tenderness, to be everything to them. Take, then, the place—command, ordain; she who must be the mother of my children must be sovereign in my house?' . . . . When I had the weakness, by excess of love for you, to make you an immense sacrifice in abandoning my children to you, picturing to myself, in a guilty blindness, that this sacrifice, on account of its greatness, would most certainly restore me your affection. Persuaded by your promises in this respect, I committed, I admit, a great fault—I ought to have died sooner than have made this sacrifice. And I made a very false calculation, for this sacrifice made to my love gave you a bad opinion of my principles, my judgment, my heart. At present you have established a complete separation between us—we are nothing more than strangers one to another. Things cannot endure in their present state. Therefore, reflect: remember that I supplicate you to give me at least a becoming position, and an interest in life. Oh, but you are weak. You have arrived at such a point that you dare no longer go out with your wife and children without being accompanied by that person for whom you have taken from me what you gave me in the first days of our marriage. You are so much under her yoke that you dare undertake nothing without her. You would consider it wrong to leave her for a moment, and your wife, the mother of your children, must live and die alone."

Letter, without Date, found in the Secretary of the Duchess de Praslin.

"I cannot understand what are your views as to the future of our children, nor by what principles you direct your conduct, nor what is the nature of your sentiments with respect to me. You will not under any pretext read my letters, nor accord me a serious conversation, nor any explanation of any kind. If it be the dread of an explanation on your private conduct, you are wrong to fear that I will enter on that subject. I for a long while expected, hoped for that moment almost as much as I desired it, but it is now an illusion completely destroyed. You have too clearly proved that you no longer love me, and that all relations must cease between us, for me to be absurd enough to expect from you any mark of affection. I therefore only demand of you, I swear it, that which is not refused to any woman, unless she be a monster of corruption: and that is, the permission to do my duty towards my children, and to enjoy the consolation that I can find in the midst of them alone, in the services that I might render them and in their tenderness, to soften the bitter regrets that wring my heart at having lost your affection; I would have given all my blood to regain your tenderness, to enjoy it again for some moments, and then to die; but I have been cowardly, selfish, guilty, I admit it, in abandoning to you all my share of rights over our children, having pictured to myself that this sacrifice, greater a hundred times than that of my life, would touch you, that you would return to me, and that you would give yourself to me a second time.

"But I take Heaven to witness, I would never have made a similar concession for any motive, if I had not been convinced that you would put them in respectable hands, and that only for their instruction. Never, never would I have willingly consented to be deprived of all relations with my children, to no longer occupy myself with their health, with their comfort. But that was not the case. Never have I been sufficiently unnatural, sufficiently infamous, to renounce the care of my children, not to live with them, and to exercise no moral influence over them. You must be very blind not to see that you are in the hands of an *intrigante*. Yes, the person who is capable of profiting by the dissensions which she remarked between us on her arrival, in order to increase her authority, which has completely separated us, which has totally separated a mother from her children, is profoundly immoral, and unworthy of the confidence which you place in her. A woman who accepts such a false position is the most dangerous example for young girls; she purchases authority at the price of her reputation. Women who make such bargains have only another step to take to lose themselves in fact as they have already lost themselves in appearance. Having had the misfortune to thrust herself into a very false position, Mademoiselle D—— ought, if she had the sentiment of modesty, or the least tact, to have reserved manners, to act becomingly towards you; instead of which, by her conduct, shameless towards you, arrogant in the house, scandalous to me, she puts herself forward in a scandalous manner.

* * * * * *

"You will admit that I lead a shocking life, that you yourself would not support it. You say that it only depends on me to change it. Eh! mon Dieu! I know very well that, if I would consent to find everthing that Mdlle. D—— does charming, to close my eyes on what I find wrong, to appear not to perceive all that there is suspicious in the mysteries which surround you, to renounce the right of having a fixed opinion on certain principles, and on what is proper; I doubt not that, if I would say 'amen!' to all that I blame, my life would be quite different in appearance; that is to say, that you would consent to speak to me more graciously, as would also Mademoiselle D——; that I should sometimes be admitted to promenades and parties of pleasure; that you would consent to talk to me from time to time as you talk to anybody else; that you would come to see me some moments if I should be unwell; that you appear to take some interest in my health or my pleasures; that you would perhaps have some attentions for me, some presents to offer me."

Letter from the Duchess to Mademoiselle de Luzy, when at Turin with her eldest Daughter.

"PRASLIN, August 25, 1846.

"I wish not to delay a moment, my dear Mademoiselle, in thanking you for your kind letter, which gave a lively pleasure, and which, so far from thinking long, I could have wished to be double. I got it this evening, and I will not deny that it was time that letters had reached me, for my head and my heart were much excited by the long silence. I am happy, as you may guess, to hear all you tell me of Isabella's happiness, but I am much astonished that you find no change in her manners.

there is a very marked one in her letters. I thank you a thousand times for the details you have given me. * * * You say that Louise and Berthe speak of me often with Isabella. It is, perhaps, to give me pleasure that you write this; in any case you have completely succeeded, for I wept with joy. Once more, my dear Mademoiselle, I thank you a thousand times from the bottom of my heart for your letter, which I truly hope will not be the last.

"SEBASTIANI PRASLIN."

To the Same, written apparently on January 1, 1847, *found in the Residence of Mademoiselle de Luzy-Desportes.*

"It is forbidden us to retire to rest without being reconciled with our neighbors; much, more, it appears to me, ought the new year to put an end to all dissensions and obliterate all disputes. It is then heartily that I offer you my hand, Mademoiselle, and ask you to forget, in order that we may live well together henceforth, all the moments of pain that I have caused you; and I promise you, also, to pass the sponge over all the circumstances which, in mortifying me, have excited me to occasion them. Every one has his faults in this world, and I am induced to believe it is too happy. This ought to render us mutually more indulgent, and to facilitate reconciliation. I am truly convinced of your sincere and tender attachment to my children, and, believe me, that no one is more disposed than I am to show gratitude and affection to those who have been devoted to them, if I am not wounded to the heart by the thought that they are estranging them from me. You know as well as I do, that it is custom which causes attachment, especially with children. Not seeing their mother, she loses her place in their hearts, as in their life they end by doubting her love, happy if at a late period their esteem and their confidence are not shaken. Certainly this was not your object; for you must have known that it would be as pernicious to the children as sorrowful to the mother to destroy bonds so sacred. From one trifle to another, one comes to do things which at first one was far from conceiving. If, instead of irritating oneself about faults which are mutually confessed, we reciprocally overlook them, I believe that every one in this world would make a good bargain. It requires only to be a good driver, and go round the stone heaps instead of over them. For my part, I confess that I often come into collision. I had long intended to write to you to renew all our acquaintance with the year. It is, therefore, with double pleasure that I have received your charming work this evening, because it proves that you are also willing to put an end to a state of things which I am convinced cannot fail to be hurtful to the children, to place yourself often in a disagreeable and false position, and place me in one very cruel to me, who live isolated for so long a time from those dear affections in the midst of which I was so happy. I anticipate with great ardor the time when my daughters will be grown up, and I confess I suffer much in seeing them what they are towards me. But I am taking a long time to say that we ought to try to abandon a wrong course, to take another, and to beg you to receive and take up this gage of a new alliance, to which I hope you will consent."

To the Duke de Praslin.

[Written in pencil—no date.]

"You have a rare and precious talent at poisoning every thing. While your conduct influenced only the happiness of my life, it was my duty to be silent, and I was so. If you imagine, with your muttered words and your threats, to make people understand that I no more approve in public than in private the conduct of a person whom I despise, and who does not merit your confidence nor mine, you are right: for I think it a scandalous shame to allow the presence near young people of a woman who has proclaimed herself as she has done. I know well enough that you have other *liaisons*, and that it is not with her that your life is occupied, but she assumes the attitude. It is this which I have the right to blame. I do not pretend to busy myself with your private conduct and affections, but neither menaces nor ill treatment will prevent my repeating, as I have a right to do, that you deceive yourself in putting your children into the hands of a woman who has no care for her reputation, and has ceased to respect herself."

Another Letter found in the Secretary of the Duke de Praslin, at Praslin.

"PARIS, June 15, 1847.

"My dear Theobald—I have waited until this moment for the result of the promises that you renewed to me, on my return from Italy, to change the organization of our home. You appear to have forgotten them, and I find myself obliged to tell you that I do not think I ought to return to Praslin, without it be to re-enter on the exercise of my rights, and to fulfil my duties of mother and of mistress of the household in their fullest extent. The system of governesses has always succeeded badly with us, and it is time, for the welfare of our children and the dignity of our home, to abandon it. So long as my daughters shall not be married, I will reside everywhere among them, I will be present at all their occupations, I will accompany them everywhere. All my plans are formed, and when you shall have reflected, you will certainly find as many motives for confidence in the education of our daughters under the care of a mother as under that of a governess. Masters will supply as easily at Praslin as at Paris the lessons of a governess, who has always stood in need of their assistance. I have foreseen everything, and all will be easily arranged. My father, I know, has offered to Mademoiselle D—— an honorable pension for life. In going with it to England, her talents and her patrons will procure her a becoming position more easily than at Paris. You would be wrong to be disquieted with the grief that our daughters would feel; it would be much shorter and much less profound than you imagine—I have certain reasons for not doubting that. For a long time back you have expressed yourself with respect to the conduct of Mademoiselle D—— in a manner to leave no doubt that you have opened your eyes to a great part at least of its grave impropriety. What would secure her retirement in an honorable manner would be a pension from my father, guaranteed by me, and her journey to England, which would explain away favorably a sudden departure. By delicacy I first sought a supporter in your family in order to open your eyes; after having waited for the result in vain for years, I must at length submit to the legitimate desire of my father to speak to you in the name of the veritable interests of our children. When you, my natural supporter, fail me, I must let myself be guided by my father. I do not doubt that, when the first *ennui* shall have passed away, you will rejoice at a crisis which will re-establish natural order in our home. If it enters into your arrangements that Mademoiselle D—— shall return to Praslin to seek her things, I will wait until she shall return before going there: if they must simply be sent to her at Paris, I will start as soon as you please for Praslin. After all the rumors which have been current, I have shown her sufficient kindness to restore her kindness, as you pointed out to me, in so far as it depended on me, in order to make her leave with honor. I have fulfilled my task: the welfare of my children, that of their establishment, will not permit me to prolong by resignation a state of things pernicious to all. Let not the fear of recrimination on these painful matters torment you. It enters into my views as much as it does into yours not to return to them. My silence on previous circumstances almost the same is a sure guarantee of this to you. The first condition of family life is peace and a good understanding. That is my object, and it will be easily obtained when no attempts shall any longer be made to separate children from their mother, and to reign by division. It is not without serious reflection, nor without the assurance that I follow the opinion of my father, that I have determined to adopt such a serious resolution. It would have obtained, I am sure, the approval of my uncle de Coigny, who is to me the representative of my mother, if I had not avoided till now to speak to him of these sad details. My wishes are that everything shall be arranged between my father, you, and myself, without the intervention of other advisers. You have often expressed to me, my dear Theobald, the desire to see things take another face, because you really feel the discomfort of our home; but you always draw back. I now count on your co-operation, as in everything which concerns the happinessof our children.

"FANNY SEBASTIANI PRASLIN."

Impressions.

Friday, June 17, 1847.—I must repeat hourly to myself that I have accomplished a sacred duty towards my daughters, in consenting to join my efforts to those of my father to send away this woman. It caused me a great deal of pain. I hate *eclat*, but every one told me, as well as my own conscience, that it was my duty! My God! what will be the future? How he is incensed. One would think he was not the guilty one. He says he loves his children, and distrusts their mother, and makes his mistresses their governesses! What a life he is leading! He is losing all his energy. May God guide my children.

Letter of Duchess de Praslin to Mademoiselle de Luzy, a copy of which was found on Aug. 20, 1847, *in the Duke's Secretary at Paris.*

"June 19, 1847.

"Mdlle.—I regret exceedingly that you are unwell, and that in such a state you have taken the trouble to write to me* for a matter which your attention to my children rendered so nat-

---

* *Letter from Mdlle. de Luzy to the Duchess de Praslin on the* 17*th or* 18*th of June*, 1847.

"Madame la Duchess,—I should have liked to express to you in person the sentiments which animate me, but I feel that under present circumstances it would be a task above my strength. Permit me to postpone to a more calm and more happy period the thanks which I desire to express to you with my own lips for the generosity with which you remunerate my feeble services. At the moment of quitting children to whom I have devoted the most lively tenderness. I find in the testimony of your satisfaction a powerful consolation, I accept with gratitude the offers of recommendation which you have the goodness to make, and I shall hasten, Madame, to avail myself of them as soon as circumstance will render it advisable for me to do so. The ill health of my grandfather, exceedingly precarious for several months past, imposes on me the duty of being with him at present. I shall demand permission to inform you at a later period of the steps which I shall think advisable to take and I pray you, Madame, to accept the assurance of my profound regret.

"H. De Luzy."

ural. If circumstances important for their interests have precipitated an event which I regarded, only a few days back, as being still distant, do not doubt that I shall in consequence seek out with greater zeal all occasions to be useful to you, and that I shall be well pleased if you point me out the way. I have heard it said that you wish to go and see Lady Hislop; if that be the case, I can offer you a letter to Lady Tankerville, who, I am certain, will earnestly second Lady Hislop in all her endeavors to forward your plans. If you thought fit to have letters for Mde. Flahaut and Miss Elphinstone, dispose of me freely. I remember you asked me to lend you a book on arriving at Praslin; I hope you will not refuse to accept that little souvenir, which I have great pleasure in offering to you. I am anxious to repeat to you, Mademoiselle, that I shall seize with eagerness on all occasions that occur, and such as you may be pleased to afford me, to be of use to you.

"S. PRASLIN."

Document found at Paris, in the Duchess's Secretaire, in a sealed Envelope, also entitled "Impressions."

"July 18, 1847.

"It is long since I have written anything, and nevertheless nothing has changed in the interval. She will leave, they say, when we go to Praslin; and in the meantime the empire she holds is most absolute. Father and children, she retains them all as in a special bond. I understand her game well enough, if she has really swallowed all shame; but for him, I cannot explain his conduct. He complains of calumny: but he confesses that appearances are bad, and he makes these appearances every day worse, and gives more grounds for all the scandalous interpretations. He pretends that their relations are misinterpreted, and yet he publicly proclaims the rupture with my father on her account.* He breaks with us, and does not

---

* *Letter from Marshal Sébastiani to the Duke de Praslin, found in the desk of the Duke de Præslin.*

"Monsier le Duke,—You have caused me great pain. You have attributed to want of feeling my closing my house to you and your children. You are obliged to render me justice. I did all that was in my power to avoid this

leave her. No character can be more enigmatical. Is it excess of corruption? or is it excess of weakness? Were it excess of weakness, could that go to the length of making him so trample on the interests of his children? What, could he have so much fear of this woman as not to dare, while she is in the house, to leave his children with their mother, or show regard to his wife? What has given her this empire over him?—it is not natural. She must have some means by which she makes her threats powerful over him. Poor man, I sincerely grieve for him. What a life he leads! What a future he is preparing for himself! If he allows himself to be thus domineered over and browbeaten by *intrigantes* at forty-two, what will he be when he grows old! And yet, how I love him! He must have been sadly changed by all these bad habits; for, on seeing what he is now, I cannot say what inspired in me this love so impassioned. He is no longer the same man; how dull is his spirit, how harrowed his heart—how much he has grown suspicious, ennuied, and irritable. Nothing animates him, nothing interests him, nothing exalts him. No generous, impassioned, or enthusiastic sentiment seems to vibrate in his heart or mind. He had rank, fortune—all that could render his existence useful, brilliant, happy and honorable. All is galvanized; he interests himself in nothing either for his country or for his children. He keeps company with governesses; he is their *cavalier servante* till he becomes their slave. Truly, I believe that he only wishes to keep Mdlle. D. (whom he has not loved for this eighteen months or two years), because he fears, if once removed

---

separation which you feel so much. I took upon myself the odious task of pretending to be ignorant of what all Paris and the journals spoke of, and for this generous conduct you address me in a letter of violent and undeserved reproaches. I never mentioned the name of Mdlle. de Luzy to any one. I am ready to say anything that may favor her interests, but be considerate, and do not ask what is impossible. I do not see my daughter for fear of prepossessing you against her. You were the first to deprive me of the pleasure of seeing my grandchildren. I do not deserve such treatment. You should consult the interests of those young people. Did I ever act towards you in such a manner as to deserve this treatment? But you are not yourself, and I excuse you. You have a good heart, listen to its impulses, and you will render me justice.

"H. SEBASTIANI.

"When you are as old as I am, you will reproach yourself with having acted harshly toward me."

hence, she would make life too hard for him. My God! what an existence! What is curious is that I am sane. He firmly believes that it is on account of jealousy that I wish the departure of Mdlle. D. He will not comprehend that my moving principle is, and will henceforth ever be, my children. He believes that it is my jealous love for him, and this flatters him. It is singular; but I do not doubt that, if he had not believed my love inextinguishable, he would have treated me less unworthily. What an illusion—what an excess of self-love! Yet it would perhaps have been possible to preserve, at the bottom of one's heart, love for a man who has treated you as he has treated me; if, on the other hand, this man excites our admiration, and elevates himself in our eyes by grand actions and great works. But a grovelling and an ordinary man, one loves only if he is just, if he is good, if he is conscientious, if he renders your life happy. It is not necessary that he should do great things, but he must know how to appreciate them. I cannot tell how far this contempt and *ennui* at all things, this total impossibility of taking a lively interest in anything, has completely cooled my feelings towards him. I thought him so different. Oh, he must have been so; I could never have loved him if he had been always what he is! Certainly, there was stuff in his heart, in his understanding; but the want of firm principles of morality and religion, and his idleness of mind, have caused him to succumb to sensual passions. And with all this, he wishes to educate his daughters! How completely has he isolated himself. He has not one real, serious friend. He has no connexions but those which have sprung from his pleasures, and which have become chains from his weakness when he wished to detach himself from them. How frightful it is! He drags after him, like a dog, the exigencies of women with whom he has been connected. And yet how *bizarre* are men. He has always sacrificed, oppressed, wounded, humiliated, ill-treated, and abandoned me, for persons he did not love. For my part, I have loved only him, and with a passion inexpressible—an ardor which astonishes me; and now I know not but that, at the bottom of his heart he, perhaps, prefers me to those women whom he despises and fears; and I—I am well disenchanted with him. He will be always unkind to me now; he is too well aware of the extent of his wrongs, and cannot comprehend that I can forgive and forget. My merit would not be so great as he thinks. I cannot be jealous except when I love, and then I can easily forgive: and since my sentiments are changed I can have no further feelings towards him but on account of the wrongs he does my children. Our position is very strange and very sad. While he has run after pleasure, I have been secluded from it. He has had enjoyments and no love—love for me has been extinguished in tears, and I have not..... But what has been worn out by one has perhaps been preserved by the other, and reciprocally..... How will all this end? I do not believe that this can ever be by a complete reconciliation, as would be desirable for our children. He will always avoid me, because he is conscious of his wrong, and I shall never seek him but from duty to my children. A feeling of shame will always prevent my making advances to a man, even though my husband, when I doubt my love for him, and when I feel that other ideas, repressed for so many years, have, rather than my affection, urged me to his arms.

"My God! you alone know what privations of the affections and all other kinds I have suffered. If I have not yielded to temptation, the glory be thine, O Lord! O abandon me not now, for without thee I shall sink! My God! My God! support me, direct me; I fear the future, the threats he has made to me, the difficulties which arise daily—but thou wilt be there, my God, and in that is my trust that thou wilt support the poor mother to whom thou hast given strength to strive for her children. Lord, help me!"

The exquisite tenderness and eloquence of these epistles have become world-wide in reputation. We regret that our limited space in this volume will not permit the publication of all the letters. In those which we furnish may be found an exhibition of that burning love and deep devotion which animated the duchess through life towards her husband. How much strength of feeling and melancholy do they not display! How much of the mother, the wife, and the woman! Nothing in language has ever more prominently portrayed the anguish of a bleeding heart, struck, as she believed it, by the neglect and inconstancy of her husband. Often in the silence of her chamber, with the lamp dimly burning, alone with her thoughts, did she sit and pen the beautiful effusions which were in after years to bring tears of sympathy to the eyes of the reader, and raise up thousands of mourners over her unhappy fate. At midnight when all the household was buried in sleep, and the poor lady heard nothing but the beating of her own heart, would she draw over to her table and indite these touching impressions and diary which we have just printed. The duchess found relief in writing in this strain. When the heart is overflowing and the mind almost mad with meditation, the patient finds satisfaction in pouring forth on paper words of sorrow. It was thus with Madame la Duchesse. There is little doubt but that her domestic sufferings were intense. An amiable and sensitive lady she must have been. Those who knew her intimately, have spoken of her as one in whom was centred all the virtues and religious enthusiasm peculiar to the French Christian. No wonder then that her writings should express vividly the interior terrible agitation of the woman. When she appealed to the honor of her husband, begged and beseeched of him to return and once more become re-united, words can scarcely be expressed more pathetically, or with more force. Her very soul seemed to gush forth at the pen's point, and the throbbing of her broken heart to have kept time with its nimble motion, as it traced on paper the history of her life and sufferings. Her words were written—

> So softly, that like flakes of feathered snow
> They melted as they fell.

An official copy of the trial, together with the letters, impressions, and diary of the duchess, and other matters connected with the tragedy, was published in Paris in the year 1847, by M. Crapelet. There is a copy of this work now extant in this city. From it and other volumes the foregoing details are compiled. Many who read this history will drop a tear to the memory of the unfortunate duchess. All will feel a sympathy for her terrible fate.

Her memory will ever be revered by history, while the unfortunate Duke who was the perpetrator of this deed of blood, will be remembered with detestation. In his disposition, the Duke was described as a man rather moody and reserved. Some went so far as to assert that the murder was committed while the culprit labored under a fit of insanity. This is certainly a most charitable view to take of the matter. It is difficult to imagine, that a man possessed of so amiable a wife could be guilty of her murder, and that murder committed in such a horrible manner, as to shock the sensibilites of the most hardened. Surely he must have been influenced by some powerful incentive. What that incentive could be, does not appear very clear. Some facts have appeared to prove that the murder was premeditated. Others point to the conclusion, that a serious wordy warfare ensued between the Duke and Duchess, relative to the letter which Madame Lemaire required in refutation of the reports, as to Mlle. Deluzy's character. On the examination it was proved that the unfortunate lady received thirty wounds. Her struggles must have been very severe, blood being scattered over all the apartment and furniture. A map of the room pointing out the spots of blood, the bed, the furniture and different positions of the parties, is annexed to M. Crapelet's official account of the various examinations. A glance at the map clearly conveys how terrible must have been the struggle between the dying wife and her murderer.

EARL FERRERS' MURDER OF HIS STEWARD.

HIS TRIAL, CONVICTION AND EXECUTION.

Lawrence Earl Ferrers, who lived during the reign of George II., was an English nobleman of a violent spirit, who had committed many outrages, and, in the opinion of all who knew him, given manifold proofs of insanity. He at length, in the year 1760, perpetrated a murder, which subjected him to the cognizance of justice. His deportment to his lady was so brutal, that application had been made to the House of Peers, and a separation effected. Trustees were nominated; and one Mr. Johnson, who had, during the best part of his life, been employed in the family, was now appointed receiver of the estates, at the earl's own request. The conduct of this man, in the course of his stewardship, gave umbrage to Lord Ferrers, whose disposition was equally jealous and vindictive. He imagined all his own family had conspired against his interest, and that Johnson was one of their accomplices; that he had been instrumental in obtaining the act of parliament, which his lordship considered as a grievous hardship; that he had disapproved him in regard to a certain contract about coal-mines; in a word, that there was a collusion between Johnson and the earl's adversaries. Fired with these suppositions, he first expressed his sentiments, by giving Johnson notice to quit the farm which he possessed on the estate; but, finding the trustees had confirmed the lease, he determined to gratify his revenge by assassination, and laid his plan accordingly. On Sunday, the 13th of January, he appointed this unhappy man to come to his house on the Friday following, in order to peruse some papers, or settle his accounts; and Johnson went thither without the least suspicion of what was prepared for his reception; for, although he was no stranger to his lordship's dangerous disposition, and knew he had some time before incurred his displeasure, yet he had imagined his resentment had entirely subsided, as the earl had of late behaved to him with remarkable complacency. He therefore, at the time appointed, repaired to his lordship's house at Stanton, in Leicestershire, at the distance of a short mile from his own habitation, and was admitted by a maid-servant. The earl had dismissed every person in the house, upon various pretences, except three women, who were left in the kitchen. Johnson, advancing to the door of his apartment, was received by his lordship, who desired him to walk into another room, where he joined him in a few minutes, and then the door was locked on the inside. After a great deal of warm expostulation, the earl insisted upon his subscribing a paper, acknowledging himself a villain; and, on his refusing to comply with this demand, he declared he would put him to death. In vain the unfortunate man remonstrated against this cruel injustice, and deprecated the indignation of this furious nobleman. He remained deaf to all his intreaties, drew forth a pistol, which he had loaded for the purpose, and, commanding him to implore heaven's mercy on his knees, shot him through the body, while he remained in the supplicating attitude. The consequence of this violence was not immediate death; but his lordship, seeing the wretched victim still alive and sensible, though agonized with pain, felt a momentary motion of pity. He ordered his servants to convey Mr. Johnson up stairs to a bed, to send for a surgeon, and give immediate notice of the accident to the wounded man's family. When Mr. Johnson's daughter came to the house, she was met by the earl, who told her he had shot her father on purpose, and with deliberation. The same declaration he made to the surgeon, on his arrival. He stood by him while he examined the wound, described the manner in which the ball had penetrated, and seemed surprised that it should be lodged within the body. When he demanded the surgeon's opinion of the wound, the operator thought proper to temporize, for his own safety as well as for the sake of the public, lest the earl should take some other desperate step, or endeavor to escape. He supported his spirits by immoderate drinking, after having retired to another apartment with the surgeon, whom he desired to take all possible care of his patient. He declared, however, that he did not repent of what he had done; that Johnson was a villain, who deserved to die; that, in case of his death, he (the earl) would surrender himself to the House of Peers and take his trial. He said he could justify the action to his own conscience, and owned his intention was to have killed Johnson outright; but, as he still survived, and was in pain, he desired that all possible means may be used for his recovery. Nor did he seem altogether neglectful of his own safety; he endeavored to tamper with the surgeon, and suggest what evidence he should give, when called before a court of justice. He continued to drink himself into a state of intoxication, and all the cruelty of his hate seemed to return. He would not allow the wounded man to be removed to his own house; saying, he would keep him under his own roof, that he might plague the villain. He returned to the chamber where Johnson lay, insulted him with the most opprobrious language, threatened to shoot him through the head, and could hardly be restrained from committing farther acts of violence on the poor man, who was already in extremity. After he retired to bed, the surgeon procured a sufficient number of assistants, who conveyed Mr. Johnson in an easy chair to his own house, where he expired that same morning in great agonies. The same surgeon assembled a number of armed men to seize the murderer, who at first threatened resistance, but was soon apprehended, endeavoring to make his escape, and committed to the county prison. From thence he was conveyed to London by the gaoler of Leicester, and conducted by the usher of the black-rod and his deputy into the House of Lords, where the coroner's inquest, and the affidavit touching the murder, being read, the goaler delivered up his prisoner to the care of the black-rod, and he was immediately committed to the Tower. He appeared very calm, composed, and unconcerned, from the time of his being apprehended; conversed coolly on the subject of his imprisonment; made very pertinent remarks upon the nature of the habeas corpus act of parliament, of which he hoped to avail himself; and when they withdrew from the House of Peers, desired he might not be visited by any of his relations or acquaintances. His understanding, which was naturally good, had been well cultivated; his arguments were rational, but his conduct was frantic.

The lord-keeper Henley was appointed lord high-steward for the trial of Earl Ferrers, and sat in state with all the peers and judges in Westminster Hall, which was for this purpose converted into a very august tribunal. On the 16th day of April, the delinquent was tried, in the midst of an infinite concourse of people, including many foreigners, who seemed wonderfully struck with the magnificence and solemnity of the tribunal. The murder was fully proved; but the earl pleaded insanity of mind; and, in order to establish this plea, called many witnesses to attest his lunacy in a variety of instances, which seemed too plainly to indicate a disordered imagination; unfounded jealousy of plots and conspiracies, unconnected ravings, fits of musing, incoherent ejaculations, sudden starts of fury, denunciations of unprovoked revenge, frantic gesticulations, and a strange caprice of temper, were proved to have distinguished his conduct and deportment. It appeared that lunacy had been a family taint, and affected divers of his lordship's relations; that a solicitor of reputation had renounced his business on the full persuasion of his being disordered in his brain; that, long before this unhappy event, his nearest relations had deliberated upon the expediency of taking out a commission of lunacy against him, and were prevented by no other reason than the apprehension of being convicted of *scandalum magnatum*, should the jury find his lordship *compos mentis;* a circumstance, which, in all probability, would have happened, inasmuch as the earl's madness did not appear in his conversation, but in his conduct. A physician of eminence, whose practice was confined to persons laboring under this infirmity, declared, that the particulars of the earl's deportment and personal behavior seemed to indicate lunacy. Indeed, all his neighbors and acquaintances had long considered him as a madman; and a certain noble lord declared in the House of Peers, when the bill of separation was on the carpet, that he looked upon him in the light of a maniac; and that, if some effectual step was not taken to divest him of the power of doing mischief, he did not doubt that one day they should have occasion to try him for murder. The lawyers who managed the prosecution in behalf of the crown, endeavored to invalidate the proofs of his lunacy, by observing, that his lordship was never so much deprived of his reason but that he could distinguish between good and evil: that the murder he had committed was the effect of revenge for a conceived injury of some standing; that the malice was deliberate, and the plan artfully conducted; that, immediately after the deed was perpetrated, the earl's conversation and reasoning were cool and consistent, until he drank himself into a state of intoxication; that, in the opinion of the greatest lawyers, no criminal can avail himself of the plea of lunacy, provided the crime be committed during a lucid interval; but his lordship, far from exhibiting any marks of insanity, had, in the course of his trial, displayed uncommon understanding and sagacity in examining the witnesses, and making many shrewd and pertinent observations on the evidence which was given. These sentiments were conformable to the opinion of the Peers, who unanimously declared him guilty.

The trial lasted for two days; and on the third the lord steward, after having made a short speech touching the heinous nature of the offence, pronounced the same sentence of death upon the earl which the malefactors of the lowest class undergo: that from the Tower, in which he was imprisoned, he should' on the Monday following, be led to the common place of execution, there to be hanged by the neck, and his body to be afterward dissected and anatomized. This last part of the sentence seemed to shock the criminal extremely; he changed color, his jaw quivered, and he appeared to be in great agitation; but during the remaining part of his life he behaved with surprising composure, and even unconcern. After he had received sentence, the lords, his judges, by virtue of a power vested in them, respited his execution for one month, that he might have time to settle his temporal and spiritual concerns. Before sentence was passed, the earl read a paper, in which he begged pardon of their lordships for the trouble he had given, as well as for having, against his own inclination, pleaded lunacy at the request of his friends. He thanked them for the candid trial with which he had been indulged, and intreated their lordships to recommend him to the king for mercy. He afterwards sent a letter to his majesty, remonstrating that he was the representative of a very ancient and honorable family, which had been allied to the crown; and requesting that, if he could not be favored with the species of death which in cases of treason distingushes the nobleman from the plebeian, he might at least, out of consideration for his family, be allowed to suffer in the Tower, rather than at the common place of execution; but this indulgence was refused. From his return to the Tower to the day of his execution, he betrayed no mark of apprehension or impatience; but regulated his affairs with precision, and conversed without concern or restraint.

On the 5th day of May, his body being demanded by the sheriffs at the Tower-gate, in consequence of a writ under the great seal of England, directed to the lieutenant of the Tower, his lordship desired permission to go in his own landau; and appeared gayly dressed in a light-colored suit of clothes, embroidered with silver. He was attended in the landau by one of the sheriffs and the chaplain of the Tower, followed by the chariots of the sheriffs, a mourning coach and six filled with his friends, and a hearse for the conveyance of his body. He was guarded by a posse of constables, a party of horse-grenadiers, and a detachment of infantry; and in this manner the procession moved from the Tower, through an infinite concourse of people, to Tyburn, where the gallows, and the scaffold erected under it, appeared covered with black baize. The earl behaved with great composure to Mr. Sheriff Vaillant, who attended him in the landau: he observed, that the gayety of his apparel might seem odd on such an occasion, but that he had particular reasons for wearing that suit of clothes; he took notice of the vast multitude which crowded around him, brought thither, he supposed, by curiosity, to see a nobleman hanged; he told the sheriff he had applied to the king by letter, that he might be permitted to die in the Tower, where the Earl of Essex, one of his ancestors, had been beheaded in the reign of Queen Elizabeth; an application which, he said, he had made with the more confidence, as he had the honor to quarter part of his majesty's arms. He expressed some displeasure at being executed as a common felon, exposed to the eyes of such a multitude. The chaplain, who had never been admitted to him before, hinting that some account of his lordship's sentiments on religion would be expected by the public, made answer that he did not think himself accountable to the public for his private sentiments: that he had always adored one God, the creator of the universe; and with respect to any particular opinion of his own, he had never propagated them, or endeavored to make proselytes, because he thought it was criminal to disturb the established religion of his country, as Lord Bolingbroke had done by the publication of his writings. When he approached the place of execution, he expressed an earnest desire to see and take leave of a certain person who waited in a coach, a person for whom he entertained the most sincere regard and affection; but the sheriff prudently observing that such an interview might shock him, at a time when he had occasion for all his fortitude and recollection, he acquiesced in the justness of the remark, and delivered to him a pocket-book, a ring, and a purse, desiring they might be given to that person, whom he now declined seeing. On his arrival at Tyburn, he came out of the landau, and ascended the scaffold with a firm step and undaunted countenance. He refused to join the chaplain in his devotions; but kneeling with him on black cushions, he repeated the Lord's prayer, which he said he had always admired; and added with great energy, "O Lord, forgive me all my errors, pardon all my sins." After this exercise, he presented his watch to Mr. Sheriff Vaillant; thanked him and the other gentlemen for all their civilities; and signified his desire of being buried at Breden, or Stanton, in Leicestershire. Finally, he gratified the executioner with a purse of money; then, the halter being adjusted to his neck, he stepped upon a little stage, erected upon springs, on the middle scaffold; and the cap being pulled over his eyes, the sheriff made a signal, at which the stage fell from under his seet, and he was left suspended. His body, having hung an hour and five minutes, was cut down, placed in the hearse, and conveyed to the public theatre for dissection; where, being opened, and lying for some days as the subject of a public lecture, at length it was carried off and privately interred.

THE RED BARN TRAGEDY.

MURDER OF MARIA MARTEN.—TRIAL, CONVICTION AND EXECUTION OF THE ASSASSIN, WILLIAM CORDER.

The murder for which this criminal underwent condign punishment equalled in cold-blooded atrocity any of the murders that are recorded in this work.

Maria Marten, the victim, was born in July, 1801, and was the daughter of a mole catcher, at Polstead, in Suffolk, England, through whom she received an education far superior to her situation in life. Possessed of more than ordinary personal advantages, she was beset by admirers, and the result was that she lost her character as a virtuous young woman; a second act of imprudence with a gentleman of fortune, residing at no great distance from her father's cottage, resulted in the birth of a child; and about the year 1826 she formed an improper connexion with Corder, the son of a respectable farmer at Polstead, who afterwards became her murderer.

The consequence of this intercourse between Maria Marten and him was that she again became pregnant, and from that time he professed to have become much attached to her, and was a frequent visitor at her father's house. The child which she bore died within a short period of its birth, and, from the fact of its having died without any known previous illness, and of Corder having disposed of the body in a manner which he never would explain, a suspicion was current that it had come unfairly by its death. However much this notion may have prevailed after the subsequent apprehension of Corder, it does not appear that any evidence was ever produced to support it; but it transpired that the unhappy girl made use of the circumstance as a means of endeavoring to coerce Corder to fulfil a promise which he had made, that he would marry her.

On the 18th of May, 1827, Corder called at the house of old Marten, expressed his willingness that the ceremony should be performed, and added that, to save time, and to keep the marriage as private as possible, he had made up his mind to have it celebrated by license. The next day was appointed for the wedding, and he persuaded the young woman to attire herself in a suit of his clothes, so as to secure the greatest secresy, and to accompany him to a part of his premises called the Red Barn, where she could exchange them for her own, and from whence he would convey her in a gig, which he had in readiness, to a church at Ipswich. She having consented to this singular proposition, Corder quitted the house, and was soon after followed by his intended victim, who carried with her the clothes in which she expected to appear at church. In the course of a conversation between Corder and the mother, before going away, he repeatedly declared his intention to make the girl his wife, and he urged as a reason why the wedding should take place at once, that he knew a warrant had been issued against her for her illegitimate children. Within a few minutes after Corder had quitted the house, he was seen by Maria's brother walking in the direction of the Red Barn with a pick-axe over his shoulder; but from this time nothing was heard of the young woman, execpt through Corder himself, who remained for some time at his mother's house at Polstead. The return of Maria Marten had been expected by her parents in a day or two, but as she had, on former visits to Corder, been absent for uncertain periods, little anxiety was felt at her non-appearance, more especially as he had stated that he should procure a temporary lodging for her. A fortnight, however, having elapsed, her mother began to question Corder, who assured her that her daughter was quite safe and well, but that he had placed her at some distance, lest his friends should discover the fact of his marriage, of which all parties knew they would not approve. Having thus from time to time evaded the inquiries made of him, he, avowing himself to be in ill health, in September departed from suffolk, with the professed object of visiting the continent; but, before quitting Polstead he had taken good care that the Red Barn should be amply stored. He took with him about £400 in money; and the several letters which were transmitted by him to his widowed mother, as well as those which he sent to the Martens, were dated from the Isle of Wight, in which place he informed the latter their daughter was living with him. It was noticed, however, that these letters, though so dated, always bore the London postmark; and as no communication was received from the daughter herself, the Martens, who had already had strong suspicions regarding their daughter's safety, became exceedingly uneasy and dissatisfied. The circumstances which eventually led to the discovery of Corder's atrocity are of so extraordinary and marvellous a character, as almost to manifest an especial interposition of Providence in bringing to light the offence and the offender. In the month of March of the following year (1828), Mrs. Marten dreamed, on three successive nights, that her daughter had been murdered and buried in the Red Barn!! Terrified at the three-fold repetition of the vision, an undefined suspicion took full possession of her mind; and so convinced did she become of the truth of the augury, that on Saturday, the 19th of April, she persuaded her husband to apply for permission to examine the Red Barn.

The grain which had been there deposited had by this time been removed, and old Marten, permission being given, proceeded in his search. He applied himself to the spot pointed out to his wife in her dream, and there he speedily turned up a piece of the shawl which he knew his daughter had with her when she quitted home. Prosecuting his search, he found at the depth of eighteen inches part of a human body. Horror-stricken, he staggered from the spot; but, on subsequently renewing his painful labor, he felt convinced that his wife's surmises were well founded, and that the remains which he had thus discovered were indeed those of his long-lost child. The body was in an advanced state of decomposition, but the dress and some peculiarities in the teeth afforded sufficient proofs of its identity.

The whole neighborhood was, of course, thrown into dismay at this most extraordinary discovery, and information of the fact was forwarded to the coroner. The body underwent a surgical examination by Mr. John Lawden, who proved to the jury assembled to investigate the circumstances, that there were sufficient appearances yet remaining to indicate that the deceased had met with a violent death. He said that there were visible signs of blood on the face and clothes, and also on a handkerchief round the neck of the deceased—that the handkerchief appeared to have been tied extremely tight, and beneath the folds a wound was visible in her throat, evidently inflicted by some sharp instrument. There was also a wound in the orbit of the right eye, and it seemed as if something had been thrust in which had fractured the small bones, and penetrated the brain. The body, when found, was partly enveloped in a sack, and had on a shift, flannel petticoat, stays, stockings, and shoes.

As may be supposed, all eyes were at once directed to Corder as the murderer, and information having been dispatched to London, Lea, a police officer, commenced an active pursuit of him. In the meanwhile, as it afterwards transpired, Corder had married a most respectable female, with whom he had become acquainted by means of advertising in the newspapers. Revolting as this mode of procuring a matrimonial alliance may appear to the delicate-minded, it is nevertheless a fact that his advertisement procured hundreds of answers, a vast proportion of which remained unopened in the hands of the respectable stationer in the city of London, who had been induced to receive them, long after Corder had made his election in favor of the lady who, so unhappily for herself, had blended her fortunes with his. Lea, the officer, traced Corder from place to place, and at length learned that he resided at Grove House, Ealing Lane, near Brentford, where, in conjunction with his wife, he was carrying on a school for young ladies. It was necessary to employ some degree of stratagem to obtain admission to the house—and Lea, on presenting himself, stated that he had a daughter whom he wished to place in the school. He was invited into the parlor, and there found the object of his search at breakfast with four ladies. He was in his dressing-gown, and had his watch before him, as he was boiling some eggs. Lea called him aside, and, after telling him that he had a serious charge against him, asked if he was not acquainted with Maria Marten, of Polstead? Corder replied in the negative, saying also that he never heard of such a person, even by name. He was then secured, and the house searched, when a brace of pistols, a powder-flask, and some balls were found in a velvet bag, which, on being shown to Mrs. Marten, was identified as having been in the possession of her daughter when she last quitted home. A sharp-pointed dagger was also found, and this was identified by a person named Offord, a cutler, as one which he had ground for the prisoner a few days before the murder. Corder was conducted to Polstead to undergo an examination before the coroner, and the greatest anxiety was evinced by the vast crowds assembled to catch a glimpse of him. He was dreadfully agitated, and the circumstances which we have described having been deposed to by various witnesses, a verdict of "Wilful murder" was the result.

The prisoner was thereupon committed to the county gaol to await his trial; but he had hardly been lodged within its walls before a new charge, namely, that of forgery upon the Manningtree Bank, was laid against him. It appears, however, that through the intervention of his friends this was eventually compromised. His wife, upon his first apprehension, was under an impression that the offence imputed to him was that of bigamy, but she was soon informed of the real nature of the allegations. Previous to his trial, she visited him nearly every day, and she continued to declare her belief that the statements in the papers were untrue, and that he would eventually be relieved by a jury of his countrymen from the foul calumnies which were published against him.

Thursday, the 7th of August following, was appointed for the trial, and the desire to witness the proceedings, or to obtain early information relating thereto, was manifested by the hundreds of well-dressed persons of both sexes assembled about the court-house.

Nor was public curiosity confined to the court-house. A multitude had early gathered round the door of the gaol, and along the road leading thence to the Shire Hall, to get a view of the accused. He was conducted from the gaol at a quarter before nine o'clock, being attired in a new suit of black, which he had put on with much care, and having his hair combed over his forehead, which he had previously worn brushed up in front. Upon being called from his cell, he made some inquiries as to the number of witnesses to be called against him, and also as to the judges by whom he was to be tried; and his que ries having been answered, he exclaimed, "Well, whatever may be my fate, I shall meet it with fortitude." He was removed in a chaise-cart from the gaol to the place of trial, and, although he hung down his head all the way, he seemed little affected by the shouting and groaning with which he was assailed on all sides. On being taken to the felon's room, beneath the building, he remarked to Mr. Orridge, the governor of the prison, "What a great number of persons! I scarcely ever saw such a crowd." At a quarter past ten o'clock, the prisoner was placed at the bar. For a few moments he conversed with his solicitor, but then he looked up to the bench, and bowed respectfully. On account of the number of challenges made by the prisoner, it was some time before a jury was empannelled. At length, however, the prisoner was arraigned. The indictment contained ten counts. In the first the murder was alleged to have been committed by the prisoner on the 18th of May, 1827, by discharging a pistol, loaded with powder and shot, upon Maria Marten, and thereby giving her a mortal wound on the left side of the face; and that by those means, wilfully, feloniously, and of his malice aforethought, he caused the death of the said Maria Marten. The second count laid the offence as having been committed by striking the deceased with a sword upon the left side of the body, between the fifth and sixth ribs, and thereby giving her a mortal wound, of which she instantly died; the third count stated that the murder was committed by striking the deceased with a sword on the left side of the face; the fourth, that it was done by sticking and stabbing her with a sword on the right side of the neck; the fifth, that the prisoner fastened a handkerchief around her neck, and thereby choked her; the sixth, that he killed her by discharging a gun, loaded with powder and shot, on the left side of her face; the seventh, that he pushed and thrust her into a hole made in the floor of a barn, and, by covering her with large quantities of earth and gravel, suffocated and choked her; the eighth was only technically different from the preceding one; the ninth laid the offence to have been committed by the joint means of sticking the deceased with a sword on the left side, and fastening a handkerchief round her neck; the tenth described it as being done by the joint force of all the felonious acts laid in the whole of the preceding counts—recapitulating the wounds, stabbing, shooting, strangulation, and smothering, as the cause of the death of the deceased.

The prisoner having pleaded "Not Guilty," in a firm and distinct voice, the trial commenced. The evidence developed the circumstances as we have detailed them. The first and sixth counts of the indictment were sustained by proving that at the time of the discovery of the body marks were distinctly visible, which showed that she had received a wound from a pistol or a gun-shot, and it was also proved by the brother of the deceased, that the prisoner, at the time of quitting the house of old Marten, on the day of the murder, carried a gun. A number of letters, written to the deceased's father by the prisoner, in reference to his intended marriage with his daughter, were also put in.

On being called upon for his defence, Corder read a manuscript paper in a low and tremulous tone. He declared that he deeply deplored the death of the unfortunate deceased; and he urged the jury to dismiss from their minds all that prejudice which must necessarily have been excited against him, by the foul imputations of the public press. He admitted that the evidence was fraught with suspicion against him; but he trusted in being able to give such an explanation of the circumstances as would develop, to their satisfaction, the real facts of the case. He then proceeded to say "No man regrets more sincerely than I do the death of the unfortunate Maria, the circumstances attending which I am now about to state; and much have I to regret that I for a moment concealed them, but I did so because I was stupefied and horror-struck at the time, and knew not how to act. You have heard of the nature of my connection with the unfortunate Maria; that connection was contrary to the will of my mother, and to conceal her situation, I took lodgings for her at Sadbury, where she was confined. In the usual time she returned to her father's house; in a fortnight after which the infant died; not, as has been intimated, by violence, but a natural death. Being anxious to conceal the circumstances from my friends and neighbors, it was agreed between her father, and mother, and myself, that Maria and I should bury the child in the fields, and we took it away for that purpose. After this Maria returned to my house at Polestead; and by means of a private staircase I took her to my own room, where she remained concealed for two days. The pistols which have been spoken of were hanging up in the room, loaded. I had before that shown her the use of them, and on returning to her father's, she, by some means unknown to me, contrived to get the pistols into her possession. It is well known that at that period Maria was much depressed in spirits, and was anxious that I should marry her, although I had reason to suspect that she was at the time in correspondence with a gentleman in London by whom she had had a child. My friends objected to the match, and I declined it at that time. But although poor Maria's conduct was not altogether free from blame, I was much attached to her, and at length agreed to her wishes; and it was arranged that we should go to Ipswich and obtain a license for that purpose Whether I did or did not say anything about a warrant having been issued by the parish officers for her apprehension, I cannot now pretend to say; but if I did, it must have been because such a report was abroad at the time. It was agreed that Maria should go in male attire to the Red Barn so often mentioned in the course of the trial. You have heard from the mother of the unfortunate Maria, that she and I had had words. As we proceeded to the barn she was in tears. To that barn we had often repaired before, and frequently passed the night there. When we reached the barn, words arose, and Maria flew into a passion. I told her that, if we were to be married, and to live together, she must not go on so. Much conversation ensued, and on changing her dress, she at length told me, that if we were married we should never be happy together—that I was too proud to marry her and take her to my mother's, and that she did not regard me. I was highly irritated, and asked her, if she was to go on this way before marriage, what was I to expect after? She again upbraided me, and being in a passion, I told her that I would not marry her, and turned from the barn, but I had scarcely reached the gate when a report of a pistol reached my ears. I returned to the barn, and with horror beheld the unfortunate girl extended on the floor, apparently dead: I was for a short time stupefied with horror, and knew not what to do. It struck me to run for a surgeon; and well would it have been for me had I done so. But I raised the unfortunate girl, in order, if possible, to afford her some assistance; but I found her altogether lifeless; and, to my horror, I discovered that the dreadful act had been committed by one of my own pistols, and that I was the only person in existence who could tell how the fatal act took place. The sudden alarm which seized me suspended my faculties, and it was some time before I could perceive the awful situation in which I was placed, and the suspicions which must naturally arise from my having delayed to make the circumstances instantly known. I, at length, thought that concealment was the only means by which I could rescue myself from the horrid imputation; and I resolved to bury the body as well as I was able. Having done so, I subsequently accounted for her absence in the manner described by the witnesses, saying sometimes one thing to one person, and at other times other things to another. I may be asked why, if innocent of the crime imputed to me, I felt it necessary to give those answers? To which I answer, that some persons are driven to do acts from fear which others do from guilt, which is precisely the case with me in this instance. It may be asked, too, why I have not called evidence to prove the facts I have stated; but, gentlemen, I put it to you whether things do not sometimes take place which are only known to the parties between whom they happen; and what direct proof can I give when the only person who knew of these facts is no more? I can for the same reason give no direct proof of the unhappy woman's having got possession of my pistols. I say pistols, because I found the other loaded pistol in the unfortunate Maria's reticule. As to the stabs and other wounds described by the witnesses, I can only say that no stab or cut was given by Maria or myself; and I firmly believe that the surgeon would never have sworn to them, were it not for the circumstances of a sword having been found in the room in which I was arrested. If any stab did appear upon the body, it must have been done with the instruments used in disinterring it."

Numerous witnesses were then called, who spoke to the prisoner's general good character. The judge summed up, and a verdict of *Guilty* was returned. At this awful crisis the prisoner was first observed to raise his handkerchief to his eyes; and during the subsequent passing of the sentence of death he was dreadfully affected. On his return to the gaol he apparently recovered his spirits, but his only desire which he expressed was, that he should be permitted to see his wife. To this request an immediate assent was given, and at two o'clock on the next day she was admitted. The meeting was of a most distressing character, and it lasted nearly an hour. During that evening Corder was constantly attended by the reverend chaplain, but he showed no inclination to confess. On the following day, [Sunday] he attended the chapel in the customary manner, and during the performance of the service appeared deeply affected. On his return to his cell, he threw himself upon his bed and wept bitterly for a considerable time. In the course of the afternoon, it was hinted to him that his defence could never be credited; but he replied to the effect that "Confession to God was all that was necessary, and that confession to man was what he called popedom or poprey, and he never would do it.' It was subsequently suggested to him that he must have had great nerve to dig the grave while the body lay in his sight, when his reply was, "Nobody knows that the body lay in the barn and in sight, whilst I dug the hole;" but then, suddenly checking himself, he exclaimed, "O God! nobody will dig my grave.' In the course of the afternoon, he had a second and last interview with his wife, and the scene was truly heartrending. He expressed the most anxious fears with regard to the manner in which she would in future be looked upon by the world; and implored her, should she ever marry again, to be cautious how she accepted a proposition reaching her through a public advertisement. The parting scene was most dreadful, and the wretched woman was carried away from the cell in a state of stupor. After Mrs. Corder had finally departed, the governor made the strongest efforts to induce Corder to confess, pointing out to him the great aggravation of his crime, should he quit the world still denying his guilt. Corder at length exclaimed, "O, sir, I wish I had made a confidant of you before; I often wished to have done it, but you know, sir, it was of no use to employ a legal adviser and then not follow his advice." The governor assented to the propriety of his advice, and his acting on it up to the time of conviction, but that now all earthly consideration should cease. The wretched prisoner then exclaimed, "I am a guilty man," and immediately afterwards made the following confession:—

"Bury Gaol, August 10, 1828, in Condemned Cell,
Sunday Evening, half-past 11.

"I acknowledge being guilty of the death of poor Maria, by shooting her with a pistol. The particulars are as follows:—When we left her father's house, we began quarrelling about the burial of the child, she apprehending that the place wherein it was deposited would be found out. The quarrel continued for about three quarters of an hour, upon this and about other subjects. A scuffle ensued, and during the scuffle, and at the time I think that she had hold of me, I took the pistol from the side-pocket of my velveteen jacket, and fired. She fell, and died in an instant. I never saw even a struggle. I was overwhelmed with agitation and dismay—the body fell near the front doors on the floor of the barn. A vast quantity of blood issued from the wound, and ran on to the floor and through the crevices. Having determined to bury the body in the barn (about two hours after she was dead), I went and borrowed the spade of Mrs. Stowe; but before I went there, I dragged the body from the barn into the chaff-house, and locked up the barn. I returned again to the barn, and began to dig the hole; but the spade being a bad one, and the earth firm and hard, I was obliged to go home for a pick-axe and a better spade, with which I dug the hole, and then buried the body. I think I dragged the body by the handkerchief that was tied round her neck It was dark when I finished covering up the body. I went the next day and washed the blood from off the barn door. I declare to Almighty God I had no sharp instrument about me, and that no other wound but the one made by the pistol was inflicted by me. I have been guilty of great idleness, and at times led a dissolute life, but I hope through the mercy of God to be forgiven.

"W. CORDER.

"Witness to the signing by the said William Corder,
"JOHN ORRIDGE."

On the next morning the confession was read over to the prisoner, and he further said, in answer to a question put to him by the under-sheriff, that he thought the ball entered the right eye.

He subsequently appeared much easier in his mind, and attended divine service in the chapel immediately before his being carried out for execution. As allusions were made in the prayers to his unhappy situation, he appeared convulsed with agony; although he appeared calm, his limbs gave up their office, and he was obliged to be carried to his cell.

At a few minutes before twelve o'clock he was removed from his dungeon, and conveyed to the press-room, where he was pinioned in the usual way. He was so weak as to be unable to stand without support. On his cravat being removed he groaned heavily, and appeared to be laboring under great mental agony. When his wrists and arms were made fast, he was led round towards the scaffold; and as he passed the different yards in which the prisoners were confined, he shook hands with most, and speaking to two of them by name, he said, "Good bye, God bless you!" They were considerably affected at the wretched appearance which he made; and "God bless you!" "May God receive your soul!" were frequently uttered. The prisoner was supported up the steps which led to the scaffold; he looked somewhat wildly around, and a constable was obliged to support him while the hangman was adjusting the fatal cord. A few seconds before the drop fell he groaned heavily, and would have fallen, had not a second constable caught hold of him. After the drop had fallen he did not struggle; but he raised his hands once or twice, as as if in prayer; the hangman pulled his legs, and he was in a moment motionless. In about nine minutes, however, his shoulders appeared to raise in a convulsive movement; but life was said to have long left him. Just before he was turned off, he uttered, in a feeble tone, "I am justly sentenced, and may God forgive me." Mr. Orridge then informed the crowd that the prisoner acknowledged the justice of his sentence, and died in peace with all men.

The mob collected on this occasion amounted to many thousands, and occupied every spot of ground from which a glimpse could be obtained. A considerable portion consisted of women; and as soon as the execution was over, vast numbers proceeded to the Shire Hall, to obtain a view of the body, which, it was understood, would be exhibited.

Accordingly, at two o'clock, the body was exposed on a table in the centre of the hall; it was naked from the navel upwards. The crucial operation had been performed, and the skin of the breast and stomach turned back on each side. The body measured, as it lay, five feet five inches in length, and presented a very muscular appearance. The face and throat were somewhat swollen and discolored, the right eye was open, and the left partially so; the mouth was also open sufficiently to show the teeth. These are the ordinary appearances of those who have died by execution. On the next day the body was delivered to the hospital for dissection, in pursuance of the sentence.

After the execution a spirited bidding took place for the rope, and as much as five dollars an inch was obtained for it! Large sums were offered for the pistols and dagger used in the murder; but the sheriff, they being his perquisites, very properly refused to part with them in such a way. A piece of the skin of the wretched malefactor, which had been tanned, was exhibited for a long time afterwards at the shop of a leather-seller in Oxford street!

In conclusion, we are bound to say that little credit was attached to the confession made on the night before the execution; for, looking at all the facts, there can be little doubt that the murder was the result of premeditation. No one can doubt the purpose of his carrying pistols on the supposed day of his nuptials, loaded as they were. That Maria Marten was enticed to the Red Barn for the sole purpose of being there murdered, is too clearly evidenced by this one fact. Frightful, however, as was his crime, and awful the treachery by which he accomplished it, it was hardly less premeditated and wicked than the proceeding by which he succeeded in inducing a virtuous woman to ally her destinies to a man known, at all events, to his own conscience, as a murderer.

The following is a copy of the advertisement through which Corder obtained his wife—

"A private gentleman, aged twenty-four, entirely independent, whose disposition is not to be exceeded, has lately lost the chief of his family by the hand of Providence, which has occasioned amongst the remainder circumstances the most disagreeable to relate. To any female of respectability, who would study for domestic comfort, and who is willing to confide her future happiness to one in every way qualified to render the marriage state desirable, as the advertiser is in affluence. Many happy marriages have taken place through means similar to this now resorted to. It is hoped none will answer through impertinent curiosity; but should this meet the eye of any agreeable lady who feels desirous of meeting with a sociable, tender, kind and sympathising companion, she will find this advertisement worthy of notice. Honor and secrecy may be depended on. As some little security against idle application, it is requested that letters may be addressed [post paid,] A. Z., care of Mr. Foster, stationer, 68 Leadenhall street, with real name and address, which will meet with most respectful attention."

The following conversation in reference to this marriage is said to have taken place after the conviction—

"Attendant—Pray, Mr. Corder, may I ask whether it is true that it was by advertisement that you were first introduced to Mrs. Corder? Corder—It is perfectly true.

"Did you receive any answers to it?—I received no less than forty-five answers, and some of them from ladies in their carriages.

"Really! Well, that surprises me.—It may well surprise you, as it did myself, but I missed of a good chance.

"Pray how was that?—I will tell you. In one of the answers which I received it was requested that I should attend a particular church on an appointed day, dressed in a particular way, and I should there meet a lady wearing a certain dress, and both understanding what we came about, no further introduction would be necessary.

"But how could you know the particular lady, as there might be another dressed in the same way?—Oh, to guard against any mistake, the lady desired that I should wear a black handkerchief, and have my left arm in a sling; and in case I should not observe her, she should discover me, and introduce herself.

"And did you meet her?—I did not. I went to the church, but not in time, as the service was over when I got there.

"Then, as you did not meet her, how could you tell that she was a respectable woman?—Because the pew-opener told me that such a lady was inquiring for a gentleman of my description, and that she had come in an elegant carriage, and was a young woman of fortune.

"Then you never saw her afterwards? No, never; but I found out where she lived, and who she was, and would have had an interview with her were it not that I was introduced to Mrs. Corder, and we never parted until we were married.

"Pray, sir, was that long?—About a week.

MURDER OF A MILLER BY HIS WIFE AND CHILDREN.

In a narrow valley between the mountains in a region of Germany (M. Fenerback, from whom are derived the materials for this account, says, that important reasons compel him to conceal the locality and the real names of the parties), about 340 paces from the last house of the neighboring village, lies the Black Mill. In this lived, until the ninth of August, 1817, the master miller, Frederick Kleinschrot, a hale hearty man of sixty years of age. His business was profitable; his capital, in money, amounted to between thirteen and fourteen thousand florins. He had lived in wedlock with his wife, Barbara, thirty years, and had had twelve children with her, five of whom, at the time above-mentioned, were still living. His eldest son was settled in another place; under the paternal roof were still the second son, Conrad, then twenty-eight years of age, who had the care of the mill; and two daughters—Margaret, twenty-three years of age, and Kunigunda, approaching her eighth year, who discharged the duties of a maid servant in her father's house. Within the curtilage of the mill stood a separate cot or building, tenanted by a day laborer named Wagner, and his wife. A lad of thirteen, who slept in a stable, completed the establishment. On the ninth of August, 1817, the miller suddenly disappeared, and had never been heard of since. On the eleventh of October, in the same year, his wife notified the fact of his disappearance to the magistrate of the district, by whose direction some inquiries were instituted, but in vain. About a year afterwards, a report was circulated that the miller had been murdered in his mill. This report was clearly traceable to some words uttered by the day laborer Wagner, to one of his fellow laborers, to the effect that the family at the mill was completely in his power, and that whenever he wanted money, they must give it him. This report derived strength from the bad terms on which the miller was known to have lived with his family. It of course reached the ears of the magistrate, but after a few examinations the inquiry was dropped, and a three years' silence on the subject took place. At the end of that period, the magistrate was dismissed for misconduct, and a functionary empowered, according to custom, to deliver over the office to the successor. Scarcely had this functionary entered upon the discharge of his duties, when a fire broke out in the judicial registry, by which many of the documents there collected were destroyed. It was suspected that the late magistrate had some hand in bringing about this conflagration, with the view of rendering his own malversations more difficult of detection. Be this as it may, the fire led to an active search for documents to supply those that were missing or consumed, and amongst others a bundle of papers relating to the missing miller came to light, and the circumstances of suspicion detailed in these papers were such as to make it evident that the late magistrate must have been bribed to secresy. A fresh investigation was accordingly instituted, and at the first examination Wagner and his wife confessed that the miller had been murdered by his sons, with his (Wagner's) assistance, the wife and daughters being privy to the crime. The body, they added, was buried in a fissure of the rocks, near one of the fields of the deceased. The tyranny of the deceased was stated as the only motive to the deed, so far as the family were concerned. A search immediately took place, and the remains of a man were found in the place indicated by Wagner. At such a distance of time the only mark by which they could be directly identified was the beauty of the teeth, for which the deceased had been remarkable. The family were taken one by one to the grave, and examined as to their knowledge of the remains. Conrad, the elder of the two sons, the moment he saw the bones, exclaimed, without waiting to be questioned, "Aye, that is my father!" and after a pause added, "but I am not the murderer." Frederick, the other son, looked at them without any symptom of confusion, and replied, "What is this? well, what may this be? they are bones, but whether they be the bones of a man or a beast, I know not; I know nothing of either." The youngest daughter, when she was conducted to the spot, cried out: "I know nothing of it; I know that of my father; but of this up here I know nothing; I am innocent, wholly innocent." When the eldest daughter's turn came, she also exclaimed: "I am innocent of the deed—I am innocent. I knew nothing of the matter till my father began to cry out fearfully; but it was then too late. I have not had a quiet hour since. Oh, God, what will become of us?"

This of course rendered all further concealment nugatory, and full confessions were soon after made by the criminals. The recitals are affecting in the extreme. The wife and children were described by all who knew them as kind, gentle and amiable; whilst the father's character appears to have been that rather of a demon than of a man. Vicious in every relation of life, a bad son, a bad father, an unfaithful husband, and a tyrannical master—he was proved to have beaten and ill-treated his own father, when living, to such a degree as to make it necessary for the old man to guard himself by bolts and locks of more than ordinary strength: to have got his maid-servant (with whom his own children were permitted to see him in bed) with child, and then given her drugs to procure abortion; besides having several other bastard children, whom he supported, whilst his legitimate family were kept in the lowest state of want; and to have frequently beaten his wife and children in a manner that left them maimed and mutilated for weeks. Thus, one of the day-laborers states, that "the old miller suffered not a day to pass without falling either upon his wife or his sons, availing himself for that purpose of the first weapon that came to hand. He once struck his wife such a blow with a hatchet, that she was obliged to carry her arm in a sling for a fortnight." The daughter, Margaret, stated, that her mother was deprived of half her reason, in consequence of a blow on the head, received from her father fifteen years before. As to servants, hardly any could be got to stay with him at all, and he was constantly changing them. "Such a monster (says the youngest son, Frederick) was our father. Alas! so long as we have been in this world, we have never known either peace or joy. Before our father's death we were tormented by him, and since his death, tormented by our own consciences." They applied to the courts of law, but were told that there was neither help nor counsel for them there. At length the idea of being their own deliverers stole upon them, and they endeavored to get rid of their own oppression by a charm. A pair of the miller's stockings were delivered to Wagner's wife, who was to hang them up in the smoke, whereupon the miller was expected to pine away and die. After waiting for some weeks the result of this experiment, more decisive means were resolved upon, and Wagner, on being applied to, agreed to dispatch his master for 2,0 florins. It appears to be doubtful who first suggested the plan; Conrad accused his mother, but the mother herself asserted that it was first suggested by the sons. It met at any rate with general assent; and Wagner undertook the commission with readiness. Arming himself with a hatchet, he one night took his post in the kitchen, through which the miller would be obliged to pass in leaving his bed-chamber, and the sons agreed to set the mill going, the noise of which would necessarily induce their father to come out. The result was exactly as they had anticipated, and immediately on the miller's entering the kitchen, Wagner aimed a blow at his head with the hatchet, but missed his head, and struck him somewhere else. Upon this the miller raised a horrible cry, and endeavored to fly back into his bed-chamber, when Wagner, throwing away the hatchet, grappled with him, and a violent and for some time doubtful struggle took place, until Wagner bethought him of his knife, which, without letting go his hold, he managed to draw from his waistcoat pocket, opened it by pressing it against his side, and then thrust the blade into the miller's body. Conrad, the eldest son, upon hearing the cry, ran into the kitchen. His father had already received the stab, but still kept his feet and groaned. Seeing this, Conrad took a billet of wood from a heap lying in the kitchen, reached it from behind Wagner, and then ran out again into the street to see if all was safe. Wagner, who had let fall his knife, then struck the miller a blow upon the head with the billet of wood, and knocked him down; but as the groans still continued, he caught up a stone that was lying upon the hearth, and dashed it against the miller's head with all his might, until the stone broke to pieces. And now, for the first time, the groaning and moaning of the miller was hushed. The sons came into the kitchen immediately afterwards, and assisted Wagner to carry the body into the bed-room. This being done, Wagner retired, it is said, to rest himself after his job: whilst Conrad went up to his mother, wailing and exclaiming: "Oh, mother, if it were but undone, it should never be done at all." She, herself, according to her own confession, shed no tears for her husband, and entertained a thorough conviction that God himself must have inspired herself and children with the design of murdering her husband. We almost fancy we hear her saying, like Beatrice, to her judges:—

"What! will human laws—
Rather will ye, who are their ministers—
Bar all access to retribution first,
And then, when Heaven doth interpose to do
What ye neglect, arming familiar things
To the redress of an unwonted crime,
Make ye the victims who demanded it.
Culprits? 'Tis ye are culprits! That poor wretch,
Who stands so pale and trembling and amazed,
If it be true he murdered Cenci, was
A sword in the right hand of justest God."

The sons had not attained to so comforting a conviction. They aided Wagner to bury their father's body; the younger even stamped the loose earth upon his grave; but the day before they had repaired together to a neighboring mountain, fallen upon their knees, bitterly repented them of the deed, and prayed God to have mercy on their sins. The sentences were as follows:—Wagner and Conrad to imprisonment in irons for life, with civil death; Frederick to fifteen years' imprisonment in a penitentiary; the mother to eight years' imprisonment in a penitentiary. The daughters were acquitted.

THE MARCHIONESS OF BRINVILLIERS, THE POISONER.

There are few persons who have walked the thoroughfares of London, who have not had their attention called to a small, delicate, plump, little hand, dimpled and beautiful, exhibited in the plaster-cast shops, for sale to artists as a model. Any one taking it in his hand would be almost charmed into a belief that he was pressing that of a beautiful and amiable woman. How would his feelings recoil, upon asking the question to whom the original belonged, when told that it was Madame de Brinvilliers, the famous poisoner!

The following account of this extraordinary and unfortunate woman—we may surely speak of her as *unfortunate*, since it is hardly possible to think of her as having been moved by anything short of some inexplicable insanity to the commission of those enormities of which she was guilty!—is compiled from the biographical dictionaries, with the addition of Madame de Sévigné's lively notices of the affair, as it proceeded at Paris. These greatly add to the interest of the narrative.

Marguerite d'Aubrai, Marchioness Brinvilliers, was born at Paris in 1651, being the daughter of d'Aubrai, lieutenant civil of Paris, who married her to N. Gobelin, Marquis of Brinvilliers. Although possessed of attractions to captivate lovers, she was for some time much attached to her husband; but at length became madly in love with a Gascon officer named Goder St. Croix, who had been introduced by the Marquis, then the adjutant of the regiment of Normandy.

Her father being informed of this affair, imprisoned the officer, who was altogether an adventurer, in the Bastile, where he was detained for a year—a circumstance which induced the Marchioness to be more outwardly circumspect, but at the same time to nourish the most implacable hatred to her father and her whole family. While in the Bastile, St. Croix learned from an Italian named Elixi, the art of composing the most subtle and mortal poisons, and the result, on his release, was the destruction, by this means, in concurrence with his mistress, of her father, sister, two brothers, and one of her own children—all of whom were poisoned the same year, 1760. During all this time the Marchioness was visiting the hospital, outwardly as a devotee, but, as afterwards strongly suspected, really in order to try on the patients the effects of the poison produced by her paramour.

The discovery of these monstrous criminals was made in a very extraordinary manner. While at work in distilling poison, St. Croix accidentally dropped the glass mask which he wore to prevent inhaling the noxious vapor, and the consequence was his instant death. Nobody claiming his effects, they fell into the hands of government; and the Marchioness had the imprudence to lay claim to a casket, and appeared so anxious to obtain it, that the authorities ordered it to be opened; when it was found to be full of packets of poisons, with ticketed descriptions of the effects they would produce. Informed of the opening of the casket, the execrable woman escaped to England, whence she passed to Liege, where she was arrested and conducted to Paris. Being tried, she was convicted of the murder of her father, sister, and brothers, and condemned to be beheaded and burnt. In this dreadful situation, she evinced extraordinary courage, amounting almost to nonchalance. On entering the chamber in which she was to be put to the question, by the torture of swallowing water, she observed three bucketsfull prepared, and exclaimed, "It is surely intended to drown me, for it is absurd to suppose that a person of my dimensions can swallow all that." She listened to her sentence without exhibiting either weakness or alarm, and showed no other weakness on her way to execution than to request that she might be so placed as not to see the officer who had apprehended her. She also ascended, unaided and barefoot, the ladder to the scaffold. Strange to say, she always possessed some sense of religion : she went regularly to confession, and when arrested at Liege a sort of general form was found in her possession, which sufficiently alluded to her criminality to form a strong presumption against her. What adds to the atrocity of her character, she was proved to have had connections with many persons suspected of the same crimes, and to have provided poisons for the use of others. Many persons of rank lost their lives about the time she was pursuing her horrible career; and the investigation seemed likely to lead to the discovery of so much guilt in this way, that it was, as a matter of policy, stopped. It was supposed that the indifference of the Marquis of Brinvilliers to his wife's conduct induced her to spare one so much in her power. She suffered on the 17th of July, 1676.

Madame de Sevigné thus describes the state of mind which characterized this monster of a woman while in prison, as well as the frightfully depraved state of feeling which she must have possessed from childhood :—

"PARIS, Wednesday, April 29th, 1676.

* * * * * * *

"Madame de Brinvilliers is not so much at her ease as I: she is in prison. She endeavors to pass her time there as pleasantly as she can, and desired yesterday to play at piquet, because she was very dull. They have found her confession; she informs us that at the age of seven years she ceased to be a virgin, and that she had ever since went on at the same rate; that she had poisoned her father, her brothers, one of her children and herself; but the last was only to make trial of an antidote. Medea has less of this guilty skill. She has owned this confession to be her own writing: it was an unaccountable folly; but she says she was in a high fever when she writ it; that it is a frenzy, an extravagance, which does not deserve to be read seriously."

"PARIS, Friday, May 1st, 1676.

* * * * * * *

"Nothing is talked of here but the transactions and behavior of Madame de Brinvilliers. Could one ever have thought of her forgetting the murder of her father at confession? And then the peccadilloes that she was afraid of forgetting were admirable. She was in love, it seems, with this same Sainte Croix; she wanted to marry him, and for that purpose gave her husband poison two or three different times. Sainte Croix, who did not care to have a wife as wicked as himself, gave the good man a dose of counter-poison; so that, after being bandied about between them, sometimes poisoned, sometimes unpoisoned again, he at last is actually making intercession for his dear. Oh, there is no end to some people's follies!"

From the following, it seems that she was not satisfied with the crimes she had already committed, but was resolved to involve innocent persons in her own just and well merited ruin:—

"Paris, Friday, July 10, 1676.

* * * * *

"Penautier has been confronted with La Brinvilliers. It was a very melancholy interview; they were wont to meet on more agreeable terms. She has so repeatedly declared, that if she was to die she would make many others die with her, that it is hardly to be doubted that she will draw this poor wretch in to be a sharer of her fate; or, at least, to be put to the *question*, which is a dreadful thing. The man has a prodigious number of friends; and those of great consequence, whom he has formerly had opportunities of obliging, while he was in possession in his two places. They leave no stone unturned to serve him, and money flies about in quantities upon the occasion; but if he should be cast, nothing can possibly save him."

The following is the account of the closing scene of the tragedy:—

"Paris, Friday, July 17, 1676

"At length it is all over: La Brinvilliers is in the air; after her execution, her poor little body was thrown into a great fire, and her ashes dispersed by the wind, so that whenever we breathe, we shall draw in some particles of her, and by the communication of the minute spirits, we may be all infected with an itch for poisoning, to our no small surprise. She was condemned yesterday; and this morning her sentence was read to her, which was to perform the *amende honorable* in the church of Notre Dame; and, after that, to have her head severed from her body, her body burnt, and her ashes thrown into the air. They were for putting her to the torture; but she told them there was no occasion for that, she would confess everything. Acrordingly, she was till five o'clock in the evening relating the passages of her life, which has been more shocking than was ever imagined. She has poisoned her father no less than ten times running, but without being able to destroy him; as likewise her brother, and several others; and all was under the appearance of the greatest love and confidence. She has said nothing against Penautier. Notwithstanding this confession, they gave her the question, ordinary and extraordinary, next morning; but this extorted nothing more from her. She desired to speak with the procurator-general; no one as yet knows the subject of this conversation. At six o'clock she was carried in a cart, stripped to her shift, with a cord about her neck, to the church of Notre Dame, to perform the *amende honorable*; after that was over, she was put again into the same cart, where I saw her lying at her length, on a truss of straw, only her shift and a suit of plain head clothes, with a confessor on one side and a hangman on the other; indeed, my dear, the sight made me shudder. Those who saw the execution say that she mounted the scaffold with great courage. As for me, I was on the bridge of Notre Dame, with good d'Escars; never, sure, was there such a concourse of people seen, nor the attention of the whole city so fixed upon any one event."

In a subsequent letter Madame de Sevigne says:—

* * * * * *

"Let me entertain you with a little more of the history of La Brinvilliers. She died as she lived, that is to say, very resolutely. She entered the place where she expected to be put to the torture; and on seeing the preparations, she said, 'they certainly intend to drown me; for, considering the smallness of my size, they can never pretend to make me drink so much.' She heard her sentence read to her without the least token of fear or weakness; only towards the latter end of it, she desired them to begin it again, telling them that the circumstance of the cart had struck her, and made her lose her attention to the rest.

"On the way to the execution, she desired her confessor to place the executioner before her, that she might not, as she said, have the sight of that rascal Desgrais, who had taken her. He was before the cart on horseback; her confessor reproved her for that sentiment, upon which she asked pardon, and submitted to endure that disagreeable sight. She mounted the ladder and the scaffold alone, and with her naked feet; and the executioner was a quarter of an hour in dressing, shaving, and ordering her for the execution, in an abusive manner, which caused a great murmur among the crowd, and was reckoned a great cruelty. The next day her bones were gathered up, as relics, by the people, who said she was a saint. She had two confessors, one of which told her that she ought to reveal everything; the other, that she ought not; she laughed at this diversity of opinion between the learned fathers, and said she believed she might very conscientiously do which of the two she pleased, and it pleased her to reveal nothing. By this means Penautier is come off a little whiter than snow; however, the public is not contented, and seems still to entertain some slight suspicion. But see the misfortune of it: this creature refused to reveal what they wanted to know, and told what nobody demanded of her. For example, she said that M. F—— had sent Glaser, the apothecary they employed in preparing their poisons, into Italy to procure an herb, which is, it seems, a choice ingredient in their mysterious compositions, and that she had heard of this pious pilgrimage of his from Sainte Croix. You see what pains is taken to load this miserable wretch with crimes, and to finish his ruin; but the truth of this information is much suspected."

A VICTIM OF JUDICIAL MURDER.

A Maltese judge of the last century, named Cambo, who was an early riser, having left his bed one morning before sunrise, hearing the footsteps of people running violently in the street, was led by curiosity to see what occasioned it at that unusual hour. Most of the houses in Valletta are furnished with balconies, covered and glazed, which, when provided with curtains, permit the inhabitants, if inclined, to observe what is going on in the street, without being themselves discovered. The judge, from one of these, though it was not yet daylight, perceived a man running in great terror from another, who followed him close behind. Directly under the judge's window the pursuer overtook the flyer, and stabbed him; the wounded man reeled and fell; in the act of striking, it is to be remarked, the assassin's cap came off, so that the judge had an opportunity of viewing his features in the increasing daylight; hastily recovering it he instantly took to flight. A few paces further on, he threw away the sheath of his stiletto, and turned into another street; the judge consequently lost sight of him.

Scarcely had he witnessed this extraordinary spectacle, than a baker, with his basket of bread for the daily consumption of his customers, made his appearance. As he walked leisurely along, the sheath of the stiletto, which lay in his path, caught his eye; he stooped, took it up, and, after examining it a little, put it in his pocket and continued his course. Just then a patrol of police, either by accident or drawn by the noise which had attracted the attention of the judge, entered the same street. In the meantime the baker, a little lower, came to the body just assassinated; the police took the same direction, and the poor man at this instant perceived them behind him; terrified at the sight of the corpse, and fearful of being suspected and arrested, he lost all presence of mind, and hid himself in the entrance of a gentleman's house near the spot; but he had not escaped the quick eye of the officers; they had seen a figure, which disappeared suddenly near the murdered person, whom they also now discovered, and very naturally conjecturing it was the assassin, began to search for him carefully on all sides, as they knew he had not run off. It was not long before they detected the unfortunate baker in his hiding-place; his incoherent and confused replies created suspicion; on searching him they found the sheath on his person; the stiletto had fallen from the wound, and lay near the body; on applying it to the sheath, they found it corresponded exactly, and less than all these circumstances would have warranted the arrest of the poor baker. He was accordingly carried to prison, and public report gave out that he was undoubtedly the murderer; nor was this prepossession any way contradicted or removed by the judge, who, though he had witnessed the whole occurrence, kept it a profound secret in his own breast. Official report was made to him within an hour after the event—still he communicated the fact to no one. The only way of accounting for his extraordinary conduct is, that he presided in the criminal court, and that there was a doubt in the existing jurisprudence, how far a judge ought to act from his own private knowledge of a case, and whether he ought not altogether to limit himself to the disposition of witnesses and other evidence brought forward on the trial, without any reference to information he might have casually received from other sources. The dull and heavy intellect of Cambo, unable to distinguish between the rule and the exception, embraced this opinion. The unhappy baker was, in due time, brought to trial. Circumstances were certainly against him; the stupid judge, who knew his innocence, particularly listened to, and punctually noted all, the apparent proofs of his guilt. He at length, to do him justice, perceived with satisfaction that the evidence was not altogether sufficiently conclusive for condemnation; but determined to proceed with all due formality, and not to deviate an iota from the ordinary routine of the court, according to the established practice of the Maltese Code of the day, which, in cases of *semi-prova*, or semi-proof, preposterously endeavored to supply the deficiencies of evidence by the forced confession of the criminal himself, he ordered the wretched man to be put to the question. Imagining in his infatuation, by this proceeding to reconcile what he esteemed his duty with his conscience; he conceived that the prisoner, being really innocent, would persist in asserting himself to be so, and thus afford him an opportunity of declaring the proof of his crime not sufficiently made out. But he was mistaken: relaxing nothing from the ordinary procedure of the court, the torture, which was that of the cord, was so cruelly and unmercifully applied, that, at the second fall, the wretched creature, yielding to the pain caused by the complete dislocation of both shoulders, called out loudly that he was guilty. So terrified was he by the apprehension of a continuation or renewal of his suffering, that when taken down to receive condemnation, as convicted, he durst not retract his forced and false confession. No alternative was now, in his own opinion, left to the scrupulous and undeviating Cambo. There was a person accused, tried, and convicted, all in due form; if he was not guilty in fact, he was so in law, and ought to have been so in reality. Perhaps the sagacious judge found that he had let matters go too far to retract at the last stage; be that as it may, the hapless wretch was condemned to death, and, horrible to relate, soon after underwent the sentence of the law.

It was not long before the dreadful truth was brought to light: the real murderer, arrested, brought to trial, and condemned to death for another crime, among other offenses confessed himself guilty of that for which the poor baker had so unjustly suffered, and appealed to Cambo himself for the truth of his assertion. In the very act of plunging his knife into the body of his victim, he had caught the judge's eye, as he stood at the window; he described his dress at the time, and mentioned the circumstance of his cap falling, when he was so near the balcony, that the judge must have necessarily remarked his features. Indeed, he had given himself up for lost, and was astonished at finding the unfortunate baker arrested, condemned, and executed in his stead, the reasons for which strange proceeding on the part of the judge he had never been able to account for.

The circumstance coming to the ears of the grand master, he sent for Cambo, and soon elicited the whole fact from that precise and straightforward functionary, who still maintained that he had only fulfilled his duty, and acted up to the letter of the law, in consigning an innocent man to a cruel and ignominious death, because it unfortunately happened that the only witness in his favor was his judge. The grand master, it seems, was of a different opinion, for he not only degraded and dismissed Cambo from all his employments, but obliged him to provide handsomely, from his private fortune, for the family of this victim of judicial murder.

WRONGFUL EXECUTION OF A FATHER FOR THE MURDER OF HIS DAUGHTER.

There are many curious and interesting cases of circumstantial evidence, or presumptive proof, upon record—cases in which, as it has subsequently been demonstrated innocent persons have suffered for the guilty; and the following may be placed amongst the most curious of these. Poor Shaw was, in all probability, an austere father, and his daughter as probably a wilful and vindictive child; but they should not be considered as less the objects of pity on that account, and especially when it is called to mind, under what circumstances they are likely to have been brought up.

William Shaw was an upholsterer at Edinburgh, in the year 1721. He had a daughter, Catherine Shaw, who lived with him. She encouraged the addresses of John Lawson, a jeweller, to whom William Shaw declared the most insuperable objections, alleging him to be a profligate young man, addicted to every kind of dissipation. He was forbidden the house; but the daughter continuing to see him clandestinely, the father, on the discovery, kept her strictly confined.

William Shaw had, for some time, pressed his daughter to receive the addresses of a son of Alexander Robertson, a friend and neighbor; and one evening, being very urgent with her thereon, she peremptorily refused, declaring that she preferred death to being young Robertson's wife. The father grew enraged, and the daughter more positive; so that the most passionate expressions arose on both sides, and the words, *barbarity*, *cruelty*, and *death*, were frequently pronounced by the daughter! At length he left her, locking the door after him.

The greater part of the buildings in Edinburgh are formed on the plan of chambers in English inns of court, so that many families inhabit rooms on the same floor, having all one common staircase. William Shaw dwelt in one of these, and a single partition only divided his room from that of James Morrison, a watch-case-maker. This man had indistinctly overheard the conversation and quarrel between Catherine Shaw and her father, but was particularly struck with the repetition of the above words, she having pronounced them loudly and emphatically! For some little time after the father was gone out, all was silent, but presently Morrison heard several groans from the daughter. Alarmed, he ran to some of his neighbors under the same roof. These, entering Morrison's room, and listening attentively, not only heard the groans, but distinctly heard Catherine Shaw faintly exclaim: "Cruel father, thou art the cause of my *death!*" Struck with this, they flew to the door of Shaw's apartment; they knocked—no answer was given. The knocking was still repeated—still no answer. Suspicions had before arisen against the father; they were now confirmed: a constable was procured, an entrance forced; Catherine was found weltering in her blood, and the fatal knife by her side! She was alive, but speechless; but, on questioning her as to owing her death to her father, she was just able to make a motion with her head, apparently in the affirmative, and expired.

Just at the critical moment, William Shaw returns and enters the room. All eyes are on him! He sees his neighbors and a constable in his apartment, and seems much disordered thereat; but, at the sight of his daughter, he turns pale, trembles, and is ready to sink. The first surprise and the succeeding horror leave little doubt of his guilt in the breasts of the beholders; and even that little is done away on the constable discovering that the shirt of William Shaw is bloody.

He was instantly hurried before a magistrate, and upon the depositions of all the parties, committed to prison on suspicion. He was shortly after brought to trial, when, in his defence, he acknowledged the having confined his daughter to prevent her intercourse with Lawson; that he had frequently insisted on her marrying Robertson; and that he quarrelled with her on the subject the evening she was found murdered, as the witness, Morrison, had deposed: but he averred, that he left his daughter unharmed and untouched; and that the blood found upon his shirt was there in consequence of his having bled himself some days before, and the bandage becoming untied. These assertions did not weigh a feather with the jury, when opposed to the strong circumstantial evidence of the daughter's expressions, of "barbarity, cruelty, death,"—and of "cruel father thou art the cause of my death,"—together with that apparently affirmative motion with her head, and of the blood so seemingly providentially discovered on the father's shirt. On these several concurring circumstances, was William Shaw found guilty, was executed, and was hanged in chains, at Leith Walk, in November, 17 1.

There was not a person in Edinburgh who believed the father guiltless, notwithstanding his latest words were, "I am innocent of my daughter's murder." But in August, 1722, as a man, who had become possessor of the late William Shaw's apartments, was rummaging by chance in the chamber where Catherine Shaw died, he accidentally perceived a paper fallen into a cavity on one side of the chimney. It was folded as a letter, which, on opening,contained the following:—"Barbarous father, your cruelty in having put it out of my power ever to join my fate to that of the only man I could love, and tyrannically-insisting upon my marrying one whom I always hated, has made me form a resolution to put an end to an existence which is become a burthen to me. I doubt not I shall find mercy in another world; for sure no benevolent being can require that I should any longer live in torment to myself in this! My death I lay to your charge: when you read this, consider yourself as the inhuman wretch that plunged the murderous knife into the bosom of the unhappy—Catherine Shaw."

This letter being shown, the handwriting was recognised and avowed to be Catherine Shaw's by many of her relations and friends. It became the public talk; and the magistracy of Edinburgh, on a scrutiny, being convinced of its authenticity, ordered the body of William Shaw to be taken from the gibbet, and given to his family, for interment; and as the only reparation to his memory and the honor of his surviving relations, they caused a pair of colors to be waved over his grave, in token of his innocence.

THOMAS GEDDELY WHO WAS EXECUTED ON ACCOUNT OF HIS RESEMBLANCE TO ANOTHER.

Thomas Geddely lived as a waiter with Mrs. Hannah Williams, who kept a public house at York, England. It being a house of much business, and the mistress very assiduous therein, she was deemed in wealthy circumstances. One morning her scrutoire was found broken open and robbed, and Thomas Geddely disappearing at the same time, no doubt was entertained as to the robber. About a twelve month after, a man calling himself James Crow came to York, and worked a few days for a precarious subsistence, in carrying goods as a porter. Many accosted him as Thomas Geddely. He declared he did not know them, that his name was James

Crow, and that he never was at York before. But this was held as merely a trick to save himself from the circumstances of the robbery committed in the house of Mrs. Williams, when he lived with her as waiter.

His mistress was sent for, and in the midst of many people instantly singled him out, called him by his name (Thomas Geddely), and charged him with his unfaithfulness and ingratitude in robbing her. He was directly hurried before a justice of the peace, but on his examination absolutely affirmed that he was not Thomas Geddely, that he knew no such person, that he never was at York before, and that his name was James Crow. Not, however, giving a good account of himself, but rather admitting that he was a vagabond and petty rogue, and Mrs. Williams and another person swearing positively to his person, he was committed to York Castle for trial at the next assizes.

On arraignment, he pleaded not guilty, still denying that he was the person he was taken for: but Mrs. Williams and some others made oath that he was the identical Thomas Geddely who lived with her when she was robbed; and a servant girl deposed that she had seen him, on the very morning of the robbery, in the room where the scrutoire was broken open, with a poker in his hand. The prisoner, being unable to prove an *alibi*, was found guilty of the robbery. He was soon after executed, but persisted to his latest breath in affirming that he was not Thomas Geddely and that his name was James Crow.

And so it proved! Some time after, the true Thomas Geddely, who on robbing his mistress had fled from York to Ireland, was taken up in Dublin for a crime of the same stamp, and then condemned and executed. Between his conviction and execution, and again at the fatal tree, he confessed himself to be the very Thomas Geddely who had committed the robbery at York, for which the unfortunate James Crow had been executed.

We must add, that a gentleman, an inhabitant of York, happening to be in Dublin at the time of Geddely's trial and execution, and who knew him when he lived with Mrs. Williams, declared that the resemblance between the two men was so exceedingly great, that it was next to impossible to distinguish their persons asunder.

SAWNEY BEANE.

THE SCOTTISH ROBBER, MURDERER, AND CANNIBAL.

History contains no parallel to the horrible cruelties and robberies that were committed by one Sawney Beane, a Scotchman, in the reign of King James the First, before he came to the crown of England, by the demise of Queen Elizabeth.

Sawney Beane was born about eight or nine miles eastward of the city of Edinburgh, in the county of East Lothian, of parents who went a hedging and ditching for their daily bread and who brought up this, their bloody-minded child, to the same occupation; but as he grew up, his disposition to idleness not permitting him to follow an honorable employment, he left his father and mother, and ran into the country; where, following a most wicked course of life, and taking up with a woman as vicious as himself, instead of living in any city, town, or village, they took up their lodging in a rock by the sea-side, on the shore of Shire Galloway, where they lived for upwards of twenty-five years, having both children and grandchildren in that time, whom they brought up so wickedly that they never separated, kept no other company but themselves, and supported themselves entirely by robbing; and, what was worse, they never committed a robbery without a murder.

They never frequented any market for provisions, but as soon as they had murdered any man, woman, or child, they did not leave the carcass behind, but carried it to their den, where, cutting it into quarters, they would pickle them, and live upon human flesh, till they got another prey of the same kind! But they had generally a superfluity, insomuch that they oftentimes, in the night-time, but at a great distance from their sanguinary mansion, threw legs and arms of some they had killed into the sea, which the tide frequently cast up at several parts of the country, to the great astonishment of the beholders. Persons who went about their lawful occupations fell often into the hands of these merciless cannibals, and never returned home again. This raised a general outcry amongst their friends and relations; insomuch that the whole country was alarmed at such a common loss of people, which frequently happened in travelling into the west of Scotland, and private spies were sent out into all parts, to find out, if possible, how these melancholy events happened. For a length of time their strictest searches and inquiries were to no purposes. However, several honest travellers were taken up upon suspicion, and wrongfully hanged upon bare circumstances, besides several innocent inn-keepers, who were also executed, for no other reason, than that persons who had been thus lost were known to have lain in their houses, and were supposed to have been robbed and murdered by them, and their bodies privately buried in obscure places, to prevent a discovery. To such an extent was this carried, that several innkeepers, on the western road of Scotland, left off their business, for fear of being made the like examples, and followed other employments; so that travellers again were put to many inconveniences for want of accommodation.

However, after several had been executed, and no one made any confession at the gallows, but declared that they were innocent of the crime for which they died, this rigorous way of proceeding was given up, and the finding out of the murderers left wholly to God.

Sawney Beane, with his wife, children, and grandchildren, still pursued their barbarous actions with impunity; and, being somewhat numerous, they would attack four, five, or six men together, if they were on foot. As for horsemen, two were the most they would ever set on, and then with such caution, that an ambuscade was laid to secure them, ride which way they would, provided one or both made their escape from the first assailants. Thus, whose fortune soever it was to fall into their barbarous hands, he or she never came off with their lives. The place was solitary where they inhabited; and, when the tide came up, the water went for near two hundred yards into their subterraneous habitation, which reached almost a mile under ground; so that if they were ever seen thereabouts by any person, it was not in the least suspected that anything human resided in such a dismal place of perpetual horror and darkness.

The number of people they had killed was not exactly known; but it was reckoned, that in the twenty-five years they had reigned in these inhuman slaughters, they had washed their hands in the blood of above one thousand men, women, and children! At length, the discovery of the cannibals was thus made.

A man, and his wife, who was behind him on the same horse, coming one evening from a fair, and falling into the ambuscade of these merciless wretches, they fell upon them in a most furious manner: the man, to save himself as well as he could, fought it bravely against them with sword and pistol, riding some of them down by main force of his horse, from which his wife in the conflict fell off, and was presently murdered before the husband's face; for the female cannibals forthwith cut her throat, sucking her blood with as great a gusto as if it had been wine, ripped up her belly, and pulled out all her entrails; which unparalleled barbarity made the poor man make the more obstinate resistance, as expecting the same fate if he fell into their impious hands. It pleased Providence that twenty or thirty passengers were riding that way from the same fair that he had been at, and Sawney Beane and his blood-thirsty clan withdrew, made the best of their way through a solitary wood, and so retired to their den.

The man, who was the first that ever came off alive after falling into their hands, told the passengers what had happened, and showed them the bloodly spectacle of his wife, whom the murderers had dragged some distance off, which struck them all with stupefaction and amazement. They carried him with them to Glasgow, and, relating the matter to the provost of that city, he immediately sent to the king about it, who in three or four days came in person thither, being desirous to see the apprehending of this villain, who for so many years had been the pest of the western part of his kingdom.

A body of about four hundred men, well armed, set out on horseback with the king, who had several bloodhounds with him, and went with the man to the wood by which he was attacked, but found no sign of any habitation all over it. They then went through it, which led down to the sea-side, when the tide being out, and going along the shore they passed by the cave of Sawney Beane, without taking any notice of it as a place of habitation, until some of the blood-hounds, running into it, and setting up a most hideous barking, howling, and yelping, the king and his attendants came back, and looked into it but seeing nothing for darkness, they could not tell what to think of it, but nevertheless imagined something more than ordinary by the blood-hounds making such a noise there, going quite out of sight, and appearing quite unwilling to come out. Torches were sent for, and a great many men ventured into it: though there were several intricate turnings and windings in this private recess from mankind, yet they at last came to the apartments of Sawney Beane, where, to their great surprise, they beheld the legs, arms, thighs, hands, and feet of men, women, and children, hung up like dried beef, and some limbs lying in pickle, a great mass of money, both gold and siver watches, rings, swords, pistols, and a great quantity of clothes, both linen and woolen, and infinite other things, which they had taken from those they had murdered.

All these they seized, took what human flesh they found there, and buried it in the sands, and brought out Sawney Beane and his murdering family, which, besides himself, consisted of his wife, eight sons, six daughters, eighteen grandsons, and fourteen granddaughters, begotten in incest. They were all pinioned and carried to Edinburgh ; all the country, as they passed along, flocked in multitudes to see this cursed tribe, who were no sooner come to their journey's end, than they were put into the Tolbooth for one night, whence the next day, being conducted under a strong guard to Leith, the men, without process or any manner of trial, had their hands and legs cut off, by which amputation they bled in some hours to death: all this torture being justly inflicted upon them in sight of the wife, daughters, and grandchildren. They were then all burned in three several fires, all dying, like the men, without repentance, but cursing and venting dire imprecations to the last gasp of life.

www.ingramcontent.com/pod-product-compliance
Lightning Source LLC
LaVergne TN
LVHW021121110826
845150LV00005B/912

* 9 7 8 1 4 2 5 5 5 1 7 8 0 *